Getting the Right Teachers into
the Right Schools

WORLD BANK STUDY

Getting the Right Teachers into the Right Schools

Managing India's Teacher Workforce

Vimala Ramachandran, Tara Béteille, Toby Linden, Sangeeta Dey,
Sangeeta Goyal, and Prerna Goel Chatterjee

© 2018 International Bank for Reconstruction and Development / The World Bank
1818 H Street NW, Washington, DC 20433
Telephone: 202-473-1000; Internet: www.worldbank.org

Some rights reserved

1 2 3 4   20 19 18 17

This work is a product of the staff of The World Bank with external contributions. The findings, interpretations, and conclusions expressed in this work do not necessarily reflect the views of The World Bank, its Board of Executive Directors, or the governments they represent. The World Bank does not guarantee the accuracy of the data included in this work. The boundaries, colors, denominations, and other information shown on any map in this work do not imply any judgment on the part of The World Bank concerning the legal status of any territory or the endorsement or acceptance of such boundaries.

Nothing herein shall constitute or be considered to be a limitation upon or waiver of the privileges and immunities of The World Bank, all of which are specifically reserved.

Rights and Permissions

This work is available under the Creative Commons Attribution 3.0 IGO license (CC BY 3.0 IGO) http://creativecommons.org/licenses/by/3.0/igo. Under the Creative Commons Attribution license, you are free to copy, distribute, transmit, and adapt this work, including for commercial purposes, under the following conditions:

Attribution—Please cite the work as follows: Ramachandran, Vimala, Tara Béteille, Toby Linden, Sangeeta Dey, Sangeeta Goyal, and Prerna Goel Chatterjee. 2018. *Getting the Right Teachers into the Right Schools: Managing India's Teacher Workforce.* World Bank Studies. Washington, DC: World Bank. doi:10.1596/978-1-4648-0987-3. License: Creative Commons Attribution CC BY 3.0 IGO

Translations—If you create a translation of this work, please add the following disclaimer along with the attribution: *This translation was not created by The World Bank and should not be considered an official World Bank translation. The World Bank shall not be liable for any content or error in this translation.*

Adaptations—If you create an adaptation of this work, please add the following disclaimer along with the attribution: *This is an adaptation of an original work by The World Bank. Views and opinions expressed in the adaptation are the sole responsibility of the author or authors of the adaptation and are not endorsed by The World Bank.*

Third-party content—The World Bank does not necessarily own each component of the content contained within the work. The World Bank therefore does not warrant that the use of any third-party-owned individual component or part contained in the work will not infringe on the rights of those third parties. The risk of claims resulting from such infringement rests solely with you. If you wish to re-use a component of the work, it is your responsibility to determine whether permission is needed for that re-use and to obtain permission from the copyright owner. Examples of components can include, but are not limited to, tables, figures, or images.

All queries on rights and licenses should be addressed to World Bank Publications, The World Bank Group, 1818 H Street NW, Washington, DC 20433, USA; e-mail: pubrights@worldbank.org.

ISBN (paper): 978-1-4648-0987-3
ISBN (electronic): 978-1-4648-0988-0
DOI: 10.1596/978-1-4648-0987-3

Cover photo: CRS PHOTO / Shutterstock.com. Used with permission; further permission required for reuse.
Cover design: Debra Naylor / Naylor Design Inc.

Library of Congress Cataloging-in-Publication Data has been requested.

Contents

Foreword — *xiii*
Acknowledgments — *xv*
About the Authors — *xvii*
Executive Summary — *xix*
Abbreviations — *xxxix*

Chapter 1 Introduction — 1
    Background — 1
    The Scope — 3
    What We Did Not Set Out to Do — 6
    Methodology — 7
    Structure of the Book — 9
    Notes — 10

Chapter 2 School Teachers in India: A Descriptive Analysis — 11
    Introduction — 11
    Teaching Workforce: The Current Scenario — 12
    Elementary Teacher Workforce: Trends in Size and Growth — 17
    Elementary Teachers, by Type of Management — 18
    Secondary Teachers: Government versus Aided Schools — 21
    Elementary Teachers, by Type of Employment — 22
    Inclusiveness — 23
    Pupil-Teacher Ratio: Trends — 27
    Educational Qualifications — 36
    Data Gaps — 36
    Conclusion — 39
    Annex 2A: Data and Methodology — 39
    Notes — 40

Chapter 3	**Who Can Become a Teacher?**	43
	Introduction	43
	National-Level Regulations	43
	State-Level Regulations and Policies for Teacher Recruitment in the Nine States	48
	Reservation Policies for Recruitment	53
	Language Requirement	55
	Criteria for Merit List Preparation	55
	Conclusion	57
	Notes	57
Chapter 4	**Teacher Recruitment**	59
	Introduction	59
	Teacher Recruitment: Direct and Indirect	59
	Minimum Standards for Becoming a Teacher	63
	Terms of Recruitment: Regular and Contract Teachers	67
	Reversal of the Trend of Hiring Contract Teachers	69
	Recruitment Process	71
	Description of the Karnataka Recruitment Process	73
	Summing Up	81
	Notes	82
Chapter 5	**Teacher Deployment and Transfers**	85
	Introduction	85
	Initial Deployment	88
	Transfer Policy and Practice	89
	Who Initiates Transfers?	90
	Who Can Be Transferred, Why, and by Whom?	91
	Deputation, Another Form of Transfer	95
	Good Practices That Could Show the Way	95
	Summing Up	104
	Notes	105
Chapter 6	**Salaries and Benefits**	107
	Expenditure on Elementary Education in India: A Brief Snapshot	107
	Comparison of Salaries across States	108
	Other Monetary and Nonmonetary Benefits	113
	Conclusion	118
	Notes	119
Chapter 7	**Teachers in School**	121
	Roles and Responsibilities: Day-to-Day Management	121
	Roles and Responsibilities of Teachers	121

	Non-Teaching Functions	123
	Support, Feedback, or Inspection?	125
	Accountability	126
	Induction and Orientation	127
	Challenges Faced in Discharging Roles and Responsibilities	128
	Roles of Contract/Para Teachers	133
	Roles and Challenges of School Leaders	133
	Summing Up	135
	Notes	136
Chapter 8	**Professional Growth of Teachers**	**137**
	Introduction	137
	Promotions	137
	Professional Development and In-Service Training	142
	Evaluation of Teacher Performance	147
	Conclusion	151
	Notes	151
Chapter 9	**Grievance Redressal Mechanisms**	**153**
	Introduction	153
	Teacher Grievance Redressal Mechanisms Established by State Education Departments	154
	Grievance Redressal through the Courts	159
	The Way Forward	167
	Annex 9A Data Sources and Their Limitations	170
	Notes	171
Chapter 10	**Unanswered Questions**	**173**
	Overview	173
	Intent and Outcome	174
	What Constitutes Policy?	176
	Enabling Circumstances for Clear Policy and Transparent Processes	177
	Role of Teachers' Unions in Influencing Policy	179
	Roots of Administrative Inefficiencies	179
	Performance Appraisal versus Assured Career Progression	180
	What Role Do Teachers' Associations and Unions Play?	181
	Downstream and Upstream Impact of the Teacher Eligibility Tests	182
	Equity, Inclusion, and Gender	182
	Pre-Service Training	183
	Do Teacher Policies Result in More Effective Teachers?	183
	Conclusion	185
	Notes	185

Chapter 11	Some Ideas to Take Forward	187
	Overarching Message	187
	Streamlined and Transparent Recruitment and Deployment	188
	Easy Access to Support Structures for Teachers	188
	Incentives for Effort and Performance	190
	Accountability and Feedback on Performance	190
	Robust Teacher Information System	191
Appendix A	Political Economy of Teacher Reforms in Karnataka and Tamil Nadu	193
Appendix B	Teacher Transfer Technology in Karnataka	229
Bibliography		241

Boxes

1.1	Areas, Issues, and Questions Explored	5
4.1	High Court Decision on Vidyarthi Mitra in Rajasthan	68
5.1	Glimpses of Teacher Transfers in Nine States	92

Figures

2.1	Year-on-Year Growth of Elementary Schools, Teachers, and Students, All-India	17
2.2	Year-on-Year Growth in Number of Elementary Teachers, by Management, All-India	20
2.3	Year-on-Year Growth in Number of Elementary Schools, by Management, All-India	20
2.4	Percentage of Aided and Government Secondary Schools Operating above Capacity	21
2.5	Percentage of Aided and Government Secondary Schools with Six Basic Infrastructure Components	22
2.6	Percentage of Elementary Teaching Workforce Comprising Para/Contract Teachers, All Elementary Schools	23
2.7	Number and Percentage of Women Teachers, All-India, Elementary	24
2.8	Percentage of Women Teachers, States, All Elementary Schools	24
2.9	Percentage of SC and ST Teachers, All-India, All Elementary Schools	25
2.10	Percentage of SC Teachers in 2010–11 and 2011–12, All Elementary Schools, Compared with the Percentage of SC Population as per Census 2011	26
2.11	Percentage of ST Teachers in 2010–11 and 2011–12, All Elementary Schools, Compared with the Percentage of ST Population as per Census 2011	26

2.12	Percentage of SC & ST Secondary Teachers in 2012–13, All Secondary Schools, Compared with the Percentage of SC & ST Population as per Census 2011	27
2.13	Numbers of Teachers and Pupils, and the Pupil-Teacher Ratio, All-India, All Elementary Schools	28
2.14	Pupils, Teachers, and the PTR in Private Elementary Schools, All-India	28
2.15	Pupils, Teachers, and the PTR in Government Elementary Schools, All-India	28
2.16	Elementary School PTR, States, All Elementary Schools, 2012–13	29
2.17	Reduction in PTR over Time, All Elementary Schools	30
2.18	Average District-Level PTR All Elementary Schools, and Percent Rural Population, 2012–13	31
2.19	Percentage of Schools in Different PTR Ranges, Elementary, 2012–13	34
2.20	Regressions of School PTRs and Enrollments, All Elementary Schools, 2012–13	35
2.21	Evolution of Educational Qualifications of Elementary Teachers, All-India, All Elementary Schools	37
2.22	Percentage of Elementary Teachers Who Have a Higher Education Degree, by State, All Elementary Schools	37
4.1	Direct Recruitment Process for Elementary and Secondary School Teachers	71
4.2	Reservation Criteria for Recruitment	75
4.3	Additional Reservation for Gulbarga Division	76
4.4	Computerized Counseling Process for Recruitment	77
4.5	Recruitment of Teachers in Mizoram, 2009	80
5.1	Application Process for Transfers within Same Unit of Seniority	97
5.2	Preparation of Provisional and Final List for Transfers	99
5.3	Counseling Process for Transfers on Request	99
5.4	Flowchart for the Counseling Process	100
5.5	Excess Teacher Transfer Process	101
7.1	Roles and Duties of Teachers: Karnataka	122
8.1	Number and Percentage of Elementary Teachers Receiving Training in Previous Year: All-India	143
8.2	In-Service Training under RMSA, Achievement against Financial and Physical Targets, 2009–13	144
B.1	Transfer Application Processing within Seniority	230
B.2	Provisional and Final List Preparation	231
B.3	Counseling Process	232
B.4	Redeployment Process	233
B.5	Redeployment Process outside the Unit of Seniority	234

Tables

2.1	Number of Elementary Teachers, Using Alternative Definitions and Data Sources, All-India	13
2.2	Profile of Elementary School Teachers, All Elementary Schools, 2012–13	14
2.3	Working Conditions of Regular and Contract Teachers in Government Elementary Schools	14
2.4	Profile of Secondary School Teachers, All Secondary Schools	15
2.5	Working Conditions in Government Secondary Schools	16
2.6	Number of Elementary Teachers, All Elementary Schools, 2003–04 to 2012–13	19
2.7	Number of Elementary Schools, 2003–04 to 2012–13	32
2.8	Increasing Standard Deviation of PTR with Every Level of Disaggregation, All Elementary Schools, 2012–13	33
2.9	Distribution of Pupil-Teacher Ratios, All Elementary Schools with PTR <150, 2012–13	33
2.10	School-Level PTRs Are Higher in Urban Schools, All Elementary Schools, 2012–13	35
2.11	Summary of Results of Regressing PTR on School Structure, All Elementary Schools, 2012–13	36
2.12	School-Level PTR Distribution, All Elementary Schools, 2012–13	38
3.1	Minimum Educational and Professional Qualifications for Teachers Laid Down by NCTE for Elementary and Secondary School Teachers	46
3.2	Minimum Educational and Professional Qualifications for Elementary and Secondary School Teachers Prescribed by the States in the Study	49
3.3	Maximum Age Limit for Senior and Senior Secondary Teachers Advertised between 2007 and 2012, Punjab	51
3.4	Minimum and Maximum Age Limits for Elementary- and Secondary-Level Teacher Recruitment	52
3.5	Criteria for Reservation Categories	54
4.1	Direct and Indirect Recruitment Practices in Sample States	60
4.2	Overview of the Applications and Dates of the Teacher Eligibility Tests Held in Madhya Pradesh, 2011–12	65
4.3	Summary of PSTET 2011, 2012, 2013, and 2014 in Punjab	66
4.4	State-Wise Position on Contract Teacher Recruitment	70
4.5	Overview of Direct Recruitment Norms for Teachers	72
4.6	Teacher Recruitments in Rajasthan in the Past 10 Years	78
5.1	Who Belongs to What Cadre?	87
5.2	Teacher Transfer Policies and Implementation	90
5.3	Classification of Schools for Teacher Deployment: Mizoram	91
5.4	Transfer Norms: Madhya Pradesh	103
6.1	Pay Scale of Government Teachers	108

6.2	Pay Scale of Government School Teachers	109
6.3	Take-Home Salaries of Teachers	109
6.4	Salary Structure of Teachers: Madhya Pradesh	110
6.5	Teachers' Salaries: Punjab	111
6.6	Breakdown of Salaries for Two Districts in Punjab	111
6.7	Salary of Contract Teachers in Eight States	112
6.8	Leave Sanctioned for Regular Teachers in the Nine States	113
6.9	Academic Leave Available to Teachers in Selected States	114
6.10	Other Benefits Available to Teachers in the Nine States	115
6.11	Government Expenditure on Education, Selected Countries	118
7.1	Percentage of Teachers Involved in Non-Teaching Assignments in Elementary Schools in Karnataka, 2009–10 to 2012–13	124
7.2	Schools Visited by CRC and Inspected, 2011–12	126
7.3	Lack of Infrastructure Facilities, 2012–13	128
7.4	Vacancies in Headmaster and Head Teacher Positions	134
8.1	Promotion Routes for Different Cadres of Teachers: Uttar Pradesh	139
8.2	Promotions for Certain Categories of Elementary Teachers over Time: Odisha	140
8.3	Annual Sanctioned and Actual Unit Costs, RMSA In-Service Funds, 2009–13	146
8.4	Elementary School Teachers Who Received In-Service Training during the 2011–12 Academic Year	147
8.5	Regression of Number of Inspections on Distance from Block Headquarters, Elementary Schools, 2012–13	148
8.6	Performance Appraisal Report: Mizoram	149
8.7	Revised (2014) Norms for State Teacher Awards: Rajasthan	150
9.1	Predominant Grievance Types, by State (High Court Cases Only)	160
9.2	Types of Grievances, by State	161
9.3	Case Outcomes, by State, Since 2009	165
9.4	Disposal Periods	166
10.1	Pupil and Teacher Attendance Rates, 2013	184
A.1	Timeline of Major Reforms in Teacher Recruitment and Transfers	197
A.2	Changes in the Priority Criteria for Transfer of Teachers	205
A.3	Number of Teachers in Tamil Nadu	208
A.4	Categories of Teachers	210
A.5	Rules Governing Different Categories of Teachers	211
A.6	Timeline of Teacher Recruitment Policies and Practices	211
A.7	Expansion of Private Teacher-Training Institutions in Tamil Nadu	215
A.8	Timeline of Teacher Transfer Policies and Practices	217
A.9	Excerpt from 2014 Government Order	219

Foreword

India is at an important crossroads today as it tries to balance the challenge of quantity, quality, and equity in education provision. How India's schoolteachers are positioned and managed is critical to turning the system around. The challenge today is to ensure that the right kind of people are recruited into teaching, managed sensitively, and most importantly, are given the administrative and academic support required to meet the goal of quality education for all.

This study was initiated by the National University for Educational Planning and Administration under the Rajiv Gandhi Foundation Chair on Teacher Management and Development in 2014–15, in collaboration with the World Bank. The principle investigator, Vimala Ramachandran, brought together a diverse group of academicians and practitioners, which greatly enriched the study. Key contributors to the study include Centre for Budget and Policy Studies (Karnataka); Centre for Educational Research and Practice (Rajasthan); Eklavya (Madhya Pradesh); Institute of Advanced Studies in Education (Mizoram); Lokdrusti (Odisha); and State Councils of Education Research and Training in Uttar Pradesh, Punjab, and Tamil Nadu. This kind of collaborative research ensured that multiple perspectives and data sources were carefully examined.

The management of the teacher workforce in India has long been a neglected area in research. This study bridges this gap. It provides the most recent evidence on how key issues pertaining to teacher management are being addressed in nine large Indian states. Importantly, it derives lessons from states that are performing relatively well in this domain.

Jandhyala G B Tilak
Former Vice Chancellor
National University of Educational
Planning and Administration
New Delhi

Keiko Miwa
Practice Manager
Education Global Practice
The World Bank

Acknowledgments

This research was conducted under the aegis of the National University of Educational Planning and Administration (NUEPA) Chair on Teacher Management and Development, established by the Rajiv Gandhi Foundation (RGF). Vimala Ramachandran held the Chair from 2013–15, the period during which the study was conducted.

We extend our sincere thanks to the Advisory Committee (RGF Chair, NUEPA), which guided us through the project: Suman Bhattacharjea, R. Govinda (Vice-Chancellor of NUEPA), M. A. Khader, Claire Noronha, Pranati Panda, K. Ramachandran, A. K. Sharma, Sreeja, V. Sudhakar, and M. P. Vijay Kumar.

We are grateful to the research partners who steered the research in the nine states:

CBPS:	Jharkhand and Karnataka: Jyotsna Jha, Puja Minni, GVSR Prasad, and Neha Ghatak
CERP:	Rajasthan: Nagendra Nagpal
CLPR:	Analysis of legal cases: Aparna Ravi and the CLPR team
DTERT:	Tamil Nadu: J. Inbaraj and S. Manivel
Eklavya:	Anjali Noronha, Arvind Jain, and Pradeep Chaube
IASE:	Mizoram: S. Hom Chaudhuri and Nikhil Mathur
Lokdrusti:	Odisha: Lohitakshaya Joshi, Abani Mohan Panigrahi, and Prasant Kumar Panda
NUEPA:	Punjab: Anupam Pachauri; Uttar Pradesh: Nikhil Mathur
SCERT:	Punjab: M. S. Sarkaria
SCERT:	Uttar Pradesh: Ajay Singh, Sanjay Agarwal, and Nikhil Mathur

We express our gratitude for the suggestions made by R. Govinda, K. Ramachandran, and M. P. Vijaykumar at a meeting in NUEPA to review the draft findings. We are extremely grateful to our peer reviewers, Yamini Aiyar, Dhir Jhingran, Amit Kaushik, Geeta Gandhi Kingdon, and Sridhar Rajagopalan for their valuable comments and suggestions.

Financial support from the United Kingdom's Department for International Development for part of this research is gratefully acknowledged.

About the Authors

Tara Béteille, Senior Economist, is part of the World Bank's Education Practice. Her work involves project design, implementation support, and research. Her areas of expertise cover school education and higher education, including teacher management policies, the political economy of education systems, and governance. Tara was part of the core team for the *World Development Report 2018: Learning to Realize Education's Promise*, and is currently leading a South Asia Companion Piece. Prior to joining the World Bank, she was a postdoctoral scholar at Stanford's Center for Education Policy and Analysis. Tara obtained her PhD from Stanford University in 2009, specializing in the economics of education. She also holds master's degrees in economics from the Delhi School of Economics and from Stanford University. Upon completing her studies at the Delhi School of Economics, Béteille joined ICICI Bank, where she led their nonprofit initiatives in education from 2000 to 2004.

Prerna Goel Chatterjee has a master's of education degree from LaTrobe University, Australia, and is a Certified Life Coach from Coach for Life, USA. She started her career working with young adults in the field of outdoor education and life skills. Currently she is Senior Faculty with the Capacity Building Unit of ASER Centre, where her main focus areas are communications and leadership skills. She also regularly conducts "Prevention of Sexual Harassment at Workplace" workshops and has worked on various qualitative research projects.

Sangeeta Dey is a Senior Education Specialist at the World Bank, where she is leading the Bank's Secondary Education Project in India, and is working on an Elementary and Higher Education Project in India and on an Early Childhood Development Project in Sri Lanka. She obtained her M.Phil. from the University of Delhi in Indian history. She has published a co-authored article on grievance redressal mechanisms for school teachers, and she co-authored a study report on "Teachers' Time on Task in Secondary Schools." Previously, she worked as Education Advisor at the United Kingdom's Department for International Development, Education Grants Officer at the Michael and Susan Dell Foundation, and Education Specialist at USAID's REACH India project, and she taught Indian history at the undergraduate level at the University of Delhi.

Sangeeta Goyal is a Senior Economist in the World Bank's Education Practice, where she works on the World Bank's programs in Bangladesh, India, Nepal, and Sri Lanka. Goyal's work includes project design, implementation support, and research covering early childhood education, technical and vocational education, and higher education. Goyal has led tracer studies in India and Nepal, examining how students fare in the labor market upon completing their studies. She has also examined the factors influencing community participation in public schools, as well as the difference in the relative performance of public and private schools. Goyal holds a PhD in economics from Columbia University.

Toby Linden is a British national who has worked for the World Bank since 1998. During his career, his work has focused on a wide variety of countries, especially in South East and Central Europe and South and East Africa, as well as India. He also was on secondment from the Bank to serve as Director of the Roma Education Fund, an international nongovernmental organization working to improve the educational outcomes of the Roma (Gypsies), who constitute the poorest minority in Europe. His publications in the education sector include the World Bank's first book on lifelong learning and papers in secondary and higher education.

Vimala Ramachandran works on elementary education, girls' education, and women's empowerment. She was involved in the conceptualization of Mahila Samakhya (Education for Women's Equality) and served as the first National Project Director from 1988–93 in the Ministry of Human Resource Development, Government of India. She established Educational Resource Unit (now known as ERU Consultants Private Limited) in 1998 as a network of researchers and practitioners working on education. From 2011 to mid-2015 she was a National Fellow and Professor of Teacher Management and Development in NUEPA. She has been engaged in research on elementary and secondary education, focusing on gender and equity issues, teacher status and motivation, and systemic barriers to realizing the equity goals of national policies and programs for elementary education; adult literacy and continuing education; and most recently, the educational needs of out-of-school youth—especially girls.

Executive Summary

The Backdrop

This study comes at a pertinent moment in the history of education in India, when there is a lot of pressure to improve the quality of schools and ensure that children learn. The Right to Education (RTE) Act 2009 mandated pupil-teacher ratios (PTRs) and teacher qualifications, and indicated what is a conducive environment for teaching and learning (Government of India 2009). Equally significant is that the RTE Act and Justice Verma Committee (2012) mandated a teacher eligibility test (TET) as the first step in the recruitment of all teachers, whether contract or on grade (Government of India 2012). In addition, several state governments have reviewed their policies on contract teachers; some others are hiring contract teachers without any long-term perspective on what would happen to them.

The National University of Planning Education and Administration (NUEPA) initiated a study to understand the working conditions of elementary and secondary school teachers in nine states in India: Jharkhand, Karnataka, Madhya Pradesh, Mizoram, Odisha, Punjab, Rajasthan, Tamil Nadu, and Uttar Pradesh. The study was conducted under the aegis of the Chair on Teacher Management and Development, funded by the Rajiv Gandhi Foundation. The World Bank was invited to join as a technical partner of the study.

"Teacher management" in this study means the recruitment policies and practices; deployment and redeployment (postings and transfers) policies and practices; salary, non-salary benefits, and related service conditions (pensions and other long-term benefits); physical working conditions of teachers; roles, duties, and responsibilities of teachers; avenues for professional growth and management of teacher in-service training; autonomy, accountability, and appraisal systems that are in place; and teachers' rights, grievance redressal mechanism (through a desk review of legal cases resolved in the past five years), and mandate of teachers' unions. The study focuses on government schoolteachers at the elementary and secondary levels. Government-aided schoolteachers were included at the secondary level, because of their strong presence in this part of the sector. The study includes all categories of teachers—regular, contract, and part-time teachers.

The study does not seek to comment on the capacity and quality of the teachers who have been recruited or how effectively they are working in Indian schools. The study instead investigates whether the government is able to recruit and deploy teachers where necessary, whether practices are informed by policies, and if all of this is being done in a transparent manner.

The study was conducted in three stages: (a) desk review of materials on teacher management and development, (b) in-depth exploration of the issues identified, and (c) dialogues with stakeholders at the state and district levels. The study adopted a methodology that was primarily qualitative in nature, through perusal of policy and other documents and interviews with stakeholders. However, the study carried out an intensive analysis of the data to capture the context of teachers and policies on teachers in India.

Teachers in India: A Descriptive Analysis

In India, there are more than 7.4 million elementary school teachers across 1.4 million government, government-aided, and private-unaided schools (of those, 5.8 million are teaching elementary sections or classes). (All data are as of 2012–13.) Of these 7.4 million teachers, 4.5 million work in government schools (3.6 million as elementary teachers), and 2.6 million are employed in schools managed privately (1.9 million teaching elementary grades, 0.4 million of which are employed in aided schools and 1.5 million in private unaided schools). The average all-India PTR in elementary schools is 28.8 (or 34.4 for teachers teaching elementary classes). PTRs range from 44.6 in Uttar Pradesh to 13.9 in Mizoram. Among the nine states under consideration, Uttar Pradesh has the largest teaching workforce, with 950,000 teachers, followed by Rajasthan, with 560,000 teachers. Mizoram has the smallest teaching workforce, with only about 19,000 teachers.

The secondary school sector is much smaller. The total size of the secondary school teacher workforce is 0.95 million, of which 0.42 million are employed in government schools and 0.49 million in private schools, the latter being split almost equally between aided and unaided schools. Karnataka has the most secondary school teachers (97,000), followed by Uttar Pradesh (89,000); Mizoram again has the least (a little over 4,000).

There are some sharp differences, but also some common features across the states. The states vary greatly in the proportions of teachers (and pupils and schools) that are under different types of management (government, aided, and private unaided), overall PTR, average school size, structure of grades within a given school, proportion of teachers who are regular as opposed to contract teachers, and proportion of teachers who are female (although the proportion has been increasing in all states over the past 10 years in elementary education).

There are some common features across the states in elementary education, namely: (a) PTRs have decreased significantly over the past 10 years, due to the appointment of teachers outpacing growth in enrollments (especially in private schools); (b) Scheduled Tribe (ST) teachers are generally well-represented (except in Madhya Pradesh), while Scheduled Caste (SC) teachers are not; (c) there has been a steady increase in the educational qualifications of all teachers; and (d) there are significant infrastructure challenges, with only a few schools meeting expectations. In addition, the characteristics of aided secondary schools in a given state are more like the government schools in that state than they are like aided schools in other states.

Perhaps the most important commonality across the states is that there are significant variations *within* states across several parameters, and these variations are as significant as the differences *across* states. For example, all the states have significant proportions of schools with PTR less than 10 *and* greater than 100. In all the states, with every level of disaggregation (from state, to district, to block, to school), the variation in PTRs increases. Therefore, most of the states need to address the inequitable distribution of teachers across schools.

A particular challenge is the large number of small schools. Eleven percent of elementary schools have only one teacher and 14 percent of secondary schools have at most two teachers. Teachers in small schools are more isolated professionally (they cannot discuss their challenges with another teacher) and face difficulties attending training (or simply taking leave). There is no system for teacher substitutes, so when a teacher is absent, the students are not taught. In secondary schools, there are far too few specialist teachers.

Who Can Become a Teacher?

The standards for teacher education and minimum educational and professional qualifications for recruitment of schoolteachers are set at the national level by the apex body, the National Council of Teacher Education (NCTE). The foundational notification was issued in August 2010. In November 2014, a new notification established the following: the Bachelor of Education (B.Ed.) program is a two-year course; an integrated four-year course leading to a Bachelor of the Arts and B.Ed. degree would be introduced; admission to B.Ed. programs was open for Bachelor of Commerce and Bachelor of Technology graduates; 20 weeks of practical work would be included in the B.Ed. course, of which at least 16 weeks would be spent in teaching; and unqualified secondary school teachers would be required to complete a three-year, part-time B.Ed. course in classroom mode during vacations.

Each state is responsible for teacher recruitment and prescribes its own minimum qualification criteria for teachers based on NCTE regulations and notifications. In practice, most states follow these national regulations, although some states have a few additional requirements. In general, teacher recruitment is undertaken by the public service commissions of the respective states. The exception is Tamil Nadu, which created the Teacher Recruitment Board in 1997.[1] Punjab has recently (2013) created a recruitment board, and Jharkhand has formed the Staff Selection Commission. Rajasthan is considering having a separate recruitment board for all non-gazetted government officers, which would include schoolteachers.

The RTE Act provides for a relaxation in the minimum qualifications required for appointment as a teacher. The central government allowed this relaxation in a few states that had a huge shortage of qualified teachers and applicants. Among the states included in this study, Jharkhand, Madhya Pradesh, Odisha, and Uttar Pradesh were granted this relaxation. However, when Madhya Pradesh requested a second relaxation after its original deadline expired, it was not granted, suggesting that states should not assume they can postpone indefinitely meeting the conditions specified under the Act for teacher qualifications.

The introduction of the TET as an eligibility criterion for teachers to be appointed is a major recent change. The qualifying score for the Central TET is 60 percent. However, a qualifying score on the TET does not confer the right for any person to be recruited, as it is only one of the eligibility criteria for appointment. NCTE regulations allow school managements (government, local bodies, government aided, and unaided) to consider giving concessions for reserved categories in accordance with their extant reservation policy, and to weight the TET scores in the recruitment process. The guidelines state that the appropriate government should conduct a TET at least once every year.

All nine states use qualification on the TET for candidates applying to teach at the elementary level. States have designed their own TETs (rather than using the Central TET) in accordance with the guidelines provided by NCTE. As of December 2014, all nine states had completed at least one or two rounds of their respective TETs (although none had conducted a TET each year). The states also prescribed minimum and maximum age limits for candidates to be eligible as teachers. The age limit criterion is quite similar across the states, with a few exceptions. In most states, the minimum age for elementary school teachers is 18 years; for secondary school teachers, it is 21 years. The maximum age (to start as such a teacher) is typically between 32 and 35 years. A few states have prescribed that knowledge of the official state language is part of the mandatory eligibility criteria—Jharkhand, Odisha, and Punjab in this study.

The merit list is the most critical part of the recruitment process. Each candidate who meets all the eligibility criteria is given a ranking, which determines the order in which teachers may choose the school to which they will be appointed. Once generated, the merit list is published, to provide opportunities for individuals to challenge their placement on the list. Construction of the merit list is a complicated process, as it needs to consider all the various criteria and reservation policies. It is perhaps not surprising that there are many court challenges to the lists, which have delayed the recruitment process in many states.

Teacher Recruitment

Teacher recruitment policies are ad hoc and there are long delays and gaps before a successful candidate can assume teaching duties. States do not have a systematic or routine process for calculating how many teachers are needed or what their specific qualifications and characteristics should be. In a handful of states, the factors underlying recruitment are closely related to political interests, making teacher recruitment resemble political strategies rather than recruitment policies. The timing of recruitment is also opaque and it is initiated once every few years. The significant number of court cases related to teacher recruitment has caused insecurity among potential teacher candidates. Even in the states where recruitment is relatively more transparent and merit-based—Karnataka and Tamil Nadu—there are considerable delays in the appointment of teachers.

A potentially positive trend over the past decade is that several states have gradually reversed the policy on hiring contract teachers in elementary schools; all new recruitments of teachers are to be on regular or permanent terms at the elementary level. However, this is not the case in secondary education, where Rashtriya Madhyamik Shiksha Abhiyan (RMSA) project funds are used to hire secondary teachers on contracts. If regularizing teachers is accompanied by stricter standards for recruitment and building greater professionalism into the cadre, then this is a welcome trend. If it is motivated by other considerations, like buying the loyalty of more teachers, then the consequences for the quality of the teaching force will be poor.

Some other trends are more worrisome. In most of the states, the teacher recruitment process continues to be opaque (politically driven). The government does not seem to have a well laid out policy to estimate the number of teachers required and a process to move from there to recruitment. This situation has led to a great deal of unrest among teachers and potential teacher candidates. This trend is present in educationally less developed states, like Rajasthan and Uttar Pradesh, as well as relatively more developed states, like Punjab.

In some states, the number of ST candidates qualifying to teach remains low, leading to high vacancies in this reserved category. This may call for a more focused approach to enhance the pool of qualified candidates from ST communities for teaching positions (the situation for the Muslim community is unknown).

Finally, the schools have no role in choosing the teachers who are appointed to them. Thus, the schools cannot express their preferences. For example, a school may seek an elementary teacher who has experience working with children with special needs or is stronger in mathematics as opposed to language. This is especially a concern when not all the vacancies in the schools will be filled. And schools may have priorities of which the appointing authority is unaware or about which he/she is unconcerned.

Teacher Deployment and Transfers

There are thousands of schools in every state that have too many teachers or too few. This is an indicator that the processes for assigning teachers to schools—initial deployment and subsequent transfers—are likely to be inefficient, politically manipulated, or nonexistent.

Transfers are important for teachers. In a system that is otherwise uniform in pay and emoluments, transfers can improve or worsen a teacher's working and living conditions considerably. If transfer requests are entertained without jeopardizing the interests of the school a teacher leaves or joins, the system does not suffer. However, when teachers can transfer regardless of school need, it distorts the overall allocation of teachers to schools and seriously compromises the education of large numbers of children.

Effective teacher transfer policies are rare in India. Where they exist (as in Karnataka and Tamil Nadu among the study countries), they are recent. Transfer policies in these two states specify the number of years all teachers must spend in rural areas, number of teachers that can be transferred in a given year, and prioritization rules for the transfer of different groups of teachers. Importantly, transfer policies in these states are implemented using an information technology–based system with checks and balances. In states like Odisha and Madhya Pradesh, a series of government orders and guidelines spell out the criteria and the process. Although the government orders and guidelines may not be categorized as "policies," they are nevertheless followed in letter and spirit.

In all the other states, the transfer practices share certain weaknesses. First, and most importantly, they are mostly ad hoc. Second, in most states, only regular teachers in government schools can be transferred. Third, teachers report needing powerful connections and paying bribes to get a transfer of their choice (or impede one against their interest) or to get a transfer relatively quickly. In Odisha, for example, political leaders are formally represented on transfer committees, and in Rajasthan transfers are given as rewards to politically helpful teachers. Fourth, if teachers who want a transfer to another school cannot be transferred because no vacancy exists, they can nevertheless get to their location of interest by requesting a deputation to an administrative office. Finally, transfers can be used to discipline errant teachers (although in practice these remain rare, the threat may be real).

Salaries and Benefits

More than 80 percent of the total elementary education budget is spent on teachers' salaries (Cheney, Ruzzi, and Muralidharan 2005; Kingdon 2010). Teachers' demands for higher pay scales and pay scale revisions after the Fifth and Sixth Pay Commissions have ensured that government teachers are paid at par with other central government employees. Along with salary hikes, teachers receive other benefits, such as annual increments (3 percent of total pay), dearness allowance, city compensatory allowance, house rent allowance, medical insurance, and pension.

In this study, all the states, except Karnataka and Punjab, are reported to have adopted the recommendations of the Sixth Pay Commission, but the states have contextualized the recommendations. For example, although Rajasthan has adopted the Sixth Pay Commission and revisions were made after the Bhatnagar Committee[2] recommendations in 2013, it has been reported that the pay scales of state government teachers are lower than those of central government employees. Punjab is currently following the recommendations of the Fifth Pay Commission of the Punjab Government,[3] but these pay scales are slightly higher than the Sixth Pay Commission of the Government of India. Elementary school teachers in Punjab are the highest paid teachers among the nine states in this study. Government teachers who were consulted for the study reported that they are mostly happy with their salaries and other benefits.

However, in some states (Odisha and Tamil Nadu), teachers with the same qualifications and teaching the same classes are paid differently. That is because their pay depends on the type of school (primary, upper primary, or secondary) in which they teach. The salary of a teacher who is teaching class VI in an elementary school will be different from the salary of a teacher who teaches the same class but in a secondary school.

The salaries of contract teachers also vary considerably across the states. Most significantly, the salary of a contract (or para) teacher continues to remain a fraction of what a government teacher earns; in some cases, it is only 25 percent of what a regular teacher earns in the same state. In addition, not only are contract teachers paid less with no extra benefits or annual increments, it has been reported that their salaries are often delayed. A key reason is that most of these teachers are hired as a part of a project (usually Sarva Shiksha Abhiyan (SSA) or RMSA) or locally hired by Zillah Parishads and, hence, their salaries are mostly dependent on the availability of project funds.

A major positive change is the electronic transfer of salaries directly into the accounts of teachers (regular and contract), which has considerably reduced the delay in payment of salaries and brought in more transparency.

Teachers are eligible for leave in all the states, although the nature and duration of the leave vary. In some states, teachers are also entitled to maternity leave, privileged leave, extraordinary leave, and unpaid leave. Contract teachers are not eligible for any leave in most of the states, although those states with the highest proportions of contract teachers generally provide them with better benefits. In Tamil Nadu, Mizoram, Odisha, Madhya Pradesh, and Punjab, contract teachers are entitled to casual leave. Mizoram is the only state where contract teachers are eligible for vacations and half-day leave.

Teachers in School

The RTE Act says that all teachers should perform the following duties: (a) maintain regularity and punctuality in attending school; (b) conduct and complete the curriculum; (c) complete the entire curriculum within a specified time; (d) assess the learning ability of each child and accordingly supplement with additional instruction, if any, as required; (e) hold regular meetings with parents and guardians and apprise them about the regularity in attendance, ability to learn, progress made in learning, and any other relevant information about their child; and (f) perform other such duties as may be prescribed.

Most state governments have incorporated the RTE provisions into their rules and regulations; therefore, these duties are applicable for all teachers in government elementary schools at least. However, translating these duties into practice in spirit is a challenge that is yet to be addressed fully. Head teachers assign teachers many non-teaching functions, such as providing administrative support, managing midday meals, managing construction, collecting and maintaining data on the school's students, organizing events, facilitating the visits of officials, distributing uniforms and books, and so forth.

Noneducational responsibilities outside school are perhaps the most talked about. Teachers have been involved in the census, elections, and disaster management, and continue to be so. Previously, teachers were used for tasks such as migration surveys, livestock surveys, family planning targets, immunizations, and so forth. RTE was meant to curtail many of these non-teaching tasks, but field-level reports indicate that teachers continue to be deployed in these sorts of tasks.

The inspection, feedback, and support systems in most states are dysfunctional. The numbers of schools have expanded far more rapidly over the past two decades than the inspection and support system. There are few officers and they have limited resources for such functions. Even in those states that mention "maintaining results" as one of the teachers' primary responsibilities of teachers (for example, Tamil Nadu and Rajasthan), the system places low expectations on the teachers. If the teachers can show that all the chapters given in the syllabus for the year have been "taught," that is considered enough toward completion of their primary responsibilities. The teacher may explain students' poor learning and development by citing various constraints, the biggest being the students' backgrounds and irregular attendance.

Another alarming problem reported by a few states in the study (including Uttar Pradesh and Mizoram) is that of "proxy teachers," whereby a teacher appointed by the government illegally "appoints" another person to work in her/his place for some consideration. Proxy teachers are more common in remote and rural areas, but are also found in urban areas. The extent of the practice of proxy teachers could not be determined during the preparation of the study, but it was openly discussed during focus group discussions.

Teachers are often not empowered to perform the roles expected of them. Induction or orientation programs are not a regular feature in any of the states. Although all positions seem to have a "probationary" period of two years, after which the teacher is to be confirmed, in practice this has no relevance. The officials and teachers are unable to state any difference between what happens or is expected from the teacher during the probationary period and otherwise. Another example is the implementation of continuous and comprehensive evaluation: in most states, continuous and comprehensive evaluation processes have been spelled out only partially. Teachers often complain about the inadequate orientation and capacity building on the issue.

Primary school teachers often find themselves in a multi-grade classroom, without adequate training. Approximately 42 percent of government elementary schools have only one or two teachers for the elementary grades. However, the teachers are not equipped to conduct multi-grade teaching effectively, despite clear policy directives at the national level. The National Curriculum Framework 2005 suggests that considerable planning is required on the part of teachers to address multi-grade situations. However, the teacher education process still treats multi-grade teaching as an anomaly.[4]

Most teachers have yet to come to terms with several provisions stipulated by the RTE, like "no detention" and "no corporal punishment." Teachers in the nine states said that such provisions have impinged on their professional rights and made their tasks more difficult. Teachers and senior officials critiqued the no-detention policy; they said that the policy removes the imperative of students to study. Educationists argue that it is the interpretation of the no-detention policy that is the problem—because the policy is equated with non-assessment of learning outcomes. Although teachers have cut down on corporal punishment, it is more out of compulsion rather than belief in the concept.

The position of head teacher is particularly difficult. All of the states included in this study have a significant number of vacancies for headmaster and head teacher positions. Rajasthan has the fewest vacancies at the primary and upper primary levels. The maximum numbers of vacancies are in states like Jharkhand, Karnataka, and Madhya Pradesh. In schools that do not have a regular full-time headmaster, not much can be expected from the leadership in the institution. Moreover, maintaining the school's student, financial, and administrative records; providing periodic and nonperiodic reporting; and liaising with the education department are some of the tasks of headmasters. Over the past decade and a half, activities like midday meals and construction of buildings have emerged as major time-consuming activities for headmasters. These responsibilities leave little time for academic support and supervision. This problem is further compounded because most schools do not have administrative, accounting, or support staff.

Professional Growth of Teachers

There are two broad ways in which teachers can grow professionally: through promotions and by acquiring new skills, knowledge, and competencies ("professional development"). Promotions and professional development cover a heterogeneous mix of activities. Promotions are ways in which teachers move to a different post (usually in a different cadre or grade of service), such as from being an elementary school teacher to becoming a secondary school teacher. Promotions therefore involve teachers leaving their current classroom teaching practice. A distinct class of promotions is those of contract teachers who become regular teachers. In all the states in the study, promotions are done solely on the basis of seniority (although some states in the past have had a merit-based element as well).

Certain types of professional development are closely related to promotions, since many promotional moves require a teacher to have qualifications beyond the ones in their current post. Several states have specific programs to assist teachers to acquire these necessary qualifications. However, there is little evidence about the take-up of these opportunities, and in some states the number of teachers who can avail of this opportunity at any one time is limited.

Beyond this specific training, however, none of the states in this study has an effective policy for in-service training of teachers. Training is carried out in an ad hoc manner, almost exclusively funded by two centrally sponsored schemes (SSA and RMSA). Training is therefore subject to the availability of these funds and the associated modalities and priorities. The incidence of training varies significantly across the states, as does the ability of the states to plan for and utilize these resources. Teachers in small schools or schools with few teachers face particular difficulties in attending training or becoming resource persons, because (in some states) when they attend training conducted outside vacation periods, students lose out on teaching time.

A couple of the states in the study have a teacher performance appraisal process, but the process is reported as existing on paper only.[5] Despite this lack of comprehensive and effective policy, several states discipline head teachers, and most states give monetary awards to "high performing" teachers. However, the rewards are usually based on students' examination performance, which further encourages teachers to go to "good" schools where it is easier to get good examination results. Thus, this incentive further distorts the allocation of teachers to schools where they are needed most.

Grievance Redressal Mechanisms

A major contribution of this study is that it gives systematic attention to the avenues available for the redressal of teachers' grievances. A clear and effective redressal procedure is important from a fairness point of view, as it allows individuals who believe they have suffered to follow a process through which the wrong may be rectified. Even if the individual's grievance is not addressed by the process, grievance procedures in themselves establish a sense of fairness and support the rule of law. For example, effective redressal procedures have standardized mechanisms for the presentation of and response to grievances. Further, they follow the principle that similar cases should be treated similarly, and that an administrative authority is required to provide reasons before denying a remedy being sought. In addition to fairness, redressal procedures help enhance accountability for policy measures and provide information to policy makers on how the policies they have formulated are working in practice.

There are two main mechanisms available for teacher grievance redressal. First, there are grievance hearings offered by state education officers at the block and district levels or at the state level by the state commissioner of education. Second, there are specialized dispute resolution tribunals in many states, for addressing service-related matters of government employees (of which teachers from government schools constitute a significant proportion). Some states also have tribunals for addressing teacher-related grievances for private and aided schools, such as the Jharkhand Education Tribunal, Odisha Education Tribunal, and Rajasthan Non-Governmental Education Tribunal.

However, the courts continue to be a major avenue for teachers to address their grievances. High Court cases that have been resolved within the past five years were analyzed. (The judgments were taken from official websites and records. The study could not obtain information on the total number of cases filed during the period.) A large majority of the judgments that were analyzed were filed as writ petitions in the High Courts by individuals—that is, by serving teachers and teacher applicants seeking to be appointed to teaching posts. Only a miniscule number of cases were filed by teachers' unions. (The study was told that unions often support a group of teachers in litigating a case even if the unions are not named as a party.) The respondents in all these petitions were various branches of the state education departments and, in some cases, also included the school in question (in the case of aided schools) and other teachers who had received benefits or been selected for a post in lieu of the petitioner teachers. A handful of judgments in each state involved appeal by the state government against decisions of tribunals or decisions by a single judge in the High Court.

There are enormous variations in the volume of cases disposed by the High Courts of the different states. The High Court of Odisha disposed 75 such cases between 2009 and June 2014, while the High Court of Karnataka disposed more than 6,000. The numbers in the remaining states were Madhya Pradesh, 160; Jharkhand, 187; Punjab and Haryana, 279; Tamil Nadu, 544; Rajasthan, 1,285; and Uttar Pradesh, 1,146.

These significant variations in case volumes could reflect different rates of filing petitions across states because of the costs or ease of filing, or that some High Courts were simply more efficient in disposing the cases that had been filed. The latter reason seems to be an important explanation in Karnataka and Rajasthan, where almost all the judgments studied disposed a group of petitions filed on related grievances, with many judgments disposing more than 100 petitions.

In contrast to the stark variations in the volume of cases, the types of grievances brought to the High Courts in different states were remarkably similar. The two predominant types of grievances related to service benefits and appointments. Of the total 9,751 cases (adjudged) across the eight states that were studied, 47.01 percent (or 4,584 cases) of these related to service benefits, followed by appointment-related disputes (33.2 percent or 3,241 cases) and disputes related to regularization of existing appointments (5.9 percent or 579 cases).

The courts do not appear to have systematically favored teachers or the state. On an aggregate basis, 31.88 percent of the cases reviewed were decided in favor of the state governments, 28.83 percent were decided in favor of teachers, and 31.02 percent were remanded to the state respondents with directions to consider the grievance and arrive at a decision.

Redress through the courts is a slow process. Only the Rajasthan High Court disposed more than 50 percent of its cases within two years. Of the 7,081 cases across the states where data were available, the study calculated the disposal period as being between the date of the filing of a petition and the date of the judgment. The High Court of Rajasthan had by far the best disposal rate, with 80 percent of cases disposed within a year, and it was the only court that disposed more than 50 percent of its cases within two years. Jharkhand had the slowest rate of disposal, with over 50 percent of the cases taking longer than five years to conclude. Other states with similarly slow disposal rates were Madhya Pradesh, Uttar Pradesh, and Tamil Nadu. Odisha and Karnataka disposed cases relatively quickly, although they still took more than two years to dispose 50 percent of their cases.

Certain types of grievances were disposed more quickly than others. Grievances relating to appointments, regularization of existing appointments, and disputes over examination standards were disposed relatively quickly, in most cases, within two years. Grievances relating to service benefits and retirement benefits took significantly longer to be resolved. These differences may partly be explained because the types of cases that were disposed more quickly involved larger numbers of teachers.

Many of the judgments appeared to stem from confusion in the interpretation of the education and service rules in the applicable state. This was particularly the case for eligibility criteria for the appointment of teachers to various posts (such as whether certain degrees could be considered equivalent to one another). Similarly, there appeared to be confusion on pay scales and the calculation of seniority under the service rules for teachers. Adding to this confusion was that there were often different rules for different types of teachers as well as different types of schools (for example, primary and secondary schools).

Several cases that were heard by the High Courts had remarkably similar fact patterns. In all these cases, a lot of time and costs of teacher-related litigation could have been saved if the state governments had implemented the decisions of the High Courts for all similarly situated teachers, rather than waiting for individual teachers to approach the High Courts in turn to get similar benefits.

Unanswered Questions

Those who manage the schools, provide resources, and teach in them have little faith in the government school system. Not one teacher the study team met sent their own children or grandchildren to a government school. There is a sense of disquiet across the country, a sense of despair when talking about the schools, teachers, and children's learning. And yet, in most states, the teachers reported that they had seen improvements in their overall status and working conditions. The past 20 years have witnessed significant developments in school infrastructure as well as general infrastructure (roads, communications, electricity, and water). The government has also paid attention to teachers' working conditions, such as the PTR, provision of teaching and learning materials, and availability of libraries and books.

Another unstated issue that the research team sensed was the attitude of the administration toward government schoolteachers. Across all levels, teachers were seen as government servants at the bottom of a hierarchical system. By virtue of their administrative role, officials exuded a sense of superiority. The relationship between teachers and administrators is contentious, with both trying to work the system in their favor. It is perhaps not surprising that teachers eagerly seek promotions to administrative posts and away from teaching in schools, such as to the Block Education Officer position.

A more in-depth study would be required to explain the combination of political and administrative circumstances that led to a more transparent system in some states, and why some states continue to manage with ad hoc systems and annual changes in norms and practices. Some states seem to have clearly laid out policies; they have set in motion transparent processes for recruitment and transfer; and, by and large, the teachers with whom the study team interacted seemed happy about the system. This study has demonstrated beyond a doubt that it is possible to develop and implement transparent systems and there are readily available models to emulate; what remains is to understand how to generate the political will to do so.

There is no shared understanding of what is meant by "good teacher performance," especially in the post–National Curriculum Framework 2005 era, in which teachers are expected to be facilitators, and the post-RTE era, in which children's right to education also entails the right to be taught in an environment without fear or punishment. Although many states take examination results as a performance benchmark at the secondary level, there is little clarity on how to assess the quality of teachers at the elementary level.

Moreover, no state in this study had a performance appraisal system in place (although some states, like Mizoram, have a system on paper and, according to the Ministry of Human Resource Development of the Government of India, Madhya Pradesh and Rajasthan have piloted a system recommended to them). International evidence shows that it is possible to make reliable and consistent judgments about the performance of teachers (based on observations of classroom practices). This is possible because of intensive and long-term training for those managers and head teachers who make such judgments and of the teachers who are being evaluated (so that they understand the process and know how to improve their performance). It is also most likely to be possible in a system in which there is professional respect between the various groups, which is not something that is generally possible in a hierarchical system.

In almost all the study's interviews and discussions, teachers' unions said that they did not engage with recruitment or transfer policies. Instead, teachers' unions mostly confine themselves to petitioning the government on teacher grievances and sometimes resort to protests and sit-ins (*dharna*). This study could not go into the role teachers' unions have played in bringing about changes in policies that affects teachers, or even the complicated process of lobbying for transfers and cushy postings. However, there is one notable exception. The reversal of the policy on contract teachers in Madhya Pradesh was attributed to the sustained pressure exerted by the teachers' union. Similarly, in Rajasthan, the teachers' union supported the case filed in the Rajasthan High Court against the contract teacher system. This area merits more in-depth, qualitative research to trace the role of teachers' unions in key policy changes.

An important insight of this study is that all nine states have adopted the RTE-recommended TET. But it was not possible to understand whether this helped the government recruit teachers who have mastery over their subject knowledge and pedagogy. Moreover, in none of the nine states was there discussion of using the TET results to inform pre-service training practices, including curriculum reform and comparing the pass rates of different pre-service training institutions. Finally, little is known about the quality of the TET in the states: whether the tests are unambiguously written; if the TET accurately measures the knowledge and skills it claims to measure; and whether it does so consistently over time (is a 60 percent pass rate equally difficult to achieve in successive rounds of the TET?).

This study shows that there has been unambiguous and significant progress in all nine states in the number of women teachers and percentage of teachers from the SC and ST communities. What is not known and could not be explored is the unstated norms and rules that pervade the system. For example, in Rajasthan there is an unstated norm to post only male teachers as headmasters of co-educational schools and female teachers as headmistresses of girls-only schools (Jandhyala et al. 2014). There could be similar unstated practices in all the states—with effects on the career progress opportunities of women or specific social groups. A more in-depth qualitative study is needed to unravel the unstated norms that affect equity and inclusion.

The grievance redressal systems outside the courts are new. The effectiveness of these tribunals in reducing the burden on their respective High Courts is unclear and beyond the scope of this study, especially as only a handful of the cases that were reviewed originated from these tribunals. However, it may be worth exploring further whether these tribunals could provide a more efficient and accessible forum for teachers to have their grievances redressed.

The ultimate test of the effectiveness of teachers is whether *all* the children they teach reach their educational potential. Whether teachers teach in the most effective way is determined by a complex set of policies and practices and how they interact with the personal characteristics of teachers and administrators. This study examines some of these policies and practices, from the selection of teachers to the accountability for their performance. Moreover, the value of the study is that the multi-state approach offers comparative insights.

Given the importance of the question of teacher effectiveness, the study returns to this issue see what light it can shine on this question. First, across many policies, the nine states have similar approaches. For example, the use of TETs and broadly following the NCTE guidelines on teacher qualifications are seen as positive developments. However, the lack of performance evaluation of teachers (and head teachers), the absence of merit considerations in promotions, and the lack of a role for schools in the various processes would not seem to promote a link to effective classroom teaching practices. These questions should be explored in more depth.

Second, the two areas in which the states differ most markedly are the processes for deployment and transfers of teachers, and teachers' salaries. Some states are clearly more policy-driven and have a more transparent system. Are teachers who are managed with respect and care more motivated than teachers who are pushed around by the system? Is the deployment and transfer system enough to make a significant difference in the performance of teachers in the classroom? One measure would be teachers' presence in the school. Here the evidence is, to say the least, mixed, with Karnataka among the worst performers (a teacher attendance rate of 80 percent in primary) alongside Uttar Pradesh (teacher attendance rate of 78 percent) (SSA 2009[6]). There is some evidence on the teaching practices in Madhya Pradesh and Uttar Pradesh and the attitudes of teachers toward teaching and the learning processes (Sankar and Linden 2014). But the practices found there could not be compared with other states in this study; this would be a very valuable exercise.

Recommendations

This study shows that the broad guidelines drawn up at the national level (such as the qualifications for teachers set by NCTE and the development of the Unified District Information System for Education (UDISE) database) have had and will continue to have an important role in facilitating a dialogue about issues related to teacher management. That said, the vast majority of teachers are state government employees, and it is the states that ultimately determine teacher recruitment and deployment policies, finance salaries, decide promotion criteria, and provide teachers support in the form of professional development and grievance redressal structures.

The overwhelming message emanating from this study is that there is an urgent need for each state to develop a comprehensive teacher management policy. The policy should include a clearly laid out recruitment protocol, transfer regime, and guidelines for related matters, such as teacher deputation to administrative duties (as block- or cluster-level administrative official), education-related duties (at the District Institute of Education and Training (DIET), Cluster Resource Centre (CRC), and Block Resource Centre (BRC), as key resource person), and promotion (as headmaster or head teacher). But a comprehensive policy is not enough; it needs to be supported by structures that allow practice to follow policy in a transparent manner, reducing the stress, delays, and confusion associated with nontransparent processes. The study identifies five key teacher management issues on which state governments should focus to improve their school education systems. The five issues are related; changes in one are likely to affect the others.

Streamlined and Transparent Recruitment and Deployment

Karnataka and Tamil Nadu provide an example of how to make teacher recruitment, deployment, and transfer more transparent and efficient. Their systems share certain common features: (a) there are clear policies for each; (b) the processes are transparent and largely conducted online using sophisticated software and management information systems; (c) there is a clearly defined timeline for the process of recruitment and transfer, which is stable across years and across change of governments; and (d) teachers at the elementary level are a block-level cadre, with considerable choice in their first assignment.

Moving beyond this, recruitment policies and practices must address two issues that have not only complicated teacher management considerably, but, more importantly, challenged the constitutional maxim of "equal pay for equal work." The first relates to the existence of multiple cadres of teachers. This complicates in several situations. At the same level, there are Zillah Parishad or Panchayati Raj Institution teachers, and there are some project-specific teachers (funded from RMSA or SSA). Or in a school, an elementary school head teacher might be responsible for the primary and upper primary cadre teachers.

The second issue is the uneven distribution of PTRs within states, and indeed within districts and blocks. All the states had a significant number of elementary schools with very low PTRs (below 1:10) and very high PTRs (above 1:100). There is therefore an urgent need for states to investigate the distribution of teachers at the school level and rationalize accordingly—making sure that the RTE-guaranteed PTR is a reality in every school. At the secondary level, the states need to develop a metric for assessing the need for subject teachers for every school and every class. The standard PTR used at the primary level does not work at the secondary level. Similarly, a metric is also needed for upper primary teachers.

Easy Access to Support Structures for Teachers

BRC and CRC structures were conceptualized as a peer support system for teachers. However, the feedback from teachers was that there is no support system. Three things are important to highlight in providing support to teachers. First, the institutions of headmaster and school principal need to be strengthened. Governments can start by recognizing the importance of these roles and ensuring that all schools have a school principal (the number of unfilled posts is scandalous) who is competent and motivated (simply appointing the most senior teacher is not a good enough policy). Governments also need to provide capacity building for all those who are serving as school principals.

Second, a systematic induction program is needed for teachers. At present, new teachers are simply expected to learn their roles and responsibilities on the job, with little formal guidance or support. To begin, states should develop a single booklet that contains all the information a new teacher needs about their roles, responsibilities, and rights. Next, new teachers should be assigned a mentor—a more senior teacher with responsibility for helping to guide the new teacher and responding to questions. And lastly, states should focus some capacity-building activities on new teachers.

Third, and more boldly, the national and state governments should engage in a dialogue about the size of the schools. The spread of schools to many rural and remote communities has without doubt had a positive impact on access for children. However, it has also had the effect of creating small schools without sufficient teachers (and without adequate support and often without sufficient physical infrastructure) to create good quality schools. Not only would teacher management be easier within fewer, larger schools, it is very likely that such schools would offer better quality education for the children. Where feasible (geographically and infrastructure-wise), children could be transported to larger schools created in a cluster of small villages.

For teachers to perform effectively, they must know that there are systems in place to protect their professional interests and aspirations. The Government of India could initiate a nationwide dialogue on grievance redressal mechanisms by drawing on good practices in different states. The Government of India could also encourage the state governments to make sure that all schools and education-related institutions, like the CRC, BRC, DIET, State Council of Educational Research and Training (SCERT), and so forth, come under the "Sexual Harassment of Women at Workplace (Prevention, Prohibition and Redressal) Act Of 2013."

Incentives for Effort and Performance

Promotions currently depend entirely on seniority and the accumulation of qualifications, not on the work teachers do to help students learn better. Even in states where policy pronouncements link rewards to performance (such as in Madhya Pradesh for confirmation of contract teachers), the study team found little evidence to suggest that the policy had translated into practice. For teachers to be effective, it is important that career progression structures reward effectiveness rather than relying on experience and qualifications.

There are no positive incentives for teachers to work in rural and remote areas, with the exception of Karnataka, where years of service in a remote area count toward a teacher's transfer opportunities. It may be a good idea to build in incentives in the form of additional allowances, housing in the school compound or the same village, priority for a posting in an urban area after a stipulated number of years, and so forth. State policy should see teaching in rural and remote areas as a positive choice that can be made by good teachers, rather than a necessity to be tolerated while waiting for a "good" posting.

A final point on career progression: the multiplicity of cadres also makes it more difficult for teachers to navigate their professional progression, as they usually must leave their present cadre to get a promotion and cannot move back. Hence, a teacher cannot build a diverse set of experiences (as primary teacher, upper primary teacher, and member of the BRC team) to be a more effective primary teacher. This needs to be addressed.

Accountability and Feedback on Performance

Teacher appraisal is perhaps the most underdeveloped but also the largest missing piece in the state teacher management systems. The lack of an effective appraisal system means that teachers get no feedback on how they are performing, and so no guidance on what their professional development needs are. As a result, administrators cannot design appropriate training programs. An appraisal system should make promotions a reward for good performance rather than simply time served. A further advantage would be to enable the small minority of teachers who continue to perform poorly to be removed from the teaching profession. It is noteworthy that this problem is not specific to government schools—private (aided and unaided) schools also face similar challenges related to poor-performing teachers. A lot of work needs to be done in this area, especially on recruitment and cadre management rules.

Improved Data Systems

Transparent, merit- and experience-driven management of the teaching cadre would be greatly improved by an integrated teacher management information system (MIS), where personnel and deployment histories are available; training history is recorded; and other teacher-specific information is available. Although it is not one of the states covered in this study, Bihar has recently developed such a system, and technical solutions are readily available. A robust teacher information system would (a) reduce delays in promotions, increments, and transfers due to administrative inefficiencies like maintenance of service books and teacher records; and (b) enable deputing teachers for training on the basis of their needs and past training experience. Equally, it would be extremely useful to administrators and researchers if the District Information System for Education (DISE) and the Unified District Information System for Education (UDISE) captured teacher-specific information. State and district officials will need greater capacity to use such a system effectively in their decision making.

Many of the issues related to teachers' accountability, to whom and for what, could be addressed if an integrated teacher MIS captured the professional trajectory of teachers. Or, to put it the other way around, the development of such an integrated teacher MIS is dependent on having shared understanding between the teachers and the state government of what teachers are accountable for and, therefore, what types of information should be collected through the MIS.

Finally, as the report shows, several administrative problems in the various states were caused by poorly developed policies or practices (for example, lack of clarity over service rules leads to delays in the payment of teachers' benefits and generates court cases). One way to address this issue would be for state governments to consult on new policies and procedures, by publishing the draft documents and inviting comments within a specific period. Beyond enhancing administrative efficiency, this approach would have the added benefit of promoting transparency.

Notes

1. The Teacher Recruitment Board in Tamil Nadu, headed by a senior Indian Administrative Service officer, undertakes all teacher recruitment pertaining to teachers in elementary, secondary, high, and higher secondary schools as well as colleges. The Board announces vacancies on its website, www.trb.tn.nic.in. The Board conducts certificate verification and written and oral exams pertaining to teacher selection. (Oral exams are conducted for college teachers.) All complaints regarding teacher recruitments, especially the TET, are also filed against the Recruitment Board.
2. Krishna Bhatnagar Committee on 6th Pay Commission, Government of Rajasthan: http://finance.rajasthan.gov.in/doc/bhatnagarcommittee/chapter-I.pdf.

3. Punjab, in the present form, came into being after the trifurcation of the larger Punjab into three states in 1965. Therefore, the first pay commission of Punjab was constituted in 1966.
4. MHRD, Government of India, officials argued that multi-grade teaching has always been an integral part of the District Primary Education Programme and SSA teacher training strategies. However, the study team was unable to find information on the number of multi-grade teacher-training programs.
5. MHRD, Government of India, officials refuted this finding of the study during a meeting on March 10, 2015. *The officials said that some states have introduced performance appraisal systems and are piloting it. For example, Madhya Pradesh and Rajasthan have piloted teacher appraisal processes.* The study team was not able to obtain information on the pilot programs from the two governments.
6. Sarva Shiksha Abhiyan EdCIL (India) Ltd., 2009, "Attendance of Students and Teachers in Primary and Upper Primary Schools: Synthesis of the Study Conducted in 20 States," New Delhi.

Abbreviations

ABL	Activity-Based Learning
ACPI	Assistant Commissioner of Public Instruction
ADMK	Anna Dravida Munnetra Kazhagam
ADW	Adi Dravida Welfare
AEEO	Assistant Elementary Education Officer
AEO	Assistant Education Officer
AIADMK	All India Anna Dravida Munnetra Kazhagam
B.A.	Bachelor of the Arts
B.A.Ed.	Bachelor of the Arts in Education
BC	Backward Class
B.Com.	Bachelor of Commerce (B.Com.)
B.Ed.	Bachelor of Education
B.El.Ed.	Bachelor of Elementary Education
BEO	Block Education Officer
BJP	Bharatiya Janata Party
BRC	Block Resource Centre
BRCC	Block Resource Centre Coordinator
B.S.	Bachelor of Science
B.S.Ed.	Bachelor of Science in Education
BT	Graduate Teacher
BTC	Basic Training Certificate
B.Tech.	Bachelor of Technology
CAC	Centralized Admission Cell
CBPS	Centre for Budget and Policy Studies
CCE	Continuous Comprehensive Evaluation
CET	Common Entrance Test
CM	Chief Minister
CPI	Commissioner of Public Instruction

CRC	Cluster Resource Centre
CRCC	Cluster Resource Centre Coordinator
CT	Certificate in Teaching
CTET	Central Teacher Eligibility Test
CWSN	children with special needs
DD	Deputy Director
DDPI	Deputy Director of Public Instruction
D.Ed.	Diploma in Education
DEO	District Education Officer
DGSE	Department of General and Secondary Education
DIET	District Institute of Education and Training
DISE	District Information System for Education
DMK	Dravida Munnetra Kazhagam
DPEP	District Primary Education Programme
DPI	Director of Public Instruction
D.T.Ed.	Diploma in Teacher Education
DTERT	Directorate of Teacher Education, Research and Training
EBC	Extremely Backward Class
ETT	Elementary Teacher Training
FGD	focus group discussion
GDP	gross domestic product
GO	government order
GOM	Government Order of Madras
GTR	Government Tribal Residentia
HOD	Head of Department
HRA	house rent allowance
HSC	Higher Secondary School Certificate
HSE	Higher Secondary Education
HSSLC	Higher Secondary School Leaving Certificate
ICT	information and communications technology
IT	information technology
JBT	Junior Basic Training
JD	Joint Director
KGBV	Kasturba Gandhi Balika Vidyalayas
LT	Licentiate Teacher
MDM	midday meal
MGR	M. G. Ramachandran
MHRD	Ministry of Human Resource Development

MIS	Management Information System
MLA	Member of the Legislative Assembly
MLC	Member of the Legislative Council
MP	Member of Parliament
NCERT	National Council of Educational Research and Training
NCF	National Curriculum Framework
NCTE	National Council of Teacher Education
NIC	National Informatics Centre
NOC	No Objection Certificate
NPE	National Policy on Education
NUEPA	National University of Educational Planning and Administration
OBC	Other Backward Classes
PAR	Performance Appraisal Report
PG	Post-Graduate
PGT	Post-Graduate Teacher
PS	Principal Secretary
PSTET	Punjab State Teacher Eligibility Test
PTR	Pupil-Teacher Ratio
PUC	Pre-University Certificate
RAA	Rural Area Allowance
RCI	Rehabilitation Council of India
RMSA	Rashtriya Madhyamik Shiksha Abhiyan
RTE	Right to Education
SC	Scheduled Caste
SD	Standard Deviation
SEBC	Social and Economic Backward Classes
SGT	Secondary Grade Teacher
SMC	School Management Committee
SOBC	Special Other Backward Classes
SS	Sikshya Sahayak
SSA	Sarva Shiksha Abhiyan
SSLC	Secondary School Leaving Certificate
SSS	Samvida Shala Shikshak
ST	Scheduled Tribe
TCH	Teacher's Certificate Higher
TET	Teacher Eligibility Test
TGT	Trained Graduate Teacher
TLM	Teaching and Learning Material

TRB	Teacher Recruitment Board
TTC	Teacher Training College
TTI	Teacher Training Institute
UDISE	Unified District Information System for Education
ZP	Zillah Parishad

CHAPTER 1

Introduction

Background

As India gears up to energize the school education system to meet the challenges of balancing quantity, quality, and equity, the role of teachers will be key to how effectively the system can turn around. Recent research in India and globally has shown that teacher effectiveness is "the most important school-based predictor of student learning and that several consecutive years of outstanding teaching can offset the learning deficits of disadvantaged students…" (Ganimian and Vegas 2011, 5).

The Global Monitoring Report on "Education for All" (2013–14) highlights the alarming fact that globally around 250 million children of primary school age are not reaching minimum standards of learning. There is a global learning crisis and this crisis hits the disadvantaged the most. The report also highlights the need to improve the quality of teaching, reiterating that the quality of learning depends on the quality of teachers. The report notes that insufficient education funding has affected education outcomes, and this will result in future economic loss. The report urged governments to boost efforts to recruit an additional 1.6 million teachers to achieve the goal of universal primary education by 2015.

The big question is whether having more teachers would solve the learning crisis. The effectiveness of teachers in the classroom, their motivation to enable children to learn, and self-image and self-esteem are closely linked. Hiring more teachers may not solve the learning problem unless governments ensure that teachers have the requisite skills, right environment, and motivation to guarantee that every child learns.

In the past decade or more, there has been some debate on what makes a good teacher. Is it their qualifications? Is it their remuneration? Is it the overall work environment? Is it functional autonomy in the school and the classroom? Is it commitment? Is it about monitoring and accountability? Or is it some combination of these factors? There are conflicting findings on these questions, but little research on what can really turn the system around to enable teachers to become dedicated professionals, respected by society for their contribution toward building generations of educated students.[1] Countries like Poland and

Singapore have made progress on these fronts, but in India very little is known about how teachers are positioned in the system, their working conditions, accountability systems, and effective autonomy where it matters the most—in the classroom.

This report was conceptualized at a significant moment in the history of education in India. The Right to Education (RTE) Act 2009 mandated specific teacher-student ratios and teacher qualifications, and issued guidelines on the factors necessary for making an environment conducive for teaching and learning. Equally significant is that the RTE Act and Justice Verma Committee (2012) mandated a teacher eligibility test as the first step in the recruitment of all teachers, whether on contract or grade. In addition, several state governments have reviewed their policies on contract teachers (contract/regular and contractual probation moving toward regularization); however, some state governments are hiring contract teachers without any long-term perspective on what would happen to them. There has also been a lot of pressure to improve the quality of schools and ensure that students learn. The annual learning assessment surveys of Pratham India (Annual Status of Education Report Survey[2]), periodic learning assessments done by the National Council of Educational Research and Training, and large-scale surveys executed by Educational Initiatives reveal in different ways that all is not well with what students are able to learn in the Indian education system.

Scanning the global literature on quality and learning, it is evident that one of the key determinants of learning is the competency, effectiveness, and motivation of teachers (Dundar et al. 2014). The literature suggests that these three teacher attributes are determined by how the education system is able to foreground the rights of children (to quality education), acknowledge the rights of teachers (working conditions), and balance the two, creatively and effectively (Cream Wright in Mpokosa and Ndaruhutse 2008). In other words, it depends on how effectively the system is being managed.

The Oxford English Dictionary meaning of the word "management" gives the word a command-oriented overtone: the "Organization, supervision, or direction; the application of skill or care in the manipulation, use, treatment, or control (of a thing or person), or in the conduct of something." Taking the elements of this definition that are pertinent to the current discussion, *good* management is more about coordinating "the efforts of people to accomplish goals and objectives using available resources efficiently and effectively." For academic research purposes, it is important to arrive at a definition of what constitutes "teacher management." A comprehensive bibliography of teacher management done by the United Nations Educational, Scientific and Cultural Organization (Gottlemann-Duret and Yekhlef 2005) identifies three major challenges as the overarching framework for teacher management:

- Provide enough teachers (to meet student demand): this includes recruitment and deployment and redistribution of teachers (transfer and posting).

- Enable teachers to do "good work" from the pupils' and teachers' point of view: this includes status and working conditions, autonomy and freedom, avenues for professional growth, and development and school leadership.
- Respond to the major existing (especially financial) constraints: different categories of teachers and their salary and periodic increments, policy decisions on contract teachers, incentives, and increments.

These elements are also reflected in the World Bank's Systems Approach for Better Education–Teachers review of what factors matter most in teacher policy globally. Although teacher development/training (content and processes) is often not included in teacher management, the mechanism for identifying the training requirements of teachers and decisions pertaining to how, for whom, and where the training will be organized are an important aspect of teacher management. There are no watertight compartments, and issues of teacher development and teacher management often overlap and intertwine with each other. However, this report focuses only on the management aspect of professional development.

Notwithstanding the spate of global research and policy-level work on teacher management, there is not enough evidence on the effectiveness of various policies and management regimes, especially in India. Specifically, there is very little documentation of how policies are implemented, and the distance between policy and practice. It is practice that ultimately determines what happens inside classrooms and whether students learn.

Keeping these issues in mind, the National University of Educational Planning and Administration, with support from the Rajiv Gandhi Foundation, initiated a study to understand the working conditions of elementary and secondary school teachers in nine states in India, namely, Jharkhand, Karnataka, Madhya Pradesh, Mizoram, Odisha, Punjab, Rajasthan, Tamil Nadu, and Uttar Pradesh.[3] These states were selected to ensure that all regions of the country are represented and suitable research agencies are available to undertake the task within a tight timeframe. This volume seeks to answer the following key questions for each of the nine states:

1. How are teachers recruited?
2. How are they deployed (appointed, transferred, and deputed)?
3. How much are teachers paid?
4. What are the various teaching and non-teaching tasks that are assigned to teachers?
5. How much autonomy do they have (and for what)?
6. Who are teachers accountable to and for what?

The Scope

At the outset, this volume primarily focuses on government schoolteachers at the elementary level and government and government-aided schoolteachers at the secondary level. Government-aided schoolteachers were included at the secondary level because of their strong presence in this part of the sector. Higher secondary teachers were kept out because, in most states, the norms governing them are distinct and, in many states, the higher secondary stage is treated administratively as part of higher education.

The volume covers all categories of teachers—regular, contract, and part-time teachers. Since the late 1980s, many states in India have appointed contract teachers (who were then known as "para-teachers") for two main reasons: (a) to respond to the rapid increase in student enrollment, address the problems of teacher absence and non-availability of teachers in rural/remote areas, and enable local governments to hire teachers (albeit with lower qualifications) on annual or short-term contracts; and (b) to enable state governments to hire more teachers with fewer financial resources. As a result, most of the educationally backward states created multiple cadres of schoolteachers. With the coming of the government's flagship elementary education program, Sarva Shiksha Abhiyan (SSA), in 2001, some states started using SSA funds to hire contract teachers. A similar trend is evident with the coming of the secondary school initiative, Rashtriya Madhyamik Shiksha Abhiyan (RMSA) in 2009. As a result, some states not only had two types of teachers—regular and contract—but also different types of contract teachers. Some contract teachers are hired by the *Zillah Parishad* (District Council) using state government resources, others are hired through the SSA/RMSA budget, and still others are hired by the school (through the School Development and Management Committee/Parent Teacher Association). Therefore, it is important to unravel and understand the evolution of multiple cadres of elementary and secondary schoolteachers.

With the enactment of the RTE in 2009, state governments have had to make changes in the entry qualifications of teachers (regular and contract), to conform with the National Council of Teacher Education (NCTE) and RTE norms. In several states, the idea of having multiple cadres of teachers doing the same work but drawing different salaries was challenged in the courts. The education community argued that giving different pay for the same work went against the spirit of the RTE Act. This has led to changes in many of the states in this study. As a result, with the interventions of the courts (Rajasthan High Court Judgment 2013), change in the perceptions of political leaders and administrators (Madhya Pradesh), and pressure from the organized teaching community (Uttar Pradesh), some states started the process of "regularizing" contract teachers. However, several states (including Jharkhand and Punjab) have not yet reviewed their policies. There are indications that many state governments are in the process of rethinking the teacher-related policies that were introduced in the 1990s and early 2000s. Given that the policies toward recruitment and management of teachers have gone through significant changes, this needs to be documented and analyzed. In doing so, the aim is to help all states (not just the nine in the study) to review their teacher policies in the light of new evidence.

The unique contribution of this volume is that it looks at and compares stated policy and actual practice. This is perhaps the most compelling justification to initiate a project to study teacher management policies in India.

Introduction

What is teacher management? This question is often posed. For clarity, this study's understanding of the concept includes the following (box 1.1):

- Recruitment policies and practices
- Deployment and redeployment (transfers and postings) policies and practices
- Salary and non-salary benefits and related service conditions (pensions and other long-term benefits)
- Physical working conditions of teachers
- Roles, duties, and responsibilities of teachers
- Avenues for professional growth and management of teacher in-service training
- Autonomy, accountability, and appraisal systems that are in place
- Teachers' rights, grievance redressal mechanisms (through a desk review of legal cases filed in the past two years), and the mandate of teachers' unions.

Box 1.1 Areas, Issues, and Questions Explored

1. Profile of all types of teachers:
   - Regular and contract teachers at the elementary and secondary levels.
   - Who can become a teacher?

2. Recruitment:
   - Who becomes a teacher?
   - Who hires them? To what cadre do they belong?
   - When was the last time the state government recruited teachers?
   - What process was followed and how much time elapsed from notification of recruitment to the actual appointment?
   - Who is the cadre controlling or managing authority?

3. Teacher deployment:
   - How are teachers deployed? Who makes decisions regarding deployment and how are those decisions taken, and at what level?
   - What is the current transfer policy in the state, and how are teachers transferred?

4. Salary and service conditions:
   - What are the salaries and non-salary benefits given to teachers (regular and contract)?

5. Working environment:
   - Physical working environment: infrastructure (toilets, school buildings, and drinking water), school facilities, library, laboratories, and availability of educational material.

6. Roles, duties, and autonomy:
   - What are the various teaching and non-teaching tasks that are assigned to teachers?
   - Who allocates the tasks and how are they communicated?
   - How are new policy changes (RTE) or new guidelines (continuous and comprehensive evaluation) communicated to teachers?
   - What are the decisions that a teacher can take for her/his class?

box continues next page

Box 1.1 Areas, Issues, and Questions Explored *(continued)*

7. Day-to-day management and administration:
   - Training and professional development.
   - How are teachers sent for training, and who decides?
   - How many days of training are mandated, and who organizes the training?
   - Are there any other mechanisms for professional support?
   - What is the system of performance evaluation of teachers?

8. School leadership:
   - School leadership and the powers and authority of headmasters.

9. Rights of teachers:
   - What is the process of grievance redressal for regular and contract teachers?
   - What different kinds of teachers' unions exist in the states, and what role do unions play in improving the conditions of teachers?

What We Did Not Set Out to Do

When this type of research is designed, the obvious question that comes to mind is whether it will reveal whether India is recruiting good teachers. *At the outset, it is important to clarify that this volume does not seek to comment on the capacity and quality of teachers who have been recruited and how effectively they are working in the schools. This volume is instead about finding out whether the government can recruit and deploy teachers where necessary, whether practices are informed by policies, and if all this is being done in a transparent manner.* Therefore, although questions about the quality of teachers are very important and should be investigated, this volume reflects on the processes that frame the management of teachers. Should future research establish that India is able to recruit sufficient numbers of effective teachers, this study will help explain why that is the case. By contrast, if it turns out that India is not able to recruit sufficient numbers of effective teachers, the present study will provide important insights into what changes are needed in current processes to improve the quality of people who are recruited to be teachers.

Further, this volume does not attempt to describe or analyze the situation of private, unaided elementary and secondary schools. Again, these issues are worth investigating, given the rapid rise of such schools, especially in elementary education. In this volume, however, there were enough questions worth investigating with respect to government and government-aided schools, such that broadening the scope further would have reduced the ability to say something meaningful on teacher management.

Methodology

Following a detailed literature review on key issues in teacher management globally and in India, the research was conducted in three stages:

- Desk review of existing materials (government orders, notifications, and related information) on teacher management and development
- In-depth exploration of issues identified
- Dialogues with stakeholders at the state and district levels.

The study adopted a methodology that was primarily qualitative in nature, through perusal of policy and other documents and interviews with stakeholders. An intensive analysis of existing data was carried out to capture the context in which the study was located.

The research was done step-by-step, as follows:

First. Beginning in April 2014, every state team conducted an extensive desk review of policy documents, government orders, gazette notifications, minutes of meetings and notices issued in the past 10 years (2003–13), and selected legal judgments delivered in the past two years (2011–13). These included documents related to teacher recruitment, transfer, salary, appraisal, professional growth, and other aspects of teacher management and development.

Second. Analysis of educational databases (District Information System for Education (DISE), Secondary Education Management Information System, and Unified District Information System for Education (UDISE)) to get a picture of the profile of teachers.

Third. Legal judgments delivered by the nine State High Courts in the past two years were gathered from the nine states for content analysis, to understand the range of grievances that teachers face and appeals against the judgments pronounced.

Fourth. The study conducted semi-structured interviews with key informants at the state level. Interviews were conducted with state-level officials from the Department of School Education, Elementary Education, and Public Instruction; the societies implementing SSA and RMSA; educational research and training institutions (Department of State Educational Research and Training, Karnataka; State Council of Educational Research and Training; and Directorate of Teacher Education Research and Training, Tamil Nadu), teacher recruitment boards (where they exist), and registered teachers associations (primary and secondary). The interviews were designed to understand the various processes undertaken and issues and challenges faced at different levels for managing various facets of teacher management and development. In total, 12 individuals were interviewed at the state level. In several states, the interviews were conducted twice—first to gather basic information and the second time to validate the information gathered through the document review and seek clarifications. *Confidentiality was assured; therefore, the names and designations of the interviewees are not listed in this report.*

Fifth. Semi-structured interviews were conducted with key informants at the district level. District-level interviews were conducted with the offices of the District Education Officer or Deputy Director of Public Instruction, District Institute of Educational Training, and block-level officers (administration and development) in two sample blocks per state. The selection of the district was done in consultation with state-level officials as well as a comparison of district- and state-level education indicators, to ensure that the sample district was representative of the state. Confidentiality was assured; therefore, the names and designations of the interviewees are not listed in this report.

Sixth. Focus group discussions (FGDs) were conducted at the block level with teachers from primary and secondary schools. In every sample district, at least two FGDs were conducted with elementary and secondary schoolteachers. *The study did not maintain a list of the teachers who participated in the FGDs, to ensure confidentiality.*

Seventh. The study sponsored a state-level workshop in September 2014, to cross-check and validate the information collected and seek the advice and guidance of experienced civil servants and leaders of teachers' unions. After completing the review of the documents, semi-structured interviews, and group discussions, a state-level discussion workshop was conducted to present the major findings and suggestions in the presence of state and district officials, teachers association representatives, and scholars and nongovernmental organizations that work on teacher management aspects in the state. Inputs from the workshop were incorporated into the report.

Eighth. The draft reports were presented at a national workshop of researchers and selected experts, to understand the specific texture of each of the nine states and cull the issues that could be covered in a national synthesis. This forum also provided detailed feedback to the research teams, so they could revise the draft state reports, provide additional information (where required), and generate common tables and matrices.

This volume is the culmination of this process. This synthesis report draws heavily on the findings of the nine state reports[4].

Structure of the Book

This volume starts with an overview of the situation as revealed through the DISE and UDISE data on teachers. Chapter 2 describes India's teaching workforce and discusses its size and the trends across elementary (primary and upper primary) and secondary schools. Taking a 10-year perspective, the analysis then focuses on the terms of (teacher) employment across the nine states. The analysis reveals that there have been some significant changes in the terms of appointment of teachers. Among the issues flagged in the chapter are the trends and variations in pupil-teacher ratios and educational qualifications. The chapter provides a succinct statistical backdrop to the research study.

Chapter 3 delves into who can become a teacher. The chapter starts with an analysis of recent NCTE notifications and the implications of the RTE Act of 2009, and then provides an overview of the situation in the nine states. The chapter flows into chapter 4, on teacher recruitment, which discusses several interesting findings on the policy framework for recruitment and the actual practice that is evident in the states. The chapter further enriches understanding on contract teachers, regular teachers, and those who are caught somewhere in-between (the contractual period before they become regular, in Madhya Pradesh and Odisha). Chapter 4 also captures the Karnataka model, which several states have been trying to emulate.

Teacher deployment and transfers have always been contentious issues in educational management—with some document-based evidence and a lot of anecdotal narratives and newspaper reports. Chapter 5 places the issues that frame teacher deployment within a policy context, and explores the extent to which the nine states adhere to their own policies. Teachers across the nine states talked about what they liked and what they did not. In several states, the discussions revolved around rent-seeking and corruption. This is a challenging and complex issue to present, backed by evidence. Unfortunately, apart from the narratives and opinions expressed in the interviews and discussions, there is indeed little concrete evidence, since issues of rent-seeking are typically hidden and not recorded. However, the chapter provides some understanding of how manipulation is possible in the absence of a clearly laid out policy and a transparent system of teacher transfers (such as in Karnataka and Tamil Nadu).

Chapter 6 focuses on salaries and benefits and the range of teacher remuneration across the nine study states. Interestingly, the more educationally developed states, such as Tamil Nadu and Karnataka, pay among the lowest salaries, although all the states (except Punjab) claim to adhere to the salaries in the 6th Pay Commission. Interestingly, Punjab, which claims to follow the 5th Pay Commission, pays teachers the best and has the lowest difference between the salaries of elementary and secondary school teachers.

Chapter 7, on teachers in schools, provides an analytical overview of the roles and responsibilities of teachers, the challenges they face in discharging them, and the implications of RTE in the lives of teachers. The chapter also discusses the evidence that was obtained on school leaders and their role.

Chapter 8 deals with the professional growth of teachers and captures the management of the training regime in the nine states. Chapter 9 describes the grievance redressal system in the nine states. The chapter distinguishes between administrative grievance redressal mechanisms and the legal route. The chapter provides a glimpse into the legal and administrative framework of India's education system, and is a first step toward a much more detailed and nuanced analysis of these mechanisms.

Chapter 10 discusses unresolved issues that emerged in the course of this study. The chapter highlights several cross-cutting themes and issues that could not be included in detail.

Notes

1. In recent research, Azam and Kingdon (2015) find that there is a lot of variation in teacher quality across teachers (as measured by their pupils' scores), and teachers' resume traits, such as qualifications, training, and years of experience have no consistent relationship with student achievement.
2. Annual Status of Education Report, 2005 to 2014, http://www.asercentre.org/.
3. The original plan was to cover 11 states; however, Maharashtra had to be dropped from the original list and, later, Uttarakhand dropped out due to internal administrative issues in the host organization.
4. The state reports are available on the NUEPA website: State reports. http://www.nuepa.org/New/completed%20reaserches.aspx

CHAPTER 2

School Teachers in India: A Descriptive Analysis

Introduction

A first step in understanding teacher management and development in India is to document the size of the teaching force and changes in key characteristics of schoolteachers over the past 10 years. This chapter uses data from 2003–04 to 2012–13, at the all-India level as well as individually for the nine states of the study.

There are some sharp differences, but also some common features across states. States vary greatly in the proportions of teachers (and pupils and schools) that are under different types of management (government, aided, and private unaided), overall pupil-teacher ratio (PTR), average school size, structure of grades/classes within a given school, proportion of teachers who are regular as opposed to contract teachers, and proportion of teachers who are female (the proportion has been increasing in all states over the past 10 years in elementary education).

The common features across states in elementary education include significant reductions in PTRs over the past 10 years, due to the increasing numbers of teachers outpacing the growth in enrollments (especially in private schools); Scheduled Tribe (ST) teachers being generally well-represented, but not, so far, Scheduled Caste (SC) teachers; a steady increase in the educational qualifications of all teachers; and significant infrastructure challenges, with only a few schools meeting expectations. In addition, among secondary schools, the characteristics of aided schools in a given state are more like the government schools in that state than they are like aided schools in other states.

Perhaps the most important commonality across states is that there are significant variations *within* states across several parameters (for example, PTR at the school or district level), and these variations are as significant as the differences *across* states. The other chapters look at how teacher policies in states have created and/or can help address these differences.

For teachers and managers of teachers, a particular challenge is the small size of schools. A significant proportion of elementary schools have only one teacher, and an even larger proportion of secondary schools have (at most) only one specialist teacher in each subject. PTRs in these schools tend to be high. Teachers in small schools are more isolated professionally (they cannot discuss their challenges with another teacher) and face difficulties attending training (or simply taking leave) because there is no system for teacher substitutes and, when a teacher is absent, students do not learn.

Teaching Workforce: The Current Scenario[1]

An "elementary school" is defined as any school that has an elementary section—but it may be part of a school that also has secondary and/or higher secondary sections.[2] Equivalently, any school with a secondary section is included in the definition of a "secondary school," although it might have primary, upper primary, and/or higher secondary sections. In practice, many states still do not use "elementary school" as a category; they refer to primary and upper primary as distinct entities.

Those planning teacher management need to be aware that different definitions of "elementary school teacher" and "secondary school teacher" yield different estimates of teacher numbers. *In this section, the numbers of elementary school teachers are based on the data presented in the Report Cards published on the Unified District Information System for Education (UDISE) website. The Report Cards define an "elementary teacher" as being any teacher (that is, teaching any section) in an elementary school (and similarly for "secondary teacher")*. Alongside these key numbers, the equivalent numbers estimated from the raw data are reported, based on an alternative definition of elementary school teachers as being only those in elementary schools *who are actually teaching elementary sections* (and similarly for secondary teachers). This narrower definition yields numbers that are much smaller. These alternative figures are presented to emphasize that using an alternative definition can lead to a significantly different understanding of the teaching workforce and its characteristics and, hence, has different policy implications.[3] For secondary school teachers, all the numbers presented in this section are based on the raw data (since the Report Cards are not published for secondary schools).

Elementary Teachers

As of 2012–13, the elementary teacher workforce in India was more than 7.4 million strong, teaching across 1.4 million government, government aided, and private unaided elementary schools (table 2.1). (If just teachers teaching elementary sections/classes are taken, as per the raw data, there were 5.8 million[4] elementary teachers.) Of these, 4.5 million teachers work in government schools[5] (3.6 million as per the raw data), and 2.6 million are employed in privately managed schools[6] (1.9 million as per the raw data, 0.4 million of which are employed in aided schools, and 1.5 million in private unaided schools).

Table 2.1 Number of Elementary Teachers, Using Alternative Definitions and Data Sources, All-India

Category	Teachers in elementary schools (Report Card data)	Teachers teaching elementary classes/sections (raw data)
Number of teachers (millions)	7.4	5.8
Number of teachers in government schools (millions)	4.5	3.6
Number of teachers in private schools (millions)	2.6	1.9
Average pupil-teacher ratio	28.8	34.4

Source: DISE Report Card data and UDISE raw data.
Note: "Private" schools include aided and unaided schools. In the available data set, it is not possible to separate these types of private schools.

The average all-India PTR, according to the Report Card data, is 28.8,[7] with a maximum PTR of 129.4 and a minimum of 4.4. The raw data show the average PTR—taken across all the elementary schools surveyed—as 34.4. However, there is significant upward and downward variation across schools; this variation is explored in more detail in this chapter.

Across the country, there are nearly 130,000 single-teacher elementary schools, most of which (79 percent) have only a primary section, or only an upper primary section (13 percent). The remaining 10,000 single-teacher schools have more than one section.

Women constitute about 46 percent of all teachers in the country, and about 21 percent of all teachers come from marginalized sections of society (SCs and STs) (table 2.2). The overwhelming majority of the teaching workforce operates as "regular" teachers, with only about 7 percent being "contract" or "para" teachers.[8] About 87 percent of all teachers have completed at least higher secondary education, and about 64 percent have at least a college degree.

Among the nine states under consideration, Uttar Pradesh has the largest teaching workforce, with 950,000 teachers, followed by Rajasthan, with 560,000 teachers. Mizoram is the smallest, with only about 19,000 teachers, but it nevertheless has the lowest PTR (13.9) by a long distance. Women are best represented in the teaching workforces in Tamil Nadu and Punjab, comprising 73 percent and 72 percent, respectively, of total elementary teachers. Women comprise less than 45 percent of all teachers in all other states except Karnataka. Jharkhand, with 32 percent, and Rajasthan, with 31 percent women teachers, have worryingly low female representation. At least 20 percent of all teachers come from the marginalized sections in five of the states under consideration, with Jharkhand (31 percent SC and ST teachers) providing the highest degree of inclusion.[9] In terms of academic qualifications, Punjab has the highest percentage of teachers who are at least graduates, at 83 percent, with Rajasthan and Tamil Nadu close behind. In terms of percentage of teachers receiving in-service training in the past academic year, the southern states of Karnataka and Tamil Nadu lead the pack, with more than 35 percent coverage, while Madhya Pradesh (9 percent), Rajasthan (12 percent), and Uttar Pradesh (13 percent) bring up the rear.

Table 2.2 Profile of Elementary School Teachers, All Elementary Schools, 2012–13

State	Number	Women (%)	SC/ST (%)	Contract (%)	Graduates (%)	Trained (%)	Avg. PTR
India	7,354,151	46	21	7	64	26	28.8
Jharkhand	170,509	32	31	49	67	29	37.9
Karnataka	306,350	58	18	1	12	39	21.3
Madhya Pradesh	464,018	41	27	0	67	9	34.4
Mizoram	19,108	44	98	25	48	26	13.9
Odisha	272,173	40	25	2	56	34	23.7
Punjab	226,570	72	17	8	83	18	15.8
Rajasthan	560,412	31	24	4	80	12	26.6
Tamil Nadu	474,211	73	16	4	75	36	28.9
Uttar Pradesh	953,807	38	15	19	71	13	44.6

Source: DISE Report Card data, 2012–13.
Note: PTR = pupil-teacher ratio; SC = Scheduled Caste; ST = Scheduled Tribe.

Table 2.3 Working Conditions of Regular and Contract Teachers in Government Elementary Schools

State	Schools without a female teacher		Schools with fewer than 2 classrooms		Single-teacher schools		Schools with 2 teachers	
	Number	%	Number	%	Number	%	Number	%
India	346,562	35.7	71,824	6.9	113,290	10.9	323,905	31.2
Jharkhand	21,436	55.9	871	2.2	6,236	15.6	19,317	48.4
Karnataka	11,350	26.1	2,495	5.5	3,886	8.6	13,616	30.0
Madhya Pradesh	56,323	54.3	4,260	3.9	20,534	18.6	49,365	44.8
Mizoram	265	15.1	11	0.6	19	1.1	93	5.3
Odisha	21,374	40.1	4,888	8.6	5,725	10.1	23,310	41.2
Punjab	2,155	11.3	451	2.4	1,149	6.0	5,535	28.9
Rajasthan	41,306	53.3	3,454	4.4	15,246	19.6	24,817	31.8
Tamil Nadu	3,223	9.0	644	1.8	2,427	6.8	15,102	42.0
Uttar Pradesh	29,108	25.1	1,139	0.7	13,107	8.2	20,224	12.7

Source: DISE raw data, 2012–13.

We now turn to the situation in government elementary schools. *The first thing to notice is that in more than a third of Indian elementary schools managed by the government, there are no women teachers* (table 2.3).[10] This finding is despite that 46 percent of teachers overall are women. At the state level, Tamil Nadu has the lowest percentage of government-run elementary schools without a female teacher. The problem is most pronounced in Jharkhand, Madhya Pradesh, and Rajasthan, where more than half of all government elementary schools have no female teachers.

More than 40 percent of all government elementary schools have only one or two teachers—and more than 30 percent of the schools in the states in this study, except Mizoram and Uttar Pradesh, fall in this category. This issue is particularly problematic in Madhya Pradesh and Jharkhand, where well over 60 percent of the government elementary schools are operating with only one or two teachers.

Secondary Teachers

For secondary schools, the total size of the teacher workforce is 0.95 million (table 2.4), with 0.42 million employed in government schools and 0.49 million in private schools, the latter being split almost equally between aided and unaided schools.

About 38 percent of all secondary school teachers are women, and just over 17 percent come from the marginalized sections (defined here as SC and ST). Nearly 89 percent of all secondary school teachers are in regular employment, while 8 percent are employed contractually.[11] More than 85 percent of all secondary school teachers are at least graduates, and nearly 44 percent are at least post-graduates.

Across the nine states in the study, most states have much fewer women than men as secondary teachers and, in all states except Mizoram, less than 20 percent of secondary schools have four core subject teachers. Punjab and Tamil Nadu register the highest representation of women, with more than 60 percent of their secondary teaching workforce comprising females. The seven other states have less than 40 percent female representation among secondary school teachers, with Uttar Pradesh having the lowest representation, at 21 percent. The maximum representation of marginalized sections among secondary school teachers (except Mizoram, with about 95 percent SC/ST teachers) is found in Madhya Pradesh, Rajasthan, and Jharkhand, each of which has more than 20 percent SC/ST teachers. Uttar Pradesh, with less than 9 percent SC/ST representation, has the lowest percentage of marginalized section teachers at the secondary level. In the proportion of secondary schools with teachers for all four core subjects,

Table 2.4 Profile of Secondary School Teachers, All Secondary Schools

State	Number	Women (%)	SC/ST (%)	Contract (%)	Graduates (%)	Schools with 4 core subject teachers (%)
India	946,786	38	17	8	86	12
Jharkhand	7,652	32	21	9	92	6
Karnataka	97,078	39	18	5	38	15
Madhya Pradesh	23,642	38	27	24	95	8
Mizoram	4,324	35	95	67	95	73
Odisha	65,273	28	10	14	86	17
Punjab	42,663	67	14	29	93	4
Rajasthan	72,886	26	22	1	89	2
Tamil Nadu	74,036	63	16	10	94	11
Uttar Pradesh	88,802	21	9	1	85	6

Source: UDISE raw data 2012–13.
Note: In Karnataka, the hiring requirements in the past included professional and educational qualifications as requirements for being a teacher, unlike the other states, which have had just the latter. SC = Scheduled Caste; ST = Scheduled Tribe.

Mizoram performs the best, with nearly 73 percent. The other states in the study have substantially less than 20 percent of total secondary schools meeting this criterion.

Six of the nine states (all but Madhya Pradesh, Punjab, and Mizoram) employ less than 15 percent of their secondary school teachers on a contractual basis; in all the states, qualifications across all teachers are high. Mizoram also presents an exception in the nature of teacher employment, with 67 percent of teachers employed on a contractual basis. This is more than twice the proportion of contract teachers in the state behind it in this regard, which is Punjab, with 29 percent contract teachers. The secondary school teacher workforce is also well-qualified in most states, with more than 80 percent of teachers having at least a college degree in all states barring Karnataka (where teacher hiring requirements in the past relied on educational and professional qualifications, as opposed to only educational qualifications in other states). In five of the nine states (Jharkhand, Punjab, Tamil Nadu, Madhya Pradesh, and Uttar Pradesh), more than half the secondary school teachers have at least a post-college graduate qualification.

Only 3.3 percent of government secondary schools meet the Rashtriya Madhyamik Shiksha Abhiyan (RMSA) norm of five teachers (two language teachers and one teacher each for mathematics, social science, and science) and a head teacher (table 2.5). Less than 1 percent of all schools meet this norm in five of the nine states of the study, and only in Mizoram do more than 12 percent meet the norm. More than 14 percent of secondary schools have only one or two teachers—and the situation in Uttar Pradesh (over 30 percent) and Jharkhand and Rajasthan (both over 20 percent) is particularly bad.

Table 2.5 Working Conditions in Government Secondary Schools

State	Schools with 5 subject teachers & a head teacher		Schools with less than 2 classrooms		Single-teacher schools		Schools with 2 teachers	
	Number	%	Number	%	Number	%	Number	%
India	3,027	3.3	22,029	24.3	6,329	7.0	6,731	7.4
Jharkhand	14	0.6	1,147	51.9	304	13.8	179	8.1
Karnataka	573	11.4	2,415	48.1	172	3.4	83	1.7
Madhya Pradesh	21	0.4	709	12.3	559	9.7	563	9.8
Mizoram	167	59.6	2	0.7	0	0.0	0	0.0
Odisha	352	7.1	2,527	50.8	191	3.8	216	4.3
Punjab	7	0.2	225	6.7	72	2.1	214	6.4
Rajasthan	41	0.3	2,167	18.4	646	5.5	1,746	14.9
Tamil Nadu	192	3.4	556	9.8	216	3.8	375	6.6
Uttar Pradesh	12	0.4	489	17.8	718	26.1	269	9.8

Source: UDISE raw data, 2012–13.

Elementary Teacher Workforce: Trends in Size and Growth

Over the past 10 years, from 2003–04 to 2012–13, the teacher workforce in elementary schools in India has almost doubled, from about 3.7 million to 7.4 million, although growth rates have varied across years. Overall, the compounded annual growth rate is 7.2 percent. There are two significant trends:

1. The increase in the number of teachers has been consistent and unbroken, with more teachers added to the workforce than have been lost each year since 2003–04.
2. The rate of growth of the teacher workforce has varied significantly, ranging from a high of 13.2 percent in 2004–05 (year-on-year) to a low of 0.5 percent in 2009–10 (year-on-year) (figure 2.1).

There are three distinct phases in the size and growth of the elementary teacher workforce. The first period extends from 2003–04 to 2007–08, and was generally a period of high, albeit decreasing, growth. The numbers of schools, students, and teachers all increased rapidly over these years, with the growth in the teacher workforce outpacing the other two.

The second phase comprises the two years of 2008–09 and 2009–10. This period saw a slowdown in the rate of expansion of elementary education. There are at least two explanations. One is that the rapid growth in previous years meant that most states had achieved near-universal elementary education, and now there were simply fewer schools that needed to be built. Another reason is that the onset of the global financial crisis dampened national and per capita income growth, and this affected state governments' ability to finance the

Figure 2.1 Year-on-Year Growth of Elementary Schools, Teachers, and Students, All-India

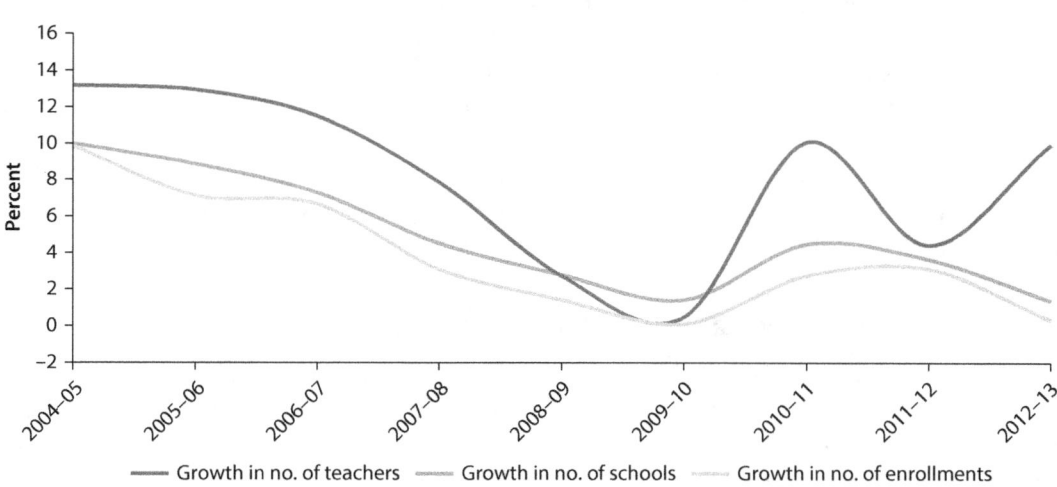

Source: DISE Report Card data, various years.

construction of schools and hiring of teachers. However, Sarva Shiksha Abhiyan (SSA) allocations from the central government continued to increase throughout the period.

The third phase started after the passage of the Right to Education (RTE) Act—which made education a fundamental right from April 1, 2010. The momentum created by the Act ensured that growth in the numbers of schools and teachers picked up sharply and immediately from 2010 to 2011. However, as in earlier periods of expansion, growth in the number of teachers once again outpaced growth in enrollments, thereby enabling a gradual lowering of the PTR toward the norm of 40:1, and eventually 30:1. This situation is explored in more detail in the next section.

Figure 2.1 highlights phenomenon of teacher growth outpacing school and enrollment growth in the first and third phases of expansion. Teacher growth fell steeply in the middle period, when the growth of elementary education slowed (tables 2.6 and 2.7). This pattern suggests that the number of teachers is affected more strongly than other elements of school education (numbers of schools and students) by an expansion or a slowdown in school education. This finding follows somewhat intuitively from the following: (a) setting up new schools involves gestation in time and money, which induces sluggishness in movements; and (b) teacher salaries comprise the principal recurring cost for schools, which is often reported by school managements as an even bigger encumbrance than capital expenditure, making teacher salaries an obvious choice for cutbacks in bad times. However, it also points to the high degree of importance accorded to the objective of reducing the PTR across elementary schools.

At the state level, the size of the elementary teacher workforce is largest in Uttar Pradesh, at 0.95 million, which is almost twice as many as the next largest teacher workforce (which is 0.56 million strong in Rajasthan) among the states under consideration (table 2.6). These are also the only states where the absolute number of elementary teachers has never decreased year-on-year.

The state data also testify broadly to the existence of the three phases in teacher growth as experienced at the national level, although different states exhibit significantly different degrees of variation in growth rates. Growth rates in the second phase are significantly lower compared with the first phase in all the states except Karnataka and Uttar Pradesh. Growth rates across states generally picked up from 2010 to 2011, with the implementation of the RTE Act, with the exceptions of Jharkhand, Punjab, and Karnataka, each of which registered negative growth in one of the two subsequent years.

Elementary Teachers, by Type of Management

For the entire period under consideration, government schools employed a large, although declining, majority of all elementary schoolteachers. At the all-India level, more than three-fourths of the entire elementary teacher workforce was employed by the government sector in 2003–04, although it fell to slightly less than two-thirds by 2012–13. At the all-India level over the past 10 years,

Table 2.6 Number of Elementary Teachers, All Elementary Schools, 2003–04 to 2012–13
Thousands

State	2003–04	2004–05	2005–06	2006–07	2007–08	2008–09	2009–10	2010–11	2011–12	2012–13
India	3,666	4,149	4,685	5,225	5,635	5,789	5,817	6,403	6,688	7,354
Jharkhand	60	71	111	132	148	151	148	167	152	171
Karnataka	238	227	228	250	260	267	279	298	387	306
Madhya Pradesh	314	377	378	399	431	436	441	437	454	464
Mizoram	12	13	13	16	16	17	16	16	19	19
Odisha	142	158	169	151	222	246	182	250	253	272
Punjab	43	91	73	85	80	103	104	205	180	227
Rajasthan	260	288	354	397	422	453	459	460	469	560
Tamil Nadu	229	250	330	360	317	327	330	334	333	474
Uttar Pradesh	400	401	527	609	644	651	698	729	799	954

Source: DISE Report Card data, various years.

there has been a clear and steady increase in the percentage of private school teachers. The number of private school teachers has grown faster than the number of government schoolteachers consistently over the past eight years (figure 2.2). This situation has been mainly due to the much faster pace of year-on-year growth of private schools than government schools since 2005–06, except in 2008–09 (figure 2.3).

In line with the characteristics of the three periods of expansion, the gap between growth in private and government schools as well as teachers has been largest in the years of significant expansion in elementary education, and generally larger in the first and third periods than in the middle one (figure 2.3). This finding seems to indicate that expansion of privately managed schools,

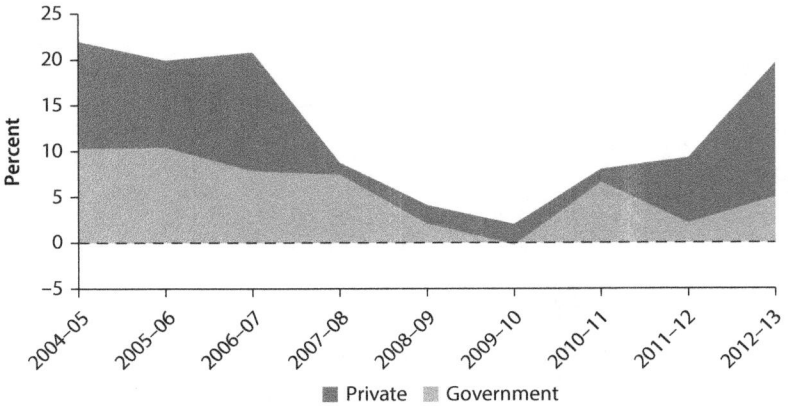

Figure 2.2 Year-on-Year Growth in Number of Elementary Teachers, by Management, All-India

Source: DISE Report Card data, various years.
Note: "Private" includes both aided and unaided schools.

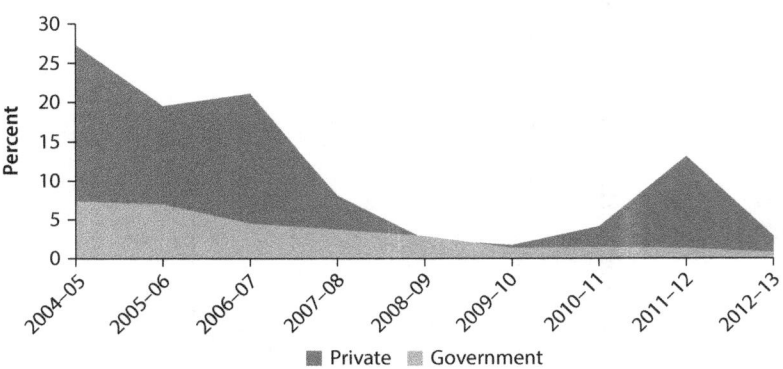

Figure 2.3 Year-on-Year Growth in Number of Elementary Schools, by Management, All-India

Source: DISE Report Card data, various years.

and teachers, has been a relatively important tool of elementary education expansion over the past decade.

Secondary Teachers: Government versus Aided Schools

Overall, at the national and state levels, aided schools share many of the characteristics of their government school counterparts. Aided and government schools have poor physical and human resources, and state governments provide very little or no support for infrastructure. Aided schools tend to be somewhat larger and located more often in urban areas. Aided schools are more like government schools than they are different, and more like those schools in their state than aided schools in other states. For example, across secondary schools in India, 53 percent[12] of aided schools and 46 percent of government schools have more pupils than their reported classrooms would permit (based on RMSA norms[13]). The corresponding figures in Karnataka are 48 percent and 40 percent, respectively; in Mizoram, 13 percent and 9 percent; and in Uttar Pradesh, 57 percent and 39 percent (figure 2.4).

A significant area of difference between aided and government schools relates to size: overall, aided schools have, on average, 207 students, compared with 170 in government schools. In some states with large numbers of aided schools, the differences are even greater (in Tamil Nadu aided schools are, on average, twice as big). This situation likely has to do with aided schools tending to be more concentrated in urban areas than government schools (although, given the geography of Indian states, most aided schools are in rural areas).

In basic infrastructure, government and aided secondary schools fare almost equally poorly (figure 2.5). The only exception here is Punjab, where government schools fare significantly better than aided ones, and infrastructure achievement is high, relative to other states, with more than 15 percent of government schools having the six infrastructure elements.[14] In seven of the other eight states,

Figure 2.4 Percentage of Aided and Government Secondary Schools Operating above Capacity

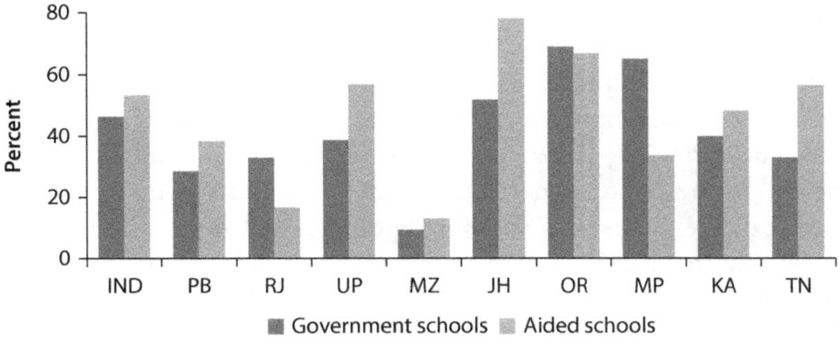

Source: UDISE raw data, 2012–13.
Note: A school is defined as operating above capacity if its school-classroom ratio > 45. IND = India; JH = Jharkhand; KA = Karnataka; MP = Madhya Pradesh; MZ = Mizoram; OR = Odisha; PB = Punjab; RJ = Rajasthan; TN = Tamil Nadu; UP = Uttar Pradesh.

Figure 2.5 Percentage of Aided and Government Secondary Schools with Six Basic Infrastructure Components

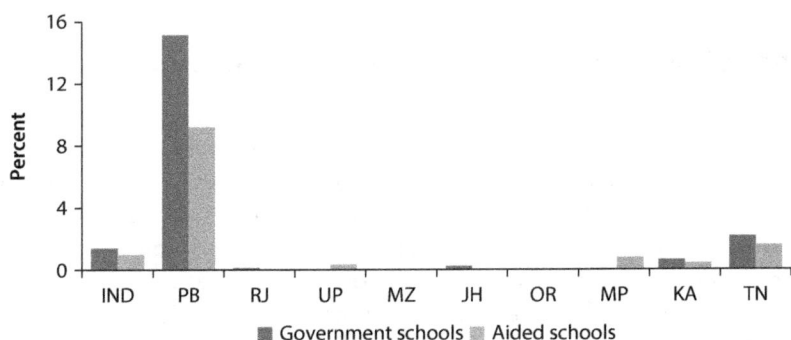

Source: UDISE raw data, 2012–13.
Note: IND = India; JH = Jharkhand; KA = Karnataka; MP = Madhya Pradesh; MZ = Mizoram; OR = Odisha; PB = Punjab; RJ = Rajasthan; TN = Tamil Nadu; UP = Uttar Pradesh.

less than 1 percent of all secondary schools—government or aided—provide all six basic infrastructure components. Tamil Nadu performs marginally better, with about 2 percent of government and government-aided schools fulfilling this criterion.

Elementary Teachers, by Type of Employment

During the period under consideration, more than 85 percent of the elementary teacher workforce in India was employed in a "regular" capacity. The percentage of "para" or "contract" teachers,[15] which was around 7.1 percent in 2003–04, reached a peak of 12.2 percent in 2011–12, before sliding back to about 7.3 percent (figure 2.6). In absolute numbers, these percentages translate into 0.5 million para/contract teachers in 2012–13, compared with 6.8 million regular teachers.

Only three states in the study have more than 10 percent of elementary teachers employed as contract teachers, but in several states, the percentages fluctuate over time. Jharkhand employed the highest percentage of para/contract teachers, at 49 percent in 2012–13. Mizoram (26 percent) and Uttar Pradesh (19 percent) are the only other states where para/contract teachers comprise more than 10 percent of the elementary teaching workforce. All three states have seen a steady rise in the percentage of para/contract teachers employed. Madhya Pradesh and Rajasthan have witnessed a steady reduction. The data also suggest that the percentage of para/contract teachers has fluctuated considerably in some states, especially Odisha and Punjab, suggesting changes in teacher recruitment policies. The trends in para/contract teacher recruitment policies are important and are explored in other chapters.

Figure 2.6 Percentage of Elementary Teaching Workforce Comprising Para/Contract Teachers, All Elementary Schools

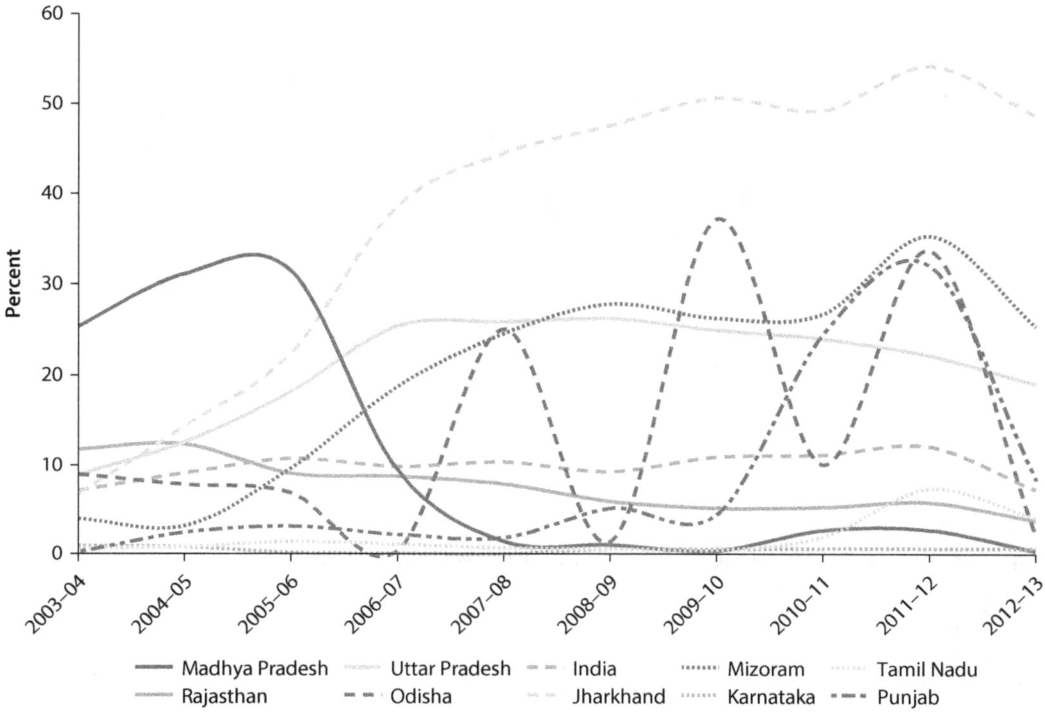

Source: DISE Report Card data, various years.

Inclusiveness

This section explores two key elements of inclusion in the elementary teaching workforce: (a) gender, or the inclusion of women, and (b) marginalized sections of society, or the inclusion of SCs and STs in the teaching workforce.

Inclusion of Women

The percentage of women in the elementary teaching workforce has steadily increased over the past decade (figure 2.7). As of 2012–13, 3.4 million women teachers constituted more than 46 percent of the elementary teaching workforce across India, up from 1.3 million and 36 percent in 2003–04.

At the state level, Karnataka, Punjab, and Tamil Nadu are clear outperformers in the inclusion of women, who constituted half or more of the teaching workforce in these states consistently over the past 10 years. The growth in the inclusion of women has been remarkable in Punjab, increasing from about 56 percent in 2004–05 to 82 percent in 2011–12 (figure 2.8). Although Mizoram has maintained female representation at around 40 percent of the teaching workforce,

Figure 2.7 Number and Percentage of Women Teachers, All-India, Elementary

Source: DISE Report Card data, various years.

Figure 2.8 Percentage of Women Teachers, States, All Elementary Schools

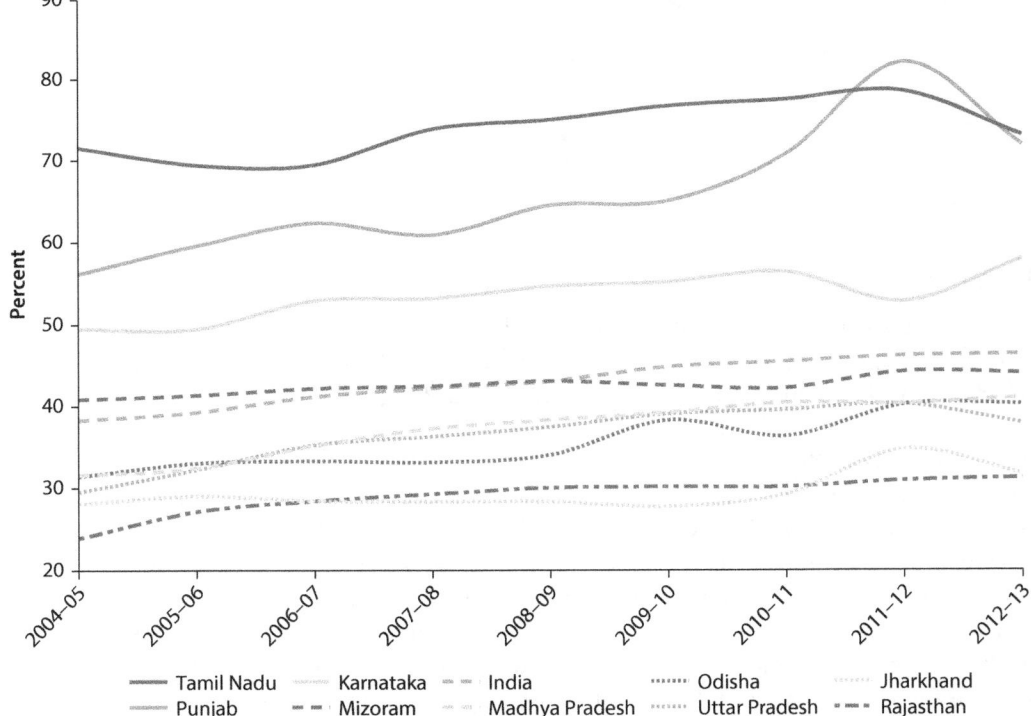

Source: DISE Report Card data, various years.

the other states have mostly remained clustered at low levels of inclusion through the entire period under consideration, with only Odisha and Madhya Pradesh showing some improvement to marginally above 40 percent.

Inclusion of Marginalized Sections of Society

The inclusion of marginalized sections, especially at the state level, is to a fair degree affected by the demographics of the territory concerned. Nevertheless, changes over time in the percentage of the overall teaching workforce constituted by SCs and STs indicate a certain degree of success or failure in making these sections of the population beneficiaries in the expansion of elementary education. At the all-India level, some success has been registered, with the percentage of SCs in the teaching workforce increasing steadily, from 9.4 percent in 2004–05 to 12.9 percent in 2011–12, and falling marginally to 12.6 percent in 2012–13 (figure 2.9). Improvement in the inclusion of STs has been less smooth and pronounced, with 8.1 percent of the teaching force comprising STs in 2004–05, versus a high of 9.5 percent in 2008–09 and 8.7 percent in 2012–13.

At the state level, Punjab registered the highest improvement in inclusion of SCs, where their representation increased from 12.1 percent in 2004–05 to over 19 percent in 2009–10 and again in 2011–12. Improvements in the representation of SCs have also been registered to varying degrees in Rajasthan, Uttar Pradesh, Odisha, Madhya Pradesh, Karnataka, and Tamil Nadu. However, SCs were underrepresented in the elementary teaching workforce in 2010–11 and 2011–12 in relation to their Census 2011 population shares, at the all-India level as well as in all states except Mizoram (which is, in any case, an outlier, with a minuscule SC population) (figure 2.10).

For STs, the inclusion in relation with their Census 2011 population shares (middle column of figure 2.11) was relatively healthy at the all-India level, for 2010–11 and 2011–12, as well as for key states with large ST populations, such as Mizoram and Jharkhand. In Odisha, Madhya Pradesh, Rajasthan, and Karnataka, however, STs are still underrepresented in the teacher workforce

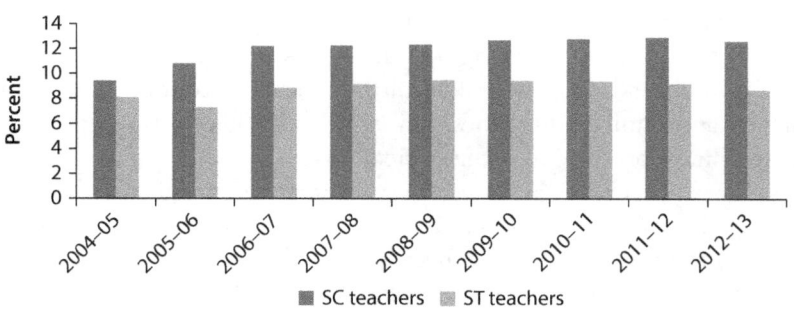

Figure 2.9 Percentage of SC and ST Teachers, All-India, All Elementary Schools

Source: DISE Report Card data, various years.
Note: SC = Scheduled Caste; ST = Scheduled Tribe.

Figure 2.10 Percentage of SC Teachers in 2010–11 and 2011–12, All Elementary Schools, Compared with the Percentage of SC Population as per Census 2011

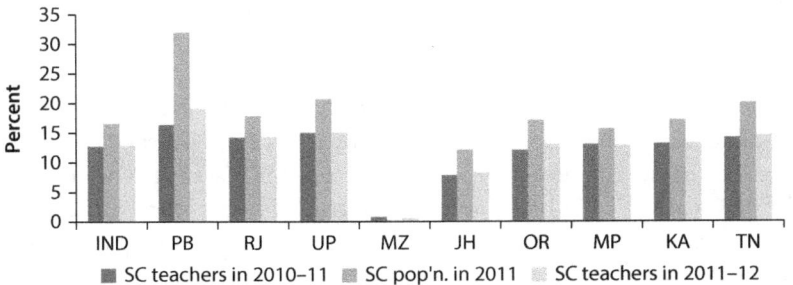

Source: DISE Report Card data and 2011 Census data.
Note: IND = India; JH = Jharkhand; KA = Karnataka; MP = Madhya Pradesh; MZ = Mizoram; OR = Odisha; PB = Punjab; RJ = Rajasthan; SC = Scheduled Caste; TN = Tamil Nadu; UP = Uttar Pradesh.

Figure 2.11 Percentage of ST Teachers in 2010–11 and 2011–12, All Elementary Schools, Compared with the Percentage of ST Population as per Census 2011

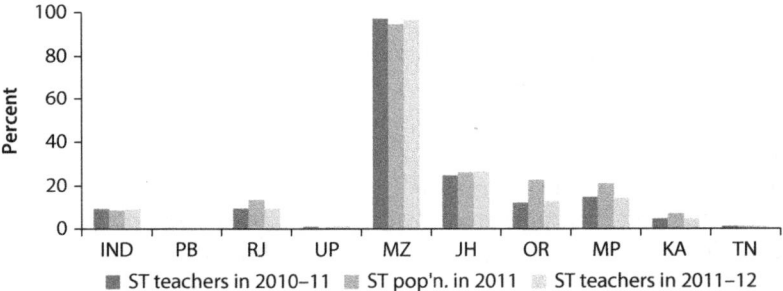

Source: DISE Report Card data and 2011 Census data.
Note: IND = India; JH = Jharkhand; KA = Karnataka; MP = Madhya Pradesh; MZ = Mizoram; OR = Odisha; PB = Punjab; RJ = Rajasthan; ST = Scheduled Tribe; TN = Tamil Nadu; UP = Uttar Pradesh.

(figure 2.11). Punjab does not have a significant ST population. Increased representation of STs in the teaching workforce has been achieved in Rajasthan, Mizoram, Jharkhand, Odisha, and Madhya Pradesh. In contrast, Uttar Pradesh, Karnataka, and Tamil Nadu witnessed varying reductions in the percentage STs in the teaching workforce over this period.

Across secondary schools, the representation of the marginalized SC and ST sections in the teaching workforce is poorer than at the elementary level. This can be seen from figure 2.12, which shows that the share of SCs and STs in the secondary teaching workforce is significantly smaller than their population share in all states except Mizoram. At the country level too, SCs and STs are clearly underrepresented in the secondary teaching workforce.

Figure 2.12 Percentage of SC & ST Secondary Teachers in 2012–13, All Secondary Schools, Compared with the Percentage of SC & ST Population as per Census 2011

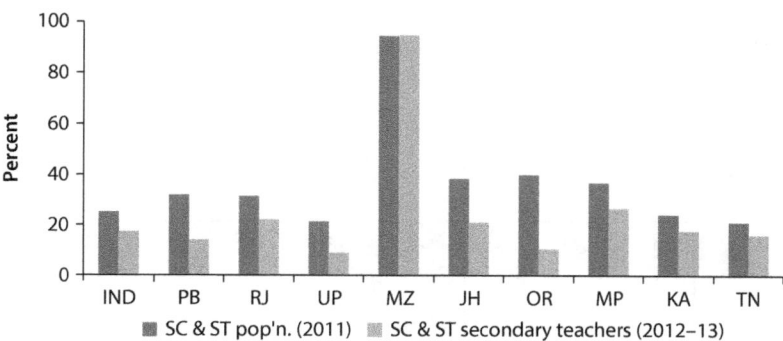

Source: UDISE raw data and 2011 Census data.
Note: IND = India; JH = Jharkhand; KA = Karnataka; MP = Madhya Pradesh; MZ = Mizoram; OR = Odisha; PB = Punjab; RJ = Rajasthan; SC = Scheduled Caste; ST = Scheduled Tribe; TN = Tamil Nadu; UP = Uttar Pradesh.

Pupil-Teacher Ratio: Trends

Reducing the PTR has been a major policy goal of the Government of India over the past 10 years.[16] The PTR norm under SSA was initially set at 40:1, or a teacher for every 40 pupils, but, in 2009, the PTR was revised downward to 30:1 with the RTE. This norm is now also to be met at the school level (not district or state). Considerable resources have been devoted to this effort and, overall, at the national level, the target has been met.

There has been a clear and steady reduction in the PTR,[17] from about 39.0 in 2003–04 to about 26.5 in 2012–13, and for all states. This was the result of faster growth of the elementary teacher workforce compared with the growth of student enrollments (this is clear from the numbers underlying figure 2.13). In line with the phases in the expansion of the teacher workforce, this reduction has also been achieved at a faster pace in the first and third time periods than in the middle period. This has meant a steady decline in the PTR (the orange line in figure 2.13).

Government schools have achieved a larger reduction in PTR, from 37.4 in 2005–06 to 27.6 in 2012–13, vis-à-vis a reduction from 31.9 to 26.6 achieved by private elementary schools. However, the PTR reduction in government schools has come about largely from steadily declining enrollments since 2007–08, whereas private schools have improved PTRs even with growth in student enrollments. This is shown in figures 2.14 and 2.15, and is synchronous with evidence in the previous section, which showed that the number of private schools (aided and unaided) is growing faster than the number of government schools.

The reduction in the overall national-level numbers to below the SSA-mandated norm masks vast disparities across individual states, districts, and schools in PTR. Uttar Pradesh has the highest PTR among the states under consideration,

Figure 2.13 Numbers of Teachers and Pupils, and the Pupil-Teacher Ratio, All-India, All Elementary Schools

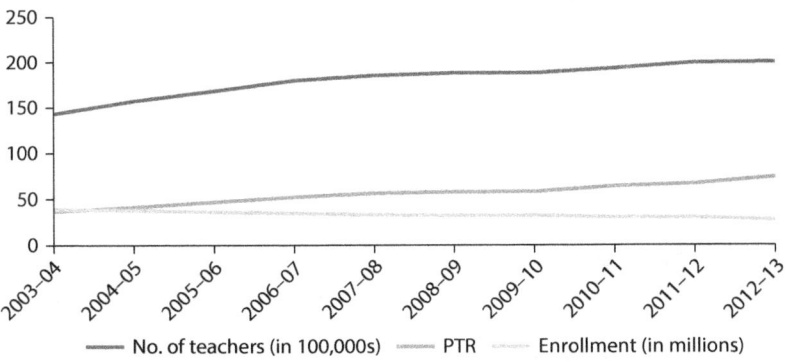

Source: DISE Report Card data, various years.
Note: PTR = pupil-teacher ratio.

Figure 2.14 Pupils, Teachers, and the PTR in Private Elementary Schools, All-India

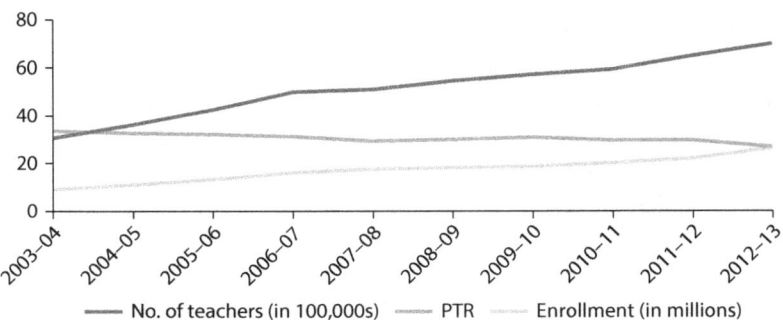

Source: DISE Report Card data, various years.
Note: PTR = pupil-teacher ratio.

Figure 2.15 Pupils, Teachers, and the PTR in Government Elementary Schools, All-India

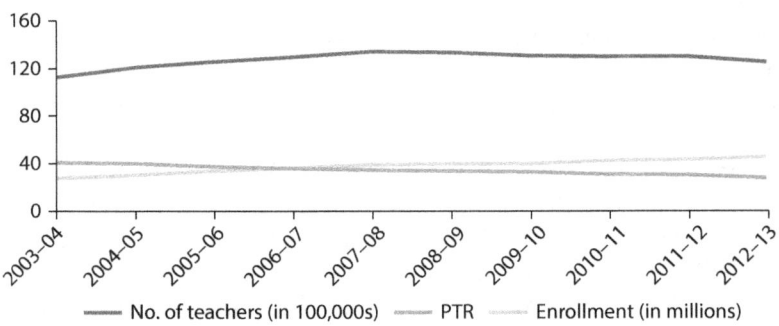

Source: DISE Report Card data, various years.
Note: PTR = pupil-teacher ratio.

at just under 40:1 (figure 2.16). Six of the remaining eight states are either very close to or below the national PTR (the horizontal line in the figure), and, therefore, under the SSA-mandated norm. All the states have successfully achieved a reduction in the elementary PTR from the 2003–04 level, as is evident from the downward trend in all the lines in figure 2.17, but the pace and extent of reduction is, again, very different across states. An impressive reduction in the PTR has taken the level in Punjab from 29.0 to 17.8 in this period. Despite a healthy rate of reduction, Uttar Pradesh's PTR, which started at 63.4, is still above the norm, at 38.9. The reduction in PTR unfolds in a very similar manner, over time and across states, for the subset of elementary schools managed by the government. Jharkhand registers the highest PTR for government elementary schools, followed by Madhya Pradesh and then Uttar Pradesh.

Pupil-Teacher Ratio for Secondary Schools

The standard PTR metric is less relevant for secondary schools, as students choose streams, and advanced subject content requires teachers specializing in the subject concerned. Given that there is no agreed alternative, the subject PTRs are used here, that is, the number of secondary students in a school divided by the number of teachers for a subject. The benchmark (which in the case of elementary schools was simply the 30:1 ratio set by RTE) will, of course, have to be subjectively and suitably revised upward, to contextualize the achievement by states and, indeed, the country as a whole, for such subject PTRs.

By this measure, there are serious shortages of core subject teachers across the country. The average mathematics PTR for India as a whole is 119, again with

Figure 2.16 Elementary School PTR, States, All Elementary Schools, 2012–13

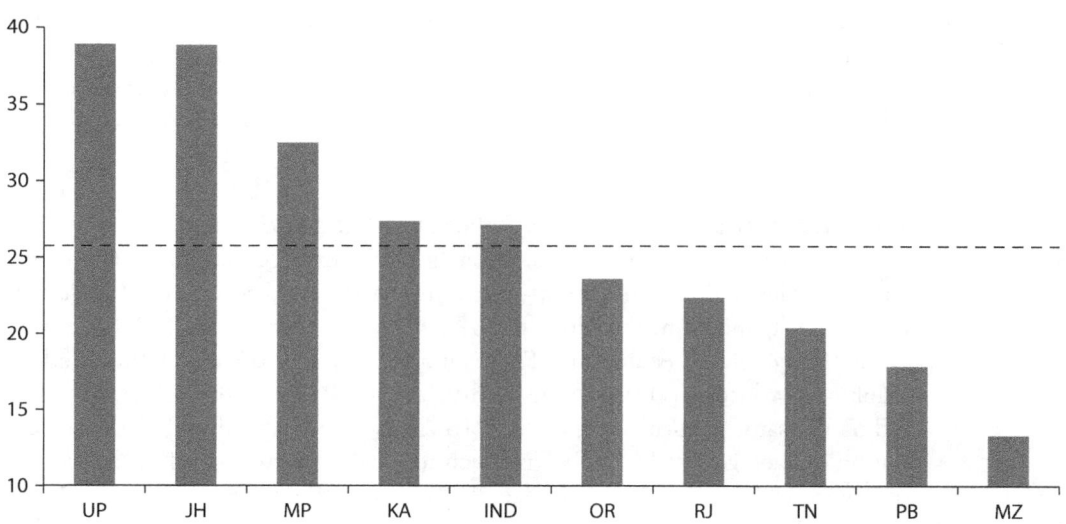

Source: DISE Report Card data.
Note: IND = India; JH = Jharkhand; KA = Karnataka; MP = Madhya Pradesh; MZ = Mizoram; OR = Odisha; PB = Punjab; PTR = pupil-teacher ratio; RJ = Rajasthan; TN = Tamil Nadu; UP = Uttar Pradesh.

Figure 2.17 Reduction in PTR over Time, All Elementary Schools

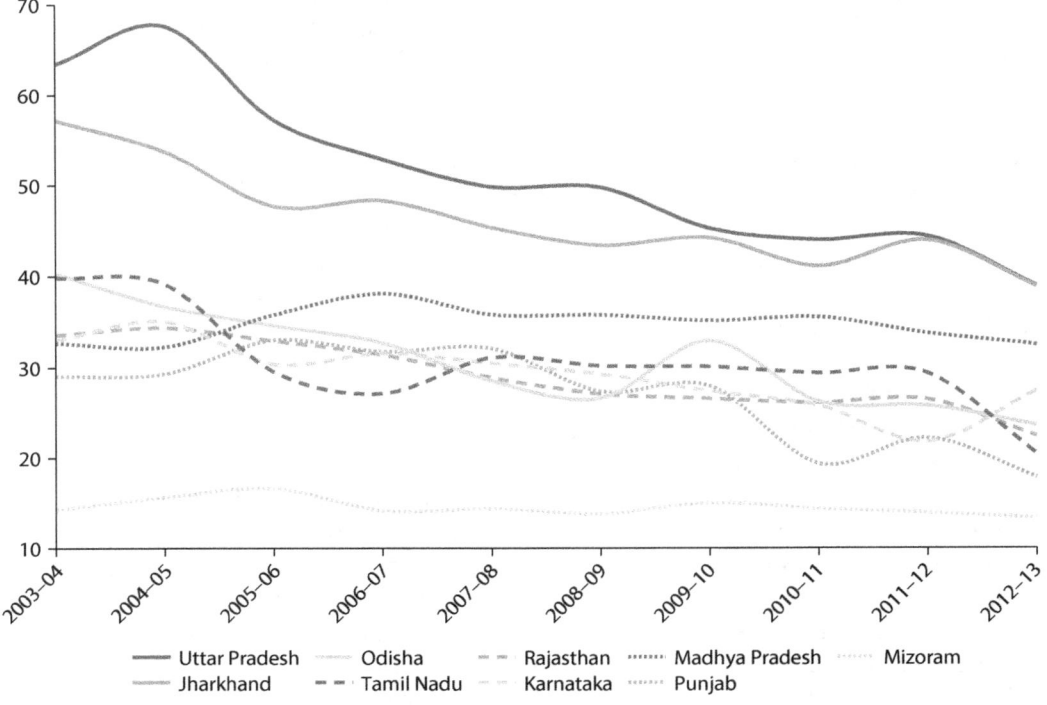

Source: DISE Report Card data, various years.
Note: PTR = pupil-teacher ratio.

significant variation across schools, with a standard deviation (SD) that is larger than the mean. Moreover, only 12 percent of all secondary schools (table 2.4), 14 percent of government secondary schools, and 21 percent of aided secondary schools have at least one teacher for each of the four core subjects—language, mathematics, science, and social science.

Elementary School Pupil-Teacher Ratio: Intra-State Variations

There is significant intra-state variation in elementary school PTRs. Moreover, with every level of disaggregation—from the state to the district, from the district to the block, and from the block to the school—the variance in PTRs increases dramatically within each state. For example, Tamil Nadu and Uttar Pradesh exhibit very different distributions of district-level PTRs. With both graphs plotted on the same vertical scale, figure 2.18 clearly shows that Tamil Nadu's distribution of average district PTRs[18] is much more closely grouped. That is, there is relatively little variation in average PTRs across the districts of Tamil Nadu (figure 2.18, panel a). The orange line in the graph indicates the average PTR for the state. The blue band, indicating the range of two SDs above and below the mean, is quite narrow for Tamil Nadu.

Figure 2.18 Average District-Level PTR All Elementary Schools, and Percent Rural Population, 2012–13

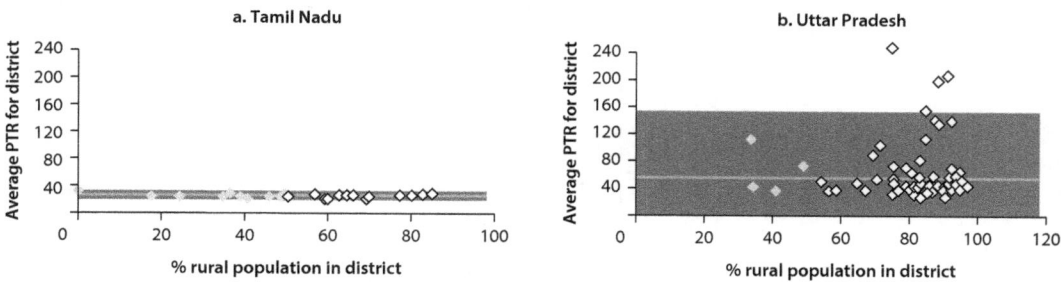

Source: DISE Report Card data.
Note: PTR = pupil-teacher ratio.

Uttar Pradesh exhibits a very different distribution, with district PTRs spread over a much wider range, from less than 30 to more than 240 (figure 2.18, panel b). This large deviation from the mean is indicated in the figure in the form of the wide blue band, which is much wider than the band for Tamil Nadu. In other words, Uttar Pradesh needs to recognize that it faces two challenges: a higher overall mean PTR, plus a much larger SD, which confirms the significantly greater heterogeneity of its district-level PTR distribution.

States' planning for teacher management and deployment should account for the inequality of PTRs being much more significant at the school level than at the district or block level. There are significant increases in variation in PTR data in each state with every level of disaggregation, from looking across district averages, to looking across block averages, to looking across school-level PTRs (table 2.8). Here too, Uttar Pradesh stands out as having a very high level of variation compared with the other states at the block and district levels, implying that the ground reality in different districts and different blocks is much less uniform in Uttar Pradesh than in the other states. In Odisha, the inequalities at the district and block level are comparable to those in most other states, but at the school level inequalities are much higher.

There are more than 19,000 elementary schools in India with PTR greater than 150. Even excluding outliers[19] (defined as PTR > 150), the range of the distribution is very large, with maximum PTRs being well over two SDs away from the mean, and minimum ones being well within two SDs (table 2.9). Moreover, as the last two columns in table 2.9 show, the absolute number of elementary schools with more than 150 students per teacher is very large, running into the thousands for states like Uttar Pradesh, Madhya Pradesh, and even Jharkhand.

Teachers are not deployed equitably across states, districts, and schools. Although some schools have more teachers than they need, many have too few to be effective. All the states have some schools with very low PTRs and some schools with very high PTRs. For example, although Uttar Pradesh has an average elementary school PTR of 41, and 30 percent of its schools have PTRs over 50,

Table 2.7 Number of Elementary Schools, 2003–04 to 2012–13
Thousands

State	2003–04	2004–05	2005–06	2006–07	2007–08	2008–09	2009–10	2010–11	2011–12	2012–13
India	3,666	4,149	4,685	5,225	5,635	5,789	5,817	6,403	6,688	7,354
Jharkhand	60	71	111	132	148	151	148	167	152	171
Karnataka	238	227	228	250	260	267	279	298	387	306
Madhya Pradesh	314	377	378	399	431	436	441	437	454	464
Mizoram	12	13	13	16	16	17	16	16	19	19
Odisha	142	158	169	151	222	246	182	250	253	272
Punjab	43	91	73	85	80	103	104	205	180	227
Rajasthan	260	288	354	397	422	453	459	460	469	560
Tamil Nadu	229	250	330	360	317	327	330	334	333	474
Uttar Pradesh	400	401	527	609	644	651	698	729	799	954

Source: DISE Report Card data, various years.

Table 2.8 Increasing Standard Deviation of PTR with Every Level of Disaggregation, All Elementary Schools, 2012–13

State	SD/mean across average district PTRs	SD/mean across average block PTRs	SD/mean across school PTRs
Mizoram	0.22	0.32	0.89
Punjab	0.15	0.21	0.91
Rajasthan	0.16	0.25	0.91
Tamil Nadu	0.09	0.18	0.91
Madhya Pradesh	0.21	0.28	0.95
Karnataka	0.28	0.32	1.15
Uttar Pradesh	1.07	1.10	1.17
Jharkhand	0.19	0.29	1.22
Odisha	0.17	0.38	1.57

Source: DISE Report Card data and UDISE raw data.
Note: PTR = pupil-teacher ratio; SD = standard deviation.

Table 2.9 Distribution of Pupil-Teacher Ratios, All Elementary Schools with PTR <150, 2012–13

State	Mean	SD	SD/mean	Schools with PTR > 150 Number	%
Jharkhand	41.10	24.52	0.60	1,096	2.4
Odisha	29.76	18.27	0.61	485	0.7
Tamil Nadu	25.92	16.86	0.65	226	0.4
Punjab	24.51	16.22	0.66	93	0.3
Uttar Pradesh	41.05	27.82	0.68	7,189	3.1
Madhya Pradesh	36.51	25.17	0.69	2,367	1.7
Rajasthan	29.00	20.48	0.71	688	0.6
Karnataka	23.88	16.98	0.71	246	0.4
India	31.10	23.08	0.74	19,361	1.4
Mizoram	15.77	13.60	0.86	1	0.0

Source: UDISE raw data.
Note: PTR = pupil-teacher ratio; SD = standard deviation.

in 5 percent of its schools, PTRs are less than 10 (figure 2.19). In five states in the study, 10 percent or more of the schools have PTRs that are less than 10; at the same time, 5 percent of the schools have PTRs that are greater than 50. Indeed, in every state in this study, there are more schools with PTRs in the range 11–30 than in the range 31–50.

Pupil-Teacher Ratio: Exploring the Factors behind Systematic Variation

The analysis conducted in this section aims to explore and understand some of the factors affecting school PTRs. The main purpose is to apply the findings to the question of allocation of elementary school teachers, that is, to which schools new or extra teachers should be allocated, so as to equalize PTRs across all schools.

Figure 2.19 Percentage of Schools in Different PTR Ranges, Elementary, 2012–13

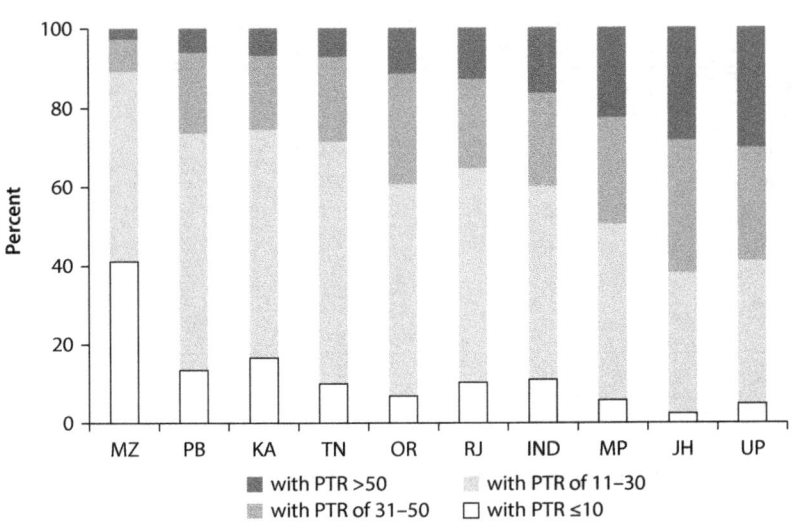

Source: UDISE raw data, 2012–13.
Note: IND = India; JH = Jharkhand; KA = Karnataka; MP = Madhya Pradesh; MZ = Mizoram; OR = Odisha; PB = Punjab; PTR = pupil-teacher ratio; RJ = Rajasthan; TN = Tamil Nadu; UP = Uttar Pradesh.

The PTRs in schools in urban districts are higher than the PTRs in rural schools in all the states, except Mizoram (table 2.10). A positive, significant coefficient indicates that being in an urban location is associated with a higher PTR for a school, compared with the PTR in a rural location. This finding is counterintuitive; however, it is important to keep in mind that urban schools tend to be larger than rural schools. A significant negative coefficient, such as that for Mizoram, indicates that in that state, being in an urban location is associated with lower PTR for a school.

States' teacher allocation policies and practices favor small schools at the expense of larger schools. Generally, only small schools achieve the PTR norm of 30:1; but they are able to achieve this only because large schools have much higher PTRs. There is indeed a positive correlation between elementary school PTR and elementary school size, and this relation is statistically significant for all the states in the study, as well as for elementary education in in all of India (figure 2.20). For the country, PTR increases by about one for every 10 additional students enrolled. The PTR norm of 30 is associated with a school size of only 100 students, which is quite small, especially for schools structured with multiple grades and sections. This association, in turn, raises the obvious question as to why larger schools are not able to achieve low PTRs. It seems that states have tried to allocate a minimum number of teachers for each school, which means that schools with fewer pupils have much better PTRs. This allocation has the consequence that much larger numbers of children who attend bigger schools suffer from high PTRs.

School Teachers in India: A Descriptive Analysis

Table 2.10 School-Level PTRs Are Higher in Urban Schools, All Elementary Schools, 2012–13

State	No. of obs.	Coefficient	SE	p-value	Sig (95%)
India	1,276,593	5.589	0.111	0.000	Yes
Jharkhand	42,974	20.729	1.205	0.000	Yes
Karnataka	56,180	12.287	0.296	0.000	Yes
Madhya Pradesh	129,713	2.971	0.321	0.000	Yes
Mizoram	2,691	−1.281	0.627	0.041	Yes
Odisha	58,851	29.779	0.959	0.000	Yes
Punjab	29,057	4.783	0.342	0.000	Yes
Rajasthan	110,502	3.571	0.239	0.000	Yes
Tamil Nadu	53,634	3.966	0.263	0.000	Yes
Uttar Pradesh	163,747	11.199	0.543	0.000	Yes

Source: UDISE raw data.
Note: The reference category is rural schools. PTR = pupil-teacher ratio; SE = standard error; Sig = significant.

Figure 2.20 Regressions of School PTRs and Enrollments, All Elementary Schools, 2012–13

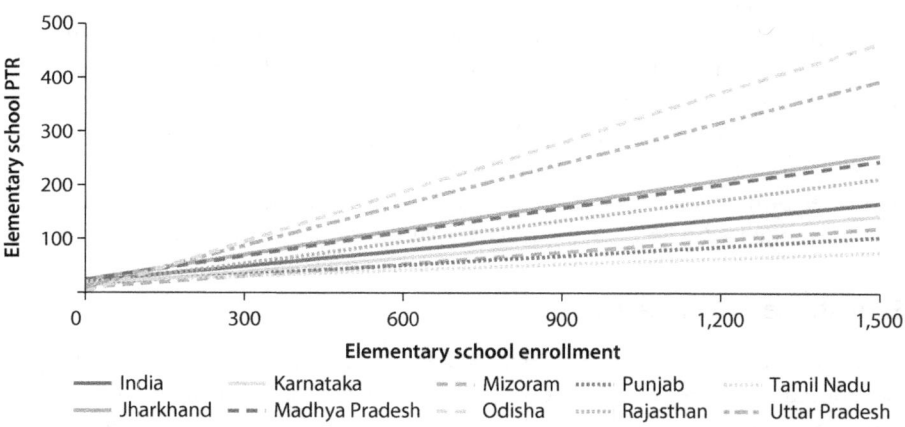

Source: UDISE raw data, 2012–13.
Note: PTR = pupil-teacher ratio.

In Odisha and Uttar Pradesh, teachers tend to be allocated to a lesser extent to larger elementary schools, resulting in faster rising PTRs as school size increases. Figure 2.20 also shows that school PTRs in Odisha and Uttar Pradesh increase with increases in school size to a degree that is substantially greater than in other states, as can be seen from the steeper slopes of the top two lines. If additional teachers are assigned in equal numbers to each school (which might be considered an equal distribution in one sense), the consequence is that schools with more pupils will continue to have larger PTRs. Tamil Nadu and Punjab seem to do a relatively good job of hiring new teachers to support new students, ensuring that among the states in the study, their elementary school PTRs rise the slowest in response to increases in enrollments.

Table 2.11 Summary of Results of Regressing PTR on School Structure, All Elementary Schools, 2012–13

Explanatory variable	Reference category					
	Primary	P+UP	Upper Primary	UP+Sec	P+UP+Sec	UP+Sec+HSec
Primary						
P+UP	4.32					
Upper Primary	5.26	0.93				
UP+Sec	5.98	1.66	0.73			
P+UP+Sec	11.74	7.42	6.49	5.76		
UP+Sec+HSec	15.52	11.20	10.27	9.54	3.78	
P+UP+Sec+HSec	19.11	14.79	13.85	13.13	7.37	3.59

Source: UDISE raw data, 2012–13.
Note: Each of the coefficients reported in the table is statistically significant. The interpretation is as follows: the top-most coefficient of 4.32 represents the increase in PTR for a school structured as primary + upper primary over the reference category of a school structured as primary only. The general rule for interpretation is that a given coefficient is attached to the explanatory variable in the row containing the coefficient, and must be interpreted with regard to the relevant reference category, which can be found at the head of the column containing the coefficient. HSec = higher secondary; P = primary; PTR = pupil-teacher ratio; Sec = secondary; UP = upper primary.

PTRs are also generally higher in schools with more complex structures. Compared with schools that are just primary schools, all other school structures, in general, have a higher PTR (table 2.11). PTRs are generally largest for the schools with the most complex structures. For example, schools that offer upper primary, secondary, and higher secondary education have, on average, a PTR of 47:1, compared with 36:1 for schools that offer only upper primary education; while schools that offer primary, upper primary, and secondary education have an average PTR of 43:1, compared with 31:1 for schools that offer only primary education.

Educational Qualifications

There has been a steady increase in teachers' educational qualifications over the past decade. At the all-India level, the proportion of teachers who have not completed higher secondary school (bottom two boxes in each column in figure 2.21) fell from over a quarter in 2004–05 to less than one-seventh, at 13.4 percent in 2012–13. At the top of the qualifications in the figure, 64.4 percent of all teachers completed at least a college degree in 2012–13, up from 51.9 percent in 2004–05, and the percentage completing a post-graduate or Master of Philosophy degree increased from 15 to 26.3 percent over this period.

Across the states, Punjab and Rajasthan have the most qualified teaching workforce, with the highest percentage of teachers who are at least college graduates (figure 2.22). In Uttar Pradesh, Tamil Nadu, Jharkhand, and Madhya Pradesh, this percentage has consistently been over 50 percent. In Mizoram and Odisha, the qualifications remain relatively poor.

Data Gaps[20]

In the discussion of elementary school PTRs, the analysis only included schools with PTRs less than 150. This was because it was assumed that PTRs greater than 150:1 are likely to be the result of inaccuracies in the data rather than

Figure 2.21 Evolution of Educational Qualifications of Elementary Teachers, All-India, All Elementary Schools

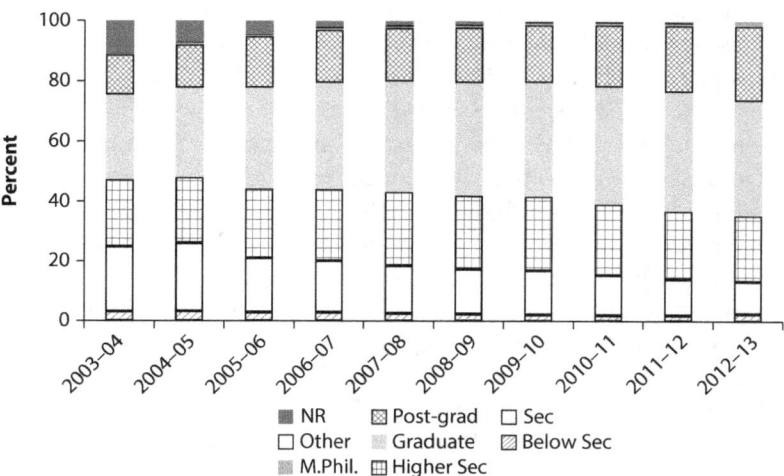

Source: DISE Report Card data, various years.
Note: M.Phil. = Master of Philosophy; NR = not reported; Sec = secondary.

Figure 2.22 Percentage of Elementary Teachers Who Have a Higher Education Degree, by State, All Elementary Schools

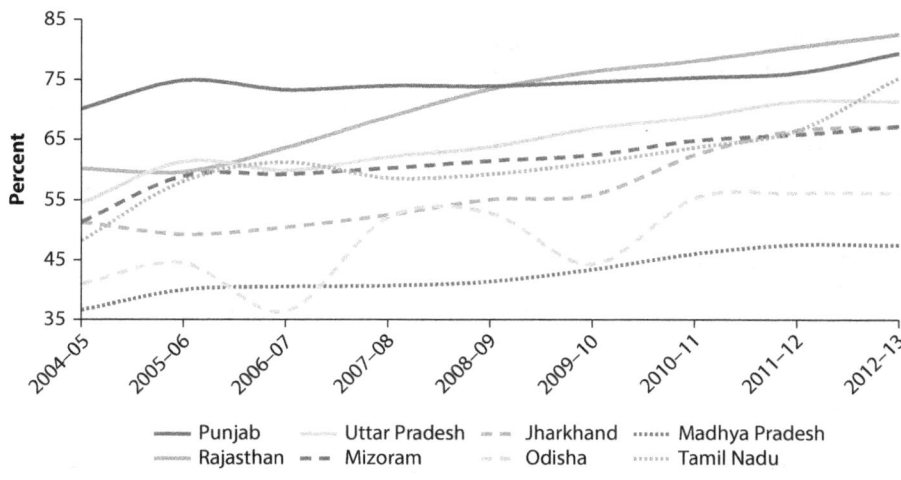

Source: DISE Report Card data, various years.
Note: Karnataka was omitted because it was an outlier, with very low teacher educational qualifications, which is due to the state's hiring policies, which emphasize professional qualifications.

representing the reality on the ground. However, excluding these schools means the analysis excludes a significant number of schools (1.4 percent of schools across India), and it is important for policy makers to understand the extent to which these are indeed data errors.

To illustrate the data gaps, this section explores the PTRs including all the data. The variance in school-level PTRs is even greater than those at the district level (as shown in table 2.12). For the nine states in the study, the minimum school-level PTRs are as low as less than 1, indicating more teachers than students, which is the case for 644 schools in India, as derived from the raw data. The maximum PTRs are apparently as high as 8,489 students per teacher in Odisha. The maximum PTRs for all the states, except Mizoram and Tamil Nadu, are well above 1,000 elementary school students per elementary school teacher. Including these schools increases the average PTR significantly in most cases: from 41 to 50 in Uttar Pradesh and from 41 to 47 in Jharkhand (comparing the relevant figures in tables 2.9 and 2.12). In Uttar Pradesh and Jharkhand, 3.1 and 2.4 percent of the schools, respectively, apparently have PTRs that are greater than 150.

The wide variance in the school-level PTR distributions for all the states can also be seen from the large size of the SD relative to the state mean. In table 2.12, this figure is shown in the SD/mean column, which illustrates the deviation of school PTRs from the state average. Values that are greater than 1 indicate that the SD is larger than the mean itself. In absolute terms, the large size of the SD relative to the mean for all states is, of course, attributable to the very large size of the maximum values relative to the mean PTR. That for most states the SD/mean is very close to or greater than 1 confirms the very wide variance in school-level PTR distributions in the nine states. The dramatic increase in the heterogeneity of the PTR distribution going from district-level PTR to school-level PTR can be seen from the values for Tamil Nadu and Uttar Pradesh. Compared with the SD/mean values of 0.10 and 0.66, respectively, for the district-level PTR distributions, the values of the SD/mean for the school-level distributions for these states are substantially higher, at 0.91 and 1.17, respectively.

Table 2.12 School-Level PTR Distribution, All Elementary Schools, 2012–13

State	Min.	Mean	Max.	SD	SD/mean
Mizoram	0.40	15.84	205	14.07	0.89
Punjab	0.20	25.21	1,841	22.84	0.91
Tamil Nadu	0.06	26.90	846	24.46	0.91
Rajasthan	0.10	30.26	1,178	27.65	0.91
Madhya Pradesh	0.14	39.89	2,101	37.94	0.95
Karnataka	0.08	25.04	1,864	28.76	1.15
India	**0.06**	**34.40**	**8,489**	**40.10**	**1.17**
Uttar Pradesh	0.10	50.36	2,362	58.84	1.17
Jharkhand	0.33	47.05	3,125	57.39	1.22
Odisha	0.14	32.10	8,489	50.35	1.57

Source: UDISE raw data 2012–13.
Note: PTR = pupil-teacher ratio; SD = standard deviation.

Conclusion

Although the size of the teaching force has been increasing continuously, and overall PTR has been declining nationally and in all states, teachers remain unevenly distributed across schools, resulting in different educational opportunities for children. In many of the schools, the PTR is below the norms laid down under RTE. In many more schools, the PTR is considerably above these norms. These findings make it important to understand how states recruit, appoint, and deploy teachers, which will be addressed in the following chapters.

Annex 2A: Data and Methodology

The objective of the analysis in this chapter is to understand the evolution of key characteristics of the teacher workforce in elementary and secondary schools from 2003–04 to 2012–13, at the all-India level as well as for the states of Jharkhand, Karnataka, Madhya Pradesh, Mizoram, Odisha, Punjab, Rajasthan, Tamil Nadu, and Uttar Pradesh.

The analysis uses District Information System for Education data, presented in the form of State Report Cards and District Report Cards for elementary schools for the academic years 2003–04 to 2012–13 ("Report Cards"). These data are publicly available on www.dise.in. Comparable data on secondary schools are available for a much shorter duration, and report a limited range of predefined variables. Hence, trend analyses for secondary schools were not performed. Instead, raw respondent-level Unified District Information System for Education data ("raw data"), available only for academic year 2012–13, are used to present a current snapshot of the teaching workforce in secondary schools. The raw data are also used to redefine certain variables of interest (vis-à-vis the definition used for the numbers presented in the Report Cards). For elementary education, the analysis based on this alternative definition is presented alongside the analysis based on data from the Report Cards.

The data from the Report Cards were downloaded from the website, and then checked and cleaned to remove inconsistencies, where possible. The main types of inconsistencies in the data, and their impact on the analysis, are the following:

- The set of variables reported is not identical across years and has generally expanded over time. Therefore, since the analysis is conducted over time, it was limited by the common denominator of the (smaller) set of variables reported in the earlier years.
- Data for the earlier years (especially 2003–04, 2004–05, and 2005–06 at the state level) are not reported under consistent variable names, and often variable and sub-variable names are not reported whatsoever (that is, there are columns and sub-columns in the data set without any headings or sub-headings). Based on the better organized data sets in later years, certain inferences have been made regarding the missing variable and sub-variable names.

- For the earlier years (especially 2003–04, 2004–05, and 2005–06 at the state level), aggregate data for the districts in a state were checked against the data reported directly at the state level for key metrics, such as the total number of schools and total number of teachers. These were found to be discrepant to a large extent in 2003–04, and the numbers for the other two years showed discrepancies of approximately 10 percent. Therefore, the data for 2003–04 are not presented. Although the state data have been used for the other two years, it is important to consider these discrepancies in interpreting the results of the analysis.
- For 2004–05, data are not reported for the states/Union Territories of Manipur, Daman and Diu, Dadra and Nagar Haveli, Goa, Lakshadweep, and Andaman and Nicobar Islands. Therefore, the data reported for all-India are only approximate (since the numbers for India are not directly reported and have, for most years, been estimated as the aggregate of the data reported for the states, where such an aggregation was possible and sensible). However, the states/UTs that have not reported data have only a very small number of schools, teachers, and pupils.
- There are various significant discrepancies in the 2010–11 state data set. For completeness, the numbers for 2010–11 are presented as reported, but they should be considered with a significant degree of caution.
- There is a discrepancy between the number of female teachers reported in the 2012–13 state data set for 2011–12 and that reported in the 2011–12 state data set. The discrepancy appears to be due to a change in the ordering of the states in the data sets across years, leading to a mismatch of numbers across states. Generally, therefore, the data for a particular year have been taken from the data set for the same year, even where such information was also available in the next year's data set.
- Apart from these cases of minor inconsistencies and missing data, necessary and reasonable assumptions (based on inference from later or previous data sets) have been made.

The cleaned raw data were aggregated into state and all-India data, which are presented in the analysis. Separate numbers for government schools only, private schools only, and all schools (government + private) were retained for the few variables where the raw data allowed it.

Notes

1. At the outset, it is important to state that we rely primarily on District Information System for Education (DISE) data. We understand that there are inaccuracies and definitional issues. However, it is still the most comprehensive data set that we have on the school system. The data for elementary schools used for this analysis come from State Report Cards and District Report Cards ("Report Cards") for elementary schools for the academic years 2003–04 to 2012–13, which present data on a selected set of DISE variables, and are available publicly on www.dise.in. Comparable data for secondary schools are available publicly only for a much shorter duration and, more significantly, only for a very limited range of DISE variables.

Therefore, for secondary schools, we rely on the Unified DISE respondent-level data, which are available for academic year 2012–13 ("raw data"), to present an analysis of the current scenario, rather than an analysis of trends over time. The section on the current scenario for elementary schools also draws on the raw data, and the numbers based on this data set (which offers much greater flexibility, for instance, for defining the variables of interest) are presented alongside those taken (as reported) from the Report Cards, to facilitate a comparison of the scenarios under alternative definitions of important variables. The other section in the paper that draws on the raw data is the section on intra-state variations in the PTR. We also draw on the literature to support these facts.

2. Schools are structured as: primary only, primary with upper primary, primary with upper primary and secondary and higher secondary, upper primary only, upper primary with secondary and higher secondary, primary with upper primary and secondary, or upper primary with secondary.

3. The data that were available to the research team did not enable all the analyses in this section to be carried out on the raw data for elementary schools; hence, the Report Card data are used.

4. This includes teachers for only those elementary schools that also report enrollment data. Therefore, this number omits approximately 170,000 teachers (3% of total), but allows comparability with the teacher numbers used for the PTR calculations that also use enrollment data.

5. This includes all elementary schools managed by the Department of Education, Local Body and Tribal/Social Welfare Department.

6. This includes private aided and private unaided schools; the break-up between these two subcategories is not provided in the Report Card data.

7. This is the average across-districts PTR for 2011–12, as there is no District Report Card available publicly for 2012–13. Since the Report Card data are presented at the district level, the average PTR is an across-districts average for the country.

8. These numbers are based on Report Card data, which report only two employment categories for teachers—regular and contract. This is different from the data collection and reporting in the raw data.

9. This point is made with the exception of Mizoram, where STs comprise an overwhelming demographic majority and, hence, also account for most of the teaching workforce.

10. This figure excludes boys-only schools.

11. These numbers do not sum to 100 percent because the secondary school data are based on the raw data, for which the Data Capture Form also allows schools to categorize teachers as part-time, and because the raw data report more than three types of employment contracts.

12. This is taken as a percentage of all aided secondary schools that have a meaningful student-classroom ratio.

13. RMSA norms: PTR is not a viable option for calculating teachers at the secondary level. That is why, under RMSA, the subject-specific requirements of the state as well as the PTR are kept in mind for the calculation of teachers. The approved RMSA norm is to provide a minimum of five subject teachers for a secondary school with up to two sections in each class. Since the RMSA scheme envisages a student classroom ratio of 40:1, a two-section school would normally mean an enrollment of 160 students. A minimum of five subject teachers will have to be provided even if the enrollment is

less than 160. Any shortfall in such schools will be made good under RMSA. For every incremental enrollment of 30 students, one additional teacher may be provided as per the RMSA norm of a PTR of 30:1. The number of sanctioned posts will be deducted from the total number of teachers so estimated, to arrive at the number of additional teachers a state will receive under RMSA for existing secondary schools. The subject-wise distribution of teachers has been left to the state government. (http://mhrd.gov.in/sites/upload_files/mhrd/files/upload_document/FAQ_0.pdf)

14. The six basic infrastructure components are: (a) at least two *pucca* classrooms and student-classroom ratio ≤ 40, (b) functional toilet block (hand wash facility and adequate number of toilet seats and urinals), (c) drinking water, (d) a room for the headmaster, (e) a library with at least 50 books, and (f) a computer-aided learning lab with at least two computers.

15. The terms "para teachers" and "contract teachers" are used interchangeably and there is no one agreed definition of what makes a teacher "para," even though the datasets analyzed here use these terms as if they were unproblematic. Are para teachers on fixed contracts? Are they recruited locally? Are their qualifications different or lower than those of regular teachers?

16. The literature on PTRs does not find convincing evidence that a reduction in the PTR is causally associated with improvement in student learning outcomes. A recent paper by Altinok and Kingdon (2012) analyzes the relationship between class size and student achievement in 47 countries, 18 of which are developing countries with an average class size of 41. This paper, and an earlier one by Hanushek (2003), show that class size does not have a significant impact on student achievement.

17. PTR = total enrollment/total teachers for the concerned territory; this is not materially different from the simple average PTR obtained from the district-level data set.

18. Estimated as the simple average of the PTRs for all elementary schools in a district.

19. These are extremely large values, which appear to be data errors, and have been addressed separately in the section on data gaps. Although comparing the SD/mean value across states would normally enable drawing some conclusions about the relative degree of homogeneity in school-level PTR distributions across states, here this must be done with due caution. This is because states such as Uttar Pradesh, Madhya Pradesh, and Jharkhand, which have the largest number of schools with PTR > 150, as well as the largest PTRs in the country, have clearly benefitted from the exclusion of all schools with PTR > 150. Therefore, the relative homogeneity of their PTR distributions in the 0–150 range can only be considered a partial picture at best.

20. Further discussion of data issues is included in annex 2A.

CHAPTER 3

Who Can Become a Teacher?

Introduction

Teacher recruitment policies at the national and state levels influence the number and quality of the pool of candidates who want to become teachers. These policies prescribe the norms for the minimum acceptable educational and training credentials of candidates who are screened from the pool of applicants toward the final selection of teachers.

This chapter describes and discusses the qualification and eligibility criteria prescribed for teacher recruitment at the elementary and secondary school levels. The criteria include educational and professional qualifications, the use of teacher eligibility tests (TETs), minimum and maximum applicable age limits, reservation quantum and categories, language requirements, and criteria for merit list[1] preparation in the nine study states. Where information has been made available, this chapter also describes the teacher recruitment practices that are followed. Some practices are aligned with, and some diverge from, the state policies and regulations.

National-Level Regulations

In India, the National Council of Teacher Education (NCTE) is the apex body for determining the standards of teacher education. NCTE issues notifications with standards for the minimum educational and professional qualifications for recruitment of schoolteachers. All the states base their teacher recruitment policies, at the elementary and secondary school levels, on the norms and standards laid down by NCTE.

NCTE Notifications on the Minimum Qualifications for Teachers Since the NCTE Act, 1993

The National Council for Teacher Education Act, 1993,[2] which came into force on July 1, 1995, provided for "the establishment of the National Council for Teacher Education with a view to achieving planned and coordinated development of the teacher education system throughout the country, the regulation and proper maintenance of norms and standards in the teacher education system and for matters connected herewith." Section 12 of Chapter III of the Act describes the functions of the Council and clause (d) of Section 12 states as one of its functions to "lay down guidelines in respect of minimum qualifications for a person to be employed as a teacher in schools or in recognized institutions" (Government of India, Ministry of Law, Justice and Company Affairs. 1993, 6[3]). Clause (d) (i) of Section 32, Chapter VII, reiterates the point that the Council may, by notification in the official Gazette, make regulations generally to carry out the provisions of this Act and such regulations may provide for the following matters, namely, one of which is (d) the norms, guidelines, and standards in respect of (i) the minimum qualifications for a person to be employed as a teacher.

Thereafter, NCTE has issued five notifications in the *Gazette of India* that communicate the regulations and subsequent amendments to the regulations on teacher qualifications. The first three notifications were published between 2001 and 2005 in the pre-Right to Education (RTE) Act phase, and laid down the regulation for the minimum qualifications for recruitment of teachers in schools:

- Notification of September 4, 2001. This notification published the regulations for determining the minimum qualifications applicable for recruitment of teachers in all formal schools established, run, or aided or recognized by the central and state government and other authorities for imparting education at the elementary (primary and upper primary/middle school), secondary, and senior secondary stages.[4]
- Notification of April 28, 2003. This was a notification of amendment to the 2001 regulation and extended those to be applicable for recruitment of teachers in all formal schools at "pre-school, nursery followed by first two years in formal school" in addition to the levels prescribed in the 2001 regulation.[5]
- Notification of August 23, 2005. This notification published a further amendment to the 2001 regulations, as amended in 2003. This amendment extended the list of minimum professional qualifications to include a Bachelor of Education (B.Ed.) (nursery) for recruitment of teachers at the pre-school and nursery level and up to the first two years in a formal school (ages 4–6 and 6–8 years).[6]

NCTE Notifications after the Right of Children to Free and Compulsory Education Act, 2009

With the enactment of the RTE Act, 2009,[7] and in exercise of the powers conferred by subsection (I) of Section 23 of the Act, the central government authorized NCTE as the academic authority to lay down the minimum qualifications for a person to be eligible for appointment as a teacher.[8] NCTE issued a notification on August 23, 2010[9] (2010 NCTE notification) that laid down the minimum qualifications for a person to be eligible for appointment as a teacher in classes I to VIII in a school (as referred to in clause (n) of Section 2 of the Act).

The major change brought in was the introduction of the TET as an eligibility criterion for teachers to be appointed.

The key additions in the 2010 NCTE notification are the following:

1. Minimum qualifying marks for the educational and professional qualifications specified (for example, for classes I to V, senior secondary (or its equivalent) with at least 50 percent marks and two-year diploma in Elementary Education).
2. Educational and professional qualifications required for classes VI to VIII spelled out clearly (for example, a Bachelor of the Arts (B.A.) or Bachelor of Science (B.S.) and Bachelor of Elementary Education (B.El.Ed.), wherever applicable).
3. Additional eligibility criteria of passing the TET, to be conducted by the appropriate government in accordance with guidelines framed by NCTE for this purpose.
4. A diploma or degree course in teacher education recognized by NCTE only to be considered.
5. Exception for teachers appointed before the date of the notification (2011): for example, teachers appointed for classes I to VIII on or after September 3, 2001 (the notification date of the NCTE 2001 regulation) need not acquire the minimum qualifications specified in the notification of August 2, 2011, provided the teacher of classes I to V, with a B.Ed., B.Ed. (special education), and Diploma in Education (D.Ed.) (special education) qualification, undergoes an NCTE recognized six-month special program on elementary education.

Thereafter, NCTE issued a notification of August 2, 2011,[10] with further amendments to the 2010 notification, in which:

1. The minimum educational qualification, that is B.A./B.S., was substituted by Graduation to allow Bachelor of Commerce (B.Com.) and Bachelor of Technology (B.Tech.) qualified candidates also to apply and the two-year Diploma in Elementary Education was added.
2. The section on minimum graduation qualifying marks required for entry to B.Ed. was further specified, and candidates with a D.Ed. (special education) or B.Ed. (special education), after appointment, are required to undergo an NCTE recognized six-month special program in elementary education.
3. Relaxation of 5 percent in the qualifying marks is allowed for candidates belonging to the reserved categories.
4. The section on exception related to the date of appointment has been expanded to state that the minimum qualification norms of this notification (2011) apply to teachers of languages, social studies, mathematics, science, and so forth, and the norms of the 2001 NCTE regulation are applicable for physical education teachers.

Table 3.1 lists the valid minimum qualifications, laid down by NCTE, for elementary, secondary, and senior secondary school teachers, as issued in the August 2011 notification (elementary) and September 2011 notification (secondary and senior secondary).

Section 23 of the RTE Act also provides for a "relaxation in the minimum qualifications required for appointment as a teacher, for such period, not exceeding five years as specified in that notification." In addition, the section states that provided that "a teacher who does not possess minimum qualifications as laid down by the academic authority shall acquire such minimum qualifications

Table 3.1 Minimum Educational and Professional Qualifications for Teachers Laid Down by NCTE for Elementary and Secondary School Teachers

NCTE standards for minimum educational and professional qualifications for recruitment of schoolteachers	
Elementary level	*NCTE notification, August 2, 2011*
Classes I to V	(a) Senior secondary (or its equivalent), with at least 50% marks, and a two-year Diploma in Elementary Education (by whatever name known), OR
	Senior secondary (or its equivalent), with at least 45% marks, and a two-year Diploma in Elementary Education (by whatever name known) in accordance with the NCTE (Recognition Norms and Procedure), Regulations, 2002 OR
	Senior secondary (or its equivalent), with at least 50% marks, and a four-year B.El.Ed. OR
	Senior secondary (or its equivalent), with at least 50% marks, and a two-year Diploma in Education (special education) OR
	Graduation[a] and a two-year Diploma in Elementary Education (by whatever name known) AND
	(b) Pass in the TET, to be conducted by the appropriate government in accordance with the guidelines framed by NCTE for this purpose.
Classes VI to VIII	Graduation and a two-year Diploma in Elementary Education (by whatever name) OR
	Graduation with at least 45% marks and a one-year B.Ed., in accordance with the NCTE (Recognition and Norms and Procedure) Regulations issued from time to time in this regard OR
	Senior secondary (or its equivalent), with at least 50% marks, and a four-year B.El.Ed. OR
	Senior secondary (or its equivalent), with at least 50% marks, and a four-year B.A./B.S. Ed. or B.A.Ed. or B.S. Ed. OR
	Graduation with at least 50% marks and a one-year B.Ed. (special education) AND
	(b) Pass on the TET, to be conducted by the appropriate government in accordance with the guidelines framed by NCTE for this purpose.
Secondary level	NCTE notification, September 4, 2001.
Classes IX and X	Graduate with B.Ed. or its equivalent OR Four years' integrated B.S., B.Ed., or an equivalent course.

Source: NCTE August 2, 2011 notification: http://www.ncte-india.org/Norms/RTE-4.pdf; NCTE September 4, 2001 notification: http://www.ncte-india.org/NOTI/noti27.htm.
Note: B.A.Ed. = Bachelor of the Arts in Education; B.Ed. = Bachelor of Education; B.El.Ed. = Bachelor of Elementary Education; B.S.Ed. = Bachelor of Science in Education; NCTE = National Council of Teacher Education; TET = teacher eligibility test.
a. Graduation is defined as a bachelor's degree.

within a period of five years." Following this provision, the central government allowed this relaxation in a few states that had a huge shortage of qualified teachers and applicants. Of the states under the study, Jharkhand, Madhya Pradesh, Odisha, and Uttar Pradesh were granted this relaxation. In the notification of September 13, 2012, issued by the Ministry of Human Resource Development to the Government of Uttar Pradesh,[11] a relaxation to recruit unqualified teachers was provided because of the unavailability of qualified teachers in sufficient numbers in the state. However, these applicants were required to pass the TET and, once recruited, they were required to complete their training within a specified period from the date of their appointment.

NCTE notification of November 28, 2014.[12] At the time of writing this chapter, NCTE issued a notification in exercise of the powers conferred by the NCTE Act, 1993, and in supersession of the NCTE Regulations, 2009, with the NCTE (Recognition Norms and Procedure) Regulations, 2014. These regulations are applicable to teacher education programs for preparing norms, standards, and procedures for recognition of institutions, commencement of new programs, addition to sanctioned intake in existing programs, eligible categories of institutions for consideration of their applications, application process and time limit, processing fees, processing of applications, conditions for grant of recognition, norms and standards for various teacher education programs, financial management, academic calendars, power to relax any of the provisions of these regulations, and repeal of NCTE (Recognition Norms and Procedure) Regulations, 2009.

Some of the highlights of the new norms for teacher professional qualifications are for the B.Ed. program to be a two-year course; an integrated four-year course leading to a B.A. and B.Ed. degree to be introduced; admission to B.Ed. programs to open for B.Com and B.Tech graduates; 20 weeks of practical work included in the B.Ed. course, of which at least 16 weeks are to be spent in teaching; and unqualified secondary school teachers required to complete a three-year, part-time B.Ed. course in classroom mode during vacations.

TET as an Eligibility Criterion for Teacher Recruitment[13]

As per the NCTE guidelines for conducting the TET issued to the states in February 2011,[14] the rationale for including passing of the TET as a minimum qualification for a person to be eligible for appointment as a teacher is threefold: (a) to bring national standards and benchmarks of teacher quality into the recruitment process, (b) to induce teacher education institutions and students from these institutions to improve their performance standards, and (c) to send a positive signal to all stakeholders that the government lays special emphasis on teacher quality.

The Central Board of Secondary Education, authorized by the central government, conducts the TET at the national level as the Central Teacher Eligibility Test (CTET). The CTET exam consists of two papers: Paper I for persons intending to be a teacher for classes I to V, and Paper II for persons who intend to be a teacher for classes VI to VIII. A person applying to teach classes I to V or classes VI to VIII is required to take both papers at the exam. Twenty percent of the questions in Paper I are on child development and pedagogy, and 80 percent on subject content (languages, mathematics, and environmental studies). For Paper II, 20 percent of the questions are on child development and pedagogy; 40 percent on languages for all applicants; and 40 percent on mathematics and science for teacher applicants for these subjects, and 40 percent on social studies for teacher applicants for this subject.

Given the heavy emphasis on subject content in the TET, it is more likely that the school- and college-level education of the candidate will have a greater impact on her/his performance on the TET than what is taught at the teacher education institutions (that is, B.Ed., D.Ed., B.El.Ed., and D/El. Ed.), which emphasize child development and pedagogy in their curriculum.

The qualifying score for the CTET is 60 percent. NCTE guidelines also allow the appropriate level of government to conduct its own TET, subject to NCTE guidelines. NCTE regulations allow school managements (government, local bodies, government-aided, and unaided) to consider giving concessions for reserved categories in accordance with their extant reservation policy and weighting the TET scores in the recruitment process. *However, qualifying the TET does not confer a right on any person for recruitment, as it is only one of the eligibility criteria for appointment.* The guidelines state that the appropriate government should conduct a TET at least once every year. The validity period of the TET qualifying certificate is up to a maximum period of seven years, but there is no restriction on the number of times a person can take the TET to acquire a certificate. A person who has qualified in the TET may also appear again to improve her/his score. All legal disputes on the conduct of the TET are subject to the jurisdiction of the appropriate government.

State-Level Regulations and Policies for Teacher Recruitment in the Nine States

In general, the public service commissions of the respective states undertake teacher recruitment. The exception is Tamil Nadu, which created the Teacher Recruitment Board in 1997.[15] Punjab has recently (2013) created a recruitment board, while Jharkhand has formed the Staff Selection Commission. At the time of writing, Rajasthan was also considering having a separate recruitment board for all non-gazetted government officers, which would include schoolteachers. States must mandatorily follow the minimum qualifications laid down under the NCTE notifications. However, the states may have additional criteria, such as age, subject specialization, language proficiency, and so forth. Therefore, among the nine study states, there are variations in eligibility criteria (educational and professional qualifications, TET qualification, minimum and maximum age limit, and reservation policies for various categories) for recruitment of teachers at the elementary and secondary levels that correspond to the states' policies (table 3.2).

Table 3.2 Minimum Educational and Professional Qualifications for Elementary and Secondary School Teachers Prescribed by the States in the Study

State	Minimum qualifications for elementary school teachers	Minimum qualifications for secondary school teachers
Jharkhand	Primary: higher secondary/intermediate passed + trained teachers for primary grades Upper primary: graduate + trained teachers for upper primary grades	Secondary: graduate with 50% marks and B.Ed.
Karnataka	Primary: Class XII/PUC + D.Ed./TCH (primary) Upper primary: B.A./B.S. + D.Ed. (yet to be implemented)	B.A./B.S. + B.Ed.
Madhya Pradesh	Primary level (grade III): 50% in higher secondary + 2-year diploma in elementary education OR 45% in higher secondary + 2-year diploma in elementary education, according to NCTE 2002 OR 50% in higher secondary + B.El.Ed. OR 50% in higher secondary with a 2-year diploma in special education. Upper primary level (grade II): graduation in the subject concerned. Diploma in elementary education or any equivalent degree OR 50% marks in bachelor's degree in subject concerned + B.Ed. OR graduation with 45% marks, according to NCTE 2002 norms OR 50% marks along with higher secondary and B.El.Ed. OR 50% in higher secondary + 4-year bachelor's degree (B.A., B.Ed./B.S., B.Ed.) OR graduation with 50% in subject concerned + B.Ed. in special education. Relaxation: 5% less for SC, ST, OBC, and disabled in qualifying marks for the qualifying educational qualifications.	
Mizoram	Primary: HSSLC with at least 50% marks or a bachelor degree or above, with a diploma in elementary education with a duration of not less than 2 years from a recognized university and approved by NCTE or HSSLC with at least 50% marks OR a graduate degree with a 2-year D.Ed. (special education) recognized by RCI. Upper primary (middle school): graduate degree or above, with a diploma in elementary education with a duration of not less than 2 years from a recognized university and approved by NCTE OR a bachelor degree or above with at least 50% marks and a 1-year bachelor in education (B.Ed.) from a recognized university and approved by NCTE OR a B.S. (science and mathematics) or above with at least 50% marks with a 2-year diploma in elementary education from a recognized university and approved by NCTE OR a 1-year B.Ed. from a recognized university and approved by NCTE or a graduate degree with at least 50% marks with a 2-year D.Ed. (special education) or B.Ed. (special education) recognized by RCI.	Secondary: graduate with B.Ed. or its equivalent OR 4-year integrated B.S., B.Ed., or an equivalent course from a recognized university
Odisha	Primary: HSC or equivalent higher secondary examination. Upper primary: TGT, the candidate must have a bachelor's degree in arts or science along with a B.Ed. degree from a recognized university.	Secondary: TGT, the candidate must have a bachelor's degree in arts or science along with a B.Ed. degree from a recognized university.
Punjab	Primary: senior secondary (10+2) with 50% marks with JBT/ETT course. Eligibility conditions have been expanded to include candidates with B.El.Ed., graduation with a 2-year diploma in elementary education, 10+2 and a 2-year diploma in education (special education), or any other qualification as per NCTE norms 2002. Upper primary: graduate with 50% marks and B.Ed. All candidates without JBT/ETT will be required to undertake a 6-month course in elementary education.	Secondary: TGT with the basic qualification of a bachelor's degree in the relevant subject with 50% marks and a B.Ed.

table continues next page

Table 3.2 Minimum Educational and Professional Qualifications for Elementary and Secondary School Teachers Prescribed by the States in the Study *(continued)*

State	Minimum qualifications for elementary school teachers	Minimum qualifications for secondary school teachers
Rajasthan	Primary level: 12th class pass (with 50% marks) +2-year diploma in education; (secondary with five subjects in which mathematics, English, and Hindi as compulsory subjects) OR 12th class pass, with 45% marks, and a 2-year diploma in elementary education as per the norms of NCTE 2002. OR a graduate and 2-year diploma in education at the upper primary level: graduate and 2-year diploma in elementary education OR graduate, with minimum 50% marks, and a 1-year B.Ed. degree.	Secondary: recognized diploma/degree in education and graduate in the related subject
Tamil Nadu	NCTE stipulated norms for: Primary: high school and a diploma in education/graduation with diploma in education. Upper primary: graduation with diploma in education Prequalification in TET mandatory	Secondary: bachelor degree in relevant subject and B.Ed.
Uttar Pradesh	Primary (assistant teacher): 1. High school exam from Madhyamik Shiksha Parishad (Uttar Pradesh) or equivalent as recognized by Uttar Pradesh government + BTC or equivalent (Notification 1981) 2. Passed intermediate exam from Madhyamik Shiksha Parishad (Uttar Pradesh) but for the candidates who have passed BTC or equivalent previously, the essential qualification will be the same as for the admission in training program (5th amendment 1993) 3. Graduate from a university established by law in India or equivalent + BTC or equivalent (8th Amendment 1998) For Shiksha Mitra—class XII upper primary (assistant teacher): for math/science (direct 50%) recruitment 1. Graduation, BTC/B.Ed. or equivalent 2. TET (6–8) qualified. 3. Graduate from university with at least one subject, science or mathematics. 4. BTC./B.Ed./B.Ed. (special education). For Anudeshak: graduate	Secondary: 1. Graduate from a recognized university of India as established by law 2. B.Ed./LT from a university or training college recognized by the state government

Source: State Reports.
Note: B.A. = Bachelor of the Arts; B.Ed. = Bachelor of Education; B.El.Ed. = Bachelor of Elementary Education; BTC = Basic Training Certificate; B.S. = Bachelor of Science; D.Ed. = Diploma in Education; ETT = Elementary Teacher Training; HSC = Higher Secondary School Certificate; HSSLC = Higher Secondary School Leaving Certificate; JBT = Junior Basic Training; LT = Licenciate in Teaching; NCTE = National Council of Teacher Education; OBC = Other Backward Classes; PUC = Pre-University Certificate; RCI = Rehabilitation Council of India; SC = Scheduled Caste; ST = Scheduled Tribe; TCH = Teachers' Certificate Higher; TGT = Trained Graduate Teacher.

Educational and Professional Qualifications

All nine study states prescribe the same minimum requirements as NCTE for educational and professional qualifications for teacher candidates at the elementary and secondary levels. There is variation in the level of detail issued in the government orders in the states with respect to eligibility criteria. Madhya Pradesh, Mizoram, and Uttar Pradesh have issued more detailed and clear qualification and eligibility criteria in comparison with the other study states. This raises the question as to how clearly the notifications are communicated in government orders or to what extent are they revised from time to time—thereby requiring more detailed explanations. Tamil Nadu and Karnataka essentially follow the NCTE guidelines and these have remained the same for several years.

To meet the RTE-prescribed pupil-teacher ratio norms, a few states have recruited teachers in large numbers within a short period. Many in the pool of available candidates do not meet the minimum professional qualifications (pre-service training). Therefore, some states have relaxed this criterion as per the provisions of the RTE Act. For example, in Punjab, candidates without Junior Basic Training or Elementary Teachers Training can become eligible if they complete a six-month course in elementary education. Madhya Pradesh has allowed candidates without pre-service qualifications to appear for the TET exam, on the condition that once recruited, these teachers will complete their required qualification within a stipulated timeframe.

Teacher Eligibility Test Qualification

The nine states have introduced the TET qualification as an eligibility criterion in their recruitment policies for candidates applying to teach at the elementary level. States have designed their own TET (rather than using the CTET) within the guidelines for conducting the TET provided by NCTE, with a few exceptions. As of writing this chapter, all states have completed at least one or two rounds of their respective TET. The TET is discussed in more detail in chapter 4.

Age Criteria for Recruitment

All nine states prescribe minimum and maximum age limits for candidates to be eligible as teachers. The age limit criterion is similar in all nine states, with a few exceptions. In most states, the minimum age for elementary teachers is 18 years, and for secondary teachers, 21 years. The maximum age (to start as such a teacher) is typically between 32 and 35 years. In Punjab, the prescribed maximum age limit for senior and senior secondary teachers has been changed in various recruitment advertisements over the years since 2007. The rationale for these differences is not clear. Table 3.3 provides this information.

Table 3.3 Maximum Age Limit for Senior and Senior Secondary Teachers Advertised between 2007 and 2012, Punjab

Year of recruitment notification	No. of teaching posts advertised (senior and senior secondary)	Age limit (without reservation) (years)
2007	4,000	42
2008	405	42
2009	7,654	37
2010 (January)	694	42
2010 (November)	3,725	37
2010	560	42
2011	3,442	37
2012	5,178	38

Source: Punjab State Report.

In the relaxation provided to the upper limit for age for the reserved categories, there is substantial variation among the states, as shown in table 3.4.

Mismatch of Minimum Age and Educational Qualification Requirement

Rajasthan and Karnataka have prescribed 18 years as the minimum age requirement for the elementary level (for the primary and upper primary education levels). However, candidates need to have at least a bachelor's degree, and this is typically obtained after the age of 21 years. Similarly, in Rajasthan, the minimum age for candidates who want to become secondary school teachers is 18 years, whereas the minimum educational qualification required is a B.A. or B.S., with a professional qualification of a B.Ed. degree. For teaching in senior secondary classes, the minimum age for teachers is 21 years; however, the minimum educational qualification is a post-graduate degree, and it is extremely unlikely that anyone would obtain this qualification before the minimum age limit. In these cases, the age limit seems redundant.

Table 3.4 Minimum and Maximum Age Limits for Elementary- and Secondary-Level Teacher Recruitment

State	Age limit for elementary school teachers	Age limit for secondary and senior secondary school teachers
Jharkhand	Minimum: 18 years; maximum: 35 years (general); 37 years (BC and EBC); 38 years (women from BC and EBC); 40 years (SC and ST); 40 years (handicapped); 43 years (handicapped women from BC/EBC); 45 years (handicapped from SC/ST); 50 years (contract teachers)	Minimum: 21 years
Karnataka	Minimum: 18 years, maximum: 40 years for general category, 43 years for OBC category, 45 years for SC/ST categories	Minimum: 21 years, maximum: same as for elementary school teachers
Madhya Pradesh	Primary minimum: 18 years; upper primary (graduate teachers): 21 years; maximum age: 35 years	Secondary and senior secondary level: 21 years; maximum age: 35 years. Age relaxation for elementary and secondary: 10 years for women (+ 5 for widows and divorcees); guest teachers and part-time vocational teachers, additional 5 years for earlier Samvida who have not taken Adhyapak (up to 15 years)
Mizoram	Minimum: 18 years; maximum: 35 years	Minimum: 21 years; maximum: 30 years
Odisha	Minimum: 18 years; maximum: 32 years. In case of SC and ST, women, and ex-servicemen candidates there is 5 years relaxation and for SEBC it is 3 years in the maximum age limit.	Minimum: 21 years; maximum 42 years. In case of SC and ST, women, and ex-servicemen candidates there is 5 years relaxation and for SEBC, it is 3 years in the maximum age limit.
Punjab	The age limit for direct recruitment as teacher, headmaster, headmistress, or lecturer is 32 years as of January 1 of the year in which posts are advertised (Government. Of Punjab 2002). However, in practice, it is not followed and the age limit changes with different recruitment advertisements. Age relaxation is allowed, as per Government of Punjab rules from time to time. However, the relaxation cannot be 10 years more than the prescribed limit (Government of Punjab 2002).	In the case of secondary and senior secondary school teachers, data from the recruitment notifications from 2007 to 2012 show varying age limits in every notification starting from 42 in 2007 to 38 in 2012.

table continues next page

Table 3.4 Minimum and Maximum Age Limits for Elementary- and Secondary-Level Teacher Recruitment *(continued)*

State	Age limit for elementary school teachers	Age limit for secondary and senior secondary school teachers
Rajasthan	Elementary: minimum: 18 years; maximum: 31 years. Upper age limit relaxed by 5 years in the case of women candidates and SC, ST, and OBC candidates. There is no age limit in the case of widows and divorced women.	Secondary: minimum: 18 years; maximum: 31 years. Upper age limit relaxed by 5 years in the case of women candidates and SC, ST, and OBC candidates. There is no age limit in the case of widows and divorced women. Senior secondary: minimum: 21 years, maximum: 31 years. Relaxation of 5 years for: male of SC, ST, OBC, SBC, and economically backward group and females of general caste. Relaxation of 10 years for: female of SC, ST, OBC and SBC. Relaxation for 5 years for state government employees. Relaxation of 15 years for employees of Rajasthan Education Subordinate services (teacher grades II and III). There is no age limit in the case of widows and divorced women.
Tamil Nadu	There is no upper age limit for the recruitment of elementary teachers since 2001, and there is no mention of minimum age for recruitment. Therefore, it is assumed that the minimum age requirement is the same as for recruitment of government servants: 18 years.	Since 2001, the upper age limit was removed; however, notifications in the TRB advertisement state "not more than 57 years." No lower limit is mentioned.
Uttar Pradesh	Primary minimum: 18 years; maximum: 30 years, 5 years age relaxation for reserved categories or as government decides from time to time. (Rules 1981), now amended as minimum age to be 21 years and maximum age 40 years (amended in 2011). For Shiksha Mitra, in addition to the above, the candidate has to be a resident of the village or at most the Nyaya Panchayat. Upper primary minimum: 21 years; maximum: 35 years, 5-year age relaxation to SC, ST, and OBC; 3-year age relaxation to ex-service men; 10-year age relaxation to handicapped; nationality Indian; resident residing in Uttar Pradesh at least 5 years. For Anudeshak, in addition to the above, has to be a resident of the district where applying.	Secondary: TGT: 1. Indian citizen 2. Minimum: 21 years; maximum: 40 years (as amended in 2014); higher secondary: PGT (government lecturer)—Indian citizen, minimum: 21 years; maximum: 32 years, now amended to 40 years (as per service rules 1992, Part-3, Regulations 7, 10).

Source: State Reports.
Note: BC = Backward Caste; EBC = Extremely Backward Caste; OBC = Other Backward Castes; PGT = Post Graduate Teacher; SC = Scheduled Caste; SEBC = Socio Economic Backward Classes; SBC = Special Backward Classes; ST = Scheduled Tribe; TGT = Trained Graduate Teacher; TRB = Teacher Recruitment Board.

Reservation Policies for Recruitment

Reservation criteria are an important item of the eligibility requirements (table 3.5). Recruitment is directly influenced by the reservation norms and policies in all states. This, in turn, has a bearing on the number of teachers recruited versus the total requirement of teachers based on the reserved positions that are filled or left vacant.

Table 3.5 Criteria for Reservation Categories

	Reservation policy (percent) with respect to:						
State	General	ST	SC	OBC	Persons with disability	Women	Other categories/comments
Jharkhand	27	26	10	14	—	—	23% ad hoc or provisional. Within the 14% reserved for backward classes, 8% is reserved for extreme backward castes (Schedule I) and 6% for backward castes (Schedule II).
Karnataka	50	3	15	32	—	50	Rural candidates (25%); ex-soldiers (10%); physically handicapped (5%); unsheltered (5%); Kannada medium (5%); general merit (50%).
Madhya Pradesh	—	SC, ST, and OBC as per population in the district			6	50	10% for ex-servicemen.
Mizoram	—	—	—	—	—	—	None, except for people with disabilities.
Odisha	—	22.5	16.25	—	—	—	Socially and Educationally Backward Classes: 11.25%.
Punjab	—	—	25	5	3	—	Rural areas 7%; border areas 3%; defense personnel, wards, spouses, and so forth 2%; children of persons killed in violence or Sikh migrants (after 1984 riots) 2%.
Rajasthan	—	12	16	21	3	30	SBC-5%; EBC 14%; outstanding sports persons 2%; tribal areas 45%; reservation for STs and SCs 5%.
Tamil Nadu	—	1	18	—	2	30	Backward Class (other than Muslims) 26.5%, Backward Class (Muslims) 3.5%, Most Backward Class/De-notified Category 20%; persons who studied in Tamil medium 20%.
Uttar Pradesh	—	2	21	27	3	—	Ex-servicemen 2%.

Source: State Reports.
Note: EBC = Extremely Backward Caste; OBC = Other Backward Classes; SBC = Special Backward Classes; SC = Scheduled Caste; ST = Scheduled Tribe; — = not available.

For recruitment, states follow the reservation policy laid down by the central government, which is also reflected in the NCTE notifications on teacher qualifications. In addition, states have their own reservation policy, including reservation for several categories, such as women, widows, ex-servicemen, and so forth, with varying percentages. Reservation criteria also vary from one state to another, reflecting the shares of the dominant castes and tribal population in the states. Some states, such as Madhya Pradesh, Tamil Nadu, and Uttar Pradesh, have made provisions for vertical (for Scheduled Caste, Scheduled Tribe, and Other Backward Classes categories) and horizontal reservations (for women, disabled persons, ex-service men, and outstanding sportspersons).[16]

Apart from these general reservation criteria in the states, some states follow a few additional reservation practices. For example, since 1996, Tamil Nadu has followed the practice of hiring women teachers for classes I to V and male teachers (only up to a maximum of 10% of the applicants) if female candidates are not available.

In various states, the roster system is used to implement the reservation policy for recruitment and promotion of teachers, for example, the 100-point roster system followed in Punjab.[17]

States have different ways of resolving the issue of reserved vacancies. In Rajasthan, despite the reservation quota of 30 percent for women, over 70 percent of teachers at the elementary level and 77 percent of teachers at the secondary level are men. Another challenge from the policy-practice perspective is that several positions for math, English, and science teachers remain vacant due to lack of available candidates from the reserved categories.

Language Requirement

A few states have prescribed qualifications in the official state language as part of the mandatory eligibility criteria.

1. Jharkhand has a requirement that the candidate successfully qualifies in at least one regional language test as part of the TET.
2. Odisha has made Oriya mandatory—candidates must have had Oriya as the medium of examination in non-language subjects at class X examination.
3. Punjab has a requirement that candidates complete their matriculation with Punjabi as a subject. Candidates who do not have this qualification are given a chance to clear the examination within a prescribed time, at the time of offer of appointment.

Criteria for Merit List Preparation

All or most of the eligibility criteria described thus far are used to prepare the merit list, which then becomes the basis for the final selection of successful candidates. The merit list is the most critical part of the recruitment process, since each successful candidate is given a ranking on the list and, as is described in chapter 4, this rank determines which teachers are appointed first, and they have the first choice of school to which they will be appointed. Once generated, the lists are published to provide opportunities for individuals to challenge their placement on the list.

The construction of the merit list is a very complicated process. Those constructing the list must consider all the various criteria and reservation policies. It is perhaps not surprising that there are many court cases challenging the lists. The following are a few examples of the specific criteria and formulae that are used to prepare the merit lists in the study states.

- *Jharkhand.* For recruitment of teachers who have passed class XII and have pre-service training, the final score used to create the merit list is made up of the sum of the following two scores:
  - The average score of academic achievement calculated as follows: marks obtained in matriculation (class X), intermediate (class XII), and the teacher

training exam are added and the sum is divided by three to obtain the average marks in percent. In this calculation, subjects taken as extra or additional are not included.
- The score assigned for marks obtained on the TET is as follows: if the TET marks are > 90 percent, then a score of 10 is awarded; for 80 percent and above but < 90 percent, a score of 6 is awarded; for 70 percent and above but < 80 percent, a score of 4 is awarded; and for 52 percent and above but < 70 percent, a score of 2 is awarded.

- In case there are many candidates with the same scores, the date of birth is used as a criterion to rank senior candidates over junior candidates. If the date of birth is also similar, then the ranking is done based on the ascending Roman alphabetic order of the candidates' first names.
- *Karnataka*. The selection of candidates is based on the Higher Secondary Examination, Pre-University Certificate, B.A., and B.S. marks; Teachers' Certificate Higher, D.Ed., and B.Ed. scores; and the percentage scores on the Centralized Entrance Test, ensuring that three kinds of reservation criterion, namely social category, sex, and individual characteristics, for overall recruitment are met. Post-2013, an additional reservation for Gulbarga division (comprising six districts: Gulbarga, Yadgir, Bellary, Raichur, Koppal, and Bidar) has been introduced due to the enactment of Article 371J (of the Constitution) in the area. This special status means that 80 percent of the seats for teachers (group C cadre) are reserved for local cadre and domicile of Gulbarga division (Government of Karnataka 2013; Rajendran 2013). This is the reservation criterion for selecting candidates only in the Gulbarga division, in addition to the abovementioned social category-wise, sex-wise, and individual characteristic-wise criteria.
- *Punjab*. The weights for deciding merit for elementary-level teachers are as follows: 10+2 (25 percent), Elementary Teacher Training test (25 percent), Punjab State Teacher Eligibility Test (30 percent), higher education (20 percent, later changed to 25 percent, as per recruitment advertisement of 2011). For the secondary level, the weights of points on the merit list are as follows: basic academic qualification: 25 percent, professional qualification: 25 percent, post-graduation: 10 percent, Master of Philosophy and Doctor of Philosophy: 10 percent, and TET: 30 percent. As per the roster, if for the last available vacancy for candidates of a particular category two or more candidates of that category have exactly the same merit, the older candidate is given preference and, if that is also the same, then both candidates are appointed (which means the sanctioned posts are increased).
- *Uttar Pradesh*. For primary- and upper primary–level teachers, the selection criteria are based on a weighted average of the class X exam results, class XII exam results, graduation results, training qualification, and TET. For secondary- and senior secondary–level teachers also, a similar weighting is given. The selection criteria for different kinds of teachers change often, based on the requirements at the time of the advertisement and changes in the government.

Conclusion

Although they are not required to do so, states in India base their teacher recruitment policies on the NCTE guidelines, but the states add requirements corresponding to their particular contexts. With the RTE coming into effect and the need to fulfill pupil-teacher ratio norms, many states have had to recruit a large number of teachers within a short period. This has resulted in a gap in some states between the minimum criteria for teacher eligibility and actual teacher characteristics. Reservation quotas also create vacancies, especially in particular subjects, and are vulnerable to manipulation by different stakeholders—including administrators and political leaders—since they can change for each recruitment drive. The use of TET has introduced some measurement of teacher knowledge as one of the criteria for determining eligibility. However, the use of TET is still in its early stages, and there has been little investigation of the format and content of the tests to determine their validity and reliability.

Some states' recruitment policies are based on the older NCTE notification for elementary school teachers, and need to be aligned to the latest one. Further scrutiny is needed of the processes followed for recruitment that deviate from the policies, to ensure that the best intent of the policies is put into practice. Of critical importance is the clear and transparent communication of the qualification and eligibility criteria in recruitment advertisements. This will reduce delays, legal and extra-legal disputes, and political influence in teacher recruitment.

Notes

1. The merit list is the final selection list of successful candidates. The results of the merit list are calculated using a combination of weighted results of the board exams for classes X and XII, bachelor's or master's degree (wherever applicable), TET, and degree or diploma in education and reservation category (wherever applicable).
2. The NCTE Act, 1993, and subsequent notifications are available at: http://www.ncte-india.org/regul.asp.
3. Government of India, Ministry of Law, Justice and Company Affairs. December 1993. National Council of Teacher Education Act of 1993, http://www.dauniv.ac.in/notices/B.Ed.NCTE%20Act%201973.pdf.
4. NCTE Regulations, September 2001: http://www.ncte-india.org/NOTI/noti27.htm.
5. NCTE Amendment Notification, April 2003: http://www.ncte-india.org/noti/determ.htm.
6. NCTE Amendment Notification, August 2005: http://www.ncte-india.org/noti/2.htm.
7. The Right to Free and Compulsory Education Act, 2009: http://www.ncte-india.org/Norms/RTE-1.pdf.
8. Ministry of Human Resource Development notification, April 2010: http://mhrd.gov.in/sites/upload_files/mhrd/files/upload_document/5.pdf.
9. NCTE Regulations, August 2010: http://www.ncte-india.org/Norms/RTE-3.pdf.
10. NCTE Amendment Notification of August 2, 2011: http://www.ncte-india.org/Norms/RTE-4.pdf.

11. http://mhrd.gov.in/sites/upload_files/mhrd/files/upload_document/rtesep2012.pdf.
12. http://www.ncte-india.org/regulation/Regulation_2014(Hindi%20&%20English).pdf and http://www.ncte-india.org/Minimum%20Qualification_2015.pdf.
13. See chapter 4 for further discussion of the TET.
14. NCTE guidelines for conducting the TET are available at: http://www.ncte-india.org/RTE-TET-guidelines[1]%20(latest).pdf.
15. The Teacher Recruitment Board in Tamil Nadu, headed by a senior Indian Administrative Service officer, undertakes all teacher recruitment pertaining to teachers in elementary, secondary, high, and higher secondary schools, as well as colleges. The board announces vacancies on its website, www.trb.tn.nic.in. The board conducts certificate verification and written and oral exams pertaining to teacher selection. (Oral exams are conducted for college teachers.) All complaints regarding teacher recruitments, especially the TET, are filed against the Recruitment Board.
16. Social reservation in favor of SCs, STs, and OBCs under Article 16(4) of the Constitution of India are "vertical reservations." Special reservations in favor of physically handicapped persons, women, and so forth, under Article 16 (1) or 15 (3) of the Constitution of India are "horizontal reservations." Horizontal reservations cut across the vertical reservations.
17. This is explained in greater detail in the Punjab State Report.

CHAPTER 4

Teacher Recruitment

Introduction

Effective teacher recruitment policies and practices are not just about ensuring high standards for who becomes a teacher (which is discussed in chapter 3). They also involve having clear recruitment policies, as well as timely and transparent procedures at all the stages of recruitment, including prompt appointment and deployment as the recruitment process culminates. Uncertainty about how and when recruitment will happen, whether merit will be rewarded, and whether school-specific needs would be met has serious implications for the quality of the teaching force. This uncertainty gives teaching a non-serious reputation, discourages applicants from investing systematically in building pre-service teaching skills, and attracts applicants with little interest in teaching. In so doing, poor recruitment policies and practices make school teaching a second-class profession.

Teacher Recruitment: Direct and Indirect

Teacher recruitment in states across the country, at the primary and secondary levels, is undertaken through a direct process (recruitment of people who are not currently in the teaching force) or indirect process (promotions of existing teachers or on compassionate grounds) or a combination of the two. In Karnataka, for instance, roughly 50 percent of all recruitments are direct, and roughly 50 percent of all recruitments (beyond primary school) are based on promotions. At the other extreme, in Mizoram, all recruitments are direct. One reason for all recruitments being direct in Mizoram is that the state is increasingly hiring contract teachers; indeed, since 1998, it has hired no teacher on regular services, but only on contract. Another reason is that there is no scope for inter-cadre movement in Mizoram, in the sense that a primary school teacher cannot become an upper primary school teacher and so forth. Since promotions are only possible if teachers are on a regular contract, Mizoram's method of recruitment is consistent with the terms of recruitment. In Odisha, in contrast, at present there is little direct recruitment, with most recruitment resulting from promotion of teachers or regularization of contract teachers. In Rajasthan, all recruitment into elementary schools is direct, and for grades IX and X, it is evenly split between direct and indirect.

In general, indirect recruitment happens based on the experience or qualifications of teachers. In Tamil Nadu, for instance, if primary school teachers want to move to upper primary, they must upgrade their qualifications—merely accumulating years of teaching is not enough. Regardless, indirect recruitment policies do not consider the performance of the teacher in improving student learning, except in Madhya Pradesh, where there is no direct recruitment into the Adhyapak (regular teacher) cadre; instead, all recruitment into this cadre happens from teachers in the contract cadre (Samvida Shala Shikshak; SSS), based on a set of objective (albeit unambitious) criteria:

1. The class(es) taught by the SSS must have attained the following results in the examinations: 50 percent pass for classes I–V; 40 percent pass for classes VI–VIII, and 30 percent pass for classes IX–XII.
2. The teachers should have the requisite professional qualifications (Diploma in Education (D.Ed.) or Bachelor of Education (B.Ed.)) for the relevant grade.
3. The teachers should have completed three years of service without any disciplinary action or leave without pay.

This study found little evidence to suggest that these criteria, especially the criterion related to student performance, are considered or followed in practice in Madhya Pradesh. The methods of recruitment also vary from state to state (table 4.1) and, in some cases, change every year.

Table 4.1 Direct and Indirect Recruitment Practices in Sample States

State	Direct	Indirect
Jharkhand	100% of primary teachers direct recruitment on contract, and ~70% of subject teachers in high school	50% of regular teacher recruitment at all levels done from cadre of contract teachers; ~25% of subject teachers in high school recruited from primary and middle schools
Karnataka	< 50% (all categories) except primary school teachers	At least 50% (all categories)
Madhya Pradesh	100% (only SSS[a] cadre recruited)	50% from parallel SSS teachers; 50% through promotion
Mizoram	100% all categories	
Odisha	100% direct recruitment to the lowest cadre (level V) teachers in primary; at the secondary level, 100% level IV by direct recruitment (employed on contract)	100% from level V to IV and from IV to III, which are district cadre posts; at the secondary level, 100% posts above level IV (meaning III, II and I) contract done by promotion; 100% senior grade posts (headmasters and so forth) by promotion

table continues next page

Table 4.1 Direct and Indirect Recruitment Practices in Sample States *(continued)*

State	Direct	Indirect
Punjab	Direct as contract teacher, no overarching policy changes from year to year	Now 100% regular indirect (from cadre of contract teachers) for regular teachers; however, policy changes from year to year
Rajasthan	100% for elementary; 50% for grades IX and X	50% for grades IX and X
Tamil Nadu	100% in primary; 50% upper primary	On upgrading qualifications, can be promoted or in some cases appear for entrance examination
Uttar Pradesh	100% primary through direct recruitment; until 2013, no direct recruitment for upper primary; since 2013, 50% direct in upper primary; in aided schools, 100% direct; no policy in secondary, but practice changes almost every year	50% upper primary; no clear policy at higher level

Source: State Reports.
Note: SSS = Samvida Shala Shikshak.
a. Samvida Shala Shikshak literally means teachers recruited on contract for a school. Madhya Pradesh has three cadres of teachers: the Samvida Shala Shikshak (SSS), the Adhyapak Samvarg (Teacher Cadre), and the Shikshak Samvarg (Teacher Cadre). In Hindi, Adyapak and Shikshak mean Teacher, and this differentiation is a bureaucratic parlance. Apart from these three cadres, there is a provision to appoint guest teachers at the school level for short periods. The Shikshak cadre is the oldest cadre of teachers held by the state government's Department of School Education. This is a district cadre and recruitment to this cadre was done at the district level. There has been no recruitment to this cadre since 1998. Direct recruitment is done only into the Samvida Shala Shikshak cadre. After working for three years as Samvida Shikshaks, teachers are absorbed into the Adhyapak cadre through a process.

Direct and indirect recruitment methods have advantages. Direct recruitment allows the government to inject fresh blood into the teaching force while also being able to raise standards (minimum qualifications) for teachers more easily than is possible once teachers are in service. Indirect recruitment has the advantage of providing career progression opportunities to teachers. Unfortunately, merit plays little role, and across states, priority in indirect recruitment is given to teachers with more years of service. The exception is Madhya Pradesh, where the policy suggests that merit is taken into account, although practice differs.

Yet, allowing direct and indirect recruitment at the same time may not be easy from the perspective of building collegiality in schools. In Tamil Nadu, for instance, the senior-most teachers teaching grades I to V expressed their displeasure at the state's recent decision to recruit 50 percent of teachers for grades VI to X through the direct method. Previously, teachers who managed to get additional qualifications through correspondence would expect to be promoted with the passage of time. With the new system in place, their professional ambitions have been thwarted, because 50 percent of such posts will now go to newly recruited teachers. The net effect is that these senior elementary teachers, who are pursuing degree courses or awaiting the results of their degrees, think of the new recruits as rivals for the post of middle school headmaster, and not as junior colleagues who need mentoring.

In general, the public service commission of the respective states undertakes teacher recruitment. The exception is Tamil Nadu, which created the Teacher

Recruitment Board (TRB) in 1997.[1] Punjab has recently (2013) created a recruitment board, and Jharkhand has formed the Staff Selection Commission. At the time of writing, Rajasthan was also considering having a separate recruitment board for all non-gazetted government officers, which would include schoolteachers. In most states, the role of the recruitment agency is to conduct the entrance examination (teacher eligibility test (TET) or equivalent), conduct the interviews, and declare the list in order of merit and reservation (as discussed in chapter 3). Once the list is prepared, it is then handed to the concerned department (primary, elementary, or secondary)—and the appointment orders are issued by the competent authority. Depending on the policy of a given state, the appointing authority communicates with the selected teachers. In Tamil Nadu and Karnataka, once the list is declared by the recruiting agency, taking into consideration merit and reservation, computerized counseling is organized and teachers are called, based on their position in the list, to discuss their preferences. The authorities, who conduct the counseling sessions, then issue the appointment letter.

In general, appointment and recruitment (once the merit list has been constructed) are undertaken by the Education Department in each state. There are three exceptions regarding appointments at the elementary level. First, in Madhya Pradesh, appointments in elementary schools come under the purview of Panchayati Raj institutions (Janpad Panchayat for primary, and Zillah Parishad for middle). Second, in Rajasthan, the Department of Education issues appointment and school placement orders for schools that are at the secondary or higher level, and the Panchayati Raj Ministry undertakes all appointments at the elementary level. This is because primary/elementary education comes under the purview of the Panchayati Raj Department. However, except for issuing the appointment letter, all other matters related to teachers are handled by the education department. Rajasthan also has a nontrivial number of schools run by the Sanskrit Department; appointments to these schools are done by that department. Third, in Punjab, in 2006, the government transferred the management of 3,449 government primary schools and 232 government secondary schools from the control of the Punjab Education Department to the Department of Rural Development and Panchayats and the Department of Local Bodies. Teachers in these schools are governed by the Punjab Panchayati Raj Teachers Recruitment and Service Conditions 2006, amended in 2011.

The rules and procedures set out in recruitment notifications, whether for direct or indirect recruitment, have been changing from year to year in Jharkhand and Uttar Pradesh. Therefore, it would be appropriate to say that these states do not have any "policy" as such.[2] All states do have a base policy or education code—for example, in Uttar Pradesh, this dates back to 1921 and amendments and changes are made to this "basic act." However, in the past 10 years (the period covered by this study), the norm seems to be to take decisions afresh whenever teachers are to be recruited—depending on the political situation in the state.

Minimum Standards for Becoming a Teacher

An essential qualification for a person to be eligible for appointment as a teacher in classes I to VIII is that he/she must pass the TET. The TET is conducted by the appropriate government (state, center, or local) in accordance with the guidelines framed by the National Council for Teacher Education (NCTE). The rationale for including the TET as a minimum qualification for a person to be eligible for appointment as a teacher includes (a) setting national standards and benchmarking teacher quality in the recruitment process, (b) inducing teacher education institutions and students from these institutions to improve their performance standards, and (c) sending a positive signal to all stakeholders that the government lays special emphasis on teacher quality.

Several states, such as Tamil Nadu and Jharkhand, were conducting eligibility tests well before the Right to Education (RTE) norms for teacher qualifications came into effect. At the time of this study, all nine states had conducted at least one round of the TET. In general, at the primary level, state TETs focus on foundation skills, and at the upper primary and secondary levels, they are subject-focused. In some states, notably Karnataka and Rajasthan, the TET is only a screening device to determine which applicants can take the entrance test for teaching. Upon clearing the TET, aspiring teachers are also required to take an entrance test in these states. At least in Rajasthan, there is discussion of unifying the TET and the entrance test, such that teachers need to take only one test to be eligible for appointment.

The TET has helped states establish a floor for teacher eligibility, but has also thrown up several challenges. Two stand out. First, although many states have set cutoffs at a level that is hardly ambitious, far too few teacher candidates are passing the TET relative to the number of vacancies the states are trying to fill. As a consequence, states have had to lower their cutoffs, questioning whether the TET can serve its original purpose of setting standards. This dilution has happened even in the best-performing states. In Tamil Nadu, for instance, a senior officer from the Teacher Recruitment Board provided insight on how the state responded proactively to help the initially ill-prepared candidates. Although representatives of the state perhaps do not see it this way, such proactivity ultimately leads to dilution in standards.

> TET has been conducted at regular intervals from 2011, because the state rule for RTE was formed only after the RTE Act 2009 came into being in 2010. TET was introduced and we have not compromised on the quality. In the first test, a very low percentage of candidates passed. Only 2,000 candidates of 600,000 managed to get through. In the first TET, the percentage of people to pass was 0.39%. But the Honourable CM gave another opportunity for the first-time applicants writing the exam. The duration of the first exam was only 2½ hours, but for 2nd exam, it was changed to 3 hours. The same test was conducted again and no fee was collected. With increased time and a positive environment, 20,000 teachers passed the TET. The second test result was 2.9%; in the 3rd TET, it was 4.37%. TRB has never compromised on the quality. It had not relaxed any marks for any community or for any

special category. The pass mark was 60%. During the third TET, the state government reduced the mark by 5% for the special and reserved category. Now, 55% is the pass mark. This has naturally influenced the results positively. More than 75,000 candidates have passed in the third TET. (Excerpt from Tamil Nadu State Report)

In Madhya Pradesh, the government claims to have set high standards for those who could take the TET, allowing only candidates with professional qualifications to apply. The Professional Examination Board (Vyavsayik Pariksha Mandal or Vyapam) conducted the Madhya Pradesh TET for the first (and only) time in 2011–12 for candidates aspiring to become elementary and secondary school teachers. Recruitment and appointment in two rounds were completed in August 2014. Interviews suggested that the online process has made this system transparent and efficient.[3] The results were declared on the online portal and the Director of Public Instruction (DPI) issued advertisements for vacant posts. DPI also takes the responsibility of consolidating all the advertisements for local bodies, to avoid redrafting and duplication of work.

Although it is clear from the advertisement for the TET that only applicants with the abovementioned professional qualifications (viz. B.Ed. and D.Ed.) need apply, as table 4.2 suggests, applications were not only accepted from people without the said professional qualifications, but they were also allowed to appear for the TET exam. Although only about 80,000 of the more than 1,300,000 applicants for grade III had professional qualifications, more than 12,000,000 sat for the exam. While it is possible that those who sat for the exam were in the final year of obtaining a professional qualification, this explanation seems unlikely, as about 465,000 cleared the exam, which is nearly six times as many as those having the qualifications.

Madhya Pradesh asked for permission from the central government to recruit untrained teachers, since the state believed that sufficient trained teachers were unavailable. Permission was granted until March 31, 2013, and so candidates without a B.Ed. or D.Ed. degree were allowed to sit for the TET exam in January and February 2012. However, various delays meant that the appointment for the first round happened only by May 2013. The central government did not agree to the state's request to extend the permission beyond March 2013 for recruiting those without professional qualifications. This meant that many vacant teacher posts could not be filled, even after two rounds of recruitment.[4]

In Punjab, of the 1,273 candidates appointed in 2013, 515 passed the Elementary Teacher Training Test (ETT), and 717 appointed candidates had the B.Ed. qualification (table 4.3). Of these 717 selected candidates, only 615 joined. Renewal of the contracts of these 615 teachers was subject to passing the six-month NCTE-recognized bridge course. Two of these 615 have done the ETT in the due course of time, but the remaining 613 teachers have been pursuing the Department of General and Secondary Education (DGSE) for arranging for an ETT bridge course. DGSE extended the timing for passing the bridge course to March 2015. In the meantime, these teachers continued to teach without being fully qualified for the job.

Table 4.2 Overview of the Applications and Dates of the Teacher Eligibility Tests Held in Madhya Pradesh, 2011–12

Cadre	No. of applications received	Among the applicants those with D.Ed./B.Ed. qualifications	No. of candidates appeared for TET	Total number of candidates who passed the examination	Among those who passed those with D.Ed./B.Ed. qualifications	Date of examination	Date of announced results	Date of revised results
SSS (grade I)	142,475	67,045	134,465	15,538	9,730	December 4, 2011	January 1, 2012	August 4, 2012
SSS (grade II)	389,938	151,629	357,042	40,353	21,969	February 19, 2012	August 6, 2012	—
SSS (grade III)	1,303,003	79,861	1,221,489	464,685	36,481	January 22, 2012	April 25, 2012	August 4, 2012
Total	18,355,416	298,535	1,712,996	520,576	68,180			

Source: Madhya Pradesh State Report.
Note: B.Ed. = Bachelor of Education; D.Ed. = Diploma in Education; SSS = TET = teacher eligibility test.

Table 4.3 Summary of PSTET 2011, 2012, 2013, and 2014 in Punjab

Date of test	PSTET (year)	Candidates appeared	Candidates passed (percent)	Recruitment
July 3, 2011	PSTET—1 (2011)	110,052	1,736 (1.57)	1,273
	PSTET—2 (2011)	127,079	8,412 (6.61)	—
June 9, 2013	PSTET—1 (2012)	60,382	4,251 (7.04)	0
	PSTET—2 (2012)	168,396	5,141 (3.05)	0
December 28, 2013	PSTET—1 (2013)	57,815	1,040 (1.79)	0
	PSTET—2 (2013)	158,273	266 (0.16)	0
August 24, 2014	PSTET—1 (2014)	47,859		
	PSTET—2 (2014)	135,836		

Source: Punjab State Report. 2015.
Note: PSTET = Punjab State Teacher Eligibility Test; — = no recruitment done.

The second important challenge in implementing the TET pertains to litigation on the correctness of the test and the extensive delays that have resulted. In Punjab, for instance, the recruitment process took almost two years. In Jharkhand, the recruitment exam for teachers was conducted in 2009, but the results have not yet been declared.

In Tamil Nadu, in a situation reflective of other states as well, a senior officer said:

> ... After conducting the test, teachers go to the court on issues connected with questions and answers, the validity of some answers, etc. Transparency leads to a lot of complications. The TRB written examination pattern is very transparent. After taking the examination, the candidate can take the carbon copy of the answer sheet. After collecting all the answer sheets from the districts, TRB publishes the tentative answers for the written Examination. Candidates have the answer sheets and answer keys are hosted on the TRB website. They can evaluate their own answer sheet. All are multiple-choice questions. TRB asks the candidate if there is any objection in the answers and they could report to TRB within 10 days' time. So if there is an objection from the candidate that it is not answer A, it is B, they produce evidence of that. The subject experts are called by TRB and they will scrutinize the answers and then TRB finalizes the answers and publishes the final results, along with the revised answers. Immediately after the publication of the answer key, many candidates will go to the court if they find the answers wrong. Many litigations are based on the answer keys.

In all states, the TET is only one of several criteria used to determine whether a candidate becomes a teacher. The other criteria typically relate to professional qualifications (as described in chapter 3).

In several states, such as Rajasthan and Karnataka, teachers who have cleared the TET are required to take an entrance test as well. In Karnataka, for instance, those who clear the TET are required to take a central entrance test. If they score 60 percent or higher on the entrance test, they can apply for a teaching position, subject to having the requisite academic qualifications.

None of the states conducts interviews of the candidates, since interview outcomes are viewed as being easy to influence through political or bureaucratic connections. This is an important change in recruitment processes, because mandatory tests and no personal interviews, perhaps, make the process more transparent and less arbitrary. At the same time, this process makes it impossible to find a good match between the expertise or interests of individual teachers and the needs or desires of individual schools. The schools have no role at any point in the teacher recruitment process.

States have made efforts to recruit candidates from socioeconomically disadvantaged groups. However, worryingly, they have had to relax the criteria for these candidates in the TET by 5 to 10 percentage points to obtain more "qualified" candidates. A major motivation for the effort to recruit more socially disadvantaged teachers is to create a teaching force that is closer to the student body socially; but, insofar as better qualified teachers make more effective teachers, lowering the standards for recruitment reduces the chances for students in their efforts to learn. States also recruit teachers on compassionate grounds, and lower recruitment criteria for them, with similar consequences for students.

Although states follow the NCTE norms on educational qualifications, it is difficult to miss the point that no state has attempted to go much beyond these norms to recruit a teaching force that is substantially more qualified. Without exception, the states seem to be satisfied with having a teaching force that comes from the lower end of the achievement distribution of any given cohort of grade XII pass/graduates.

Terms of Recruitment: Regular and Contract Teachers

One of the features of the drive to universalize elementary education has been to open more schools and attempt to staff these schools in accordance with the RTE norms. Appropriateness has meant at least three things: (a) the state should be able to afford the salary and other costs associated with the additional teachers; (b) formal qualifications may need to be modified to ensure that a steady supply of teachers exists for new schools; and (c) there is more local hiring of teachers, to ensure less social distance and more accountability between teachers and students. These three conditions have been met by most states by hiring teachers on fixed pay and timebound contracts, with none of the benefits associated with regular employment, such as pension and leave.

Every state in India has recruited at least some contract teachers over the past 15 years, except Karnataka. Most recently, Rajasthan, one of the earlier states to adopt the contract teacher model, announced that it would not recruit any more contract teachers as of 2014. Box 4.1 provides a detailed account of the court case that led to the decision to terminate the contract teacher cadre (Vidyarthi Mitra) in the state, in which the court found the recruitment of unqualified people as teachers to be "illegal and unconstitutional."

In terms of the numbers of contract teachers and their relative proportion vis-à-vis regular teachers, in some states, such as Jharkhand, contract teachers form up to half of the teaching cadre. In general, however, the number of contract teachers does not exceed the number of regular teachers in any state.[5]

The practice of hiring contract teachers has opened several debates (and court cases) in India on de-professionalizing the teaching cadre versus building greater accountability into the system.[6] The proponents of the de-professionalization

---

Box 4.1 High Court Decision on Vidyarthi Mitra in Rajasthan

TILOK SINGH & ORS. VS. STATE OF RAJASTHAN & ORS. (S.B. CIVIL WRIT PETITION NO.10339/12) & 89 CONNECTED MATTERS

Important parts of the decision are as follows:

---- This Court is firmly of the opinion that the Scheme introduced by the State Government providing for the engagement of even unqualified/untrained persons as Vidyarthi Mitra for their posting against the posts of Teacher Gr. III, Senior Teacher and School Lecturer dehors the relevant recruitment Rules and the eligibility criteria laid down by the NCTE exercising the power under the relevant statute, the provisions of the Act of 2009, and against the constitutional scheme of public employment, cannot but deemed to be illegal, arbitrary and falls foul of Article 14, 21 & 21A of the Constitution of India.

41. Since the Scheme providing for the engagement of Vidyarthi Mitra against the vacant posts of Teachers is found to be unconstitutional, no directions can be issued by this court to permit the continuance in employment of the petitioners and their likes under the said Scheme, which will obviously amount to perpetuating an illegality. Of course, the petitioners who have discharged the duties as Vidyarthi Mitra but have not been paid the honorarium for the period they have worked are entitled to relief to this extent inasmuch as the State Government cannot be permitted to deny the payment due to them as honorarium for the period they have discharged the duties against the posts of Teachers as Vidyarthi Mitra in various schools run by the State.

42. In the result, the writ petition No.8154/10 is allowed. The writ petitions preferred by the petitioners assailing their termination from service, claiming continuance/re-employment as Vidyarthi Mitra and against the insistence of the Government for execution of the fresh contract, are dismissed. The Vidyarthi Mitra Scheme, introduced by the State Government for engagement of "Vidyarthi Mitra" on contractual basis on fixed honorarium against the posts of Teachers Gr. III, Senior Teachers and School Lecturers, is declared illegal and unconstitutional. The respondents are restrained from engaging the Vidyarthi Mitra under the Vidyarthi Mitra Scheme against the posts of Teachers Gr. III, Senior Teachers and School Lecturers. The respondents are directed to proceed with the recruitment process to fill in all the vacant posts of Teachers and School Lecturers in various services/cadres forthwith and complete the process as early as possible, in any case, within a period of six months from the date of receipt of certified copy of this order. It is made clear that pending completion of the regular recruitment process, the State shall not be precluded from engaging the eligible persons on the various

box continues next page

Box 4.1 High Court Decision on Vidyarthi Mitra in Rajasthan *(continued)*

posts of Teachers on urgent temporary basis in accordance with the relevant recruitment Rules. The State shall also ensure that henceforth the determination of the vacancies of Teachers in various services/cadres is made every year as mandated by the relevant recruitment Rules and all efforts shall be made to fill up the vacancies preferably before the next academic session starts in the schools run by the State. The petitioners who have not been paid honorarium for the period they had worked with the respondents as Vidyarthi Mitra, shall be paid the amount due within a period of two months from the date of receipt of certified copy of this order. It is made clear that on account of the Vidyarthi Mitra Scheme being declared illegal and unconstitutional, the petitioners and their likes who had worked with the respondents as Vidyarthi Mitra, shall not be deprived of the benefits already accrued to them. No order as to costs.

Source: Rajasthan State Report.

---

argument believe that this practice has allowed the state to recruit low-cost and low-quality teachers and put them in schools in poorer areas, where the likelihood of parents complaining is relatively low. Another side to the de-professionalization argument is that although well-qualified teachers may be hired on contract, with little job security, it lends an ad hoc character to their employment. This ad-hoc-ism can hardly be motivating. Equally worrying is that the social status of a teacher decreases when people start commenting that anyone with minimum educational qualification can become a teacher. Proponents of the accountability argument believe that open-ended contracts for teachers have led them to believe they have a job for life, and their performance (or lack thereof) is unlikely to jeopardize their career. Term contracts, in contrast, are likely to keep such teachers on their toes, and motivate them to perform. Where contract teachers are given the opportunity to become regular teachers if they perform well (as in Madhya Pradesh, at least in theory), a contract position serves as a probationary period of clear and fixed duration, during which time a person's fitness to be a teacher can be assessed.[7]

Reversal of the Trend of Hiring Contract Teachers

In sharp contrast to the early 2000s, when there was an increasing trend in states hiring contract teachers on one- to two-year contracts, the trend appears to be reversing in several states. Although many states continue to hire contract teachers, there is an increasing trend to regularize them, based on years of service or/and additional qualifications acquired. In some states, there is also a trend toward increasing the qualifications required to become a contract teacher. In Jharkhand, for instance, there is no difference in recruitment norms for contract teachers and regular teachers. In Madhya Pradesh, all new teachers are hired initially on contract for a period of three years. After three years of service, these teachers become due for regularization. Initially, it was expected that once such

Table 4.4 State-Wise Position on Contract Teacher Recruitment

State	Regular	Contract
Jharkhand	Yes	Yes, as per government decision, 50% posts reserved for contract teachers
Karnataka	Yes	No, since 1989
Madhya Pradesh	Yes	Yes, at all levels, during probation and they are made regular after 3 years
Mizoram	No since 1998	Increasingly all contract teachers at all levels
Odisha	Yes	Yes, at all levels during probation; they are made regular after 6 years
Punjab	Yes	Yes, initial contract is 1.5 years, then 3 years, and then regularized
Rajasthan	Yes	No, since 2013—after order of the High Court of Rajasthan
Tamil Nadu	Yes	Yes, since 2002, as part-time teachers in specific subjects like arts, crafts, and physical education and training
Uttar Pradesh	Yes	Only in information technology and vocational in secondary; gradual phasing out of contract teachers

teachers were regularized, they would be put on probation for two years to complete all relevant in-service teacher training. However, this criterion was never implemented. Similarly, in Odisha, contract teachers are regularized after completing six years of service. In Uttar Pradesh too, the government has decided to "regularize" the contract teachers and refrain from hiring more contract teachers. Table 4.4 provides an overview of the regularization of contract teachers in the sample states.

The trend toward regularization has come from three sources. The first is the recognition after RTE 2009 and the NCTE guidelines for teachers, that all teachers need to be qualified as per NCTE guidelines. If teachers can improve their professional qualifications, then there has to be some recognition or reward for this. The second is a change in the political scenario in the state, where the political party takes a decision to reverse the long-standing policy of the previous government (such as in Madhya Pradesh), or there is pressure from teachers' unions on the government to treat all teachers equally. The third is the judgment of the High Court based on the petition of teachers or public-interest litigation.

This study found little evidence to suggest that formal criteria were clearly defined or faithfully met in the decision to regularize contract teachers. Instead, the evidence suggests that many contract teachers have not acquired the relevant qualifications, but, being well connected politically, they were regularized. In some states, the contract teachers were assisted through part-time courses to acquire professional qualifications, and, for example, in Mizoram, they were given several chances to clear the required examinations.

During state-level discussions, the teachers' union leaders and teachers also spoke about easy access to the formal degrees and diplomas required for regularization. In Punjab, there was a recent case wherein many of the teacher candidates were found to possess bogus degrees.[8] Teachers in Jharkhand talked about a degree market where a proxy candidate appears for examinations on behalf of the teachers. Similar experiences were also narrated in other states. However, given that this is a grey market, there is little concrete evidence to confirm the availability of bogus degrees and diplomas.

Recruitment Process

Recruitment processes in the states in the sample can be categorized into two broad types: (a) systematic and efficient, and (b) politically driven.

Karnataka, Tamil Nadu, Madhya Pradesh, and Odisha typify systematic and efficient systems. In these states, estimates are made of the need for teachers—with each school sending its requests to the block, where they are collated and sent to the district. The district officials then apply the RTE guidelines (district-wide ratio) and send their demand to the state government. These estimates are then sent to the Cabinet or Finance Department for approval. Depending on the budget situation of the government, the estimate may be revised downward. Once the estimate is approved, vacant positions are advertised online and the process of recruitment formally starts.

The next subsection describes the case of Karnataka, since it is the most systematic and foolproof. Indeed, Odisha is in the process of adopting the Karnataka pattern. Direct recruitment processes for teachers in elementary and secondary government schools are very similar in the state, with slight variations in appointing authorities, geographical unit for application, calculation of number of vacant posts, and age and educational qualifications. The major differences between elementary and secondary school teacher recruitment are highlighted. Recruitment at both levels is undertaken as per the guidelines prescribed in Government of Karnataka (2001a), as described in figures 4.1 and 4.2, and in table 4.5.

Figure 4.1 Direct Recruitment Process for Elementary and Secondary School Teachers

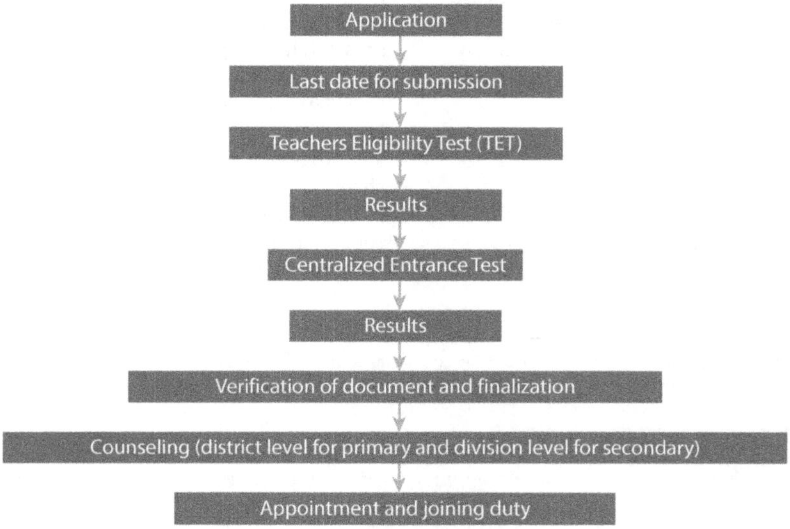

Application
↓
Last date for submission
↓
Teachers Eligibility Test (TET)
↓
Results
↓
Centralized Entrance Test
↓
Results
↓
Verification of document and finalization
↓
Counseling (district level for primary and division level for secondary)
↓
Appointment and joining duty

Source: Karnataka State Report, prepared by CBPS, 2014.

Table 4.5 Overview of Direct Recruitment Norms for Teachers

Norm	Elementary schools	Secondary schools (government and aided)	Honorary teachers
Geographical unit for application[a]	District level	Division level[b]	School/block
Competent authority	Block Education Officer (*appointing authority*)	Deputy director of public instruction, district level (*appointing authority*)	School HM (*appointing authority*)
	Deputy director of public instruction (*selection authority*)	Joint director of public instruction, division level (*selection authority*)	Block Education Officer (*selection authority*)
Calculation of vacancies	PTR = 40 at the school level	Subject-wise staffing	Appointed based on need
Educational qualifications	Class XII/PUC + D.Ed. TCH (primary) B.A./B.S. + D.Ed.[c] (upper primary)	B.A./B.S. + B.Ed.	Usually retired teachers, local experts
Minimum age	18 years	21 years	None
Maximum age	40 years for general category 43 years for OBC (2A, 2B, 3A, 3B) category 45 years for SC/ST categories	40 years for general category 43 years for OBC (2A, 2B, 3A, 3B) category 45 years for SC/ST categories	None
Retirement age	60 years	60 years	Appointed only one academic year ending on April 10
Reservation	(i) Social category-wise: SC (15%); ST (3%); OBC (32%); general (50%) (ii) sex-wise: women (at least 50%); men (remaining) (iii) individual characteristic-wise: rural candidates (25%); ex-soldiers (10%); physically handicapped (5%); unsheltered (5%); Kannada medium (5%); general merit (50%)	(i) Social category-wise: SC (15%); ST (3%); OBC (32%); general (50%) (ii) sex-wise: women (at least 50%); men (remaining) (iii) individual characteristic-wise: rural candidates (25%); ex-soldiers (10%); physically handicapped (5%); unsheltered (5%); Kannada medium (5%); general merit (50%)	None
Counseling for selection of block	Yes	Only for government schools	None
Database	State-level computerized database called HRMS	HRMS only for government schools; individual managements maintain database for aided schools	None

Note: B.A. = Bachelor of the Arts; B.S. = Bachelor of Science; D.Ed. = Diploma in Education; HM = headmaster; HRMS = Human Resource Management System; OBC = Other Backward Classes; PTR = pupil-teacher ratio; PUC = pre-university college; SC = Scheduled Caste; ST = Scheduled Tribe; TCH = Teachers' Certificate Higher.
a. This unit is also utilized for recruitment through promotion.
b. There are four divisions in Karnataka: Bangalore Division (nine districts in the southeast), Gulbarga Division (six districts in the northeast), Mysore Division (eight districts in the southwest), and Belgaum Division (seven districts in the northwest).
c. Yet to be implemented.

Description of the Karnataka Recruitment Process

Elementary School Teachers
The guidelines spelled out in the Recruitment Notification (Government of Karnataka 2001b) guide the recruitment of elementary teachers (primary and upper primary). This notification specifies the eligibility criteria of age and qualifications, types of posts available, salary and non-salary benefits, retirement age, details about online application, admission and selection process, and reservation criteria. The subsequent recruitment notifications, for each district, also list the vacancies available. The rest of this subsection describes the steps undertaken during the direct recruitment process.

Identification of Vacancies
The Block Education Officer (BEO) identifies the vacancies at the block level as per the required pupil-teacher ratio (PTR) norms. Currently, PTR = 40:1 is followed to calculate vacancies in Karnataka. A proposal to amend the PTR to 30:1, to calculate the vacancies, has been submitted to the government and approval for the same is awaited (key informant interviews on June 11, 2014). Block-level vacancies are consolidated at the block level. The same is being conveyed to the deputy director of public instruction at the district level (interview with senior government official, April 8, 2014). All district-level demand for new teachers is sent to the Commissioner of Public Instruction. The final decision on the number of teachers to be recruited and when to initiate the recruitment process is undertaken by the Office of the Commissioner of Public Instruction in consultation with the Finance Department, Ministry of Primary and Secondary Education, and Chief Minister.

Once the number of vacancies is finalized, the department moves it up to the Finance Department, which takes a view on what size of additional burden the state exchequer can bear. Based on this assessment, the total number of new posts for the year is decided by the Education Department in consultation with the Finance Department. At times, the number specified for recruitment is less than the demand, due to existing vacancies. In that situation, each district or block is allocated new recruits as a proportion of the existing vacancies (S4, May 6, 2014). The process by which vacancies in individual schools are filled is not clear.

The gap between the required and sanctioned numbers of new recruits is filled by hiring honorary teachers or transferring excess teachers from other government or aided schools.[9] After the decision on recruitment is taken, the recruitment notification for each district, along with the list of block-wise vacancies, is published. This notification includes information on the eligibility criteria, selection process and criteria, pay scale, reservation for different categories, and specific deadlines.

Eligibility Criteria for Application (Full-Time Teachers)
Class XII (pre-university college (PUC) or equivalent) and Diploma in Education D.Ed./Teachers' Certificate Higher is the basic requirement for applying for elementary school teacher posts in Karnataka.

Applicants can apply for that medium of instruction in which they have cleared their State School Leaving Certificate or learned as their first or second language in PUC (higher secondary). Those applying for Kannada medium schools need to clear the Kaava/Jaana/Ratna Kannada examinations, which are conducted by Kannada Sahithya Parishat. The minimum age requirement for primary and upper primary teachers is 18 years (completed as of the last date of submission of application). The upper limit for applications is 40 years for the general category, 43 years for the Other Backward Classes (OBC) (2A, 2B, 3A, 3B) category, and 45 years for the Scheduled Casted (SC) and Scheduled Tribe (ST) categories (Government of Karnataka 2001b, 2013a, 2013d).

Application Process
An online application form for Rs 400 (general category) and Rs 200 (SC, ST, and OBC categories) (Government of Karnataka 2013a) is filled and submitted by a given date. Physically challenged candidates are exempted from this fee (Government of Karnataka 2007). Those applying for more than one subject or medium and/or more than one district need to fill multiple forms. Based on the forms, eligible candidates appear for a district-level TET (Government of Karnataka 2013b) conducted by the Recruitment Cell, Bangalore. To clear the test, general category candidates need a minimum mark of 60 percent; SC, ST, and OBC candidates need a minimum of 55 percent; and physically challenged and ex-soldier candidates need minimum of 50 percent (Government of Karnataka 2013d). Those who clear the TET have to appear for a centralized entrance test. Applicants with at least the minimum mark for their category on the entrance test are considered for recruitment.

Selection and Appointment Process
The selection of candidates is based on State School Leaving Certificate, PUC, B.A., and B.S. marks; Teachers' Certificate Higher, D.Ed., and B.Ed. scores; and percentage scores on the centralized entrance test (detailed in the subsection on the application process), ensuring that the overall recruitment meets three kinds of reservation criterion, namely, social category, sex, and individual characteristics (figure 4.2).

These criteria have been designed to be mutually exclusive, implying that the mentioned percentages need to be fulfilled for the overall selection of teachers. For example, if 1,000 teachers are to be recruited, the final selection will ensure that there are 150 SC candidates, 30 ST candidates, and 320 OBC candidates; it will also ensure that at least 500 women constitute the selection list; and among the 1,000 recruited, at least 250 will be from rural areas, 100 ex-soldiers, 50 physically handicapped, 50 unsheltered, and 50 from Kannada medium.

Figure 4.2 Reservation Criteria for Recruitment

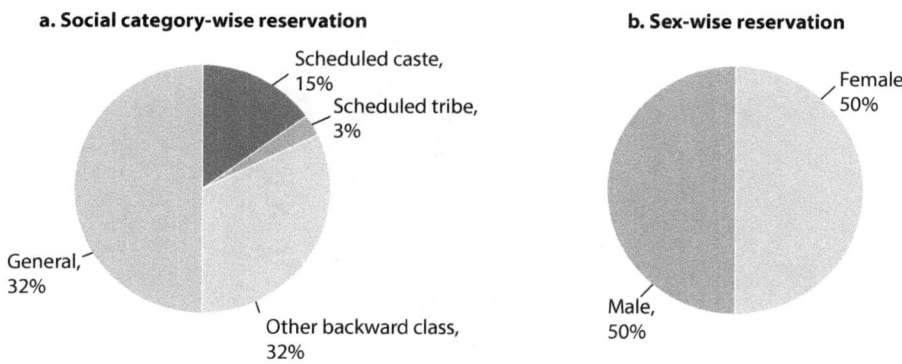

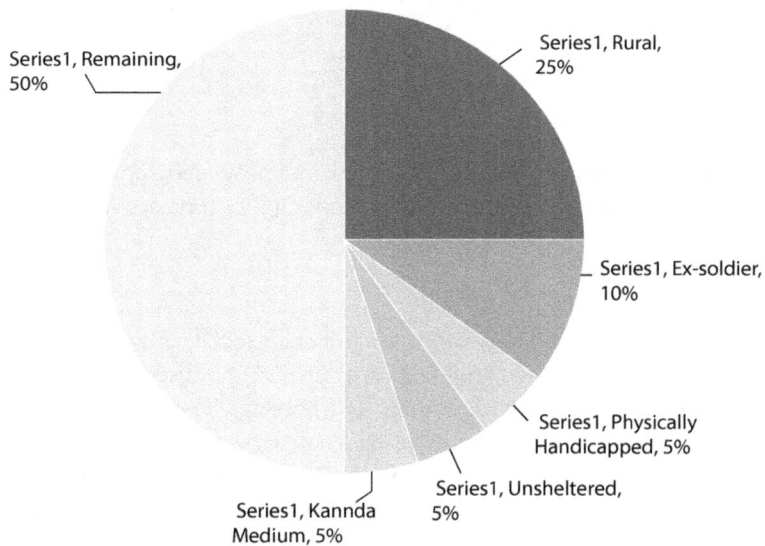

Source: Government of Karnataka 2011, 2012, 2013d.

Post-2013, an additional reservation for Gulbarga division (comprising six districts: Gulbarga, Yadgir, Bellary, Raichur, Koppal, and Bidar) has been introduced, due to the enactment of Article 371J (of the Constitution) in the area. This special status means that 80 percent of the seats for teachers (group C cadre) are reserved for local cadre or domicile of Gulbarga division (Government of Karnataka 2013c; Rajendran 2013). This acts as a reservation criterion for selecting candidates only in the Gulbarga division, in addition to the abovementioned social category-wise, sex-wise, and individual characteristics-wise criteria.

These criteria act as parameters in short-listing and selecting candidates. Merit lists for each social category are prepared separately. The merit-wise list is utilized during counseling for the final selection of candidates (based on the

Figure 4.3 Additional Reservation for Gulbarga Division

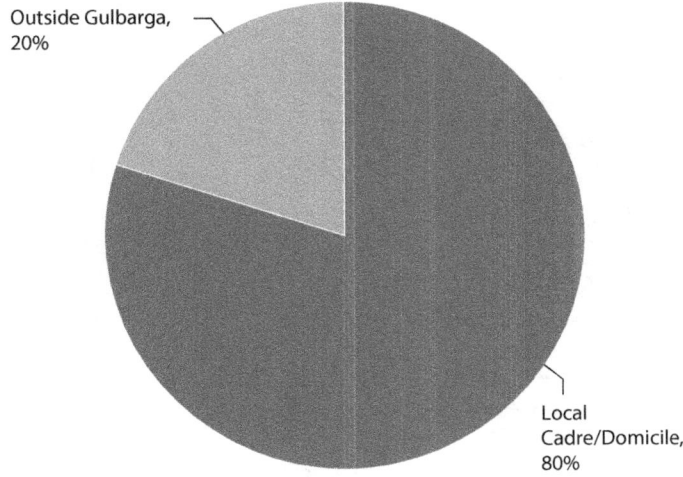

Source: Rajendran 2013.

percentages mentioned).[10] Figure 4.3 explains how geographic information system-enabled software ensures that the reservation criteria are fulfilled for each geographic unit.

Counseling Process

After the preparation of separate merit lists for each social category, the academic certificates of the short-listed candidates are verified and district-level computerized counseling is held for deciding their first postings. The computerized counseling for final selection is conducted using a software program that ensures that the required number for each criterion is met. The names of the short-listed candidates are entered in the program, which categorizes the candidates on the basis of their social category, gender, individual characteristics, and geographical unit of application (district/division).

Short-listed candidates choose their block based on their district selection. Merit candidates from the SC, ST, and OBC categories are given first preference in block selection. They are shown the vacancy list in their selected district and choose the block. Their selection is reflected immediately in the number of remaining vacancies in that block. After the required number for each of the three reserved categories is fulfilled, merit candidates from the general category choose their block (figure 4.4).

General category applicants are posted immediately after counseling. Those applying under various reserved categories must produce the necessary documents before final appointment (D1, April 8, 2014; D3, April 9, 2014). This process takes about four months. There are often delays due to administrative issues, like verification of documents related to marks, caste, income, and medical certificates (D1, April 8, 2014).

Figure 4.4 Computerized Counseling Process for Recruitment

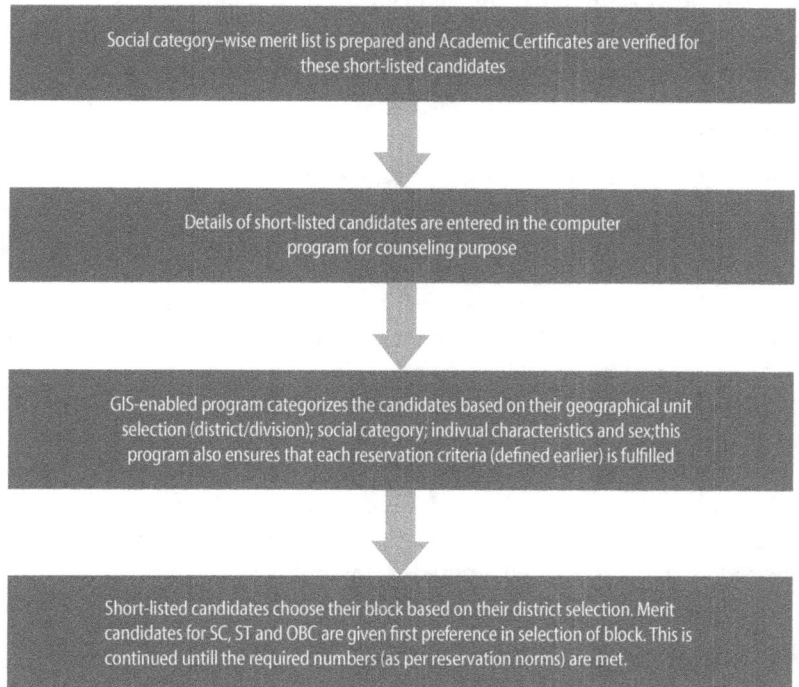

For elementary teachers, the selection authority is the deputy director of public instruction (at the district level); the appointing authority is the BEO. Post-counseling and selection, a generic list of all the selected candidates is displayed, inviting objections, if any, to the same. After receiving objections, if any, the final list of candidates is displayed and the selected candidates are appointed to schools within their selected block. They are initially posted in a rural school for the first five years of service (D1, April 8, 2014; D3, April 9, 2014). However, no personal interviews are undertaken for the final appointment of the teacher to avoid favoritism. Teachers select their schools during the counseling process and this is done in the presence of the BEO.[11]

Post-Recruitment Maintenance of Records
After the recruitment of a teacher, his or her data are maintained in an online centralized human resource management system database at the block level. This database is managed at the state level. Some of the variables maintained in the system are the following: name, date of birth, entry date, designation, qualifications, caste, service record (how many years in school, rural, urban), subjects taught, physical handicap or medical condition, salary details (including different allowances, loans, insurance deductions, pension deductions,

and so forth), leave credits and encashment, seniority list, retirement details, release of or arrears in salary or allowances, complaints against the teacher, vacancies in that particular school, and the teacher's contact details and family background (Interviews with officials done on April 8 and 9, 2014).

The System in Other States

In contrast to the transparent and efficient systems in Karnataka, Tamil Nadu, Madhya Pradesh, and Odisha, in states such as Rajasthan, Jharkhand, Uttar Pradesh, and Punjab, the teacher recruitment process is heavily influenced by political interests. Although the process in Rajasthan appears systematic on paper, beginning in April every year with a careful assessment of vacancies in the forthcoming academic year, recruitment drives commence only in response to political considerations, regardless of need. Indeed, most of the major recruitment drives in the state have come shortly before election time (table 4.6). Importantly, the fluctuation in the numbers recruited suggests that the careful calculation of vacancies that is supposed to take place every April perhaps does not take place, or, if it does, it has little to do with actual recruitment decisions.

In Jharkhand, the vacancy rate in elementary schools is nearly 40 percent on average; yet, schools are often upgraded for political reasons, leading to even

Table 4.6 Teacher Recruitments in Rajasthan in the Past 10 Years

Year of recruitment	Posts	Number of posts filled	Recruiting agency	Status
2004	Teacher grade III	33,000	RPSC	Process completed
2006	Teacher grade III	70,000	RPSC	Process completed
2007				
2008	Teacher grade II	8,900	RPSC	Process completed
2011	Teacher grade II	11,000	RPSC	Result pending; dispute in answer key
2012–13	Teacher grade III	32,963	Zillah Parishad	Some cases pending due to court cases
2013–14	Teacher grade III	20,000	Zillah Parishad	Exam conducted and result withheld; dispute on TET eligibility criteria
	Vidyarthi Mitra	22,311 (all grades total)	At school level	—
2014	Teacher grade I	—	RPSC	Exam held on July 13, 2014
	Contract teacher (Vidyarthi Mitra)	Discontinued and fresh appointment not given	—	Started agitation; Education Minister on July 15, 2014 said we are studying decision of the court and soon final decision will take place
2014 (Proposed)[a]	Teachers in grades II & III	Teacher grade II: 9,000 Teacher grade III: 20,000	Rajasthan Subordinate Service board	Proposed

Note: NIL = no posts filled; RPSC = Rajasthan Public Service Commission; TET = teacher eligibility test; Zillah Parishad = district-level elected local government institution; — = not available.
a. Education Minister, on July 22, 2014 in Rajasthan Assembly, declared that before August 31, 2014, all vacant posts of teachers will be filled (newspaper report).

more vacancies. There are currently 1,232 schools with no teachers. In Punjab, although there are clear criteria for teacher recruitment, in practice, the decision for new recruitment depends on budgetary provisions available with the state government for the financial year, and political decisions in response to pressure groups of prospective applicants. The study suggests that as per the RTE entitlement, there is a shortfall of 2,632 teachers at the primary level and 8,858 teachers at the upper primary level in Punjab.

These posts include block primary Education Officer and center head teacher posts, which are teaching cadre posts and have been lying vacant. An implication of these posts lying vacant is that schoolteachers are deputed to take up the block primary Education Officer and center head teacher responsibilities, leading to the number of teachers falling short of the active teaching requirement at the school level. Amritsar, Gurdaspur, and Pathankot are three districts where there are 494, 285, and 199 posts more than required, respectively, at the primary level (taking into account the RTE norms). Since the primary school teacher cadre is a district cadre, it seems that more teachers than required were recruited in these districts, or the primary schools closed. The study does not have enough data to arrive at an inference about the reason.

The study also revealed that until 2013, most recruitment in Punjab took place through temporary recruiting committees. It often happened that the chairperson of the recruitment body selected and deputed the staff of her/his personal choice to the recruitment body. If the chairperson retired, the new chairperson would do away with the staff deputed by the previous chairperson and select new staff of her/his choice. This practice of replacement of staff resulted in delays and errors. The temporary structure and fluid membership of the structure resulted in several errors in declaration of rules and terms for recruitment or interpretation of rules. Indeed, there have been several court cases against the state for appointing teachers without the requisite qualifications or for regularizing teachers before the mandated number of years. Further, the responsibility falls on the new team to respond to litigations and inquiries arising due to any error because of misinterpretation of rules, negligence of rules and procedures, or justification of decisions by the previous recruitment team.

In Uttar Pradesh, again, there is complete lack of clarity on how vacancies are calculated and the criteria to be used for determining eligibility. During the course of the study, several respondents said that the frequent changes in norms, timing of recruitment drives, and so forth are meant to accommodate the interests of politically powerful teachers (and their relatives).

Finally, in Mizoram, the process of teacher recruitment is relatively muddled, with several departments involved in determining how many teachers should be recruited. As a result, the recruitment process is quite a long, drawn out process, requiring negotiation, concurrence, and approvals at multiple levels. As figure 4.5 shows, the recruitment process set in motion by the Education Department in 2009 took two years before the teachers were finally issued appointment orders, and far fewer teachers were recruited than had been proposed by the department.

Figure 4.5 Recruitment of Teachers in Mizoram, 2009

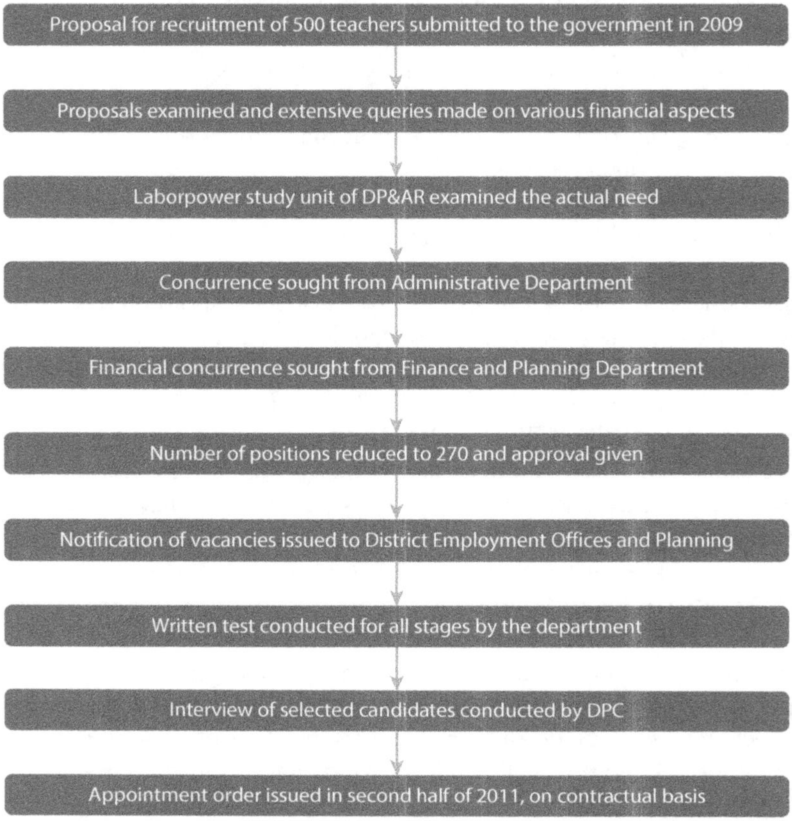

```
┌─────────────────────────────────────────────────────────────────────────┐
│ Proposal for recruitment of 500 teachers submitted to the government in 2009 │
└─────────────────────────────────────────────────────────────────────────┘
                                    ↓
┌─────────────────────────────────────────────────────────────────────────┐
│ Proposals examined and extensive queries made on various financial aspects │
└─────────────────────────────────────────────────────────────────────────┘
                                    ↓
┌─────────────────────────────────────────────────────────────────────────┐
│ Laborpower study unit of DP&AR examined the actual need                 │
└─────────────────────────────────────────────────────────────────────────┘
                                    ↓
┌─────────────────────────────────────────────────────────────────────────┐
│ Concurrence sought from Administrative Department                       │
└─────────────────────────────────────────────────────────────────────────┘
                                    ↓
┌─────────────────────────────────────────────────────────────────────────┐
│ Financial concurrence sought from Finance and Planning Department       │
└─────────────────────────────────────────────────────────────────────────┘
                                    ↓
┌─────────────────────────────────────────────────────────────────────────┐
│ Number of positions reduced to 270 and approval given                   │
└─────────────────────────────────────────────────────────────────────────┘
                                    ↓
┌─────────────────────────────────────────────────────────────────────────┐
│ Notification of vacancies issued to District Employment Offices and Planning │
└─────────────────────────────────────────────────────────────────────────┘
                                    ↓
┌─────────────────────────────────────────────────────────────────────────┐
│ Written test conducted for all stages by the department                 │
└─────────────────────────────────────────────────────────────────────────┘
                                    ↓
┌─────────────────────────────────────────────────────────────────────────┐
│ Interview of selected candidates conducted by DPC                       │
└─────────────────────────────────────────────────────────────────────────┘
                                    ↓
┌─────────────────────────────────────────────────────────────────────────┐
│ Appointment order issued in second half of 2011, on contractual basis   │
└─────────────────────────────────────────────────────────────────────────┘
```

Note: DPC = Departmental Promotion Committee; DP&AR = Department of Personnel and Administrative Reforms.

Figure 4.5 clearly shows that decisions about recruitment are not just a matter for the Education Department, which cannot decide on the number of teachers needed and initiate the recruitment process on its own. Various other departments of the state government review the proposal and share their views. The Department of Personnel and Administrative Reforms and the Department of Finance play key roles in these decisions. That the number of posts was brought down from 500 to 270 indicates that the concerns and imperatives of other departments are quite different.

Across states, there is a long gap between recruitment and appointment. The exception is Odisha, where appointment typically happens within a couple of months of recruitment. In states such as Mizoram and Punjab, it can take several years, and even in relatively more efficient states such as Karnataka and Tamil Nadu, appointment can take between six months and a year. The main reasons for the delays include court cases relating to unqualified candidates being recruited, errors in TET, and document verification. Regardless, these delays are likely to be demotivating for teachers, potentially encouraging them to look for other jobs, and unhelpful for students who wait for teachers to teach them.

Summing Up

This chapter suggests that states, in general, have low entry requirements for teachers, with recruitment policies and procedures not designed to attract the most academically talented people. Moreover, except for two states—Karnataka and Tamil Nadu—teacher recruitment policies in India are ad hoc. States do not have a systematic or routine process for calculating how many teachers are needed, and what their specific qualifications and characteristics should be. In several states, the factors underlying recruitment are closely related to political interests, making teacher recruitment resemble political strategies rather than recruitment policies.

Even in the states where recruitment is relatively less ad hoc (like Madhya Pradesh and Odisha), there are considerable delays in the appointment of teachers. In Karnataka, for instance, where the process of recruitment is relatively transparent and merit-based, there are long delays and gaps before a successful candidate can assume teaching duties. As a consequence, students go for months without a teacher. During this period, the School Development and Management Committee hires part-time or guest teachers (without the required qualifications) to fill the gap. In Tamil Nadu, the recruitment process is streamlined and transparent—however, teachers and teachers' union leaders say that there are a few instances when vacant posts are filled without due process, invoking extraordinary circumstances. However, these instances are very few.

The chapter notes several important trends in recruitment practices that could hold promise for improving the quality of the teaching force. The first relates to a reversal in the terms and conditions of recruitment, from contract to regular. Beginning in the late 1990s, states in India started hiring contract teachers, that is, teachers hired for a specific period, with qualifications and pay that were below those of permanent regular cadre teachers. In states such as Rajasthan and Madhya Pradesh, there was a freeze on recruiting permanent teachers; all recruitment of teachers was, henceforth, to be on a contract basis. Over the past decade, several states have gradually reversed the policy on hiring contract teachers; now there is a freeze on contract teacher hiring. All new recruitments of elementary teachers are to be on regular/permanent terms at the elementary level. However, it is important to note this is not the case at the secondary level, where Rashtriya Madhyamik Shiksha Abhiyan project funds are used to hire secondary teachers on contracts. If regularizing teachers is accompanied by stricter standards for recruitment and building greater professionalism into the cadre, then this is a welcome trend. If it is motivated by other considerations, like buying the loyalty of more teachers, then the consequences for the quality of the teaching force will be poor.

A second feature—a worrisome one—is that in most states (whether educationally backward states like Rajasthan and Uttar Pradesh or mid-level states like Punjab), the teacher recruitment process continues to be opaque (politically driven) and the government does not seem to have a well laid-down policy to estimate the number of teachers required and a process to move from there to recruitment. This situation has led to a great deal of unrest among the teachers and potential teacher candidates.

A third trend, which is visible across the country, is the adoption of the TET for recruitment. This, in turn, has highlighted not only the poor quality of the schools and college education of potential teachers, but also the professional training degrees. That the TET has now become universal is a positive trend; however, in some states (Madhya Pradesh, Odisha, Jharkhand, Uttar Pradesh, and Rajasthan), the number of qualifying candidates may restrict the availability of qualified candidates. In some states, the number of ST and SC candidates qualifying remains low, leading to high vacancies in the reserved category. This may call for a more focused approach to enhance the pool of qualified candidates for teaching positions from the ST and SC communities. It may also be worthwhile to explore whether the situation is the same with regard to Muslim candidates.

Finally, the schools have no role in selecting the teachers that are appointed to them. Thus, the schools cannot express their preferences given their existing group of teachers, for example, for an elementary teacher who has experience in working with children with special needs or who is stronger in mathematics as opposed to science. This situation is especially a concern when not all the vacancies will be filled; schools may have priorities of which the appointing authority is unaware or about which he/she is unconcerned. Equally significant is that there is no clear process for assigning schools to newly-recruited teachers—which, essentially, implies that there is no guarantee that teachers would be preferentially assigned to the most deserving schools wherein the need is the highest.

Notes

1. The Teacher Recruitment Board in Tamil Nadu, headed by a senior Indian Administrative Service officer, undertakes all teacher recruitment pertaining to teachers in elementary, secondary, high, and higher secondary schools, as well as colleges. The board announces vacancies on its website, www.trb.tn.nic.in. The board conducts certificate verification and written and oral exams pertaining to teacher selection. (Oral exams are conducted for college teachers.) All complaints regarding teacher recruitments, especially the TET, are also filed against the Recruitment Board.
2. When this was presented to the Ministry of Human Resource Development, Government of India, in March 2015, the Secretary noted that all teacher recruitment happens with the approval of the Cabinet and any decision that is taken by the Cabinet is "policy."
3. http://www.vyapam.nic.in.
4. The Ministry of Human Resource Development, Government of India, did not agree to this point and said that as there is no shortage of qualified candidates, the question

of asking for relaxation does not arise. When we pointed out the vacancies in reserved (ST) positions, the ministry said that there could be some other reason. Relaxation of norms was not the problem.

5. As noted in chapter 2, the exception is Mizoram, in which almost all teachers are on a contract basis.
6. In addition, of course, an argument for contract teachers is based on urgent need in some states to fill teaching positions, given the expansion of student enrollment.
7. In addition to these arguments, several econometric studies examine the effectiveness and the cost of regular and contract teachers (Atherton and Kingdon 2010; Goyal and Pandey 2010; Muralidharan and Sundararaman 2010). These studies point out that there is no difference between contract and regular teachers, especially with respect to effectiveness, while contract teachers cost far less.
8. Reference to newspaper stories in September 2013: http://education.mathrubhumi.com/php/news_events_details.php?nid=12864 and http://rajnewinfo.blogspot.in/2013/12/5178-teachers-fake-degrees-scam-punjab.html; Bihar: http://ibnlive.in.com/news/bihar-sacks-15000-teachers-for-faking-degree/81372-3.html; Jharkhand: http://timesofindia.indiatimes.com/city/ranchi/For-Rs-20k-get-a-fake-BEd-degree-and-a-job/articleshow/18124955.cms.
9. It is also important that the sanctioned strength of schools is not revised periodically to reflect enrollment or movement of students to other schools, including private schools.
10. As noted in chapter 3, post-2013, an additional reservation for Gulbarga Division (comprising six districts: Gulbarga, Yadgir, Bellary, Raichur, Koppal, and Bidar) has been introduced due to enactment of Article 371J (of the Constitution) in the area.
11. It is especially important to understand this process when there are fewer teachers recruited than vacancies available within the block.

CHAPTER 5

Teacher Deployment and Transfers

Introduction

This chapter examines the system of teacher deployment (initial postings) and transfers in India. Teachers' initial postings have traditionally been centrally determined in India, in the sense that a teacher cannot choose the school where he/she would like to teach (with the exception of Karnataka and Tamil Nadu, where teachers choose the school—among those that are displayed as having vacancies—during counseling). The schools (and thereby headmasters) have no choice in determining which teachers they can hire. Depending on the state, teacher appointment and deployment decisions are made by state, district, or block-level officials.

Post-appointment, teachers often change schools for a variety of reasons. In general, government schoolteachers change schools (or are transferred) due to promotion, rationalization, special (personal) request, new vacancies created because of retirement, or disciplinary action/punishment. In some states, transfers are made for political reasons—and teachers may be shifted every few years. As a result, a teacher's initial posting, posting midcareer, and posting at the end of their career may all be different.

Understanding teacher transfers is important for several reasons.

- First, transfers can help correct the distortions in initial deployment through rationalization of posts. For example, if a school ends up having more teachers for one subject and none for another, this situation could be corrected by the system through transfers. Similarly, such a system could also address skewed pupil-teacher ratios (PTRs) and provide adequate numbers of teachers where they are needed.
- Second, if transfers are done carefully and in a fair and transparent manner, the option of transferring can motivate and encourage teachers. Transfers could be a reward for good work, especially for teachers who spend several years in schools located in difficult areas, such as rural and remote locations. This could act as a motivating force if opportunities for change are available to all teachers in an impartial manner and there is a system to reward good work.[1]

Transfers are also done during promotions, to fill the vacancies that are created by promotions. In some states, the headmaster cadre in primary school, upper primary school, or both (joint) is drawn from the elementary teacher cadre. In some states, teachers who have the requisite qualifications may be assigned or promoted to work with the Block Resources Coordinator, Cluster Resource Centre or even the District Institute of Educational Training as teacher educators, trainers, and master trainers.

- Third, transfers could work in a discouraging or debilitating manner when teachers try to move to better locations or better-resourced schools and their ability to do so is influenced by criteria other than merit. This situation may occur when practices like rent-seeking and building patronage networks determine who is transferred, when, and to what place.
- Fourth, transfers for disciplinary action, whereby teachers who are being "punished" are sent to remote areas or schools that are considered more challenging, could send the wrong message to students, who end up being "punished" for no fault of theirs.[2]
- Fifth, if large numbers of teachers attempt to move to schools they consider desirable, such as urban and well-resourced schools, from rural and remote schools and poorer schools, then the children in the latter are likely to suffer. More importantly, teachers invest their energy in moving out or staying in a preferred location. This system reinforces existing hierarchies in schools.

The larger sociopolitical context in which teachers operate is important. Given the large number of teachers, their role in the electoral process (as returning officers during elections), frequent interactions with other voters (that is, parents), and reach in rural and remote areas, teachers are seen as an asset by political parties and other interest groups. In several states in this study, interviews with key informants and focus group discussions revealed that transfers and postings are used to build patronage networks by politicians as well as teachers, and are an important source for rent-seeking and corruption. It is in this context that teacher deployment policies and practices are central to any discussion on the working conditions of teachers.

It is also interesting to note that teacher transfers are done more frequently at the elementary level and not so often in secondary schools. Across the nine states covered in the study,[3] transfers and postings seem to trouble elementary teachers far more than secondary teachers, as there is relative stability at the secondary level.

The teacher deployment process is influenced by two factors: (a) the cadre in which the teachers belong (block, district, divisional, or state), and (b) whether the teachers are on contract or have been categorized as regular teachers. There is huge variation across the nine states, as is evident from table 5.1. The significance of the cadre is that promotions and the opportunity to request a transfer are dictated solely by seniority in the cadre. A teacher's cadre circumscribes the geographical area over which he/she can be transferred when the state is undertaking a rationalization exercise. When a teacher's cadre is at the block level,

Table 5.1 Who Belongs to What Cadre?

	Elementary teachers			Secondary teachers			
	Block or municipal cadre	District or Zillah cadre	State cadre	Block cadre	District or divisional cadre	State cadre	Specific to state
Jharkhand		All regular teachers are district cadre				All regular teachers in a state cadre	Contract teachers assigned to a specific school[a]
Karnataka	Block-level cadre for elementary teachers				Divisional-level cadre for secondary teachers		Seniority list for elementary maintained in district
Madhya Pradesh	Samvida and Adhyapak are Janpad cadre	Shikshak are district cadre		Samvida and Adhyapak are Janpad cadre	Shikshak are divisional cadre		No transfers when they are Samvida or Adyapak
Mizoram			Regular and non-regular elementary teachers are state cadre			Regular and non-regular secondary teachers are state cadre	
Odisha	Elementary cadre (regular)				Secondary cadre (regular)		All categories of non-regular teachers are appointed to a school
Punjab		Zillah Parishad teachers	SSA teachers and regular teachers		Zillah Parishad teachers	Secondary regular teachers and RMSA teachers	No clarity on who belongs to which cadre, fluid situation
Rajasthan		Elementary teachers			Divisional-level cadre for secondary teachers		School-level cadre for contract teachers when they existed
Tamil Nadu	Elementary teachers are block cadre				Secondary teachers are district cadre		
Uttar Pradesh		Elementary teachers are district cadre				Secondary teachers are divisional cadre	Shiksha Mitra are school cadre

Note: RMSA = Rashtriya Madhyamik Shiksha Abhiyan; SSA = Sarva Shiksha Abhiyan; Zillah Parishad = elected local self-government institution at the district level.
a. Government of Jharkhand Resolution no. 273, dated February 16, 2013, quoted in the State Report.

the teacher can only be moved from one school to another within that block, unless the teacher requests to be moved outside the block or has been given a disciplinary/punishment posting. But when a teacher's cadre is at the state level, he/she can be transferred anywhere in the state (at least in theory). It is easier for a teacher to remain close to their hometown or family if the teacher can be transferred only within a block vis-à-vis the entire state. As the chapter shows later, this factor has important implications for the opportunities for corruption and patronage associated with teacher transfers.

- In Karnataka, Madhya Pradesh (for some teachers), Odisha, and Tamil Nadu, elementary school teachers are essentially block-level cadres.[4] This means that during initial deployment, a teacher is allotted to a cadre and this becomes her/his home cadre. Transfers beyond the cadre can be done, but the teachers may have to forfeit their seniority and be placed as newcomers in the new district or block. This acts as a disincentive to seeking a transfer.
- In Uttar Pradesh, Jharkhand, Madhya Pradesh (some teachers), Punjab, and Rajasthan, all regular elementary teachers belong to a district cadre, which is where they are initially deployed and their seniority list is maintained. Transferring outside the district could involve loss of seniority. However, in Punjab and Jharkhand, the situation is unclear, as there is no transfer policy. In Rajasthan, transfers of elementary school teachers happen within the district and if they are posted by the government, they can then retain their seniority, but if they seek to transfer outside their home district, they lose their seniority.
- The situation of secondary teachers is slightly different. In Karnataka, Madhya Pradesh, and Rajasthan, it is a divisional level cadre (meaning a cluster of districts). In Odisha, Punjab, and Tamil Nadu, it is a district cadre. In the rest, secondary teachers are part of a state cadre.
- In Mizoram, which is a very small state, all teachers—elementary and secondary, regular or non-regular—are part of a state cadre.
- *In no state in India do government teachers belong to a school-level cadre.* The exceptions are contract teachers and guest teachers who are appointed to a school (meaning that they cannot be transferred) and secondary aided teachers.

Initial Deployment

A teacher's initial deployment on appointment depends on the teacher's cadre (state, district, or block), as well as the recruitment and appointment process followed in her/his state. In Karnataka, Tamil Nadu, and Madhya Pradesh (Samvida and Adhyapak), teachers at the elementary level belong to a block-level cadre. In Karnataka and Tamil Nadu, teachers can choose the block in which they would like to teach and, depending on their rank in the entrance process, they can also select the school in which they would like to teach (from among the existing vacancies displayed during the counseling process). In Madhya Pradesh,

Samvida and Adhyapak teachers can give their choices in order of preference and this is taken into consideration during initial deployment. In contrast, at the secondary level in states like Uttar Pradesh, Mizoram, and Odisha, teachers are part of a state-level cadre, which means they can be posted at a school anywhere in the state.

Initial deployment is done in several ways. In Tamil Nadu and Karnataka, a computerized counseling process is used to enable the teachers and the administration to agree on where the newly appointed teacher would be posted. In most other states—at the elementary and secondary levels—teachers give their preference and the decision is taken by the administration. The process may be based on rank or it could involve the intervention of political leaders or teachers' union representatives. Initial deployment is quite critical in the life of a teacher; therefore, where the process is opaque, teachers may spend time and money to ensure they are deployed in the district or block of their choice. Therefore, at the start of their careers, many teachers end up forging links with middlemen or local patrons, who help teachers get a posting of their choice. As will be shown later in this chapter, this process, once set in motion, becomes a critical factor in the professional life of a teacher.

Transfer Policy and Practice

Not all teachers can be transferred, whether for rationalization or disciplinary reasons, and not all teachers can request a transfer. Across the states, teachers in aided schools and contract teachers cannot be transferred, except for teachers in secondary aided schools in Karnataka. In some states, teachers in aided schools can ask to move to another school run by the same management. However, teachers in aided schools cannot move from one management to another. In Madhya Pradesh, for instance, where all new teachers are hired on contract for three years before becoming eligible for regularization, no transfers are possible when they are on contract. In general, only regular government teachers (Shikshak Samvarg and Adhyapak Samvarg) can be transferred or request a transfer.

Other than specifying which category of teachers can or cannot be transferred, except for Karnataka, Tamil Nadu, and Mizoram, the states do not have a policy that is specific to teacher transfers. Table 5.2 provides details on the transfer policies in the sample states.

Of all the states, the teacher transfer policies in Karnataka and Tamil Nadu are the most systematic and transparent. Madhya Pradesh and Odisha have government orders (GOs) that clearly spell out the transfer process. Mizoram also has a policy that provides a broad guideline, but it is not always followed. Jharkhand, Uttar Pradesh, Rajasthan,[5] and Punjab do not (as yet) have a transfer policy. Annual GOs are issued to authorize what can or would be done in that year. These annual guidelines specify who can be transferred, who can ask for a transfer, who will be given priority, and the timeframe in which transfers would be carried out. These annual guidelines are not always based on any long-term policy, but on the

Table 5.2 Teacher Transfer Policies and Implementation

	Teacher transfer policy	Online system	Political interference
Karnataka	Regulation of Transfer of Teachers Act 2007	Yes	Not evident
Jharkhand	No	No	Reported, no formal process
Uttar Pradesh	No	No	Reported, no formal process
Mizoram	Mizoram education (transfer and posting of teachers) rules, 2006	No	Reported, all transfers sent to MP/MLA for no-objection
Rajasthan	No	No	Reported, no formal process
Madhya Pradesh	Yes, GO specifically for transfers	No	Reported, no formal process
Odisha	Yes, GO issued from time to time	Under discussion	Formal representation in transfer committees
Punjab	No	Yes, but not used	Reported, no formal process
Tamil Nadu	GO 209, 1997, counseling process notified in 2001	Yes	Not evident

Note: GO = government order; MLA = Member of the Legislative Assembly; MP = Member of Parliament.

immediate pressures working on political leaders and administrators. Newspaper reports and our discussions with teachers, teachers' union leaders, and administrators across these states suggest that the annual transfer guideline typically is a culmination of the lobbying of competing interest groups.

Having a transfer policy could be seen as a first step toward nurturing a transparent and teacher-sensitive working environment. However, announcing a policy is not sufficient if it does not protect teachers from the need to cultivate political connections. In Odisha, although the policy is quite clear, it provides a formal mechanism for the elected representative (Member of Parliament (MP) or Member of the Legislative Assembly (MLA)) to be consulted. In Mizoram, notwithstanding the 2006 policy, political leaders (MP and MLA) can refuse to permit teachers in their constituency to be moved out. In Rajasthan, the "desire" of a political representative is a compelling reason for transfer. As a result, Rajasthan has seen waves of transfers (when thousands of teachers were transferred in one go) and periods when all transfers were prohibited by order of the Chief Minister of the state. Over the years, several research studies have documented how teacher transfers are closely intertwined with rent-seeking and political patronage (Béteille 2009; Ramachandran et al. 2004; Sharma and Ramachandran 2009).

Who Initiates Transfers?

Another important dimension of teacher transfers is the question of who initiates them and why. In Odisha, Tamil Nadu, and Madhya Pradesh, transferring teachers is not a routine annual exercise. Here the teachers are transferred on request or for a specific purpose (rationalization, post–Right to Education (RTE) Act). Sometimes a rule stipulates the frequency of requests for transfers. For example, in Odisha, teachers must have served a certain number of years in a location before they can ask for a transfer. In Tamil Nadu, teachers can make a request for an inter-district transfer only once in their entire career. In Mizoram (table 5.3),

Table 5.3 Classification of Schools for Teacher Deployment: Mizoram

Category	Location of schools	Minimum tenure	Consideration of transfer (after completion of minimum tenure)
A	All schools within limit of Aizawl and Lunglei	6 years	May be considered for transfer to a category D, C, or B school, according to necessity, as decided by appropriate authority
B	Schools in the district headquarters other than Aizawl and Lunglei, towns and villages along National Highway 54	5 years	May be considered for transfer to a category A school by application, or to a category C or D school, according to necessity as decided by appropriate authority
C	Schools in villages connected by all-weather roads	4 years	May be considered for transfer to a category A or B school by application, or to a category D school, according to necessity, as decided by appropriate authority
D	Schools not falling in A, B, or C	3 years	May be considered for transfer to a category A, B, or C school, subject to availability of a vacant post

Karnataka, Tamil Nadu, and Odisha, schools are categorized as difficult/easy, remote/urban—and each of these categories is assigned a numerical value. Teachers with long tenure in such locations are eligible to request a transfer. The worrying part is that there are no such norms or guidelines in many states and the annual transfer guideline is done in an ad hoc manner. Teachers in these states said that they feel powerless or helpless without the right political connections or access to adequate finances to fund their transfer.

Who Can Be Transferred, Why, and by Whom?

Across all states, contract teachers cannot be transferred (in effect, they belong to a school cadre, although they cannot typically choose their school). However, in Rajasthan (until 2014), with close to 50 percent of teachers on contract, despite a no-transfer policy for contract teachers, we were informed that transfers could be done if there is sufficient motivation and pressure from the "right" quarters.

Regular teachers can be transferred for the following reasons:

1. *Administrative reasons.* Transfers may be implemented to rationalize PTRs in schools and/or ensure the presence of all subject teachers. In Odisha, teachers cannot be transferred outside the Kalahandi-Balangir-Koraput (deficit) districts, thereby limiting the opportunities for teachers working in the area. A similar scenario prevails for teachers working in 10 identified backward districts in Rajasthan; the teachers must complete their service in the districts for 10 years before being eligible for a transfer.
2. *Request of teacher.* The request may be (a) on medical grounds; (b) to join a spouse who is also a government servant; (c) due to illness, from a list of severe medical reasons; (d) for personal reasons, such as marriage or being an unmarried woman; (e) for persons with disability; and (f) for other compelling reasons that may be notified from time to time.

3. *Mutual transfer.* Two teachers may agree among themselves and then submit a mutual transfer request. In such cases, both teachers may lose their seniority if they are transferred outside their home cadre, and they may have to bear the financial cost of the transfer (moving and relocating). Such transfers can happen across blocks and districts. In almost all the states, there is a limit on the number of times a teacher can ask for a mutual transfer. In Punjab, it is once in three years. In Odisha, it is once in a lifetime as a teacher.
4. *Disciplinary grounds or in the public interest.* These types of transfers are rarely invoked. During this study, we came across instances of disciplinary transfers in Karnataka.
5. *Swap transfers.* These are permitted in almost all states that have aided secondary schools, provided the teachers are from schools run by the same management or if the managements of two schools agree. The government is not involved in this kind of transfer.

In many of the states studied, the official reason for a transfer is likely to be one of the listed reasons, but the actual transfer happens due to political reasons or interference. In some states, the government, from time to time, stipulates a percentage of teachers from each cadre, district, or division (as the case may be) who can be transferred. The percentage is not the same across the states, but it was 5 percent of the cadre in Karnataka. In some states, there is also a clear jurisdictional norm for transfers. For example, in Odisha, secondary teachers can be transferred only within a revenue district (sometimes this is different from an educational district).

Karnataka, Tamil Nadu, and Odisha have clearly defined time schedules for transfers. In all three states, transfers must be completed before the end of summer vacation (June or July). No such timeframe seems to be adhered to in Uttar Pradesh and Punjab. In Jharkhand, there is a timeframe on paper, but it is not clear to what extent it is followed (box 5.1).

Box 5.1 Glimpses of Teacher Transfers in Nine States

Odisha

In Odisha, there are two separate committees: one for Intra-Panchayat Samiti (PS) transfers and the other at the district level for intra-district transfers. There is political representation on all these transfer committees: the President of the Zillah Parishad is always a member of these committees, as are a Member of the Legislative Assembly (MLA), Member of Parliament (MP), or their nominees. Even in 2005, when there was no representation of any political representative on the PS-level transfer committee, there was specific mention to give due weight to the recommendations of the Sarpanch. In 2007 and 2009, the MLAs were made chairpersons of the PS-level transfer committees. The 2013 transfer guideline advised the transfer committee to collect recommendations from MLAs and MPs. Since 2010, there has been only one

box continues next page

Box 5.1 Glimpses of Teacher Transfers in Nine States *(continued)*

committee at the district level. The earlier system of transfers and rationalization within the PS and education district has been replaced by transfers within the education district only. The policy is still evolving.

Uttar Pradesh

In 2013, the annual transfer circular (known as Samayojan and Transfer) gave priority to teachers with a disability, widowed or divorced, those (self or family) suffering from serious disease, mutual transfers, state and national awardee teachers, those who have served the maximum time in their place of posting, and husband-wife.

Madhya Pradesh

There is a complex system of four types of teachers, each with three levels, and a different body manages each type of teacher. Two types are managed by not one but various different bodies. For example, the Samvida Shala Shikshak and the Adhyapaks Samvarg are managed by the Zillah or Janpad Panchayat or the Nagariya Nikaya (municipal corporation) and the School Education or Tribal Welfare Department, depending on who manages the schools where the teachers are posted. The Shikshak—the older cadre—is managed by the School Education or Tribal Welfare Department. The Atithi Shikshak is managed by the school management committee. Only regular teachers (Adhyapak Samvarg and Shikshak Samvarg) can be transferred.

Tamil Nadu

The block is the basic unit for elementary school teachers. Transfers happen usually within a block, then from one block to another, and then to another district. Seniority-related issues are clearly stipulated in the transfer policy. Transfers are not routine business, but are initiated when there is a request from a teacher or when there are vacancies. A no-objection certificate from the school is essential for transfers. From 2001 to 2012, this was done manually in the presence of teachers at the district level. Now it is an online process where teachers who want a transfer assemble at the counseling unit. Since 1997, when teachers get transferred from one unit to another (one block to another or from elementary to high school), they are placed as the junior-most and have to sever all the seniority rights they had in the previous position.

Rajasthan

Teacher transfers in the state are characterized by ad hocism. Guidelines are issued from time to time specifying the order in which teachers should be transferred depending on category (widow, terminally ill, and so forth), as well as duration in a rural area. However, these guidelines are rarely followed. In 1994, the Bordia Committee proposed a detailed policy and plan for transfers, but this was not adopted. In 2005, a new transfer policy was adopted, but this was abandoned within a year due to political pressure. As of 2013, again guidelines have been issued. Although teachers apply for transfers through the formal process, there is a system of "desires," whereby connections with MLAs are the only way in which teachers believe transfers will be processed quickly. There is no regular time for transfers. The following types of teachers cannot be transferred: those who have joined government service from aided

box continues next page

Box 5.1 Glimpses of Teacher Transfers in Nine States *(continued)*

schools (when aided schools were abolished), those appointed post–April 2011 and on probation, contract teachers, and teachers from 10 restricted districts that face shortages. Teachers in these districts can only be transferred after completing 10 years of service, assuming the transfer ban is lifted.

Mizoram

Teachers are a state cadre and deployment is done by the Directorate. The state government can place teachers wherever it wishes. Transfers are guided by the 2006 policy. Schools are classified into four categories (A, B, C, and D) and minimum tenure is fixed for each category: A, six years; B, five years; C, four years; and D, three years. The most remote schools are in category D. There is a provision for compulsory posting in category D schools, and there are no restrictions on inter- or intra-district transfers. Transfers are normally initiated through teacher applications. Although technically the Directorate can transfer teachers for administrative reasons, such as rationalization, there have been no instances (in the past 10 years) of such transfers.

Karnataka

Transfers on request are done every year, as per the vacancy list. A minimum two-teacher norm is followed. All transfers are as per the Karnataka State Civil Service Act of 2007. Transfers usually start in March and are completed by the opening of school in June. The first round of transfers and redeployment is done with respect to excess teachers; subsequently, vacancies that arise are notified. Then transfers on request are initiated, based on the 2007 Act. Mutual transfer requests are also considered at this time, but are taken up last. All transfer applications must be sent through the head of institution, then service records are verified, after which the transfer process is initiated. The same process as the process for deployment is followed. A merit list is prepared and displayed for five days to see if there are any objections. Then the final list is made available. Transfers outside the seniority list (from one district or division to another) are done after the regular transfers are completed and vacancy lists notified. There are also transfers for disciplinary action—teachers posted to remote and difficult areas—which are the only type of transfer that is not done through computerized counseling and where a post can be shifted to a school to make this happen. However, this is extremely rare.

Jharkhand

The Jharkhand state government adopted the same transfer and redeployment rules as existed in undivided Bihar (before 2000). Currently, teachers are transferred and deployed through Zillah Prarambhik Shiksha Samitis. The District Commissioner chairs this committee and the Deputy Superintendent of Education is the member-secretary, followed by other members. Mostly teachers are transferred on administrative or personal grounds. These district-level sthapna sammittees were given the power to transfer teachers twice in a year (May-June and November-December). The duration of posting at any post and location generally is for a period of three years. However, for some locations, this may be reduced to two years. Transfers are usually done in the teachers' home or neighboring blocks. For inter-district transfers of teachers, the Director Primary is the competent authority. In the past seven years,

box continues next page

Box 5.1 Glimpses of Teacher Transfers in Nine States *(continued)*

no mass transfers have taken place in Jharkhand. There is a provision for couple transfers in the rules laid down by the Personnel Department. Para teachers are not transferred and redeployed, as they are managed and controlled by the local bodies that recruit them for a specific school.

Punjab

A new transfer policy is announced every year. As a result, the system varies from year to year, and this is a high-level political decision. The one constant is that regular and contract employees can apply for transfer. Employees can be transferred only once in an academic session. Equally, when teachers ask to be transferred from one Zillah Parishad to another, they could lose their seniority. However, if it is a case of disciplinary action or a transfer due to management reasons, the transfer requests can be considered even before completion of three years. Newly married and unmarried women are given preference for transfer.

Source: Respective State Reports, 2014.

Deputation, Another Form of Transfer

In Punjab, teachers informed us that when they are unable to get a transfer or have missed their chance, they could arrange for a deputation to their preferred location through personal networking. Some of the teachers said that they have been deputed to work in the Sarva Shiksha Abhiyan or Rashtriya Madhyamik Shiksha Abhiyan Directorate, or sent to the State Council of Educational Research and Training or Cluster Head Teacher. They also informed us that science and mathematics teachers are more likely to be deputed to these nonteaching positions, because of their ability to manage numbers and data. The deficit of teachers is quite serious in the Indo-Pakistan border areas of Punjab; this was cited as an example of teacher-politician connections that prevented the administration from posting teachers in deficit schools.

Good Practices That Could Show the Way

Teacher transfers are a fairly complex and contentious process in states that have not yet worked out a long-term policy. It is also the one issue that evokes a lot of debate among teachers, teachers' union leaders, and administrators. Teachers in states that do not have a transparent policy and process are of the view that this is the root cause of low motivation and the most important reason for teachers to nurture patronage networks. Administrators complain that teachers are so adept at networking to move from or to another location that they are not answerable to anyone in the administration. Parents in school-level committees say that they are powerless to enforce regular attendance, because teachers depend on support from powerful people in the system. Lack of accountability, teacher absenteeism, and low time spent on teaching and learning are all blamed as effects of teacher transfers.

At this juncture, it may be pertinent to look a little closer at Karnataka.

The Karnataka Story

Karnataka's practices, at least in the past decade, have been policy-driven. All transfers (elementary and secondary teachers and headmasters) are implemented as per the Karnataka State Civil Services (Regulation of Transfer of Teachers) Act 2007 (Karnataka Act No. 29 of 2007) (Government of Karnataka 2007a). This Act derives most of its provisions from the Transfer Guidelines (Government of Karnataka 2001) issued for transfer of all government employees in the state. This was followed by rules guiding the implementation of the Act (Government of Karnataka 2007b). One of the key aspects of teacher transfers in Karnataka is that only 5 percent of the total number of the sanctioned posts of teachers in a particular cadre within that unit of seniority can be transferred in a given year. The total number of transfers outside the unit of seniority cannot exceed 1 percent of the total cadre strength of the unit (D1, April 8, 2014; Government of Karnataka 2007a; S1, February 12, 2014; S4, May 6, 2014; S5, May 6, 2014).

Transfers are initiated in March and finalized by the start of the new academic year (D1, April 8, 2014). The Deputy Director of Public Instruction of the district and the Joint Director of Public Instruction of the division are the competent authorities for finalizing transfers of elementary school teachers and secondary school teachers, respectively (D1, April 8, 2014; Government of Karnataka 2007b; S4, May 6, 2014). Apart from issuing transfer and releasing orders, the competent authority also ensures that the first appointment of all teachers is in a rural area, and that no teacher is transferred outside the rural area before completion of five years of service in the rural area (from the date of appointment). During this period, transfers from one unit of seniority to another are also prohibited. There are exceptions—in case for example, of female widowed teachers, physically handicapped or disabled teachers, medical treatment of teachers or their spouse or children for serious ailments (such as open-heart surgery, cancer, or kidney failure), and married teachers whose spouses live outside the unit of seniority. However, in cases of teachers wanting to be together with their spouses, they should have completed three years of service and can avail of this only once during their service time (Government of Karnataka 2007a). In case the competent authority or any other officer makes an order of posting or transfer in contradiction with the Teachers Transfer Act 2007, disciplinary action is taken against him/her.

What is the sequence of transfers? The first round of transfers includes redeployment of excess teachers to needy schools. The number of excess teachers in schools is calculated based on two factors. One is to maintain the PTR in the schools. Until the 2013–14 academic year, 40:1 PTR was used to calculate excess teachers and vacant posts. However, a proposal to decrease the PTR to 30:1, in compliance with RTE, has been sent to the ministry for approval. And two is to fill subject-wise vacancies in upper primary schools for teachers appointed after 2001.[6] While calculating excess teachers in schools, the minimum two-teacher norm is maintained as per the National Policy on Education (Government of India 1986). During the second round of transfers, the remaining vacant posts are taken into account. Notification of such vacancies is done through notice boards. Transfers on request (within and outside seniority) are done based on the guidelines prescribed under the Teacher Transfers Act 2007 (Government of Karnataka 2007b). Mutual transfers are finalized along with transfers on request (figure 5.1).

The process of transfers on request is conducted using a software program (specially designed for government teacher transfers in Karnataka), which ensures that the maximum allowed percentage of teachers (5 percent per year) is not breached. The program incorporates the priorities, as per the Act, in processing the transfers, maintaining the service details of all teachers and facilitating computerized counseling for final placement.

Figure 5.1 Application Process for Transfers within Same Unit of Seniority

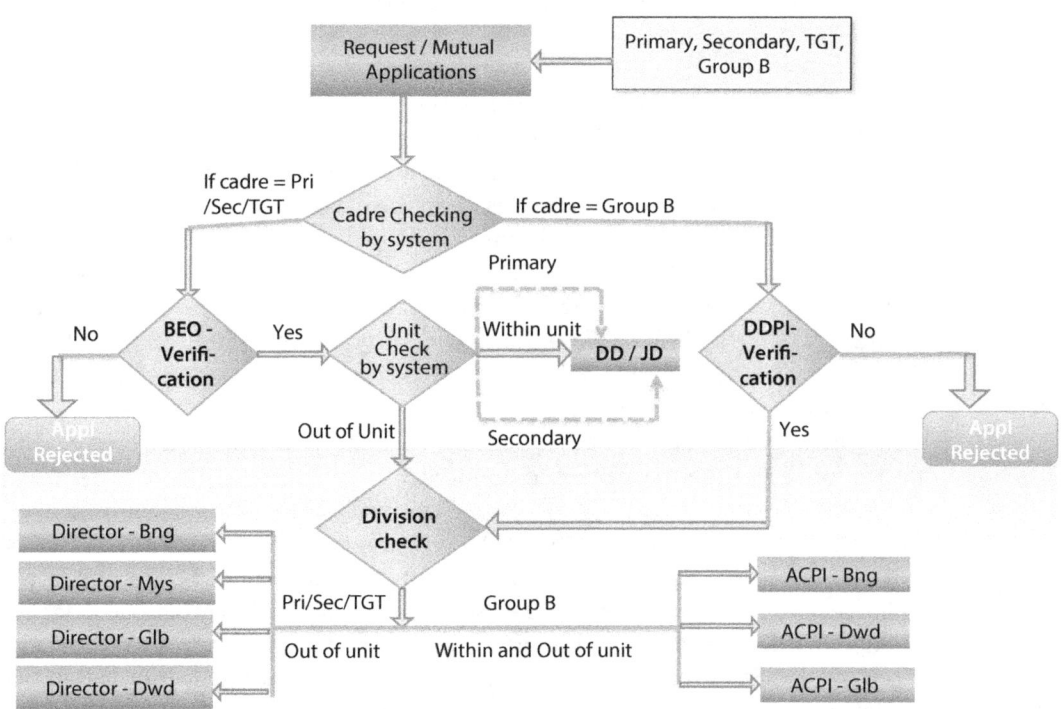

Source: Management Information System (MIS) Section, Sarva Shiksha Abhiyan Karnataka.
Note: ACPI = Assistant Commissioner Public Instruction; BEO = Block Education Officer; Bng = Bangalore Division; DD = Deputy Director; DDPI = Deputy Director Public Instruction; Dwd = Dharwad Division; Glb = Gulbarga Division; JD = Joint Director; Mys = Mysore Division; TGT = Trained Graduate Teacher.

All applications for transfers are sent through the head of their institution After verification of service records to ensure the minimum five years of service in rural areas, the application is forwarded to the Block Education Officer (for elementary school teachers) and Deputy Director of Public Instruction (for secondary school teachers). After the certification of the documents is submitted with the application, the application is entered in the computer program for initiating the transfer process. A priority list, as specified in the Act, is prepared based on the following order of priority (Interview with official, April 8, 2014; Government of Karnataka 2007a):

1. Cases of terminally ill (such as open-heart surgery, cancer, and kidney failure) applicants
2. Cases of physically handicapped or disabled teachers with more than 40 percent disability (medical certificate required)
3. Cases of widowed female teachers
4. Cases of married teachers whose spouse is posted outside the seniority unit and after completion of three years of service (this provision can be availed only once during the service); highest priority is given when both spouses are government employees
5. Other female teachers
6. Elected office bearers of recognized associations of government schools
7. Other male teachers.

Within each of the priority categories, the priority list is prepared by multiplying the number of years of service of the applicant in all cadres in the places classified as A, B, and C zones,[7] as per their unit of seniority (figure 5.2). Zone A is given the least weight and zone C is given the maximum weight. Teachers with more weight due to more time spent in difficult areas are given higher priority. In the case of a tie, the seniority of the individual is taken into consideration. In the case of a tie in seniority, the older teacher is given priority (Government of Karnataka 2007a, 2007b). Based on the priority list and specified weights, the competent authorities (Block Education Officer and Deputy Director of Public Instruction) prepare a provisional list. This list is displayed for five days so that objections can be raised. The authorities examine the objections received and reject or accept the transfer based on merit.

Applicants on the provisional list are notified of the date for computerized counseling. An updated vacancy database is shown to the applicants on the day of the counseling as per the priority list (figures 5.3, 5.4, and 5.5). The applicants choose a position at a school on the list of vacant posts for transfer. The database is updated for the next teacher on the priority list (Government of Karnataka 2007b; Jha, Saxena, and Baxi 2001). This process is repeated until the upper limit of the number of transfers is reached or all the applicants are exhausted within the timeframe communicated by the heads of departments.

Once the process is complete, the competent authority issues transfer orders reflecting the choice of the applicant and then deletes that vacancy from the list.

Teacher Deployment and Transfers

Figure 5.2 Preparation of Provisional and Final List for Transfers

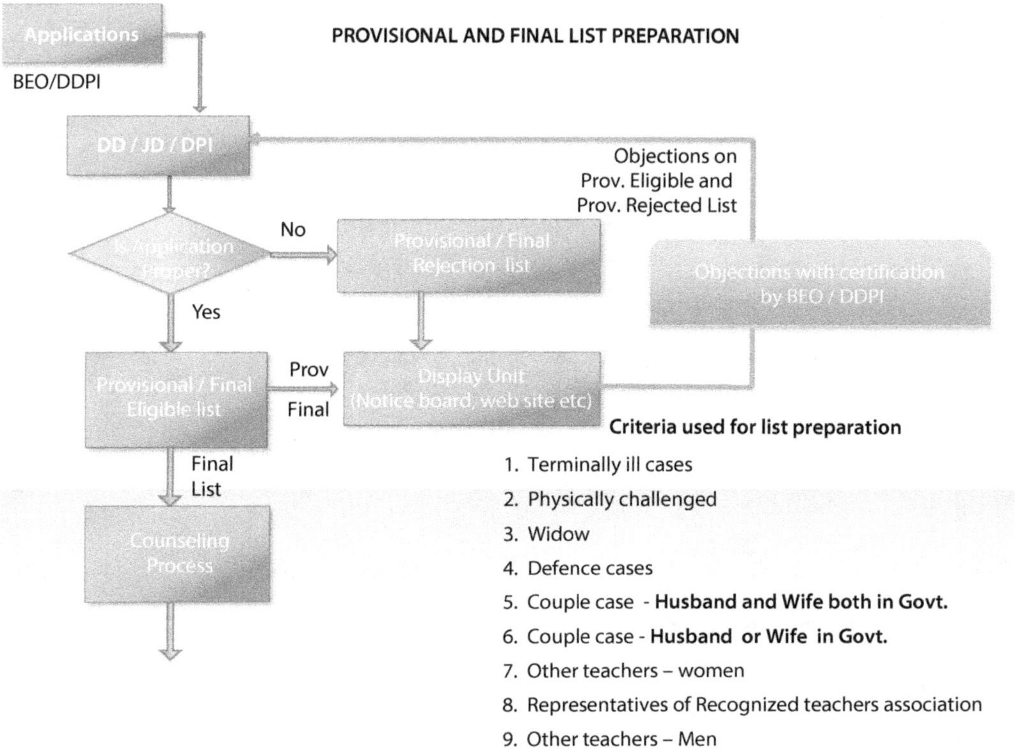

PROVISIONAL AND FINAL LIST PREPARATION

[Flowchart showing: Applications (BEO/DDPI) → DD/JD/DPI → Is Application Proper? → No: Provisional/Final Rejection list → Display Unit (Notice board, web site etc); Yes: Provisional/Final Eligible list → (Prov) Display Unit, (Final) Counseling Process. Objections on Prov. Eligible and Prov. Rejected List → Objections with certification by BEO/DDPI → back to DD/JD/DPI]

Criteria used for list preparation

1. Terminally ill cases
2. Physically challenged
3. Widow
4. Defence cases
5. Couple case - **Husband and Wife both in Govt.**
6. Couple case - **Husband or Wife in Govt.**
7. Other teachers – women
8. Representatives of Recognized teachers association
9. Other teachers – Men

Source: Management Information System Section, Sarva Shiksha Abhiyan Karnataka.
Note: BEO = Block Education Officer; DD = Deputy Director; DDPI =Deputy Director Public Instruction; DPI = Director of Public Instruction; JD = Joint Director.

Figure 5.3 Counseling Process for Transfers on Request

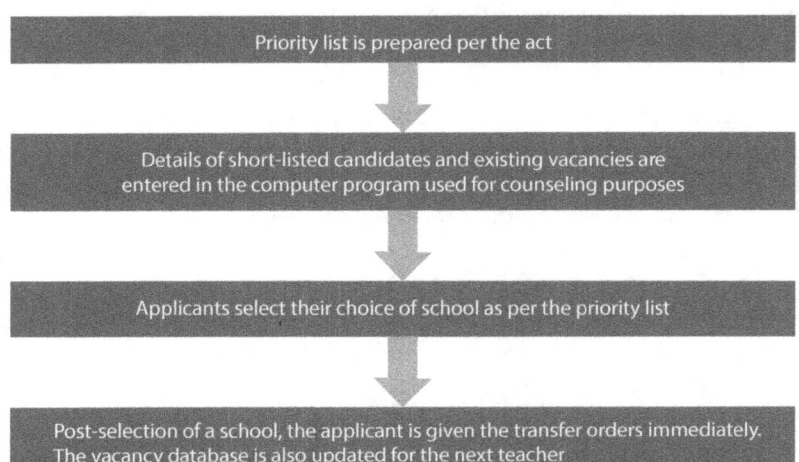

1. Priority list is prepared per the act
2. Details of short-listed candidates and existing vacancies are entered in the computer program used for counseling purposes
3. Applicants select their choice of school as per the priority list
4. Post-selection of a school, the applicant is given the transfer orders immediately. The vacancy database is also updated for the next teacher

Figure 5.4 Flowchart for the Counseling Process

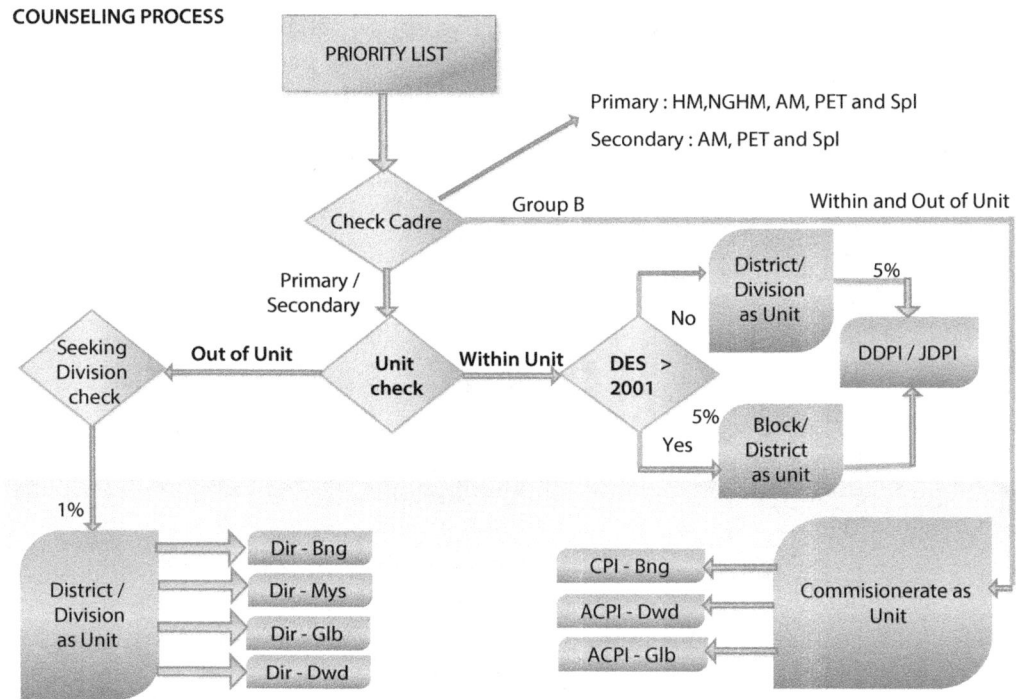

Source: Management Information System Section, Sarva Shiksha Abhiyan Karnataka.
Note: ACPI = Assistant Commissioner Public Instruction; AM = Assistant Manager; Bng = Bangalore Division; CPI = Commissioner of Public Instruction; DDPI = Deputy Director Public Instruction; DWD = Dharwad Division; Glb = Gulbarga Division; HM = headmaster; JDPI = Joint Director Public Instruction; Mys = Mysore Division; NGHM = Non-Graduate Head Master; PET = Professional Entrance Test.

A copy is sent to the relevant official and another is given to the applicant. The final list of teachers to be transferred, along with the places of transfer is displayed on the notice board. No transfer is allowed after the display of this list. If any transfers are made after the display of the list, the relevant competent authority is held personally responsible and disciplinary action is taken against him/her. The competent authority formally releases the teachers, who receive transfer orders, after verifying their service particulars.

Transfers of teachers outside the seniority unit are implemented based on the Government of Karnataka policy of 2005. Such transfers (apart from the exceptions mentioned above) are undertaken after the district-level counseling for transfers within the seniority unit is completed. The competent authority shares information about the remaining vacant positions in the district or division for inter-district and inter-division transfers. Inter-unit transfers take place only for schools in zones A and B.

Figure 5.5 Excess Teacher Transfer Process

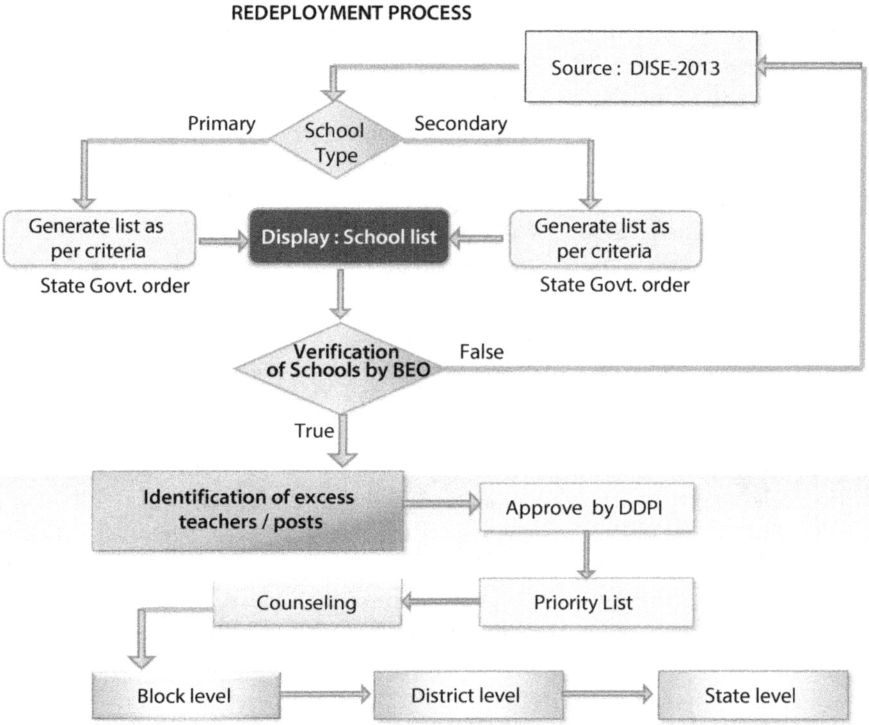

REDEPLOYMENT PROCESS

```
                        Source: DISE-2013
        Primary    School Type    Secondary
                   ↓
Generate list as        Display: School list       Generate list as
per criteria                                       per criteria
State Govt. order                                  State Govt. order
                   ↓
              Verification          False
              of Schools by BEO  ────────→
                   ↓ True
Identification of excess  →  Approve by DDPI
teachers / posts                  ↓
              Counseling  ←   Priority List
                   ↓
Block level  →  District level  →  State level
```

Source: Management Information System Section, Sarva Shiksha Abhiyan Karnataka.
Note: BEO = Block Education Officer; DDPI = Deputy Director of Public Instruction; DISE = District Information System for Education.

Transfers for disciplinary action

Sometimes teachers are transferred to educationally backward and remote areas on disciplinary grounds. Such transfers are considered after the second round of transfers. A teacher who is working in an urban area and faces a timebound penalty under the Karnataka Civil Services (Classification, Control and Appeal) Rules, 1957 (Government of Karnataka 1957) or criminal charges can be transferred to zone C. If there is no vacancy in zone C, a vacancy can be created by transferring an eligible teacher from zone C to zone B or A. This is the only kind of transfer that is not done through computerized counseling (Government of Karnataka 2001). Field interactions indicated that this is rarely practiced. Initially, warnings are given; if the teacher still does not comply, then the teacher concerned can be transferred on disciplinary grounds.

Transfers for public interest. If the government feels it is necessary to transfer a teacher from or to a particular school or area for smooth functioning, the government can do so by citing public interest as a reason. However, no evidence was gathered in the course of this study that would indicate that this process happens frequently.

The following are important features of Karnataka's transfer policy:

- First, there is an upper limit on the number of transfers that are permissible in an academic year. These transfers take place just once in a year, and happen before the new school year starts.
- Second, all teachers are expected to have served in rural areas for five years before they are eligible for transfers. In the case of transfer requests, the more time a teacher has spent in a difficult location, the higher are the chances that her/his transfer request will be granted.
- Third, there is an online system that implements the policy seamlessly.

The Odisha Story of Evolving Clarity

It is, indeed, noteworthy that in Odisha, there is almost no mention of teacher transfers in the Odisha Education Act of 1969, Odisha Education Service Rules 1971, or Odisha Subordinate Education Rules of 1993. This was corrected in 2005 when the Odisha government sent officials to Karnataka and Tamil Nadu to understand their teacher transfer systems and gradually started issuing orders that provided a policy framework for the transfer of teachers. Today, the transfer policy in Odisha is quite clear and, in many ways, the government is trying to move toward a more transparent system—albeit slowly and step-by-step. There are three notable characteristics of the system in the state:

1. Teacher transfer committees at the block, district, and state levels provide for formal representation of elected representatives (MLA or MP), thereby formalizing political oversight of teacher transfers.
2. Not more than 10 percent of teachers in the district can be transferred in one year.
3. Contract teachers are eligible for transfer within a specific area; the rules regarding such transfers are evolving.

Discussions with officials and teachers' union representatives in Odisha revealed that policies are changing. They plan to come out with a comprehensive policy, covering all aspects of deployment and transfer, soon.

Contentious and Complex Situation in Rajasthan

Teacher transfers have long been a contentious issue in Rajasthan. Several studies in the past 10 years have documented this highly contentious terrain (Béteille 2009; Ramachandran et al. 2004; Sharma and Ramachandran 2009). The situation is similar in Uttar Pradesh, Punjab, and Jharkhand, where, in the absence of a clear policy or norm, teachers are victims of a transfer-posting regime and work the system to their advantage (but to the detriment of schools).

Rajasthan has some overarching policies, including the Rajasthan Education Code 1957, Rajasthan Education Service Rules 1970, Rajasthan Education Subordinate Service Rules 1971, Departmental Rulebook 1997, and guidelines and policies that were issued in 2005 and 2013. Notwithstanding these policies, transfers have been highly politicized in the state. Teachers across the state believe that, irrespective of the political party in power, teacher transfers are always subject to political influence. In interviews with district and state officials, they also agreed that politicians believe that influencing transfers is a right. Teachers and administrators informed us that rent-seeking and patronage networks are an inherent part of teacher transfers.

Given that teacher transfers are a politically sensitive issue in Rajasthan, the recent government has placed a total moratorium on transfers since 2012. A senior officer placed in the directorate said that: "It is like Madhu Makhi Ka Chatta (a beehive) and once you touch it will be difficult to manage." Generally, the government puts a ban on transfers but then relaxes it for a short duration. In a focus group discussion with teachers, one teacher said that teachers have started receiving calls from "agents" informing them that the "ban" would be lifted soon. When we asked them who these agents were, they informed us that most of them were politically networked teachers.

The Status in Madhya Pradesh

Madhya Pradesh has separate rules for transfers of regular teachers and contract teachers (on probation) (table 5.4). Administrative transfers for the regular cadre

Table 5.4 Transfer Norms: Madhya Pradesh

Norms	Adhyapak Samvarg	Shikshak
Timing of transfers	• There does not seem to be any date for transfers in the new 2014 policy. • In 2008, when the decision regarding Adhyapak Samvarg transfers was taken, transfers were opened in July 2008.	• Open only between May 1 and June 15 every year
Priority list	Priority list for on-request transfers: • Any person (or spouse) suffering from cancer, brain tumor, open-heart surgery, bypass surgery, paralysis, or kidney transplant • Persons with disability, with more than 40% disability • If both husband and wife are in government service, they may be transferred to the same location • Women who are widowed or divorced • Other categories of women • Other categories of men.	• Administrative transfers for rationalization • Mutual transfers, certified and NOC given by head of institution where posted • For husband and wife wanting posting together in one institution, they can apply to DEO and be posted where there are posts vacant • Priority for voluntary transfer is the same as in Adhyapak Samvarg
Competent authority	• All matters related to transfers and deployments at the inter-district level are handled by the Commissioner of Public Instruction or Commissioner of Tribal Welfare, depending on management of the institution, and for the intra-district level between one local body and another, by the District Collector. • Within the local body, Varisht Adhyapak (grade I), CEO, Zillah Panchayat. • For Adhyapak and Sahayak Adhyapak (grades II and III), the CEO Zillah Panchayats.	
Upper limit for transfer	• In a situation where one position has two eligible applications for transfer, preference will be given on a priority basis.	

Note: CEO = Chief Executive Office; DEO = District Education Office; NOC = No-Objection Certificate.

are usually done for rationalization of posts from teacher-surplus institutions to teacher-scarce institutions. This type of transfer is allowed from urban to rural areas, but not the other way around. The rules that govern teacher transfers are the same as for other government employees, namely the State and District Level Officers/Employees Transfer Policy 2012-13 Serial Number F 6-2/2012/One/9, dated May 1, 2012.

Since transfers are restricted and the appointments are made to particular schools, there are still large numbers of schools where there is an adverse PTR and there are a large number of single-teacher schools as well. There is now a policy to transfer for rationalization particularly into rural schools; however, given the overall shortage of teachers, such rationalization has not been effective. Freshly recruited teachers are given a choice (from among vacant positions) and they rarely opt for rural and remote schools.

During focus group discussions and interviews, teachers and teachers' union leaders expressed concern over distance from home to school for those teachers who work in remote/rural areas. Teachers feel that it would be helpful if the they were provided residential facilities in rural areas, as they would then not have to travel long distances. In Madhya Pradesh, there are no policies or regulations that stipulate the number of years a teacher has to serve in a rural and remote area. As a result, teachers without influence or resources end up serving in difficult areas, while those with influence or resources manage to avoid rural and remote postings.

Summing Up

In every state, there are thousands of schools that have too many or too few teachers. This situation is an immediate indicator that staffing plans for schools are likely to be inefficient, manipulated, or nonexistent. As previous work shows, transfers are important for teachers (and not just for schools aiming to be fully staffed). In a system that is otherwise uniform in pay and emoluments, transfers can improve or worsen a teacher's working and living conditions considerably.

At the end of the day, not all teaching assignments are created equal; some are in urban areas with better amenities and/or easier students. Therefore, teachers who are assigned to a school in which they do not wish to teach are given the opportunity (at least in theory) to apply for a transfer to another school. If such requests are entertained without jeopardizing the interests of the school, and a teacher leaves or joins, the system does not suffer. However, when teachers can obtain a transfer regardless of the school's need, it distorts the overall allocation of teachers to schools, seriously compromising the education of large numbers of children.

As this study shows, effective teacher transfer policies are rare in India. Where they exist (Karnataka and Tamil Nadu), they are recent. Transfer policies in these two states specify the number of years all teachers must spend in rural areas, number of teachers that can be transferred in a year, and prioritization rules for the transfer of different groups of teachers. Importantly, transfer policies in these states are implemented using an information technology–based system that has checks and balances. In states like Odisha and Madhya Pradesh, a series of GOs and guidelines spell out the criteria and the process. Odisha is indeed an interesting case, where political leaders are formally represented on transfer committees, thereby making their involvement "official." Although a series of GOs and guidelines may not be categorized as "policies," they are, nevertheless, followed in letter and spirit. Both states have tried to streamline the system in the past two years. In all the other states, transfer practices share the following similarities:

- First, they are mostly ad hoc.
- Second, in most states, only regular teachers in government schools can be transferred.
- Third, teachers often need powerful connections and report paying bribes in these states to obtain a transfer of their choice (or impede one against their interest) or get a transfer relatively quickly. In some states, such as Rajasthan, transfers are given as rewards to politically helpful teachers. In states other than Karnataka, Tamil Nadu, Madhya Pradesh, and Odisha, adverse reassignments are used as threats against politically uncooperative teachers.
- Fourth, if teachers who want a transfer to another school cannot be transferred because no vacancy exists, they can, nevertheless, get to their location of interest by requesting a deputation to an administrative office.[8]
- Finally, transfers can be used to discipline errant teachers (although in practice such transfers are rare). This practice focuses on punishment, and shows little regard for the interests of the students who receive the errant teacher.

As this chapter shows, if teachers want to leave a school for another assignment, they find a way. This process consumes a considerable amount of their time, energy, and financial resources, and depletes needy schools of teachers. Designing a transfer policy along the lines of states such as Karnataka and Tamil Nadu is crucial, but requires strong political will. Madhya Pradesh and Odisha are trying to streamline the system. It is likely that it will take some time before a comprehensive recruitment and deployment policy is adopted by these states. It also requires technical skills to design a policy that is fair and offers opportunity to those who are most in need or eligible for transfers. Importantly, the policy will require software to facilitate transfers, checks and balances to ensure that the system is using the correct information to generate transfer lists, and teachers who are comfortable using technology.

Notes

1. Indeed, if there were a system of rewarding teachers working in difficult circumstances, then transfers could be a way for teachers to volunteer to move to such schools.
2. This is a consequence of the difficulties of removing poorly performing teachers from the workforce; none of the states in this research reported a significant chance of

government schoolteachers being dismissed from service. In the absence of such mechanisms, moving poorly performing teachers to another school might appear the only option. Dr. Dhir Jhingran commented: "In Assam, transfer of teachers, based on adverse comments by a visiting supervisor, was quite common (in the 1990s and 2000s). Often these transfers were stopped because the teacher would approach an MLA or some other political leader. Since this kind of reversals of transfer became common, the DEO reduced the practice of such transfers. However, some District magistrates continue to do this."

3. The nine states covered in this study are: Jharkhand, Karnataka, Madhya Pradesh, Mizoram, Odisha, Punjab, Rajasthan, Tamil Nadu, and Uttar Pradesh. (Detailed state reports are available: http://www.nuepa.org/New/completed%20reaserches.aspx).

4. In some cases (for example, Karnataka), although the cadre may be block level, the seniority list may be maintained at the district level.

5. We were informed during the course of this research that Rajasthan is planning to announce a policy soon. No announcement had been made as of December 31, 2014.

6. Post-2001, the department appointed subject-wise teachers for upper primary schools. While calculating excess teachers, the year of appointment is taken into consideration. For those teachers appointed before 2001, PTR is used as the basis for calculating excess teachers in a school. For subject-wise teachers, vacancy for that particular subject is taken into account.

7. Zone A: Zillah HQ/Taluk HQ/Highways/Bangalore City area; zone B: 5 to 15-kilometer radius from Zillah HQ/Taluk HQ/Highways/Mysore-Hubli-Dharwad Municipal Corporations; zone C: beyond 15 kilometers from Zillah HQ/Taluk HQ/Highways/Areas with population less than 5 lakhs (Government of Karnataka 2013).

8. Clearly, the RTE has not changed the situation and there is no fear of RTE norms.

CHAPTER 6

Salaries and Benefits

Over the past decade, in India and globally, massive investments and reforms have been put in place to increase teacher effectiveness. One of the major focuses of these reforms has been salaries. This chapter provides an analysis of salaries and other benefits given to teachers (both regular and contract) in India. The chapter also includes a brief discussion on the impacts of the Fifth and Sixth Pay Commissions on teachers' salaries.

Expenditure on Elementary Education in India: A Brief Snapshot

Currently, India spends less than 3 percent of its gross domestic product (GDP) on education. However, there has been considerable increase in the overall education expenditure in the past 10 years. Since 2000–01, the central government's education budget has increased significantly, especially after the introduction of centrally sponsored schemes, such as Sarva Shiksha Abhiyan (SSA), Mid-Day Meal, and Rashtriya Madhyamik Shiksha Abhiyan (RMSA). Elementary education budget allocations doubled, from Rs. 68,853 crores in 2007–08, to Rs. 147,059 crores in 2012–13 (PAISA 2012). A major reason for this increase was the introduction of an education cess of 2 percent in 2004, which was raised to 3 percent in 2009 (Mukherjee and Sikdar 2012; *The Hindu* 2014).

Of the total elementary education budget, a huge percentage of allocations are spent on teachers' salaries. According to some reports, teachers' salaries constitute more than 80 percent of the total budget allocations (Cheney, Ruzzi, and Muralidharan 2005; Kingdon 2010). In the past, teachers have demanded higher pay scales. Pay scale revisions after the Fifth and Sixth Pay Commissions were expected to ensure that teachers in state government schools were paid at par with other central government employees. The main objective of the Pay Commissions was to remove any anomalies in salaries by reducing the number of pay scales. For example, the Fifth Pay Commission reduced the number of pay scales from 51 to 34, and the Sixth Pay Commission further reduced the

Table 6.1 Pay Scale of Government Teachers
Indian rupees

Category	Fourth pay commission (1986)	Fifth pay commission (1996)	Sixth pay commission (2006)
Primary school teacher (selection scale)	1,640–2,900	5,500–9,000	PB-2 of 9,300–34,800 along with grade pay of 4,200
Trained graduate teacher (selection scale)	2,000–3,500	7,500–12,000	PB-2 of 9,300–34,800 along with grade pay of 4,800
Post-graduate teacher (selection scale)	2,200–4,000	8,000–13,500	PB-3 of 15,600–39,100 along with grade pay of 5,400

Source: The data are based on information from http://dpe.nic.in/important_links/dpe_guidelines/wage_policies/glch4aindex/glch04a8 and http://karnmk.blogspot.in/2012/11/4th-5th-and-6th-cpc-pay-scales-and.html.
Note: The values in the table are estimates, as they could not be confirmed from government sources. Each state adapts the central pay scale according to its needs. PB = pay band.

number to 20. These changes resulted in higher pay scales for teachers. Table 6.1 compares the salaries of teachers before and after the Fifth and Sixth Pay Commissions.

Along with salary hikes, the Fifth and Sixth Pay Commissions included other benefits, such as an increase in the annual increment (3 percent of total pay), increase in the percentage of dearness allowance and house rent allowance (HRA), medical insurance scheme for new government employees, and revised pension schemes. However, in comparison, the salary of a contract (or para) teacher continues to remain a fraction of what a government teacher earns. In some cases, the salary of a contract teacher is only 11 percent of what a regular teacher earns in the same state. Based on the findings from the State Reports,[1] the next two sections compare the salaries and benefits (monetary and nonmonetary) available to regular and contract teachers.

Comparison of Salaries across States

In this study, all the states, except Karnataka and Punjab, reported that in principle, they had adopted the recommendations of the Sixth Pay Commission. However, each state has contextualized the recommendations and, hence, there are some differences in the salaries of teachers (tables 6.2 and 6.3). For example, even though Rajasthan adopted the Sixth Pay Commission and revisions were made after the Bhatnagar Committee recommendations in 2013, the pay scales of state government teachers are lower than those of central government employees. Similarly, Odisha adopted the Sixth Pay Commission in 2009, but teachers are given a lower pay scale (pay scale Rs. 5,200 to Rs. 20,200 and grade pay of Rs. 2,200), which teachers feel is a blatant violation of the Sixth Pay Commission.

Differences in salaries become more glaring when they are compared with the take-home salaries of teachers (new appointees, salary after 15 years, and salary after 25 years of service). Table 6.3 shows the take-home salaries of teachers in eight states.

Table 6.2 Pay Scale of Government School Teachers
Indian rupees

State	Sixth Pay Commission	Primary		Upper primary		Secondary	
		Basic pay	Grade pay	Basic pay	Grade pay	Basic pay	Grade pay
Tamil Nadu	Yes	5,200–20,200	2,800	9,300–34,800	4,600	9,300–34,800	4,600
Karnataka[a]	No	13,600–26,700		13,600–26,700		17,650–32,000	
Jharkhand	Yes	9,300–34,800	4,200–4,600	9,300–34,800	4,200–4,600	9,300–34,800	4,600
Odisha[b]	Yes	5,200–20,200	2,200	5,200–20,200	2,200	9,300–34,800	4,200
Rajasthan	Yes	9,300–34,800	3,600	9,300–34,800	3,600	9,300–34,800	4,200
Mizoram	Yes	9,300–34,800	4,200	9,300–34,800	4,600	9,300–34,800	4,600
Uttar Pradesh	Yes	9,300	4,200	—	—	12,540	4,600
Punjab[c]	Fifth Pay Commission	10,300–34,800	4,200	—	—	10,300–34,800	5,000
Madhya Pradesh	—	5,200–20,200	2,400	9,300–34,800	3,200	NA	NA

Source: State Reports on Working Conditions of Teachers in India.
Note: — = not available.
a. In Karnataka, only consolidated salaries were given.
b. In Odisha, there are different levels of service in the elementary cadre. On promotion from level V to level IV, the scale remains the same and grade pay increases from 2,200 to 2,400. From level IV to level III, the scale increases to 9,300, and the grade pay increases from 2,400 to 4,200. From level III to level II, only the grade pay increases, to 4,600.
c. Punjab does not have any specific recruitment for upper primary teachers. They are appointed for classes I to V, VI to X, and XI to XII.

Table 6.3 Take-Home Salaries of Teachers
Indian rupees

State	Primary			Secondary		
	Salary of new appointee	Salary after 15 years	Salary after 25 years	Salary of new appointee	Salary after 15 years	Salary after 25 years
Tamil Nadu	15,345	28,660	50,140	26,370	48,750	84,410
Karnataka	18,794 (R) 21,814 (U)	26,098 (R) 30,198 (U)	33,672 (R) 38,892 (U)	24,272 (R) 28,102 (U)	34,618 (R) 39,978 (U)	44,762 (R) 51,622 (U)
Jharkhand	28,650 (R) 31,600 (U)	39,780 (R) 43,260 (U)	44,400 (R) 48,100 (U)	37,494 (R) 39,208 (U)	57,523 (R) 60,160 (U)	78,637 (R) 82,247 (U)
Odisha	14,031	26,659	27,347	25,625	37,806	43,034
Rajasthan	26,013	NA	NA	28,331	NA	NA
Mizoram	16,504	NA	NA	NA	NA	NA
Uttar Pradesh	29,293	39,683	44,783	37,226	47,716	52,996
Punjab[a]	35,936 (R) 36,588 (U)	59,113 (R) 60,194 (U)	79,288 (R) 80,742 (U)	40,602 (R) 41,340 (U)	66,868 (R) 68,092 (U)	89,699 (R) 91,346 (U)

Source: State Reports on Working Conditions of Teachers in India.
Note: Take-home salary includes basic pay, grade pay, dearness allowances, House Rent Allowance, city compensatory allowances, any other benefits, and deductions. Take-home salaries for teachers might differ from district to district. The values in the table are only a generalized indicator for each state. NA = not available; R = rural; U = urban.
a. Salaries are given for Mohali district, because the salaries of teachers vary across districts.

Table 6.3 does not include information on Madhya Pradesh, because the cadre system in Madhya Pradesh is far more complicated in comparison with other states. In Madhya Pradesh, teachers are recruited as Samvida Shala Shikshak on a fixed-term contract and are paid Rs. 5,000 if they are primary school teachers and Rs. 7,000 if they are middle or high school teachers.

Table 6.4 Salary Structure of Teachers: Madhya Pradesh
Indian rupees

Cadre	Primary				Middle			
	LDT	Sahayak Adhyapak	SSS grade III	Atithi Shikshak	UDT	Adhyapak	SSS grade II	Atithi Shikshak
Salaries	5,200–20,200 +2,400 (grade pay)	4,500–25,000+ 1,250 (grade pay)	5,000	100 per day	9,300–34,800 +3,200 (grade pay)	4,500–25,000+ 1,600 (grade pay)	7,000	150 per day

Source: Madhya Pradesh State Report on Working Conditions of Teachers in India.
Note: LDT = Lower Division Teacher; SSS = Samvida Shala Shikshak; UDT = Upper Division Teacher.

After three years, if a teacher continues to be a part of the system, they receive an increment of 15 percent on the fixed amount. Although the Adhyapak Samvarg pay scales were revised substantially in February 2013, they are lower than the pay scales of regular teachers who are drawing salaries as per the Sixth Pay Commission (table 6.4). However, in the latest order by the Urban Administration and Development Department, it was announced that the salary of Adhyapak Samvarg would be at par with that of regular teachers by September 2017.

Among the nine states in the study, the data on Punjab are especially noteworthy. Although Punjab follows the Fifth Pay Commission, pay scales are equivalent to the Sixth Central Pay Commission.[2] Additionally, elementary school teachers in Punjab are among the highest paid teachers in all nine states (table 6.3), possibly because the basic pay scale is slightly higher than that of the Central Pay Commission (table 6.2). Interestingly, in some districts, like Patiala, the salaries of teachers in rural areas are marginally higher than those posted in urban areas, because teachers also receive the Rural Area Allowance (RAA) in addition to the HRA (table 6.5). However, teachers' salaries may not necessarily be higher in all rural areas, because in certain urban areas, HRA is higher than RAA+HRA (table 6.6). Despite the high salaries, Punjab continues to grapple with skewed recruitment and transfer policies and, as shared by teachers during group discussions, rent-seeking is rampant, which adds to the challenges that teachers face.

Another issue that came out in the study was that in some states (Odisha and Tamil Nadu), teachers with the same qualifications and teaching the same grades are paid differently. That is because their pay depends on the type of school (primary, upper primary, or secondary) in which they teach. In other words, the salary of a teacher who teaches grade 6 in an elementary school will be different from one who teaches the same grade but in a secondary school.

Salaries and Benefits

Table 6.5 Teachers' Salaries: Punjab
Indian rupees

	Primary (Junior Basic Training cadre)			Secondary (Master cadre)		
District/ habitation	Salary of new appointee	Salary after 15 years	Salary after 25 years	Salary of new appointee	Salary after 15 years	Salary after 25 years
Mohali urban	36,588	60,194	80,742	41,340	68,092	91,346
Mohali rural	35,936	59,113	79,288	40,602	66,868	89,699
Patiala/Rajpura urban	39,956	58,168	78,015	39,956	65,796	88,258
Patiala/Rajpura rural	40,602	59,113	79,288	40,602	66,867	89,698
Patiala/Sanaur	34,633	56,952	76,379	39,126	64,419	86,404

Source: State Council of Educational Research and Training, Punjab.

Table 6.6 Breakdown of Salaries for Two Districts in Punjab

	Junior Basic Training cadre		Master cadre		Home rent allowance (%)	Rural area allowance (%)	Dearness allowance (%)	Mobile allowance	Medical allowance
District/ habitation	Initial basic pay	Grade pay	Initial basic pay	Grade pay					
Mohali Urban	12,090	4,200	13,450	5,000	20	0	100	250 per month	500 per month
Mohali Rural					10	6	100		
Patiala/Rajpura Urban					12.5	0	100		
Patiala/ Rajpura Rural					10	6	100		
Patiala/Sanaur					8	0	100		

Source: State Council of Educational Research and Training, Punjab.
Note: Where cells are empty, it is because the data from the first row are applicable.

Salaries of Contract Teachers

In most states, government teachers reported that they are mostly happy with their salaries and other benefits. However, just like those of regular teachers, the salaries of contract teachers vary considerably across states (table 6.7). In addition, not only are contract teachers paid less than regular teachers, with no extra benefits or annual increments, the salaries of contract teachers are often delayed. An important reason is that most contract teachers are hired as part of a project (usually SSA or RMSA) or locally hired by Zillah Parishads and, hence, their salaries are mostly dependent on the availability of project funds.

Electronic Transfer of Salaries

A major change that has taken place in salary disbursement is the electronic transfer of salaries directly into the accounts of teachers (regular and contract), which has considerably reduced the delay in payment of salaries and brought in

Table 6.7 Salary of Contract Teachers in Eight States
Indian rupees

State	Teacher category	Elementary Consolidated pay	Secondary Consolidated pay
Tamil Nadu	Under SSA, part-time special teachers are hired for Arts, PET, Music, and so forth	5,000/- per month	—
Karnataka	No contract teachers	Not applicable	n.a.
Jharkhand	Contract teacher hired under SSA/JEPC	5,700/-untrained, 6,200/-trained & 6,700/-trained +TET	—
Odisha	Shiksha Sahayak (under SSA)	5,200	—
	Junior Teacher (under SSA)	7,000	—
Rajasthan	Vidhyarthi Mitra Level I (under PRI)	4,800	—
	Vidhyarthi Mitra Level II (under PRI)	4,800	—
	Vidhyarthi Mitra Secondary (under PRI)	—	5,300
Mizoram	Trained undergraduate (primary)	16,200	—
	Trained graduate (UPS/secondary)	20,568 (UPS)	20,568 (secondary)
Uttar Pradesh	Shiksha Mitra	3,500	—
	Anudeshak (UPS)	7,000	—
	IERT	19,200	—
Punjab	SSA primary	28,000	—
	SSA upper primary/RMSA	31,500	31,500

Source: State Reports on Working Conditions of Teachers in India.
Note: IERT = Inclusive Education Resource Teachers; JEPC = Jharkhand Education Project Council; PET = Physical Education Teacher; PRI = Panchayati Raj Institutions; RMSA = Rashtriya Madhyamik Shiksha Abhiyan; SSA = Sarva Shiksha Abhiyan; TET = Teacher Eligibility Test; UPS = Upper Primary Schools; — = not available.

more transparency. However, teachers in Punjab have raised serious concerns related to delay in salaries. According to them, salaries are delayed by three to six months for every cadre of teacher. Similarly, the salaries of centrally-sponsored scheme teachers in Mizoram, and SSA and Panchayati Raj Institution teachers in Rajasthan are often delayed. This is because their salaries are dependent on project funds and often there are delays in the allotment and release of funds.

Are Salaries Withheld?

Except for Karnataka and Rajasthan, in most states, salaries are not withheld for any reason. In Karnataka, although it is rare, salaries can be withheld for major and minor penalties, such as not filing income tax returns, not submitting medical certificates on time (after taking leave on medical grounds), or if there is a major complaint (including criminal cases) that has been registered against a teacher. In such cases, only half the dearness allowance is given to the teachers until the case is resolved. Similarly, in Rajasthan, the salary of a teacher can be withheld if the teacher has been absent from duty without informing the authorities or without approval of the leave. During such times, teachers receive only the monthly maintenance allowance, which is equal to half the monthly pay.

Other Monetary and Nonmonetary Benefits

A range of monetary and nonmonetary benefits is provided to regular teachers, although it varies across states (tables 6.8, 6.9, and 6.10). As is evident from table 6.8, teachers are eligible for leave in all the states, although the nature and duration of the leave varies. The main categories of leave in all the states are casual, earned, paid, half-pay, and medical. Apart from these, in some states, teachers are also entitled to privileged leave, extraordinary leave, and unpaid leave. Contract teachers are not eligible for any leave in most states. The exceptions are Tamil Nadu, Mizoram, Madhya Pradesh, and Punjab, where contract teachers are entitled to casual leave, as well. Mizoram is the only state where contract teachers are eligible for vacation and half-day leave.

Maternity leave for regular teacher is 180 days in all the states. Male teachers are entitled to15 days of paternity leave, except in Tamil Nadu where they are entitled to only one week. In comparison with regular teachers, contract teachers are entitled to leave (casual, maternity, paternity, and vacation) only in some states. Another interesting phenomenon that was observed is the availability of childcare leave for teachers. In some states, childcare leave includes leave in the case of miscarriage (Uttar Pradesh) and leave in the case of adoption (Tamil Nadu and Uttar Pradesh).

Further, regular teachers are entitled to academic leave (table 6.9), to encourage teachers to pursue higher education. For example, in Karnataka, teachers can

Table 6.8 Leave Sanctioned for Regular Teachers in the Nine States
Days

	Casual	Earned	Paid	Half pay	Medical
Tamil Nadu	12+3 restricted	17 per year or 240 in entire service	—	—	90 days for every 5 years or maximum of 540 in entire service
Karnataka	10	10	—	—	—
Jharkhand	16	14	60	Yes	—
Odisha	15	13 per year or 300 in entire service	—	180 in entire service	180 in entire service
Rajasthan	15	—	—	20	All government teachers are entitled to medical leave
Mizoram	8	No	No	20	No
Uttar Pradesh	14	—	—	20	—
Madhya Pradesh	13	—	—	—	—
Punjab	Female: 20 days, male: 10 days, up to 10 years of service; 15 days up to 15 years of service; and 20 days after 15 years of service	8	10	20	10 per year

Source: State Reports on Working Conditions of Teachers in India.
Note: — = not available.

Table 6.9 Academic Leave Available to Teachers in Selected States
State Teacher category and description of leave

Tamil Nadu	Regular: study leave to complete higher education (paid leave for a period up to 1 year)
Karnataka	Regular: study leave to complete higher education (paid leave for a period up to 4 years)
Odisha	Regular: to take the examination
Rajasthan	Regular: academic leave for participation in seminars, exams, and so forth; academic leave for higher study/degree, maximum 2 years
Mizoram	Regular: 12 months at a time and 24 months during the entire career
Uttar Pradesh	Regular: study leave for 2 years; academic leave for participation in seminars, exams, and so forth
Madhya Pradesh	Contract: leave with pay if they are enrolled in a regular course

Source: State Reports on Working Conditions of Teachers in India.

take paid leave up to four years (three years for a Bachelor of the Arts or Bachelor of Science, one year for Bachelor of Education, and two years for post-graduate course) for further study. The government also bears the real costs of their higher education (tuition and examination fees) and, on re-joining service, teachers are given a promotion based on the degree acquired, as per their service and seniority and the vacancies available. This facility (paid leave and promotion) is provided only if the teacher signs a contract to work for the government for at least 10 years after the completion of the degree. Similarly, in Tamil Nadu, teachers are given incentives (in the form of increments) to complete higher education. Madhya Pradesh is the only state where contract teachers are also eligible to take paid leave if they enroll in a regular course.

Apart from these benefits, regular teachers are eligible for allowances that include city compensatory allowances, travel and medical benefits, loans and advances, insurance, pension, special increments, awards, and so forth. (Table 6.10 provides more details.)

As is evident from table 6.10, some states give cash awards to teachers if the performance of their students has been satisfactory. There are also various district, state, and national awards for teachers in many states. Although awards and recognitions have a positive impact on the motivation of teachers, sometimes the bar may be too high (as in Rajasthan currently), as a result of which there are more awards than eligible teachers. Sometimes, the awards may favor teachers teaching subjects where students score higher marks more easily, such as mathematics.

A major issue that was flagged during this study was the issue of rent-seeking. Although various states pointed out this issue, it was most prominent in Punjab. During group discussions, teachers and even senior administrative officials shared that rent-seeking is a norm in claims such as arrears, medical claims, and even pensions.

Table 6.10 Other Benefits Available to Teachers in the Nine States

	Loan/advance	Pension/PF	Special increment	Awards
Tamil Nadu	Interest-free festival advance (Rs. 2,000); house-building advance with low interest rates (up to 25 lac); computer loans; two-wheeler and car loan of up to Rs. 2 lac; education advance to teachers' children for higher education; advance toward various diseases; TANSI advance; winter clothes purchase advance (Rs. 1,000).	CPF, PF for staff of aided schools since 1986 (maintained in same manner as state government employees); aided and local body teachers come under the Liberalized Pension Scheme.	Teachers can receive four increments in their teaching career, if they acquire higher degrees. Rs. 2,500 given to teachers who complete 25 years of flawless service.	Dr. Radhakrishnan awards for teachers who have completed 15 years of service and have produced excellent board exam results (cash award of Rs. 5,000).
Karnataka	Housing loan facility through HUDCO; interest-free vehicle loan; interest-free festival loan; KSIC and other Karnataka government cooperative discounts.	Provident savings funds.	Time bound increment after 10, 15, 20, 25...years of service; stagnation increment: additional increment on completion of 25 and 30 years of service for those teachers who have not been given a single promotion.	District and special awards to teachers through Karnataka State Teachers Benefit Fund, Rajiv Gandhi Memorial awards, district- and state-level literacy and cultural activities.
Jharkhand	Not available.	Not available.	Teachers retire at the age of 60 years with PF; gratuity and leave encashment benefits (for those recruited before January 12, 2004). For those teachers who were recruited after December 2004, contributory PF and gratuity benefits are available after retirement.	Time-bound increment (rarely paid); additional increment for 25, 30, and 35 years of service (rarely paid).
Odisha	Festival advance, depending on allotment.	Regular teachers prior to 2005 have pension; after that, there is the New Pension Scheme on contributory mode. All contractual teachers are covered under EPF.	On promotion, one additional increment.	Governor's Award and President's Award for deserving teachers.

table continues next page

Table 6.10 Other Benefits Available to Teachers in the Nine States *(continued)*

	Loan/advance	Pension/PF	Special increment	Awards
Rajasthan	Loan from Provident Fund for temporary withdrawal for medical treatment, education of children, repair of house. Amount is equal to 50% of her/his deposit in PF account or total salary of 5 months (basic salary), whichever is less. Permanent withdrawal is for house construction, higher education of children, and so forth. Employee is entitled only after completion of 15 years of service and maximum limit of withdrawal is 50% of total deposit in PF account.	There are two pension schemes, those for teachers employed prior to 2004 and those after 2004. In the former scheme, teachers were eligible after 15 years; in the latter, they are eligible upon retiring (10% of salary and DA is deducted and the same amount is contributed by the government).	Government teacher as a state employee gets relaxation in the maximum age in the recruitment process if he/she applies for other government post in the state.	62 state awards are given on Teachers' Day based on performance. Recently, the state has revised the norms for consideration for awards. Teachers' unions are demanding review of the new norms, as they feel the new norms are very stringent and a lot fewer teachers would qualify for the awards.
Mizoram	Not available.	Regular teachers have pension (converted to CPF in 2010 for new recruits only), contribution to PF.	Double increments to teachers promoted to HMs at the primary and upper primary school levels.	Not available.
Uttar Pradesh	Not available.	All teachers are covered by the state insurance scheme. Premiums against the state insurance are deducted from the salary and on accidental death of the teacher, the total policy amount is payable to the family of the teacher. Teachers who joined before April 1, 2005 come under the GPF scheme. A deduction of 10% of their basic salary is contributed to GPF every month. For those who joined service prior to 2005, (full pension on completion of 20 years); those who joined after 2005, CPF 10% of basic salary. These shares are contributed by employees and employers each and the sum accrued is managed by fund managers appointed by the government.	The Government of Uttar Pradesh has decided to absorb all 1.71 lakh Shiksha Mitras as regular teachers, which means they will receive salary at par with assistant teachers. In the first phase, 58,826 Shiksha Mitras have already been absorbed as assistant teachers after completing the BTC course through distance mode. A second batch of 64,000 teachers was undergoing the BTC program, again through distance mode. They were expected to join service by the end of 2014 or early 2015. The final batch of 46,000 teachers were set to begin their BTC.	Not available.

table continues next page

Table 6.10 Other Benefits Available to Teachers in the Nine States *(continued)*

	Loan/advance	Pension/PF	Special increment	Awards
Madhya Pradesh	Loan and medical insurance for Shikshak and Adhyapaks.	Adhyapaks are also eligible for gratuity and the government has instituted a new pension scheme for them. Adhyapak recruited after 2011 come under the contributory pension scheme (not clear whether it will be monthly payment or lump sum amount). Shikshak Samvarg get regular pension as other government employees. SSS do not receive a pension.	The Adhyapak and Shikshak cadres get two advance increments for family planning operations after one child and one advance increment after a family planning operation after two children. The Samvida Samvarg is on a fixed salary for the period of three years. If the period is extended for another three years, a one-time 15% increase is given for the next period of three years.	Not available.
Punjab	Loan can be taken from GPF refundable and nonrefundable.	Full pension after completion of 25 years of service.		State award may be applied after completing five years of service. National award may be applied after completion of 15 years of service by normal teachers but the condition of 15 years is relaxed by five years for teachers teaching in remote / rural areas

Source: State Reports on Working Conditions of Teachers in India.

Note: BTC = Basic Teaching Certificate; CPF = Contributory Provident Fund; DA = Dearness Allowance; EPF = Employees Provident Fund; GPF = General Provident Fund; PF = Provident Fund; HM = headmaster; HUDCO = Housing and Urban Development Corporation; KSIC = Karnataka Silk Industries Corporation; TANSI = Tamil Nadu Small Industries Corporation.

Conclusion

To achieve universal elementary education, the Kothari Commission (1966) reported that India should invest 6 percent of its income in education. Current figures show that India spends around 3 percent of its GDP on education (table 6.11). According to the latest report by Accountability Initiatives (Dongre, Kapur, and Tewary 2014), expenditure on education is only about 2.5 percent of GDP, of which 1.75 percent comes from public expenditure and the rest from private expenditure. More developed economies, such as China and Singapore, also spend a similar percentage of their GDP on education (Jain and Dholakia 2009); however, a big difference is that both China and Singapore have been able to achieve universal education, while India continues to struggle.

Many reports have indicated that more than 80 percent of the education budget is spent on salaries. It is well-documented that teachers in India receive higher salaries compared with teachers in other countries (De and Endow 2008; Jain 2009; Kingdon 2010; Dongre, Kapur, and Tewary 2014). In India, teachers' salaries constitute a major proportion of education expenditure by state. For example, Rajasthan spends nearly 88 percent of its education budget on teachers' salaries, and in Madhya Pradesh it is close to 75 percent. Expenditure on school infrastructure is 5 and 11 percent in Rajasthan and Madhya Pradesh, respectively, which leaves very little money for other inputs to improve the quality of education.

Furthermore, in the past decade, regular teachers' salaries have increased by more than 100 percent in some states. For example, Kingdon (2010) finds that after the implementation of the Sixth Pay Commission, the salaries of regular primary school teachers in Uttar Pradesh increased by 115 percent; by 101 percent for high school teachers, and by 103 percent for senior secondary school principals. Likewise, Jain and Dholakia (2009) calculated that the increase in salaries was close to 285 percent in 2006 and was further increased by 200 percent in 2011. According to some reports, government teachers enjoy higher pay grades than non-teaching occupations in India (Kingdon 2010; World Bank 2014).

Table 6.11 Government Expenditure on Education, Selected Countries
Percent of gross domestic product

Country	2007	2008	2009	2010	2011	2012
Bangladesh	2.56	2.39	2.23	—	—	—
Cambodia	1.60	—	—	2.60	—	—
Hong Kong SAR, China	3.45	3.26	4.39	3.51	3.42	3.51
India	—	—	3.21	3.32	3.85	3.79
Indonesia	3.04	2.90	3.53	2.99	—	3.57
Malaysia	4.37	3.96	5.97	5.12	5.94	—
Nepal	3.52	3.81	4.66	4.72	—	—
Philippines	2.60	2.69	2.65	—	—	—
Singapore	—	2.78	3.03	3.11	3.07	3.13

Source: http://data.uis.unesco.org/. (Data extracted May 14, 2015.)
Note: — = not available.

One consequence of these large increases in teacher salaries is an increasing social and economic distance between teachers and students, especially in rural areas. Most teachers belong to upper social groups, while students studying in government schools usually come from socially and economically backward groups. In India, on average, a teacher earns five times more than the average per capita income, and this ratio is higher than the national average in some states. It is quite possible that when teachers belong to upper social groups and are more affluent than students, it can result in prejudices toward students. In addition, a significant percentage of teachers are absent and/or engaged in non-teaching activities (World Bank 2009; Muralidharan et al. 2014), which further adds to the fiscal burden.

Notes

1. This study was done in nine states of India: Jharkhand, Karnataka, Madhya Pradesh, Mizoram, Odisha, Punjab, Rajasthan, Tamil Nadu, and Uttar Pradesh. Detailed State Reports are available at: http://www.nuepa.org/New/completed%20reaserches.aspx.
2. Punjab, in the present form, came into being after the trifurcation of the larger Punjab into three states in 1965. Therefore, the first pay commission of Punjab was constituted in 1966. Hence, Punjab's First Pay Commission corresponds to the Second Pay Commission of the center.

CHAPTER 7

Teachers in School

Roles and Responsibilities: Day-to-Day Management

This chapter discusses three aspects of the working conditions of teachers in schools, which have a direct bearing on how teachers feel about their work. First, the chapter looks at the roles and responsibilities of teachers as prescribed and practiced, how teachers become aware of the same, and how teachers are given feedback and support. Second, the chapter examines the challenges faced by teachers in schools. Finally, the chapter investigates issues faced by school leaders and their relationship with teachers.

Roles and Responsibilities of Teachers

The terms "teacher" and "teaching" invoke a classroom full of students who are being taught. However, the role of a teacher, especially that of a government teacher, is far more diverse. According to section 24 of the Right to Education (RTE) Act, all teachers should perform the following duties:

- Maintain regularity and punctuality in attending school.
- Conduct and complete the curriculum.
- Complete the entire curriculum within a specified time.
- Assess the learning ability of each child and, accordingly, provide additional instructions, as required.
- Hold regular meetings with parents and guardians and apprise them of the regularity in attendance, ability to learn, progress made in learning, and any other relevant information about their child.
- Perform other such duties as may be prescribed.

Most state governments have incorporated the RTE provisions into their own rules and regulations and, therefore, these duties are applicable for all teachers in government elementary schools. However, translating these duties into practice in spirit is a challenge that is yet to be addressed fully in almost all the states. Figure 7.1 depicts the diversity of teacher roles as it plays out in practice in Karnataka.

Figure 7.1 Roles and Duties of Teachers: Karnataka

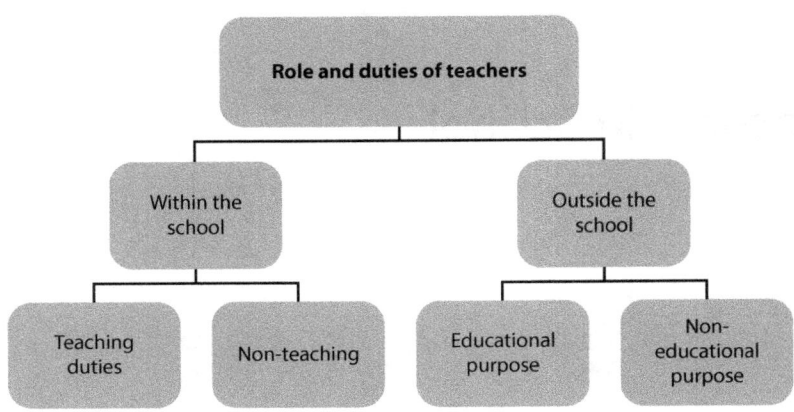

Sources: Centre for Budget and Policy Studies, Bangalore 2014 (http://www.nuepa.org/New/completed%20reaserches.aspx); Karnataka State Report.

Teaching comprises various facets, including planning and preparation, classroom activities, assessment, and reporting. In addition, the National Curriculum Framework (NCF) 2005 visualizes active engagement with parents as one of the important roles of a teacher. Almost all states assign these responsibilities to teachers, with emphasis on "maintaining results." There is a spectrum of the degree of detail different states have gone into while assigning such responsibilities. At one extreme is Tamil Nadu, which has specified the daily and weekly schedule of government elementary school teachers in the state. Then there are states like Rajasthan, which have a broad definition of teacher roles. For example, the job charts specify the following duties for grade II teachers (source: State Reports):

1. Maintain the results of classes VIII and X in consonance with the overall results (more than minimum 30 percent).
2. Organize a minimum of two co-curricular activities each year.
3. Participate in a training, orientation, creative writing, or professional enhancement activity once a year.
4. Participate in school administration activities, class teacher, work-in-charge, examination-in-charge, subject-in-charge, and so forth, and take responsibility for a minimum of one activity.
5. Prepare question papers, evaluate answer books, conduct practical exams, and so forth.
6. Facilitate inspection by the District Institute of Educational Training lecturer once every three months.

Finally, there are states like Mizoram, where no job charts seem to exist. In the absence of a job chart, it is left to the teachers and officers to define the roles of the teachers on a day-to-day basis. Naturally, this leads to a vague definition of the roles (source: State Report).

Karnataka, perhaps, has the most balanced and comprehensive definition of teacher roles. In a series of notifications published during 2014, teaching duties were defined as follows (source: State Reports):

1. Framing the weekly timetable for the class
2. Ensuring that all students have the relevant textbooks (provided by the government)
3. Preparing lesson plans as per the timetable
4. Explaining topics and chapters using simple teaching and learning materials
5. Maintaining student-related records (socioeconomic profile of students, parent-related information, attendance, and academic (Continuous and Comprehensive Evaluation (CCE)) records)
6. Providing remedial classes for slow learners
7. Conducting and assessing tests.

Non-Teaching Functions

The *non-teaching functions within schools* include providing administrative support, organizing events, managing midday meals, managing construction, collecting and maintaining data on students, facilitating visits of officials, and distributing uniforms, books, and so forth. Typically, these are functions of the headmaster, but, given that in most states support staff have not been appointed in government schools, it is natural that the headmasters turn to teachers. Some of these tasks are quite sensitive, as they involve managing large sums of money, supervising other workers, and maintaining multiple records.

Teachers are also involved in various *functions outside the school* that may be classified into educational and noneducational. Training programs; attachment with Cluster Resource Centers (CRCs), Block Resource Centers (BRCs), and the District Education Officer's (DEOs) office; curriculum development; marking board examination answer sheets; and so forth are some of the educational engagements of teachers outside the schools. At one level, these tasks augment the capacities of teachers and may lead to their growth. At the same time, these tasks are likely to divert teachers' attention from the pupils at their school.

Noneducational responsibilities outside school are perhaps the most talked about. Teachers have been involved in the census, elections, and disaster management, and continue to be. For some time, the diversity of such tasks had become quite alarming and teachers were being used for tasks such as migration surveys, livestock surveys, family planning targets, and immunization.

Teachers informed us (in discussions conducted in the nine states) that after RTE 2009, their nonteaching duties have been streamlined and clearly specified. However, we did not come across any government order or notification to this effect. In Tamil Nadu, the teachers informed us that in addition to elections and census-related duties, they also distribute textbooks and uniforms. These are viewed as "educational/school-related tasks." As these materials do not come in one go, this work carries on for several months. Equally, teachers in several states said that they have to go to the block office to collect the textbooks and uniforms.

In Mizoram, the teachers particularly mentioned the midday meal (MDM) program, and said that they receive little administrative support when they must go outside the school to purchase items or organize fuelwood.

In Jharkhand, since the RTE, apart from the mandated duties like the census, survey of out-of-school children, and elections, teachers are not assigned any other duties outside the school. However, this is not true for all the states. During one focus group discussion (FGD) with teachers in Odisha, they reported that:

> Non-teaching duties (post-RTE) has reduced on paper, but not so on the ground. Work related to civil works and MDM are quite excessive... The Headmaster/Headmistress has the responsibility of procuring and maintaining bill vouchers in this regard. It is, of course, a regular practice that the HM cannot/does not alone do it and he/she involves other teachers also. Experience shows that MDM is quite a sensitive issue and there are many registers such as Cash Book, Daily Expenditure Record, Bill Vouchers, Purchase Register, Stock Register, *Janch* (Verification) Register to be maintained by them. The present per student budget allocation for MDM was Rs. 3.79 for primary and Rs. 5.65 for upper primary that have recently been increased to Rs. 4.03 and Rs. 6.04 excluding rice. This is insufficient to maintain prescribed quality of MDM. Moreover, the factors such as maintaining equation with the Self-Help Group/SMC, arranging firewood etc. are quite cumbersome affairs and this really puts the teachers on the back foot... when the supervising officials come their monitoring and supervision remain confined mostly to MDM and civil work. They verify bills, vouchers, record, quality etc. and do not bother/find time to monitor academic aspects of the school. (Odisha State Report)

The Karnataka State Report has compiled statistics from the Unified District Information System for Education to demonstrate this point, as shown in table 7.1.

In Madhya Pradesh, it was reported that a window has been kept open for utilizing the services of teachers for other purposes, albeit with the consent of the education department. At the field level, however, there are reports where

Table 7.1 Percentage of Teachers Involved in Non-Teaching Assignments in Elementary Schools in Karnataka, 2009–10 to 2012–13

Teachers	2009–10	2010–11	2011–12	2012–13
Number involved in non-teaching assignments	20,514	35,738	34,096	4,974
Total number	280,282	297,502	387,130	306,117
Percentage involved in non-teaching assignments	7.32	12.01	8.81	1.62

Source: Compiled from Unified District Information System for Education data for 2009–10, 2010–11, 2011–12, and 2012–13.

teachers continue to be deployed beyond the tasks stipulated in the RTE. Such deployment is sometimes at the behest of teachers as well, as this allows them to be located at their preferred location (Madhya Pradesh State Report).

According to a recent study on teachers' time-on-task, conducted by the World Bank in three states of India—Andhra Pradesh, Madhya Pradesh, and Uttar Pradesh—actual teaching time is only 81 to 87 percent of 223 to 231 school-calendar days (Sankar and Linden 2014). The balance of the time is spent on various non-teaching and non-school tasks. The study goes a step further and explores whether teaching-time is spent on student-centric activities or otherwise, through classroom observations. Of all the teaching-time observed, only 24 percent was deemed to be student-centric. This finding is not surprising for anyone who has observed government schools in India, where teachers and the education system have not internalized NCF 2005 in spirit.

In addition, the diversity of roles—*learning facilitator versus school administrator versus civil servant versus community mobilizer*—creates a *suboptimal identity* where the teacher experiences conflict between the different roles that he/she is expected to play. Naturally, this has a negative impact on teaching. It also affects accountability for the learning outcomes of students.

Support, Feedback, or Inspection?

The *inspection, feedback, and support* systems in most states were found to be dysfunctional. Teachers and administrators said that the number of schools has expanded rapidly over the past two decades. For example, in Uttar Pradesh, the number of schools has more than doubled since 2000; however, the inspection and support system has not grown proportionately. Although there are no hard data on the ratio of administrators to teachers, in several states, the District and Block Education Officers we interviewed mentioned this as a serious issue. For example, in Lunglei District of Mizoram, the officers said that the staffing patterns of the district and block offices have not changed in the past 20 years, although the number of teachers has increased and so has the range of administrative duties that must be performed. The attempt made through the Sarva Shiksha Abhiyan, to create CRCs and Block Resource Centers has not worked. This was because appropriate staff could not be placed at these centers, or the short-sightedness of senior officers led to loading the centers with administrative work. Consequently, many schools are never visited (table 7.2). Only a few schools are visited regularly; invariably these are easily accessible "model" schools of some sort. As table 7.2 shows, 49 percent of schools across the country were not inspected at all in 2011–12, and 32 percent were not visited by CRCs.

Even the schools visited by the officers or CRCs are not provided feedback or given academic inputs. Most of the time is consumed in completing administrative formalities or, worse, fault-finding. This situation has been persisting for years and the government has made limited efforts to address it. This unintentional *laissez-faire* kind of autonomy given to teachers by the government not only

Table 7.2 Schools Visited by CRC and Inspected, 2011–12

State	Percentage of schools visited by CRC coordinators	Percentage of schools inspected
Jharkhand	79	45
Karnataka	96	44
Madhya Pradesh	71	54
Mizoram	90	51
Odisha	78	42
Punjab	32	28
Rajasthan	54	61
Tamil Nadu	86	67
Uttar Pradesh	52	40
All India	68	51

Source: Elementary Education in India, District Information System for Education Analytical Tables 2012–13.
Note: CRC = Cluster Resource Center.

contributes to making the schools ineffective, it also makes it convenient to place the blame on the teacher as and when some issue comes to light. Equally, teachers find it easy to deflect the onus onto the system or administration.

Although some states mentioned "maintaining results" as one of the teachers' responsibilities (for example, Tamil Nadu and Rajasthan), even when that is the case, the system places very *low expectations* on the teachers. If teachers can show that all the chapters given in the syllabus for the year have been "taught," that is considered sufficient toward completion of their primary responsibilities. The teacher is allowed to explain poor learning and development of the student by citing various constraints, the biggest being the students and their backgrounds. No value is given to commitment and innovation. Although autonomy is conceptualized in the policy documents as an important element of professionalism, teachers rarely express the need for or consider that they lack autonomy.

Accountability

A related issue is the *lack of a sense of accountability* among teachers. Teacher absenteeism is a fairly common complaint of the government and community against teachers. This has been confirmed by research as well, namely, Kingdon and Muzzammil (2008), PROBE (1999, 2011), Dreze and Gazdar (1996), and Sharma and Ramachandran (2009). The Ministry of Human Resource Development (MHRD) commissioned a study on students' and teachers' attendance in primary and upper schools across the major states of the country (Government of India, MHRD, and SSA 2009). The study found that the average attendance of primary and upper primary teachers in 2006–07 was 81.7 percent and 80.5 percent, respectively. The attendance system of most states is weak, and the states do not have data on teachers' attendance. Lack of data also means that little action can be taken; even where data are made available through independent surveys and studies, there is serious lack of administrative and political will to address this issue.

Another alarming problem that was reported by two states in the study (Uttar Pradesh and Mizoram) is "proxy teachers," whereby a teacher appointed by the government illegally "appoints" another person to work in her/his place for some consideration. The teacher uses this opportunity to take up another occupation or for some personal reasons, like house construction. Proxy teachers are more common in remote and rural areas, but this practice is also found in urban areas despite the proximity of government offices and officials. The extent of the practice of proxy teachers could not be determined during the preparation of this study, but it was openly discussed during FGDs.

Such practices of teachers are possible because of the *absence of effective monitoring and low probability of disciplinary action*. Teachers find a way to get around whatever limited monitoring is done. All state governments have provisions for disciplinary action, but it becomes very difficult to indict a teacher and take any serious action. A different interpretation of rules, pressure from teachers' unions, humanitarian reasons, and so forth are all invoked when a situation of dereliction of duty or misconduct comes to light. The officer or committee considering the case tends to consider the political affiliations of the teacher, status of vacancies in the school, and so forth while taking the decision. Almost all officers at the district and block levels who were interviewed during the study cited such instances, on the condition of anonymity. As discussed in chapter 5, on teacher deployment, the provision of transfer for disciplinary action is rarely invoked. More often than not, the teacher is able to get away. Every such instance further encourages teachers to be errant. At the same time, it was also reported during FGDs with teachers and teachers' unions that *officers could misuse their powers* to harass certain teachers. Some cases were reported in Uttar Pradesh and Rajasthan, although most such cases do not come to public notice, as the teachers are afraid to rake the issue further. This is one area where it is difficult to find "hard evidence."

Induction and Orientation

Teachers are expected to learn their roles and responsibilities on the job, as *induction or orientation programs* are not a regular feature in any of the states. Although all the positions seem to have a "probationary" period of two years, after which the teacher is to be confirmed, in practice, this has no relevance. The officials and the teachers are unable to state any difference between what happens or is expected from the teacher during the probationary period and otherwise. Madhya Pradesh has taken the idea of probation to another level, by converting the initial three years of service into contractual appointment. By doing this, the state has kept open the option of taking severe action against teachers, which could act as a deterrent for otherwise errant teachers and force them to focus on their responsibilities. The study could not obtain adequate evidence to explore this issue further.

Challenges Faced in Discharging Roles and Responsibilities

Responsibilities without Capacity Building and Adequate Support

Typically, the system engages with an issue early in the launch of the new intervention and then expects the teachers to take it forward regardless of whether they have been adequately empowered to do so. The implementation of continuous and comprehensive evaluation (CCE) is a clear example of this. In most states, CCE processes have been spelled out only partially and teachers often complain about the inadequate orientation and capacity building on the issue. Another interesting issue that came to light in Mizoram was that of the conversion of a government school from Mizo language to English medium following demand from the community. To the credit of the state government, it has instituted a system of screening where the State Council of Educational Research and Training assesses the English capabilities of the teachers of the applicant school and recommends whether the school should be converted. Notwithstanding the subversion of the screening process that was reported in some cases, the teachers of the converted school are expected to teach the entire syllabus of all the subjects in English, with no capacity building or support from any quarter.

Lack of Infrastructure and Teaching Aids

The status of school infrastructure in India has improved significantly, including in states that have started quite late. Yet, when measured against what would be desirable, a lot more needs to be done.

As table 7.3 demonstrates, many schools lack basic facilities like electricity, libraries, and playgrounds. Despite the emphasis ostensibly placed on information and communications technology, many schools do not have computers, even in the southern states like Karnataka and Tamil Nadu. A similar situation prevails in secondary schools, as discussed in chapter 2. Teachers in such schools must surmount these challenges while attempting to help young children learn and grow.

Table 7.3 Lack of Infrastructure Facilities, 2012–13

Facilities lacking in schools	Percentage of schools in states								
	JH	KN	MP	MZ	OD	PJ	RJ	TN	UP
Drinking water facilities	10	5	5	11	6	1	7	2	3
Girls' toilets	17	1	8	3	32	5	3	5	3
Boys' toilets	40	4	28	76	79	21	23	38	5
Electricity connection	89	4	77	51	77	1	52	4	62
Computers	92	72	88	73	91	50	78	47	90
Libraries	23	4	40	64	24	14	43	5	27
Playgrounds	69	38	44	51	71	19	52	25	27

Source: Drawn from Elementary Education in India, District Information System for Education Analytical Tables 2012–13.
Note: JH = Jharkhand; KA = Karnataka; MP = Madhya Pradesh; MZ = Mizoram; OR = Odisha; PB = Punjab; RJ = Rajasthan; TN = Tamil Nadu; UP = Uttar Pradesh.

It was observed and reported during FGDs that working spaces and furniture for teachers inside or outside the class are virtually nonexistent. There is no monitoring mechanism for such indicators and the District Information System for Education does not capture the availability of furniture and other teacher-specific facilities. Teachers who are posted in remote areas or where the habitations are very small often struggle to find a decent place to stay in such locations and are, consequently, forced to undertake long and arduous journeys. Given that many schools are located in rural areas, which lack basic as well as aspirational amenities, teachers feel frustrated about living and managing their families in such areas.

Teacher Vacancies

Teacher vacancies continue to plague the system, putting undue pressure and responsibilities on the teachers. Although state governments have been giving a lot of attention to recruitment in the past few years, motivated by the RTE, and state-level pupil-teacher ratios have improved substantially, a school-level analysis reveals that the problem is yet to be solved. This situation is discussed at length in chapter 2 of this report. The creation of new posts and recruitment are long and cumbersome processes influenced greatly by the willingness of the leaders of the state and the financial situation of the state government (discussed in chapter 3). Further, state governments find it difficult to rationalize teachers across districts and regions (discussed in chapter 4). It is common to find stark differences in the pupil-teacher ratios between urban and rural schools, since most teachers wish to be located in urban areas. As a result, teachers in deficit schools are forced to take on the responsibilities of the vacant positions. Although many teachers reportedly make spirited and praiseworthy efforts, these are likely to be suboptimal.

Multi-Grade Teaching[1]

Primary school teachers often find themselves in a multi-grade situation, due to the lack of adequate teachers, an inadequate number of students in different grades, or inadequate classrooms in the school. As noted in chapter 2, approximately 42 percent of government elementary schools have only one or two teachers for the elementary grades. However, the teachers are not equipped to conduct multi-grade teaching effectively, despite clear policy directives at the national level. NCF 2005 suggests that teachers must undertake much more careful class and lesson planning when working in such scenarios. However, the entire teacher education process still treats the multi-grade situation as an anomaly. A research monograph by Blum and Diwan (2007) cites a teacher educator from Delhi as stating:

> Multi-grade has a really negative reputation in India. In many places, both urban and rural, that I have visited, schools have big classes of 80 or more students in each grade. The teachers receive some discussion about how to manage multi-grade, but it is really theoretical and it doesn't address all the different situations that teachers may face in their postings…

The same monograph also cites a leading National Council of Educational Research and Training (NCERT) policy maker:

> There is a general confusion about multi-grade in India. Is it a quality improvement measure—in which case you need skilled teachers working in small schools—or is it just an attempt to make the best of the bad situation, which many schools are currently in?

Therefore, it is not surprising to find that most teachers see multi-grade teaching as an impediment, which further complicates the issue. A few state governments—Karnataka and Tamil Nadu (through ABL) and Rajasthan (through Lehar Programme)—have taken proactive measures to support teachers in multi-grade situations. In general, however, teachers do not see this positively.

Continuous Comprehensive Evaluation

CCE has emerged as a big challenge for teachers and the education system alike. Teachers in the nine states talked about the bane of CCE. Notwithstanding that several states have conducted orientation and training programs for teachers on CCE, teachers and administrators opined that, given the existing pedagogic practices in India, the concepts of "comprehensiveness" and "continuity" in evaluation are difficult to comprehend. Consequently, the effort to transplant CCE into the traditional pattern of education has not met with success—except in pilot projects where the government, nongovernmental organization, or United Nations Children's Fund partners have worked with teachers to develop the formats for CCE.

The teachers see CCE as something that has increased their workload significantly in terms of checking of examination papers and assignments and maintaining different records pertaining to students. There is a strong feeling among teachers that the abolition of examinations (in elementary education) and their replacement by CCE has resulted in poor student and teacher performance. This idea is contested by government officials, especially MHRD and its academic counterpart, NCERT. As so far there has been no study or evaluation of the implementation of the CCE system in India, it is premature to make any definitive statement on CCE.

Mismatch between Curriculum and Students' Abilities

As has been widely reported, teachers are often faced with the situation where the students are unable to engage with the curriculum prescribed for a certain grade (World Bank 2014). This happens because the students lack the prior knowledge or experience that has been assumed by the curriculum formulators. Often, basic language and numeracy skills are missing in upper primary classes. In such a situation, teachers, quite naturally, blame the students and their background, the teachers of previous classes, and the education system, which has allowed students to move up the grades without acquiring the necessary skills. The problem is further exacerbated for students who are absent for long periods due to seasonal migration or health reasons. Ten years of the Annual Status of

Education Report Survey (2005–14) have repeatedly pointed out that over 50 percent of children in class V are not able to negotiate a class II text for reading or simple arithmetic (ASER 2005–2014). A recent study commissioned by MHRD, on inclusion and exclusion of children in schools and classrooms, captured the prevalent attitudes of teachers toward children from disadvantaged and marginalized social groups (Ramachandran, Naorem, and State Research Teams 2012).

Although it may be argued that teachers should expect to encounter such situations and be able to ensure student learning, this is obviously not a happy situation for a teacher. The concepts of bridge courses or remedial teaching exist in the system to address such problems; however, these have not proven to be effective. Teacher development processes do not address this issue. In this unfortunate situation, it is the students who often bear the brunt of the frustration of the teacher, because dissatisfied teachers are not good teachers.

Single-Teacher Schools

Single-teacher schools continue to be present in the system. This is especially true for remote, rural areas, as most teachers do not want to be posted in such areas. In such schools, teachers and students struggle to meet the multiple responsibilities of running the schools. Teachers must teach multiple grades simultaneously without adequate empowerment for the same. Every time the teacher is called for any responsibility outside the school, the school practically shuts down for the day/s. Making up for lost time is very difficult in such schools.

Midday Meals

Despite RTE provisions and subsequent notifications by the state government as well as an order from the Supreme Court on not giving teachers the responsibility of managing the midday meal, headmasters and teachers continue to be given this responsibility. This involves multiple challenges: ensuring rations are available on time and there is a functional cooking space available on a daily basis, managing the cooking staff, ensuring hygiene, ensuring all students receive at least the stipulated quantity, maintaining records, managing the funds flow situation, facilitating audits, and so on. Naturally, this takes significant time and energy away from teaching functions. It is also a sensitive responsibility, as demonstrated by some recent unfortunate incidents, like the Chhapra, Bihar, school meal poisoning on July 16, 2013; Bangalore, Karnataka on September 21, 2014; and Naiveli, Tamil Nadu, on July 18, 2013. This adds to the frustration that many teachers undergo.

Some states have reported good practices in this area, where self-help groups, formed under various departments, have been given the responsibility to provide the meals. This has eased the pressure on the headmasters and teachers.

Construction

Construction is another area in which teachers must struggle. It is quite common to find ongoing construction activities in the schools for expanding or repairing the infrastructure. These activities must be supervised and managed by the headmaster and teachers. Like midday meals, this too is a sensitive issue where the teachers have to handle materials, money, construction workers, and records.

Implications of the RTE Provisions

Most teachers have yet to come to terms with several provisions stipulated by the RTE, like "no detention" and "no corporal punishment." Teachers in the nine states said that such provisions have impinged on their professional rights and have made their tasks more difficult. Although teachers have cut down on corporal punishment, it is more out of compulsion than any real belief in the concept. Teachers and senior officials critiqued the no-detention policy; they said that this takes away the imperative of students to study. Although teachers recognize the principle behind the concept, they continue to feel the need for the possibility of retaining a student in a class if her/his learning level is inappropriate. The teachers have not been empowered to see these clauses in the light of the larger transformation that is being attempted through the RTE.

Management of School Management Committees

Various instruments and institutional forms have been used to facilitate the involvement of parents and communities around schools and their functioning, with the aim to build ownership as well as strengthen school accountability. The RTE has put a legal stamp on this issue with the provision that each school has a School Management Committee (SMC), with the mandate to manage all aspects of the school. The RTE has also specified that parents of children studying in a given school will form at least 75 percent of the SMC. The school system is coming to terms with this shift in power from the headmasters and officials to the parents and community. A recent National University of Educational Planning and Administration study (Singh 2011), which explored the status of school-level management committees in 14 states, reported that the headmasters continue to direct and control the committees. However, during discussions with teachers and headmasters, it emerged that in some places, the community has started asserting itself in civil works and school functioning.

During discussions conducted for this study, some teachers also talked about interference and harassment at the hands of SMC members. Although we do not have hard evidence to back this claim, and because the research tools did not specifically explore this issue, it is difficult to make any general statement on the relationship between teachers and the community. Looking at this objectively, not all of what is reported as interference would be undesirable. That was the whole reason such provisions were introduced in the first place. What needs to be done, however, is to build the capacities of teachers and headmasters to engage with SMCs and communities in a meaningful way, academically and administratively, and build the capacity of SMCs to contribute effectively (Dundar et al. 2014). School development planning presents an opportunity where the teachers and the community could be brought together effectively.

Roles of Contract/Para Teachers

Many contract/para teachers have been introduced in the education system over the past two decades. In several states, they are underqualified and low-paid, with their primary responsibility being to support regular teachers or undertake specific tasks. The introduction of contract/para teachers has allowed governments to bolster teacher strength without having to wait for augmenting teacher education capabilities, at a much lower cost. Such was the attractiveness of this mechanism that slowly the same state governments reduced regular appointments and started recruiting more and more contract/para teachers. Since contract/para teachers were contractual and, therefore, less prone to protest (in theory), the responsibilities of the non-regular teachers were enhanced by the headmasters and officials much beyond their initial brief. It came to a pass where contract/para teachers were performing the same duties as regular teachers, with much less pay. This led contract/para teachers to organize themselves and seek better salaries and regular status, which has been successful in many states. The presence of underqualified persons as teachers confused regular teachers and the society, and convoluted teacher management norms.

Roles and Challenges of School Leaders

Teachers look to school leaders for direction on the routine functions of the school, and to school leadership as an important growth avenue. However, the policy and practice of school leadership leaves a lot to be desired on both counts. Generally, school leadership is more defined at secondary schools than at elementary schools; primary schools are the worst off. In the states covered by the study, only Tamil Nadu seems to have empowered the institution of school leadership reasonably. Some of the key aspects of school leadership that came to light during the study are described in the following subsections.

Large Number of Vacancies

Without exception, all the states in the study have significant numbers of vacancies for the positions of headmasters and head teachers. As table 7.4 shows, Rajasthan has the least number of vacancies at the primary and upper primary levels. The maximum number of vacancies are in states like Jharkhand, Karnataka, and Madhya Pradesh. These vacancies have been computed only for schools that have a minimum enrollment of 150 for primary and 100 for upper primary.[2] If schools with lower enrollments are included, the vacancy percentage is likely to be even worse.

Such high levels of vacancies clearly indicate that governments have not taken this position seriously. A senior teacher is usually given the charge of a school and this arrangement continues for years. Sometimes, such vacancies arise due to inadequate feeder cadre, but many times, it can be attributed to administrative neglect and apathy. Often, positions are not created, recruitments and promotions are not done on time, and minor issues of seniority are allowed to escalate

Table 7.4 Vacancies in Headmaster and Head Teacher Positions

	Vacancies in headmaster and head teacher positions in elementary schools (%)	
State	Primary enrollment > 150	Upper primary enrollment > 100
Jharkhand	82	81
Karnataka	80	50
Madhya Pradesh	70	56
Mizoram	49	26
Odisha	67	71
Punjab	51	56
Rajasthan	16	20
Tamil Nadu	28	50
Uttar Pradesh	48	27
All India	45	46

Source: Drawn from Elementary Education in India, District Information System for Education Analytical Tables 2012–13.

into court cases that linger for years. In schools that do not have a regular full-time headmaster, not much can be expected from the leadership institution.

Limited Powers

In schools where there is a headmaster, the individual is constrained by the limited powers devolved to her/him. School leaders are delegated certain powers, such as granting leave, assigning responsibilities to teachers, and so forth. School leaders have few financial powers.

Inadequate Incentives, No Separate Cadre

Several instances were reported from states like Mizoram and Uttar Pradesh where eligible teachers preferred not to be promoted to the position of headmaster. Such teachers feel that the incentives, if any, were too little for the large additional responsibilities and workload of a headmaster. Most states do not have a separate cadre for headmasters, at least at the elementary level. Apart from the salary and other service conditions that a cadre usually defines and enhances, it also helps in creating a distinct identity that is essential for performing the duties effectively. At the same time, it could also be argued that having separate cadres has its problems, since school leaders should have had some teaching experience as well.

A recent study in Rajasthan reveals that women teachers were hesitant to take on the function of headmistress or head teacher, as that involved many hours of administrative work, financial responsibilities, political pressures, and related problems of dealing with men at different levels of society. And there is an unwritten practice in Rajasthan of not posting women as headmistresses in co-educational schools (Jandhyala and ERU Research Team 2014). This trend has imposed severe restrictions on the professional growth of women teachers and aggravated the overall shortage of teachers willing to assume additional administrative responsibilities.

Expanded Managerial Roles

Maintaining the student, financial, and administrative records of the school; periodic and nonperiodic reporting; and liaising with their nodal department are some of the tasks that headmasters have always carried out. For the past decade and a half, activities like midday meals and construction of buildings have emerged as major time-consuming activities for headmasters. All of this obviously leaves little time for academic support and supervision. This problem is further compounded because most primary and elementary schools do not have administrative, accounting, or support staff. This issue was reported by several states, including Karnataka, Mizoram, Jharkhand, and Rajasthan.

Neglected Academic Role of School Leaders

Apart from the time constraint, the system does not really expect the headmasters to play an academic role. If the headmaster can maintain records, submit reports, and provide utilization certificates, the system deems him or her to be an efficient headmaster. Real accountability for students' learning is not enforced on the headmaster. Tamil Nadu and Rajasthan appear to be the exceptions in this case. In Rajasthan, a few headmasters were reportedly suspended because of the poor results of their schools.

Inadequate Investments in Building Capacities

Karnataka (Azim Premji Foundation supported Educational Leadership and Management program), Tamil Nadu (UK-India Education and Research Initiative for secondary school teachers and headmasters), and the Central Square Foundation-supported India School Leadership Institute reported new initiatives to build the capacities of school leaders. In addition, in both these states, teachers receive paid leave to acquire higher qualifications. A certain percentage of headmaster positions is set aside for teachers who have upgraded their qualifications (see chapter 8 on professional growth). In other states, some capacity-building initiatives have been reported from time to time, but, in general, headmasters are left to learn the ropes on their own. Most states do not even conduct an orientation or induction program for headmasters on their roles and the expectations from them.

Summing Up

The Indian reality is quite unique—teachers are expected to play a diverse role in the school, in the classroom, and in the community. Although the RTE has certainly emphasized the teaching function of teachers, a lot more needs to be done to define the roles and responsibilities of teachers and insulate them from tasks that divert them from their primary responsibility of teaching. Support and supervision are effectively two sides of the same coin. But the hard reality is that teachers in Indian schools are neither supported nor supervised, thereby affecting the effectiveness of the schooling system. It may be fair to say that the learning crisis today could, among other reasons, be attributed to this ambiguity. Equally, this could also be one of the factors that contribute to the lack of accountability of teachers.

Notes

1. During a presentation of this research to MHRD, the Secretary stated that the "government has spent a lot of funds on multi-grade and CCE training. Therefore, the teachers' claim, that multi-grade related training is insufficient, is not correct. This report should highlight the funds that have been spent on training and how many teachers have attended multi-grade training…" We tried to access information on multi-grade training done in the nine states. With the exception of Tamil Nadu, where the ABL program is being implemented, and Karnataka, where NaliKali is being implemented, we did not find any data on "multi-grade" training. Equally, there is no robust Management Information System on the number of teacher trainings attended by teachers along with the topics covered. This remains a serious lacuna.
2. As specified by the RTE.

CHAPTER 8

Professional Growth of Teachers

Introduction

This chapter discusses two broad ways in which teachers can grow professionally: through promotions and by acquiring new skills, knowledge, and competencies ("professional development"). Promotions and professional development cover a heterogeneous mix of activities. The chapter ends with a review of teacher performance evaluation systems.

Promotions

Promotions are ways in which teachers move to a different post, usually to a post that is in a different cadre or grade of service. Therefore, a promotion typically includes a move to a different, and higher, salary scale. The most common type of promotion is for an elementary school teacher to become a secondary school teacher. However, a wide range of other moves are considered promotions, including the following:

- *Primary to upper primary.* In some states (for example, Tamil Nadu), primary and upper primary school teachers are in different cadres, and so movement between them is considered a promotion. In Odisha, there are five elementary grade cadres, with moves between these grades considered as promotions.
- *Becoming a head teacher.* The process of becoming a head teacher varies across states. In most cases, the most senior teacher (by years of service) is appointed the head teacher of a school. Sometimes this is the most senior teacher at the particular school (as with primary and upper primary school head teachers in Rajasthan); in other cases, it is the most senior person in the block or district (as in Karnataka).
  - In Jharkhand, there are no sanctioned posts for head teachers in primary-only schools. In these schools, the senior-most teacher acts as head teacher to manage the school formalities, but this is not considered a promotion. In upper primary schools, the post of head teacher is filled through promotion of Bachelor of the Arts (B.A.) and Master of Arts trained teachers.

- *Becoming an inspector.* Secondary school teachers can become inspectors or District Institute of Education and Training faculty (in Karnataka).
- *Becoming an Assistant Elementary Education Officer (AEEO)/District Education Officer (DEO).* In Tamil Nadu, middle school head teachers can be promoted to the post of AEEO; high school head teachers can become DEOs.
- *Becoming a Block Resource Coordinator Centre (BRCC) officer or Cluster Resource Centre Coordinator (CRCC) officer.* Elementary school teachers can become BRCC or CRCC officers and, in Odisha, this is considered a promotion. In Karnataka, this is not considered a promotion at the elementary level; however, becoming a resource person is a promotion in secondary education.

Teachers in some positions or in aided schools cannot access promotions. As can be seen for the case of Uttar Pradesh (table 8.1), the situation is typically quite different for teachers in aided schools. Teachers in aided schools can only be promoted within their school (Tamil Nadu and Uttar Pradesh) or by getting a job at another aided school upon that post being advertised (Uttar Pradesh). Generally, no promotions are available to contract teachers (except being promoted to being part of the cadre of regular teachers, which is discussed further in this chapter) Some subject-specific teachers, such as those for vocational subjects, have no career path as subject teachers.

The frequency of promotions varies considerably across types of promotion and states, because of state policy and the number of posts available to be filled. Some states have a policy that states that appointments as secondary school teachers are only possible based on promotion. The remainder of the secondary school positions are filled by "direct recruitment," that is, through new people becoming teachers for the first time. The two most common patterns are an even split, with 50 percent filled by promotion and 50 percent by direct recruitment; and all posts filled on promotion. In Rajasthan, for example, 50 percent of secondary school teachers are appointed "on promotion." In Odisha, all vacancies for levels I to IV (of five levels) in the elementary school cadre are filled on promotion; and the same is true of all secondary school teachers in Karnataka. This figure was 25 percent in Jharkhand, but proposals in 2014 would enable 50 percent new graduate-trained posts in elementary schools to be filled on promotion. In Uttar Pradesh, as of 2013, instead of all upper primary posts being filled on promotion, only 50 percent of science and mathematics teacher posts were filled in this manner.

A similar pattern emerges for the appointment of head teachers. In Rajasthan, there is a distinction between head teachers of senior secondary schools, which are all filled on promotion, and secondary schools, 50 percent of which are filled by promotion and 50 percent by direct recruitment. In Karnataka, for promotions to head teachers of secondary schools, 25 percent are filled through the Karnataka Education Service Examination and the remaining posts from promotion of high school teachers.

The balance of promotion and direct recruitment and the policy on qualifications can change over time, and the periodicity of change varies considerably.

Professional Growth of Teachers

Table 8.1 Promotion Routes for Different Cadres of Teachers: Uttar Pradesh

No.	Type of teacher (cadre of teacher)	Promotional avenues
1	Assistant teacher, primary school	Promoted as head teacher of primary school or assistant teacher at upper primary school
2	Assistant teacher, upper primary school Head teacher, primary school	May be promoted as head teacher of upper primary school
3	Shiksha Mitra	No promotion
4	Anudeshak, upper primary school	No promotion
5	Assistant teacher, aided primary school	No promotion, but may apply for head teacher after completion of five years of service in same school or other schools in case post is advertised by that school
6	Assistant teacher, aided upper primary school	No promotion, but may apply for head teacher after completion of five years of service in the same school or other schools in case post is advertised by that school
7	Teacher (KGBV)	No promotion
8	Itinerant teacher (CWSN)	No promotion
9	Government LT (TGT)	May be promoted as lecturer, if possesses required qualification to be lecturer
10	Government Lecturer (PGT)	May be promoted as head teacher of government high school
11	Aided school LT (TGT)	May be promoted as lecturer, if possesses required qualification to be lecturer, and the school is an intermediate college
12	Aided school lecturer (PGT)	No promotion, but will get a chance to be principal of the same college if number one or two in seniority; secondary selection board will call him/her for interview by default
13	ICT teacher	No promotion
14	Vocational teachers	No promotion
15	Attached primary teacher	Can be promoted up to lecturer (Act 1921)
16	Sanskrit aided school	Promotion to higher grades, LT grade to lecturer and to head of institution (Act 2009, chapter-2, Regulations 3 and 6(2))

Source: State Council of Educational Research and Training, Lucknow 2014: Uttar Pradesh State Report.
Note: CWSN = children with special needs; ICT = information and communications technology; KGBV = Kasturba Gandhi Balika Vidyalaya; LT = Licentiate Teacher; PGT = Post-Graduate Teacher; TGT = Trained Graduate Teacher.

For example, in Odisha, the rules on promotion did not change for almost 35 years (between 1975 and 2009), but then changed again in 2014 after only five years (table 8.2). These changes served to make it more difficult to obtain promotions, by extending the number of years required to be served and/or increasing the educational qualifications needed to be promoted.

A further complication is that some states require a certain number of years of service in a particular grade before being considered eligible for promotion. For example, in Odisha, to become an Assistant Block Education Officer, which is a level II position, a teacher must have been in a level III position for at least two years. In Uttar Pradesh, the minimum tenure an elementary assistant teacher

Table 8.2 Promotions for Certain Categories of Elementary Teachers over Time: Odisha

Level IV			Level III		
1975	2009	2014	1975	2009	2014
8 years of service in level V; no weight for qualification	60% Matric/+2 CT, 40% B.Ed.	50% Matric/+2 CT, 50% B.Ed.	Must have 5 years of service in level IV	Minimum 1 year of service in level IV; 50% Matric +2 CT, 50% B.Ed., total 13 years of service in levels V + IV	100% B.A./B.S. or B.Ed., minimum 2 years in level IV (in case of non-availability, 6 years of service in levels V+IV

Source: Odisha State Report.
Note: B.Ed. = Bachelor of Education; B.A. = Bachelor of the Arts; B.S. = Bachelor of Science; CT = Certificate in Teaching.

had to serve before becoming eligible for promotion used to be 10 years, but this was recently reduced to five years, given the large number of vacancies at senior levels.

The availability of promotions is dependent not only on the policy on promotions, but also on the number of open positions that are being filled. Although a teacher may have acquired all the necessary qualifications to be a teacher in a promoted post, promotions may not be possible. In Jharkhand, for example, promotions were expected every 12 years, and in Mizoram, every eight years. Now, in Karnataka and Jharkhand, promotions from elementary to secondary school teachers are reported as being rare. However, Karnataka has recently changed the norm for the number of students at a primary school that entitles the school to a post of head teacher. From the 2014–15 academic year, a head teacher is assigned to a school with 60 pupils, not 120 as in the past. This change has resulted in many vacancies for primary school head teachers. A similar event occurred in Tamil Nadu in 2012, when 344 upper primary schools were upgraded to high schools and de-linked from their primary schools. These 344 "new" primary schools acquired head teachers; the senior-most secondary grade teachers in the unit of appointment were appointed to the head teacher positions.

In Mizoram, administrative inefficiency has prevented promotions. A major bottleneck has been the haphazard maintenance of the Annual Confidential Reports or Performance Appraisal Reports (PARs). When the PARs have to be organized and analyzed for processing promotion requests, these are often not available and need to be found or, worse, rewritten. Another fallout of the mismanagement of PARs and the Service Books has been that there has been a lack of clarity on the seniority among teachers. This situation has led to general delays in the publication of the seniority lists. The problem has been compounded by litigation initiated by teachers who felt aggrieved. The seniority lists have been published recently (2014), after a long gap, in compliance with the judgment given by the High Court.

Given the rarity of promotions, Karnataka and Rajasthan provide additional salary increments after certain periods of service. In Karnataka, from 2012, those who have continued in the same post for 25 years (30 years) without a single promotion are granted a second (third) additional increment in the scale of pay. Recently, it was announced that a fourth increase would be granted after 35 years of service without a promotion. In Rajasthan, the periods of service meriting increments are 10, 20, and 30 years for teachers in grade I, and 9, 18, and 27 years for teachers in grades II and III.

Promotions involve teachers leaving their current classroom teaching practice. An elementary teacher who is promoted as a secondary teacher remains teaching. However, in many cases, a promotion involves a teacher ceasing to be a classroom teacher and taking a different type of position (such as head teacher, inspector, or block resource person). It is unfortunate, that a good teacher is unable to remain in a teaching post, if her career is to advance.

The most common promotions are those of contract teachers becoming regular teachers, and unqualified teachers becoming regular teachers after acquiring the requisite qualifications. These types of promotions are, by far, the largest class of promotions in those states that have contract teachers or that had recruited unqualified teachers in the past. These classes of promotions are considered separately in this chapter, because they will eventually cease to take place, since many states have decided to abandon the practice of recruiting contract teachers and hiring unqualified teachers.

In Odisha, the preliminary recruitment is as a Sikshya Sahayak (SS) and, after three years of continuous and satisfactory service, the SS becomes a Junior Teacher. Again, after three years of continuous and satisfactory service, the Junior Teacher becomes a regular teacher under the Zillah Parishad cadre. This means it takes six years for a candidate to become a regular teacher. Until recently, there were two categories of regular teachers at the elementary level: regular teacher elementary cadre level V, and regular teacher Zillah Parishad cadre. In the scale of pay and other benefits, there was no difference. But only teachers in the elementary cadre level V were covered under the Advanced Career Progression Rule and Promotion, and so were eligible for promotions. However, in July 2014, all existing Zillah Parishad cadre teachers were converted to level V elementary cadre teachers (although future Zillah Parishad cadre teachers are not automatically converted).

In all the states in this study, promotions are done primarily based on seniority. Usually, seniority is defined as the number of years in the cadre, and usually (such as in Karnataka) within reserved categories. In Mizoram, seniority is based on the teacher's date of joining the school.[1] In Tamil Nadu, secondary teachers' seniority is within the block.

In the past, some states have had a merit-based element as part of the promotion process as well. For example, this was the case in Rajasthan until 2002–03, which combined merit and seniority. In the process, for every post to be filled by promotion, five candidates, on seniority basis, were considered by the departmental promotion committee. On entering the preview criteria, further selection of the candidate was based on her/his merit. In 2002–03, responding to criticism of merit-based promotions, the government withdrew the process and converted it into a simple seniority-based promotion system. The basis of the criticism was that in the merit-cum-seniority process, there is a lot of scope for subjectivity, and it offers scope to politicians and bureaucrats to exploit teachers on certain practices. This is consistent with the discussion in chapter 4, where this research found that interviews have been removed from the teacher selection process to minimize any scope for manipulation.

There is an important connection, from the teachers' perspective, between transfer and promotion policies. In many cases, when teachers are transferred from one district to another, they automatically become the least senior person in that district cadre, thus significantly affecting their ability to be promoted in the future. In some cases, there is a rationale, from the state's perspective, for such a policy. For example, the policy discourages teachers from seeking transfers to urban areas and, thereby, helps maintain the level of the teaching force in rural (and more difficult to staff) schools.

Professional Development and In-Service Training[2]

Since many promotional moves require a teacher to have qualifications beyond the ones in their current post, certain types of professional development are closely related to promotions. For example, in Karnataka, lower primary teachers acquiring an undergraduate degree can be promoted to higher primary schools; higher primary teachers completing a Bachelor of Education (B.Ed.) degrees can be promoted to secondary schools. Those teaching in secondary schools can be promoted to pre-university colleges (senior secondary) after completion of a master's degree in their respective subject. Again, promotions are dependent on vacancies being available.

Several states have specific programs to assist teachers to acquire these necessary qualifications (although there is little evidence about the take-up of these opportunities).[3] Karnataka has the most comprehensive and generous policy. Here, teachers, with a minimum of five years of experience and who are younger than 45 years, can opt to pursue higher education to earn a B.A., Bachelor of Science (B.S.), B.Ed., post-graduate, Master of Philosophy, or Doctor of Philosophy in their chosen stream. The government provides paid leave (sabbatical) for a period up to four years (three years for B.A. or B.S., one year for B.Ed., and two years for a post-graduate course) and their post is filled temporarily. Along with their salary, teachers are also given a half day of dearness allowance. The government also bears the real costs of the teachers' higher education (that is, tuition and examination fees).

Moreover, on re-joining teaching service, the teachers are given a promotion based on the degree acquired, as per their service and seniority and the vacancies available. This facility (paid leave and promotion) is provided only if the teacher signs a contract to work for the government for at least 10 years after the completion of the degree. The policy restricts the number of teachers who can utilize this benefit; currently, only up to 15 teachers per block can apply to pursue higher education. As per the policy, all teachers can apply for this provision;

however, currently only those pursuing a higher degree in English, mathematics, and science are granted permission, due to the large number of vacancies for these subjects. Hence, only 750 teachers have applied for this provision (there are more 300,000 elementary school teachers in Karnataka).

None of the states in this study has an effective policy for in-service training of teachers. Training is carried out in an ad hoc manner, almost exclusively funded by two centrally-sponsored schemes, Sarva Shiksha Abhiyan (SSA) and Rashtriya Madhyamik Shiksha Abhiyan (RMSA). Therefore, training is subject to the availability of these funds and the associated modalities and priorities. The incidence of training varies significantly across states. Further, there is no database that records not only the number of training programs conducted, but also the issues and topics covered in the training.

States receive significant resources for in-service training of teachers under SSA and RMSA. For example, in fiscal year 2012–13, Rs. 1,273 crores was approved for states under SSA, although only about half that (Rs. 619 crores) was spent.[4] The figures for RMSA were much smaller—only Rs. 18 crores was allocated for teacher training, although this still constituted the bulk of state spending on this item.[5]

There was little progress in the absolute number of teachers across India receiving training between 2005–06 and 2012–13. From the point of view of quality of education, teachers' in-service training is complementary to the educational qualifications they bring to their role. However, little progress was made in absolute number of elementary teachers across India receiving training between 2005–06 and 2012–13, although the numbers picked up markedly in 2007–08 and again in 2011–12 (figure 8.1). Making the picture grimmer is the

Figure 8.1 Number and Percentage of Elementary Teachers Receiving Training in Previous Year: All-India

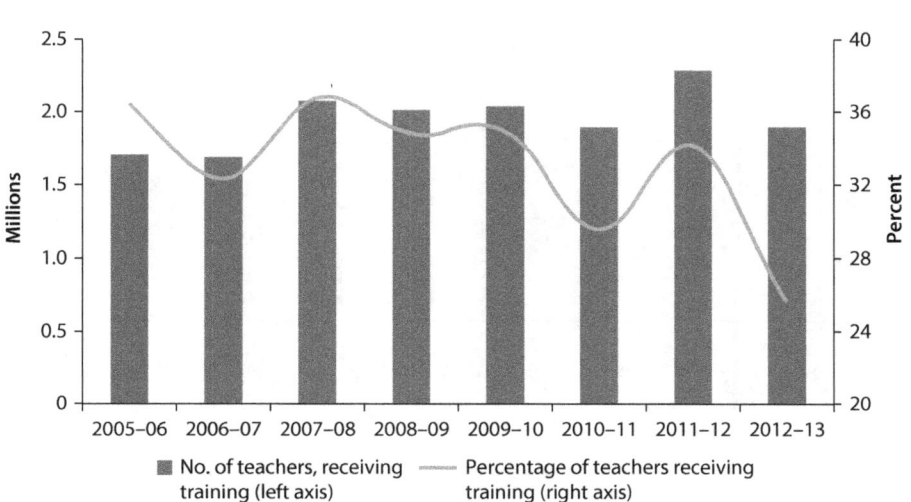

Source: Calculations based on information from various Sarva Shiksha Abhiyan joint review missions.

significant decline over this period in the percentage coverage of in-service training—from 36.4 percent of all teachers across India in 2005–06, and 34.2 percent in 2011–12, the proportion in 2012–13 fell to 25.8 percent.

Across the states under consideration, only Odisha, Karnataka, and Tamil Nadu trained more than 30 percent of their elementary teachers in 2012–13. Rajasthan, Uttar Pradesh, and Madhya Pradesh trained fewer than one in seven elementary teachers. Over time, the percentage coverage has declined significantly (compared with 2005–06), and to worrying levels in Rajasthan, Uttar Pradesh, Madhya Pradesh, and Punjab.

A closer look at funding under RMSA reveals wide divergence of practice across states. Among the major states, over the past four years, physical achievements (the amount of training achieved compared to the amount planned) varied from over 80 percent for Maharashtra to a mere 3 percent for Bihar. Funds utilization varied from 78 percent in Gujarat to 4 percent in Bihar (figure 8.2). For the four years 2009–13, states and Union Territories received approval for training of 2,582,646 teachers, of which 1,342,200 teachers (52 percent) were in fact trained. States with more secondary school teachers have higher sanctioned approvals, and higher numbers of teachers trained. (The correlation between number of secondary school teachers in 2012–13 and the sum of sanctioned and actual training across the four years is positive and significant.)

The performance of the states in achieving annual physical targets has been close to 60 percent, except in 2010–11, when it declined to around 40 percent.

Figure 8.2 In-Service Training under RMSA, Achievement against Financial and Physical Targets, 2009–13

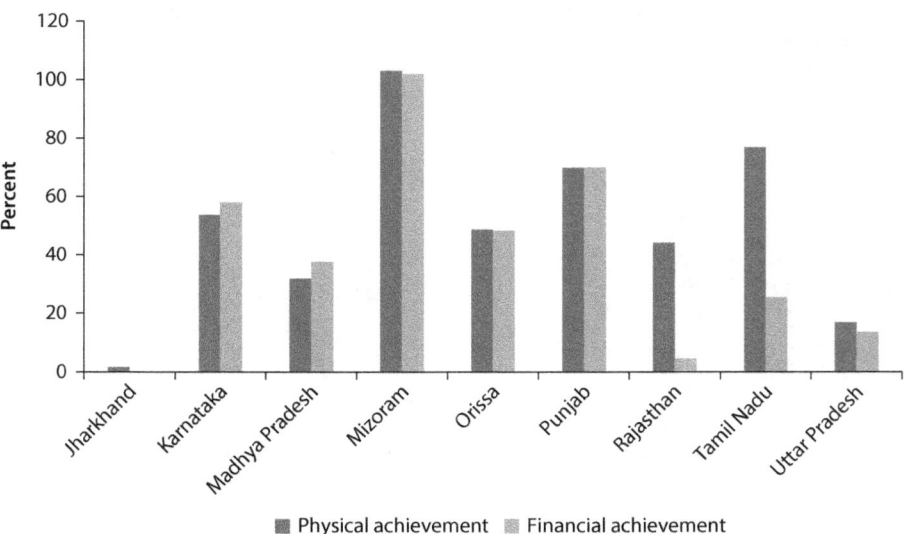

Source: RMSA joint review missions, various years.
Note: RMSA = Rashtriya Madhyamik Shiksha Abhiyan.

There was persistence in high and low performance by states (in achieving their targets for numbers and budgets for in-service teacher training) between 2009 and 2013. Although some states achieved between 70 and 100 percent of their targets (in physical terms), for others the results were mixed, and some states have not started teacher in-service training activities.

The financial performance of the states has also improved over time. For the country as a whole, 7 percent of sanctioned funds were spent overall by the states in 2009–10, 29 percent in 2010–11, 36 percent in 2011–12, and 51 percent in 2012–13. However, there is a great deal of variation in the spending percentages across states each year as well as across the years. Overall, the states spent 36 percent of their sanctioned amounts on teacher training between 2009 and 2013.

Mizoram is the best-performing state in training for secondary teachers among the states in this study. Mizoram managed to achieve all its physical and financial targets over the four years. In contrast, there has been no teacher training under RMSA in Jharkhand. Most of the states in this study achieved almost the same extent of physical and financing progress. However, in Rajasthan and Tamil Nadu, there was significant physical progress (44 percent and 77 percent, respectively) but this was achieved without spending most of the financial resources that were sanctioned (25 percent and 14 percent, respectively).

There is wide variation in unit costs for training secondary teachers across states over time and in any particular year, and for a particular state over time. In 2009–10 and 2010–11, the average sanctioned unit cost across of the states was around Rs. 1,000 (approximately Rs. 200 per day for five days). For the next two years, 2011–12 and 2012–13, it was around Rs. 1,500 (approximately Rs. 300 per day for five days).

The data suggest several concerns with the planning of in-service training for secondary teachers across the states. First, there is significant variation in the actual money that states spend per teacher. This might reflect differences in the type of training being offered, or local costs (such as for facilities or materials) might vary. However, RMSA provides for only five days per teacher and even within one state, unit costs can vary across years (compare Karnataka in 2011–12 when the unit costs were Rs. 3,157, with unit costs of Rs. 1,072 the next year) (table 8.3). Second, there is a great deal of difference in almost every state (except for Mizoram) between the sanctioned unit costs and the money per teacher that was actually spent; sometimes, states spend much more than planned, sometimes much less. This finding is particularly striking in the last two years, since states were allocated different unit cost amounts (presumably based on their own respective plans). Lastly, despite repeated failures to spend the money that has been allocated, some states (such as Jharkhand and Rajasthan) continue to plan for and request allocations. Only in the last year has Rajasthan spent any of the money allocated to it.

To instill new teaching practices and ideas in schools, it is not enough that individual teachers attend training; good practice indicates that a critical mass of teachers need to be trained in any given school for that practice to take root and be implemented consistently. However, the states' practices of selecting teachers

Table 8.3 Annual Sanctioned and Actual Unit Costs, RMSA In-Service Funds, 2009–13
Indian rupees

State	2009–10 Sanctioned	2009–10 Actual	2010–11 Sanctioned	2010–11 Actual	2011–12 Sanctioned	2011–12 Actual	2012–13 Sanctioned	2012–13 Actual
Jharkhand	1,000	0	1,000	0	2,390	0	1,738	0
Karnataka	1,000	0	1,000	0	1,555	3,157	1,987	1,072
Madhya Pradesh	1,000	0	1,083	—	1,574	195	2,650	1,500
Mizoram	1,000	1,000	1,000	989	1,866	1,707	1,656	1,656
Odisha	1,000	0	1,000	—	1,500	963	1,500	1,500
Punjab	1,000	306	1,000	396	1,493	1,635	1,498	2,387
Rajasthan	1,000	0	1,000	—	1,500	0	1,500	1,500
Tamil Nadu	1,000	996	1,000	—	3,663	1,061	1,718	1,099
Uttar Pradesh	1,000	0	1,000	—	1,573	484	1,500	1,533

Source: Selected data from Goyal and Dey 2014.
Note: RMSA = Rashtriya Madhyamik Shiksha Abhiyan; — = not available.

to participate in training have resulted in a situation in which schools have few trained teachers, a very high percentage trained, or the same teacher(s) trained repeatedly. Across India, 35.7 percent of elementary school teachers were reported as having received training in the 2011–12 academic year. However, almost two-thirds of the schools (59.5 percent) had 10 percent or fewer of their teachers trained, while about 30 percent (29.8 percent) of the schools trained almost all, that is, more than 90 percent, of their teachers. This pattern is repeated across all the states. Moreover, in most states, more than half of the schools had less than 10 percent of their teachers trained. This suggests that schools either train teachers or they do not; or perhaps state policy and practice is to train only a few teachers in every school.

Perhaps not surprisingly, Tamil Nadu, which managed to train 70 percent of its teachers, was the only state in which more than half of the schools reported training more than 90 percent of their teachers (table 8.4). And not surprisingly, smaller schools tend to train a larger proportion of their teachers, which has the effect that teachers in rural areas (where small schools tend to be located) have a greater chance of being trained than teachers in urban areas. It may be the case that states assume that once a teacher is trained, he or she will disseminate the new practices to other teachers in the school. However, the evidence suggests that this "cascade" model of training is not very effective.

Finally, none of the states in this study has a formal system whereby, when a teacher attends training (or indeed any other event during school teaching time), a substitute teacher is provided during their absence. Instead, children are typically not taught that subject on the days when the teacher is absent. In a larger school, there is some possibility that another colleague might cover for the absent teacher. But teachers in small schools or in schools with few teachers face difficulties in attending training or becoming resource persons because, when they attend training, students lose out on teaching time. Of the government

Table 8.4 **Elementary School Teachers Who Received In-Service Training during the 2011–12 Academic Year**

State	Percent trained			
	0–10	11–90	91–100	Avg. % of teachers trained
India	59.5	10.7	29.8	35.7
Jharkhand	58.3	9.2	32.4	37.4
Karnataka	51.2	3.1	45.7	47.6
Madhya Pradesh	82.6	5.7	11.7	14.6
Mizoram	61.1	19.8	19.1	31.1
Odisha	45.3	14.3	40.4	48.7
Punjab	65.0	14.7	20.3	29.1
Rajasthan	76.6	11.8	11.6	18.0
Tamil Nadu	24.1	13.7	62.2	70.3
Uttar Pradesh	77.2	9.7	13.1	18.5

Source: Unified District Information System for Education, 2011–12.

elementary schools, 10.9 percent have only one teacher, and 12 percent of secondary schools have only one teacher in four subjects (mathematics, science, social science, and Hindi). This is another piece of evidence that suggests that the working conditions of teachers in larger schools are better.

Evaluation of Teacher Performance

There are two broad ways in which teacher performance is used for annual evaluations and at the time of promotions. Most states in this study had no formal appraisal process, but teachers were still subject to some degree of informal reviews of their performance from multiple sources. In all the states, the head teacher is formally expected to monitor the day-to-day work of teachers in the classroom. Cluster- or block-level resource persons are expected to visit schools and observe teachers and provide feedback to them. Although these systems are formally in place, the implementation processes remain weak (table 8.5). Often other officials in the educational administration structure visit schools randomly to check (although they usually focus on data and administrative issues and do not observe teacher performance in the classroom). In some states, like Tamil Nadu, there are times when the entire government machinery, from the Minister and Principal Secretary, is involved in visiting and monitoring schools. This happens in fits and starts.

School Management Committees (in elementary schools) and School Management and Development Committees (in secondary schools) have the formal responsibility to monitor teacher performance. However, in discharging this responsibility, these committees usually restrict themselves to ensuring that teachers reach school on time, maintain and share students' records, and maintain school accounts accurately (Karnataka).

Four states in this study have a teacher performance appraisal process, but it is reported as existing on paper only. These states are Karnataka, Madhya Pradesh, Mizoram, and Rajasthan. For example, in Madhya Pradesh, the policy is

Table 8.5 Regression of Number of Inspections on Distance from Block Headquarters, Elementary Schools, 2012–13

State	Coefficient	Statistically significant difference?
India	0.007	Yes
Jharkhand	−0.002	No
Karnataka	−0.001	No
Madhya Pradesh	0.003	Yes
Mizoram	−0.001	No
Odisha	−0.006	Yes
Punjab	0.007	Yes
Rajasthan	0.008	Yes
Tamil Nadu	−0.007	Yes
Uttar Pradesh	0.010	Yes

Source: Unified District Information System for Education.
Note: a positive number indicates that being far away increases the chances of being visited.

that those contract teachers who wish to become regular teachers at the end of three years of service can only do so if their performance is satisfactory with no disciplinary issues or extended absences. However, teachers report that all contract teachers who complete three years of service and wish to shift their status to become regular teachers are able to do so.

Mizoram has an elaborate appraisal system, but, again, this is reported as not being implemented in practice. It is a four-tier process, which begins with a self-appraisal by the teachers, followed by an appraisal by her/his reporting officer, then a reviewing officer, and finally an accepting officer (table 8.6). Given the complexity of this system and the number of teachers for whom it is meant to apply, it would be surprising if the system were activity and widely used.

Rajasthan is moving back to a system of teacher appraisal. Currently, an annual PAR is required of all government employees every year. However, given that decisions about promotions no longer take performance into account, the PAR system is reported as having fallen into disuse. An initiative in 2014 sought to reintroduce teacher appraisal, based on guidelines from the Ministry of Human Resource Development. The appraisal system covers teachers and head teachers, and includes a self-assessment and supervisor evaluation. Odisha was also reported as planning the introduction of a new system.

Despite the lack of comprehensive and effective policy, several states discipline head teachers and most states provide monetary awards to "high-performing" teachers (usually based on students' examination performance). In Jharkhand, Karnataka, Rajasthan, and Tamil Nadu, teachers can receive awards. In Karnataka, there are three types of awards:

- *District awards.* District Awards carrying a cash prize of Rs. 3,000 are given to teachers who have rendered meritorious service. The total number of awards is 357 (primary school teachers: 202, and high school teachers: 155). The selection of teachers for the awards is done by the district-level committees. Teachers are not supposed to apply directly for this award.

Table 8.6 Performance Appraisal Report: Mizoram

Section I Filled by administrative division/personnel department	Section II Self-appraisal	Section III Appraisal by reporting officer	Section IV Review by reviewing authority	Section V Acceptance by accepting authority
• Name and service details • Reporting, reviewing, and accepting authorities • Period of absence or leaves • Training programs attended • Awards/honors • Details of PAR of previous years, property returns, and medical examination	• Brief description of duties • Annual work plan and achievements • Any exceptional contributions • Factors that hindered performance • Training needs • Various declarations • Details of transfer and posting during the period under report	• Concurrence or otherwise with responses in section II related to accomplishments of work plan and unforeseen tasks • Comments on exceptional contributions mentioned in section II • Any significant failures by officer under appraisal • Concurrence or otherwise with training needs • Assessment of work output on three parameters, on a scale of 1–10 (40% weight) • Assessment of various personal attributes, on a scale of 1–10 (30% weight) • Assessment of functional competency, on a scale of 1–10 (30% weight) • Comment on integrity • Pen picture, overall qualities of officer in 100 words • Comment on transfer and posting • Overall grade, on a scale of 1–10	• Concurrence or otherwise with assessment made by reporting officer with respect to work output and other attributes • Concurrence or otherwise with assessment made by reporting officer with respect to extraordinary achievements or significant failures • Reasons for variance, if any • Pen picture by reviewing officer • Overall grade, on a scale of 1–10	• Concurrence or otherwise with remarks of reporting/reviewing authorities • Reasons for variance, if any • Overall grade, on a scale of 1–10

Source: Institute of Advanced Study in Education, Aizawl 2014: Mizoram State Report.
Note: PAR = Performance Appraisal Report.

- *Special awards.* State-level awards of Rs. 5,000 each are sanctioned to eight teachers for scientific and innovative work. Applications for this award are invited from eligible teachers from primary and secondary education in August and September every year, through paper notification.
- *Rajiv Gandhi Memorial Award.* Rs. 12,000 each is awarded to the two Best Science Teachers (primary and secondary) at the state level. Applications for the award are invited from eligible teachers in August and September every year, through paper notification.

In addition, teachers are given a cash award for 100 percent pass rate of their students. In Rajasthan, the basis for giving awards changed in 2014 (table 8.7). The new norms make student performance the only criterion for giving an award to teachers. Although this has the advantage of putting the focus on student

Table 8.7 Revised (2014) Norms for State Teacher Awards: Rajasthan

Norms prescribed in the old/existing policy (up to June 5, 2014)	Norms prescribed in the new policy (June 6, 2014)
(i) Results of children in the service tenure (ii) Publication of a book, research thesis, paper, research work, or project (iii) Innovation in teaching process, use of TLM in effective teaching (iv) Contributed in the development of work related to school building, classrooms, laboratory, hostel, library, or other (v) Exceptional contribution in co-curricular and curricular activities (vi) Developed relationships with students, parents, and community (vii) Overall personality of the teacher (This policy was effective from August 21, 1989, Rajasthan Education Code 1957)	(i) Teachers of classes I to VIII, 90 percent children in the A grade in last 3 consecutive years (A grade is given to students who score between 86 and 100 percent marks (ii) For secondary classes, the results of the teacher's classes should be above 90 percent for the past consecutive five years. (iii) For primary classes, the criterion is based on the performance of each child; for secondary classes, the overall result of the class is considered (iv) For physical education teachers, the criterion is that students should have received the Olympic, Arjun, or National Award once in five years

Source: Rajasthan State Report.
Note: TLM = teaching and learning material.

performance as the ultimate objective of teaching, these awards clearly favor those teachers who are lucky enough to be teaching in schools with students from more advantaged backgrounds or high-scoring subjects. Therefore, these awards discourage teachers from working in more difficult circumstances. Teachers' unions also complain that the new norms mean fewer teachers will receive awards. This system is yet to be implemented.

Tamil Nadu only offers one teacher award, the Dr. Radhakrishnan Award. Teachers who have completed a minimum period of 15 years of service, produced excellent results on their board examinations, and developed a healthy rapport between the community and schools are selected through a district-level committee. A state-level screening committee also examines the merit of each applicant. Each year, on September 5, the Best Teacher Awards are presented by the Minister for School Education. Each award consists of Rs. 5,000 cash, a silver medal, and a merit certificate.

In 2014, the Government of Rajasthan took action against exceptionally poor results on board examinations. The Education Minister suspended around 100 head teachers and principals. However, the suspension was revoked soon after (June 2014) and these head teachers and principals were transferred to other schools. On July 22, 2014, the state declared in the Legislative Assembly that soon action would be taken against the heads of schools (total 1,400 schools) for zero percent results on the 10th and 12th boards in 2014 (newspaper report, July 24, 2014). This is a positive development in the sense of focusing head teachers on student outcomes, and schools that report zero percent results are clearly doing very poorly. However, as was seen elsewhere in this study, head teachers generally have little control over inputs at the school level (for example, they have no role in selecting the teachers appointed to their schools and they are not able to discipline teachers effectively), and so their direct responsibility for examination results and their ability to make a difference is somewhat limited.

Conclusion

Promotions are, in theory, a way to recognize those teachers who have performed well. They are also an incentive for teachers to perform well. The process for contract teachers to become regular teachers appears to fit this pattern, since only those contract teachers with satisfactory service are regularized. Done effectively, this system could mean that contract teachers serve a sort of probationary period, whereby their ability to be effective teachers is evaluated and those who do well become regular teachers. The threat of not being regularized could work as an incentive to become an effective teacher. However, all contract teachers who meet the service requirements (for example, three years in Madhya Pradesh) become regular teachers without a formal evaluation of their teaching performance.

There is also no link between performance and promotions of regular teachers. The reasons are many. Most fundamentally, all promotions for regular teachers are done based on seniority, with no link to performance. In addition, the availability of promotions varies considerably for different types of teachers and over time. Given that state governments are wary of disturbing a hornet's nest, they leave regular teachers, who are unionized and enjoy political support, alone. The teachers' union leaders who participated in the state discussions were quite confident that seniority-based promotions would continue and there would not be any performance-based promotions.

Notes

1. In Mizoram, there was an unfortunate side effect of this rule during the process of provincialization of schools. Teachers in schools that were provincialized often had higher seniority than teachers in other preexisting government schools, reducing the overall seniority of the latter teachers.
2. This section draws on Goyal and Dey (2014).
3. See also table 6.9 in chapter 6. Note that the term "untrained teachers" is often taken to mean "unqualified teachers." In this chapter, "trained" (and "untrained") refer to receiving (or not) in-service training, usually of a few days' duration and not linked to acquisition of qualifications.
4. Source: data collated from audit reports from SSA as posted on the Ministry of Human Resource Development website.
5. Source: Staff calculations from data reported to the fourth joint review mission of the RMSA program.

CHAPTER 9

Grievance Redressal Mechanisms

Introduction

An aspect of the working conditions of teachers that has received little systematic attention is the avenues available for redressal of their grievances. The absence of studies and information on grievance redressal processes is applicable to the delivery of various services in India, despite grievance redressal procedures being essential for ensuring basic fairness and legal accountability (Gauri 2013). A clear and effective procedure for redressal of grievances is important from a fairness point of view, as it allows individuals who believe they have suffered to follow a process through which the wrong may be rectified. Even if the individual's grievance is not addressed by the process, grievance procedures, in themselves, establish a sense of fairness, as they support the rule of law. For example, most formal redressal procedures have standardized mechanisms for the presentation of and response to grievances. Grievance redressal procedures are also based on certain basic principles, such as that similar cases should be treated similarly and an administrative authority is required to provide reasons before denying a remedy being sought. In addition to fairness, redressal procedures help enhance accountability for policy measures and provide information to policy makers on how the policies they have formulated are working in practice.[1]

For teachers, grievance redressal could take many forms, ranging from approaching the headmaster of the school, to approaching a teachers' union for assistance, to taking a complaint to a Block Education Officer or District Education Officer, and/or to filing a petition in court. This chapter addresses the questions as to what are the different grievance redressal mechanisms available to teachers and how they work in practice. The chapter outlines two kinds of procedures that teachers in government and government aided schools have used in seeking redress for their grievances: (a) the system that is embedded in the administrative system, including quasi-judicial mechanisms, such as tribunals, and more informal grievance redressal sessions conducted by officials at the block and district levels, and (b) the legal system through the courts.

The chapter is organized as follows. The next section describes grievance redressal mechanisms in the eight study states,[2] established by the state education departments—the system embedded in the executive/administrative arm of the government. The mechanisms include use of the administrative hierarchy (beginning with the school head teacher) and the special dispute resolution tribunals established in some states. The following section describes and presents an analysis of teacher issue–related litigation in the High Courts of eight of the nine study states (Mizoram excluded). The last section concludes with an overview of the issues discussed in the chapter and some reflections on the way forward. Annex 9A describes the data sources and their limitations.

Teacher Grievance Redressal Mechanisms Established by State Education Departments

There are two main executive/administrative mechanisms available for teacher grievance redressal. First, there are grievance redressal sessions offered by state Education Officers at the block and district levels, or the state level by the state commissioner of education. Second, there are specialized dispute resolution tribunals in many states, for addressing service-related matters of government employees (of which teachers from government schools constitute a significant proportion). Some states also have tribunals for addressing teacher-related grievances for private and aided schools, such as the Jharkhand Education Tribunal and the Rajasthan Non-Governmental Education Tribunal.

Grievance Redressal Sessions by State Education Departments
Karnataka
The Office of the Commissioner, Public Instruction, holds *Shikshana Adalats* in different districts of the state, which are one-day drives during which the Commissioner acts as a grievance redressal body by accepting applications, representations, and complaints from teachers working in all types of schools. The *Adalats* have no written rules of procedure and applications do not need to have a specific format and could, in some cases, even be oral. The intention is to hold these sessions every fortnight, but this seldom happens in practice, as their scheduling depends on the availability of the Commissioner and other officers.

The issues that are typically addressed in these *Adalats* include salary and time-bound increments. Depending on the nature of the problem and the authority concerned, the Commissioner refers the matter to the block- or district-level authorities to address the issue. The time limit for disposal of each representation is 15 days. From conversations with the Commissioner's office, it was understood that most unresolved matters found their way to the Karnataka Administrative Tribunal.

Tamil Nadu
Over the past two years, the Tamil Nadu government has instituted a regular grievance redressal forum at the block and district levels to address certain common grievances of primary school and aided school teachers. These sessions

are held by Assistant Elementary Education Officers (AEEOs) on the first Saturday of each month, wherein a grievance is resolved by the AEEO and relevant orders passed, or the matter is passed to the District Education Officer, who takes up grievances on a district-wide basis on the second Saturday of each month. Grievances that cannot be resolved at the district level are passed to the Directorate for further consideration. The initial motivation of the government in instituting these sessions was not so much to provide teachers with a forum to address their grievances, but rather to ensure that the working days of AEEOs were not otherwise disrupted by having to hear and resolve teacher grievances on a daily basis. However, conversations with officials in the education department suggested that the number of teacher grievances had decreased in the past few years, which they attributed, at least in part, to the grievance redressal sessions.

Rajasthan[3]

In Rajasthan, teachers have the option to approach their immediate supervisor (headmaster or principal) to voice their grievances. The State Education Code 1957/Departmental Rules 1997 and Headmaster Guide Book 2014 specify that it is the duty of headmasters and principals to address and dispose of their grievances in a stipulated period. In case the issue is beyond the jurisdiction of the headmaster or principal, they are supposed to forward the same to the next-level officer in the hierarchy of the district or state and so on.

In 2004, when passing judgment on a petition (no. 712/2004), the High Court of Rajasthan directed the state government to form a permanent committee to resolve service-related issues in the pre-litigation stage. In compliance with this decision, the state government formed a permanent committee comprising the following members:

1. Secretary of the concerned department
2. Secretary, legal, representative of the finance department (not less than special secretary)
3. Representative of Department of Personnel (not less than deputy secretary rank)
4. Head of department concerned.

In addition, teachers can use the offices of their unions to represent their issues and concerns to the state.[4] Following the enactment of the Right to Education (RTE) Act, committees at the block and district levels were set up in Rajasthan to deal with the grievances of elementary school teachers in government schools. Teachers can first file their complaints at the block level and, if not satisfactorily resolved, they may file again at the district level.

In 2011, the Department of Administrative Reform of the Government of Rajasthan set up a portal, SUGAM, for all government employees to air their grievances. The portal provides for online registration of grievances, which are followed up on a daily basis.

Odisha[5]

The State Government of Odisha offers two avenues for grievance redressal for teachers. First, a grievance day is held every Monday at the state level and the Secretary-cum-Commissioner hears grievances along with other state-level officials for prompt disposal of cases. The second avenue is a toll-free helpline that functions from 8 a.m. to 8 p.m.

The Sankalp Manual, published by the Department of Education, specifies time periods within which officers at each level (block and district) are to address complaints. The manual also includes time periods within which officials are required to comply with requests such as the sanction of increments, sanction of leave, assured career progression, provisional pension, rehabilitation assistance, retirement benefits, and similar matters.

Jharkhand[6]

In Jharkhand, a separate grievance redressal cell or department for teachers in the Human Resources Department does not exist. The State Government of Jharkhand follows the standard procedure adopted by the government as laid down in the rules common for all government employees. At times, there are annual campaigns organized (not mandatory) by the District Commissioners along with Human Resources Department officials to resolve teachers' issues on a one-time basis. But such drives are rare. In addition, the state has given teachers the right to form associations to represent their issues and concerns. In Jharkhand, there are six registered teachers' associations: (a) Jharkhand Rajya Prathamic Shikshak Sangh, (b) Akhil Jharkhand Prathamik Shikshak Sangh, (c) Rashtravadi Shikshak Sangh, (d) Para Shikshak Sangh, (e) Jharkhand Rajya Madhyamik Shikshak Sangh, and (f) Alpsankhyaka Shikshak Sangh. These associations are active in influencing state education policies, especially those related to teachers.

Uttar Pradesh[7]

In Uttar Pradesh, teachers have formed cadre-wise unions for representation of their issues and grievances, to take up their issues with local-level officers and the government.

Under Rule 1979 (recognition of service associations) of the Government of Uttar Pradesh, all state-level employee associations have to be recognized by the government for dialogue. In Uttar Pradesh, the following teachers' associations are recognized: Uttar Pradesh Prathamik Shikshak Sangh, Uttar Pradesh Upper Primary Shikshak Sangh, and Uttar Pradesh Rajkiya Shikshak Sangh. Other similar associations do not fulfill the recognition criteria according to the rule.

Most teachers' unions have their school-level (secondary schools) or block-level units to look after the interests of their members. These units take up individual or common teacher grievances with the principal or the Block Education Officer. Most unions hold regular meetings with the district-level and state-level officers to sort out teacher grievances at the administrative level. These include

General Provident Fund advance, salary arrears, withholding of salary, transfers, suspension, disciplinary action, and other related issues.

The Uttar Pradesh Legislative Council has nine teacher members who are selected from the pool of secondary school teachers (mostly from aided schools) in the state. This provides the teachers with an additional forum for representation through the members of the Legislative Council.

Madhya Pradesh[8]

The teacher grievance redressal system in Madhya Pradesh has undergone significant changes in the past 15 years. Since 2008, with the absorption of para and contract teachers into the system, senior teachers, regular teachers, and assistant teachers could, in principle, appeal for redressal to the appointment authority, additional Chief Executive Officer of School Education, or Tribal Welfare Authority as the competent authority and the District Collector as the appellate authority.

In 2009, the School Education Department decided to address teacher issues—for working and retired teachers—through an online portal (which included a teacher database). All teacher cadres can submit their grievances through the portal and retrieve their redressal report using a unique identification code assigned to them. Reports on written complaints are also available online. For restitution of cases, the following rules are followed:

- The Joint Director and other senior officers monitor the cases filed.
- State-level redressal of cases can use methods such as video conferencing.

In 2011, the Madhya Pradesh State Rules and Regulations included clauses for redressal of teacher grievances, based on the provisions of the RTE Act. The sequence/levels through which a grievance would be addressed included the School Management Committee, including the head teacher; state-nominated local officials who would be expected to address concerns within a 30-day period; and a committee formed by the Collector, Superintendent of Policy, Chief Executive Officer, Chief Medical Officer, Health Officer (district), Municipal Corporation Commissioner, and the Tribal Welfare and Additional Commissioner. The District Education Officer would be the convener of this committee, which would meet quarterly. In addition, under the RTE Act, all schools that fall under a specified jurisdiction (schools under Tribal Welfare or Scheduled Caste (SC) Welfare) would have their own grievance redressal systems.

In practice, however, even with the revision of the grievance redressal mechanisms over time toward more efficiency, it has not worked well. The number of cases has grown since 2005, without proper monitoring and resolution taking place. Some recent attempts have been made to reduce the accumulated number of cases, such as through camps (the first one organized in June 2014) for resolving grievances for all cadres of teachers.

Punjab[9]

In Punjab, teachers can use a module of the e-Punjab school web portal to lodge their grievances. Teachers can check on the status of their grievances anytime online. Senior officers of the department monitor and review monthly all pending grievances.[10]

Teachers in Punjab who are members of unions also use union services for putting forward their demands and grievances to the state. Unions often agitate on behalf of their members and there is evidence that the state has sometimes acceded to these demands.

Dispute Resolution Tribunals

In several of the states studied, teacher grievances could also be heard by service tribunals constituted to hear service-related disputes of government employees. The service tribunals appear to be functioning better in some states than others. Some states, such as Tamil Nadu in 2005, have abolished their services tribunals.[11] Where they function effectively, such tribunals could be helpful in taking the load off the High Court. The tribunals could also provide teachers with a more specialized forum in which their service-related grievances could be heard. For example, the Karnataka Administrative Tribunal and the Rajasthan Civil Services Appellate Tribunal are two such forums that hear various service benefit matters of government schoolteachers.

Some states also have specialized education tribunals, although these typically hear the grievances of teachers in private schools. For example, the Jharkhand Education Tribunal hears the disputes of teachers of aided and unaided private schools, as do the Rajasthan Non-Government Educational Tribunal and the Odisha State Education Tribunal. The case of the Odisha State Educational Tribunal is worth studying. This tribunal was originally constituted through the Odisha Education Act of 1969. The tribunal was assigned the responsibility of resolving disputes between teachers, school management, and the government in private and aided schools. However, the tribunal lacked major enforcement powers, and thus it was largely redundant. According to the State Education Department, about 5,000 writ petitions and 1,793 contempt of court proceedings piled up in the Odisha High Court because of nonexecution of the tribunal's orders. Subsequently, in the case of *Dilip Kumar vs. State of Odisha*, the High Court took cognizance of these issues and entrusted this power to the tribunal through the Civil Procedure Code, such that the tribunal had enforcement powers similar to those of a civil court (*New Indian Express* 2010).

The effectiveness of these tribunals in reducing the burden on their respective High Courts is unclear and beyond the scope of this study, especially because there were only a handful of cases in our review that originated from these tribunals. However, it may be worth exploring further whether these tribunals could provide a more efficient and accessible forum for teachers to have their grievances redressed.

Grievance Redressal through the Courts

This section presents the results of a study of more than 9,000 judgments of the High Courts of the eight study states relating to teacher grievances between 2009 and June 2014. The analysis looks to answer three questions. (a) What were the types of grievances that caused teachers to approach the High Courts in their respective states? (b) What were the outcomes of these cases? (c) How long did these disputes take to conclude, typically measured as the time between the filing of a petition or the date of an order being challenged and the date of the judgment?

The Landscape of Grievances

A very large majority of the judgments analyzed were filed as writ petitions in the High Courts by serving teachers and teacher applicants seeking to be appointed to teaching posts. Surprisingly, only a miniscule number of cases were filed by teachers' unions, although it was said that unions might often support a group of teachers in litigating a case even if they were not named as a party. The respondents in all these petitions were various branches of the state education departments and, in some cases, also included the school in question (in the case of aided schools) and other teachers who had received benefits or been selected for a post in lieu of the petitioner teachers. A handful of judgments in each state involved appeals by the state government against decisions of tribunals or decisions by a single judge in the High Court.

The first surprising finding was the enormous variation in the volume of cases disposed by the High Courts of the states. Although a part of these differences may be explained by variations in size and population across states as well as because some High Courts may have chosen to report more judgments than others, these differences alone do not explain all the variation. The High Court of Odisha disposed only 75 such cases between 2009 and June 2014, while the High Court of Karnataka disposed more than 6,000. States that fell in the middle of the spectrum included Madhya Pradesh (160), Jharkhand (187), Punjab and Haryana (279), and Tamil Nadu (544). Rajasthan had 1,285 judgments and Uttar Pradesh had 1,146.

These significant variations in case volumes could reflect that teachers in some states filed far fewer petitions in the High Courts than their counterparts in other states, or some High Courts were simply more efficient in disposing the cases that had been filed. A factor that could explain how some states were more efficient in disposing cases is the tendency of the High Courts in these states to club together and dispose a large number of related petitions in one judgment. This was particularly the case in Karnataka and Rajasthan, where almost all the judgments studied disposed a group of petitions filed on related grievances, with many judgments disposing more than 100 petitions. Although the practice of clubbing is followed in most states, there are no specific rules on how petitions are to be clubbed together, and the business of clubbing is typically left for the court registrar to decide.

Another explanation could be a question of access. Litigating in the High Court requires resources and knowledge. The High Courts may be more accessible to teachers in some states than others, depending on the resources and support (for example, from teachers' unions) available for filing petitions and contesting cases in the High Courts. In cases where the High Courts are especially difficult to access, teachers may choose to find alternative forums for redressal of their grievances, which could, perhaps, explain why the volume of teacher-related litigation varied significantly across the states.

In contrast to the stark variations in the volume of cases across states, the types of grievances brought to the High Courts in different states were remarkably similar. The two predominant reasons that caused teachers and potential teachers to approach the High Courts were related to service benefits and appointments. Of the total 9,751 cases that were reviewed across the High Courts of the eight states, 47.01 percent (or 4,584 cases) related to service benefits, followed by appointment-related disputes (33.2 percent or 3,241 cases) and disputes related to regularization of existing appointments (5.9 percent or 579 cases).[12] Other issues that featured prominently (although not as frequently as service benefits and appointments) related to termination, transfers, promotions, and retirement benefits. Tables 9.1 and 9.2 set out the three most predominant grievance types for each state, and the breakdown of the different types of grievances that were decided by the High Courts in the eight states, respectively.

Common Themes in Appointment and Service Benefit–Related Grievances
Appointments

Appointment-related grievances can be divided into three sub-types. The first sub-type is related to grievances over the eligibility criteria for appointments. Often, this involved disputes over whether a certain qualification could be

Table 9.1 Predominant Grievance Types, by State (High Court Cases Only)

State	Predominant grievance type		
Jharkhand	Appointments (31.01%)	Service benefits (29.41%)	Retirement benefits (14.97%)
Karnataka	Service benefits (65%)	Appointments (22.9%)	Regularization (3%)
Madhya Pradesh	Retirement benefits (45%)	Appointments (31.25%)	Service benefits (12.5%)
Odisha	Termination (48%)	Appointments (29.33%)	Transfers (10.67%)
Punjab and Haryana	Appointments (60.93%)	Transfers (12.19%)	Termination (11.11%)
Rajasthan	Appointments (69.96%)	Regularization (12.14%)	Service benefits (10.58%)
Tamil Nadu	Service benefits (42.10%)	Appointments (22.24%)	Examination standards (13.60%)
Uttar Pradesh	Appointments (46.29%)	Regularization (18.95%)	Service benefits (14.85%)

Table 9.2 Types of Grievances, by State

Case type	JH	KA	MP	OD	PJ&H	RJ	TN	UP	Total
Service benefits	55	3,962	20	1	11	136	229	170	4,584
Appointment	58	1,391	50	22	170	899	121	530	3,241
Regularization	6	188	0	0	1	156	11	217	579
Transfer	0	183	2	8	34	22	12	12	273
Termination	11	54	7	36	31	10	10	80	239
Retirement benefits	28	1	72	7	9	11	26	11	165
Promotion	11	3	3	1	5	5	40	85	153
Examination standards	1	0	0	0	3	45	74	3	126
Contempt	1	60	0	0	9	0	0	5	75
Suspension	3	0	3	0	0	0	5	24	35
Insurance	0	19	1	0	0	0	0	0	20
Miscellaneous	13	214	2	0	6	1	16	9	261
Total	187	6,075	160	75	279	1,285	544	1,146	9,751

Note: Punjab and Haryana are covered by one High Court. JH = Jharkhand; KA = Karnataka; MP = Madhya Pradesh; OD = Odisha; PJ&H = Punjab and Haryana; RJ = Rajasthan; TN = Tamil Nadu; UP = Uttar Pradesh.

considered equivalent to the required qualification for a post. In other cases, these disputes stemmed from confusion over implementation of the guidelines on teacher qualifications proposed by the National Council for Teacher Education (NCTE) following the enactment of the RTE Act. For example, the Rajasthan High Court disposed several petitions[13] that were filed by teacher applicants asking the state government to relax the cutoff date after which the minimum qualifications laid down by NCTE would apply.[14] The petitioners were teacher applicants to government elementary schools who did not have these qualifications and contended that they would have been eligible for appointment had the state not delayed the selection process. The court dismissed these petitions, stating that the state government cannot relax the cutoff date, as this would be contrary to the RTE Act and the minimum qualifications required of teachers under the rules prescribed by NCTE.

In another group of decisions disposed by the Madras High Court in Tamil Nadu, teacher applicants challenged the Director of School Education's order to grant appointments to applicants with a one-year or three-year degree in the relevant subject.[15] The Madras High Court engaged in a detailed discussion of the rules and eligibility criteria and concluded that although the term "graduate" (which was the requirement for the post) was not defined in the rules, the term is generally understood to be a holder of a valid university degree, which the University Grant Commission rules define as being a three-year degree. Hence, the petitions were allowed and the court quashed the Director of School Education's order to grant appointments to candidates with one-year degrees.

The second sub-type relates to grievances over the selection process and the procedures followed. For example, teacher applicants raised questions as to whether the advertisement had properly described the relevant post and whether the criteria for selection stated in the advertisement were followed. Interestingly, there were instances in quite a few states (including Tamil Nadu and Punjab) where the selection criteria were changed while the selection process was underway. The High Courts of all the states gave a lot of regard to whether due process and the principles of natural justice were followed during the selection process. The courts were willing to quash the results of the selection if, for example, there was any evidence of impropriety or not following the rules during the selection process. In 2012, the High Court of Punjab and Haryana disposed of 69 petitions filed by teacher applicants challenging the selection process for physical training instructors pursuant to an advertisement issued by the Haryana Staff Selection Commission in 2006.[16] The High Court quashed the entire selection process, as it was revealed that the selection criteria were different from those published in the initial advertisement for the posts. Further, the High Court noted with concern that it had learned that all selection decisions were made by the chairperson of the commission alone, rather than by the members of the commission as a whole.

The third sub-type is cases related to reservation criteria. These were often disputes over whether a candidate from a reserved category should be given preference over a candidate from another reserved category. The High Courts generally decided these disputes on the basis of the rules regarding appointments for reserved category candidates. There were disputes involving candidates from a wide variety of backgrounds—SCs, Scheduled Tribes, and Other Backward Classes, but also persons with disabilities, freedom fighters, and women. Another issue that often arose in the reservation cases was related to whether reserved category candidates were entitled to a relaxation of the eligibility criteria and, if so, to what extent. The High Courts generally upheld the NCTE guidelines that allowed for up to 5 percent relaxation of marks for reserved category candidates. As was the situation in a case decided by the Rajasthan High Court,[17] the High Courts were unwilling to allow further relaxation, as this was considered contrary to the NCTE guidelines.

Service Benefits
Disputes regarding service benefits encapsulated a wide variety of service-related matters. These included nonpayment or untimely payment of salary, leave encashment, and disputes over pay scale and seniority. Most of these judgments were very fact-specific decisions that generally tended to be decided by the High Courts on a case-by-case basis and on the merits. One type of case that safeguarded the rights of teachers was those involving challenges to government decisions to reclaim excess amounts paid to them (for example, where the pay scale was wrongly calculated the first time around). In these cases, the courts typically relied on principles of fairness and did not allow the government to reclaim excess amounts already paid to teachers, although the government was entitled to change the pay scale going forward.

There was also a subcategory of service benefit disputes that dealt with larger policy issues. Many of these cases, which often related to how seniority was to be calculated for determining pay scale, suggest that the service rules for teachers in many of the states were not entirely clear. Adding to this confusion was that there were often different rules for different types of teachers as well as different types of schools (for example, for primary and secondary schools). Consequently, there were several cases where teachers approached the courts to extend government orders on service benefits that related to one category or group of teachers to the group to which the petitioners belonged as well. In many of these cases, the High Courts did not allow these petitions on the basis that it was at the discretion of the state government whether to extend these benefits to other groups of teachers.

Teachers Appointed on an Ad Hoc Basis

A theme that emerged in several of the states was related to teachers who had been appointed on an ad hoc or contract basis. These teachers were referred to by different terms in different states (contract teachers in Rajasthan and Punjab, untrained or para teachers in Jharkhand) and there does not appear to be a uniform definition for such teachers across states or even within a particular state. These grievances were not as numerous as those that were related to appointments or service benefits. However, it would be worth looking into these grievances in greater detail, as some of the judgments involving such ad hoc or contract teachers had wider policy implications, although some were appealed against in the Supreme Court.

The primary type of grievance involving contract or ad hoc teachers related to such teachers approaching the High Courts to have their appointments regularized. In most instances, the High Courts (in Karnataka, Rajasthan, and Uttar Pradesh) did not interfere with the state education departments' decisions, especially in situations where the contract teacher had been originally appointed for a temporary post. A common theme running through many of these judgments was the notion that, unlike regular teachers, teachers appointed on an ad hoc basis were not governed by any set of rules regarding their appointments or benefits and, therefore, decisions on these teachers were left largely to the executive decisions of the respective state governments.

The Supreme Court was more willing than the High Courts to make specific pronouncements on ad hoc and contract teachers. For example, the Supreme Court held, in unequivocal terms, that untrained teachers in Jharkhand, who were appointed by the state with the promise that they would receive training, could not be penalized in their benefits on account of the state government's delay in providing the training. Similarly, the Supreme Court was critical of the Government of Haryana for failing to appoint regular teachers and, instead, relying on "guest teachers."[18]

At the same time, the Supreme Court's ability to delve into the merits of the claims of contract teachers is limited, as contract teachers and other teachers appointed on an ad hoc basis do not have any statutory rights. The appointments of contract teachers are done by the state education departments purely as administrative decisions. In general, contract teachers were not very successful in the 1990s and 2000s, as the courts maintained that these are policy decisions of the state governments. For example, this was how the case that was appealed from the High Court of Madhya Pradesh was viewed.[19] Here, the Supreme Court held that as the contract teachers had been appointed pursuant to an education program and not pursuant to any statutory rules, the teachers were not entitled to pay parity with other classes of teachers or even the minimum pay scale. However, after the RTE Act and in 2014, the Rajasthan High Court ordered the government to do away with the system of contract teachers.

Grievances of Teachers in Aided Schools

Although it is not a dispute category in itself, the cases reviewed included grievances of teachers from aided schools. In Karnataka, the majority of the cases analyzed involved aided schools. Almost all these were service benefit grievances and largely centered around three themes. One of the themes, which applied to several cases in Karnataka, related to how seniority was to be calculated for teachers in aided schools for the purpose of determining benefits. In most cases, the question was whether aided institutions were liable to provide service benefits to employees calculated from the date of their appointment or from the date on which the institution in question started to receive grant-in-aid. In a landmark judgment decided in 2006 in *VTS Jeyabal and others vs. State of Karnataka and Others*,[20] the High Court of Karnataka held that employees of aided institutions were entitled to service benefits for the entire period from the date of their appointment, including the time when the institution was not yet admitted to receive aid. The Division Bench of the Karnataka High Court and the Supreme Court confirmed the decision in *Jeyabal* on appeal.[21] Several writ petitions in the timeframe of this study were disposed with directions to the state government to consider applications as per *Jeyabal*.

This decision in *Jeyabal* and several other connected decisions placed the onus on the state government to implement the grant of service benefits to teachers in aided schools from the date of their initial appointment. In one such case, the government estimated the cost of implementation of these judgments to be around Rs. 7,000 crores to the exchequer (*The Hindu* 2013). Several contempt petitions were filed, since the government had failed to implement the orders on service benefits. Following this, the Karnataka State Legislature enacted the Karnataka Private Aided Educational Institutions Employees (Regulation of Pay, Pension and Other Benefits) Act, 2014. This Act essentially circumvents the court orders and provides that the service during the non-grant-in-aid period "shall not be reckoned for purpose of pay, leave or seniority."[22] The Statement of Objects and Reasons for the Act detailed the court orders on the retrospective provision of service benefits, but observed that there is "no justification" for granting such service benefits and further that such provision "would involve very huge financial implications to the state exchequer."[23] Therefore, the State

Legislature has, so far, successfully circumvented all court orders regarding the provision of service benefits.

Another theme involved the differences between sanctioned and non-sanctioned posts in aided schools. In some states, teachers holding non-sanctioned posts challenged the differential benefits available to teachers in sanctioned and non-sanctioned posts as a violation of equality under Article 14 of the Constitution. The High Courts in most states dismissed these petitions on the basis that it was a policy decision of the state.

A final theme related to the status of aided schools. For example, there were several cases that revolved around the question of whether an aided school that had stopped receiving grant-in-aid was still required to pay the same kinds of benefits. In such cases, the High Courts held that if a school had stopped receiving aid due to a lapse on its part, it could not stop paying teachers the benefits to which they were entitled.

Case Outcomes

Table 9.3 displays the outcomes of decisions in numbers and the percentage of cases that were decided in favor or against teachers in the eight states since 2009.

As table 9.3 suggests, the outcomes of the judgments were relatively evenly split between teachers and the state. There was no suggestion that the High Courts generally tended to favor the teachers or the state respondents. On an aggregate basis, 31.88 percent of the cases reviewed were decided in favor of

Table 9.3 Case Outcomes, by State, Since 2009

	Case outcome					
State	For teachers	For the state	Remand to the state	Partial relief for teachers[a]	Other/misc.[b]	Total
Jharkhand	75 (40.1%)	56 (29.95%)	42 (22.46%)	13 (6.95%)	1 (0.53%)	187
Karnataka	1,880 (30.95%)	943 (15.92%)	2,759 (45.42%)	53 (0.87%)	440 (7.24%)	6,075
Madhya Pradesh	24 (15%)	90 (56.25%)	40 (25.00%)	3 (1.88%)	3 (1.88%)	160
Odisha	48 (64%)	7 (9.33%)	19 (25.33%)	0 (0%)	1 (1.33%)	75
Punjab and Haryana	131 (46.95%)	41 (14.70%)	80 (28.67%)	2 (0.72%)	25 (8.96%)	279
Rajasthan	85 (6.61%)	1,181 (91.91%)	13 (1.01%)	6 (0.47%)	0 0.0%	1,285
Tamil Nadu	192 (35.29%)	300 (55.15%)	35 (6.43%)	2 (0.37%)	15 (2.76%)	544
Uttar Pradesh	376 (32.81%)	491 (42.84%)	36 (3.14%)	175 (15.27%)	68 (5.93%)	1,146
Total	2,811	3,109	3,024	254	533	9,751

a. Cases where the court granted some but not all the relief sought by a teacher.
b. Includes cases that were disposed based on precedent (where the specific relief being granted was unclear) and cases that were infructuous or the outcome was not clear from the face of the judgment.

the state, 28.83 percent were decided in favor of the teachers, and 31.02 percent were remanded to the state respondents, with directions to consider the grievance and arrive at a decision.[24] Although in some states the state or teachers prevailed in a significant majority of cases, it is difficult to draw any inferences from these data as to whether certain High Courts were more sympathetic to teachers. Some of the results have been further skewed by large groups of clubbed decisions. The case of Rajasthan is particularly telling on this point, as 788 petitions were clubbed together and dismissed in one judgment,[25] which is largely responsible for making it an outlier among the states, with 92 percent of the judgments going in favor of the state.

However, the overall prevalence of the "remand to respondents" category (31.02 percent) suggests that in a third of the cases, the High Courts were not willing to pass any orders on the merits of the teachers' grievances. Instead, the court simply remanded the matter back for the relevant official in the state education department to consider within a specified period, sometimes with guidelines on how the petition was to be considered.

Disposal Periods

Calculating the time taken for a petition to be disposed by the High Court proved to be one of the more challenging aspects of the study, given the lack of data. Where data were available,[26] the study calculated the disposal period based on the period between the date of filing of a petition and the date of the judgment. Table 9.4 provides the percentage of cases that were disposed in each state within the period ranges specified (again, for cases disposed in the past five years).

Table 9.4 shows that the High Court of Rajasthan had, by far, the best disposal rate, with 80 percent of cases disposed within a year. It was the only court that disposed more than 50 percent of its cases within two years. Jharkhand had the

Table 9.4 Disposal Periods

Period (months)	JH	KN	MP	OD	PJ&H	RJ	TN	UP
	(percentage of cases disposed)							
0–6	3.39	11.92	20.41	10.14	22.28	6.78	25.78	20.6
7–12	6.78	7.40	6.12	21.74	4.95	77.12	8.01	6.45
13–18	8.47	8.51	6.12	1.45	2.97	0.09	7.32	10.42
19–24	8.47	23.64	6.12	4.35	0.99	0.75	5.57	9.93
25–30	3.39	17.36	4.08	42.03	54.46	1.41	3.14	2.48
31–36	1.69	0.24	4.08	0	1.49	12.05	2.79	2.98
37–42	5.08	3.52	10.20	1.45	1.49	0	4.18	1.99
43–48	6.78	12.00	4.08	4.35	0.50	0	5.57	1.49
49–54	3.39	12.31	0	7.25	0.50	0.09	2.44	0.99
55–60	0	0.24	2.04	1.45	0	0.09	2.09	1.99
60+	52.54	2.87	36.73	5.80	10.40	1.60	33.1	40.7

Note: JH = Jharkhand; KN = Karnataka; MP = Madhya Pradesh; OD = Odisha; PJ&H = Punjab and Haryana; RJ = Rajasthan; TN = Tamil Nadu; UP = Uttar Pradesh.

slowest rate of disposal, with over 50 percent of the cases taking longer than five years (60 months) to conclude. Other states with similarly slow disposal rates were Madhya Pradesh, Uttar Pradesh, and Tamil Nadu. Odisha and Karnataka disposed cases relatively quickly, although they still took more than two years to dispose 50 percent of their cases.

The data also reveal that in many states, certain types of grievances were disposed more quickly than others. Grievances relating to appointments, regularization of existing appointments, and disputes over examination standards were disposed relatively quickly, in most cases, within two years. By contrast, grievances relating to service benefits and retirement benefits took significantly longer to be resolved. This was particularly the case in Madhya Pradesh, Rajasthan, and Tamil Nadu.

An interesting feature about the appointments, regularization, and examination standards cases was that they usually involved multiple petitioners as well as larger questions of state policy or challenges to orders that were applicable to a number of teachers. By contrast, most of the service and retirement benefits cases, except for service benefit grievances on pay scale and seniority, involved fact-specific grievances of individual petitioners. A combination of factors could be the possible reasons for the difference in disposal periods, including that more resources (including support from the teachers' associations) are poured into cases where multiple petitioners are involved, and it is in the interests of the state respondent to have these policy-related grievances resolved quickly.

The Way Forward

Teachers can use various mechanisms to present their grievance issues and concerns. In most states, teachers can approach the school principal and various Education Officers at the block, district, and state levels, to air and seek resolution of their grievances. In addition, in most states, teachers are members of unions or associations, which also interact with the state to represent the concerns of their members. In Uttar Pradesh, teachers have representation in the state Legislative Council, giving them an additional forum for discussion on teacher-related issues. Some states have exclusive dispute resolution tribunals for hearing and disposing of such matters. All these mechanisms are largely used for administrative issues, such as deployment, salaries, and transfers. No information was found that would indicate that these mechanisms are also used for matters relating to teacher learning, student-related inputs, or outcomes at the school level. Given the lack of data, the study also cannot comment on the distribution of grievances that are resolved through these mechanisms and those that are resolved through the courts.

On the redressal of grievances through the court systems, disputes over appointments and service benefits dominated teacher litigation in almost all the study states. To some extent, these issues are contentious for many categories of employees and potential employees. It would perhaps be expected that these are the types of issues that have been and will continue to be vigorously litigated.

At the same time, the analysis of High Court decisions involving teachers in the eight study states revealed some patterns that could suggest some ways forward toward reducing the volume of teacher-related litigation while at the same time ensuring that the legitimate concerns of teachers are addressed.

Many of the judgments appeared to stem from confusion in the interpretation of the education and service rules in the state concerned. This was especially the case for the eligibility criteria for the appointment of teachers to various posts. For example, there was confusion over the degrees required for appointments and whether certain degrees could be considered equivalent to one another. Another common area of confusion was over the state governments' implementation of the guidelines on teacher qualifications that NCTE had formulated in the light of the RTE Act. These cases suggested that several state governments were unclear on the weight to be given to the teacher eligibility test in selecting candidates for posts, the date from which the criteria laid down by NCTE would apply, and the level of relaxation that could be granted to reserved category candidates. Yet another frequent bone of contention with appointments related to the rules followed during the selection process for candidates. Indeed, in some states, including Punjab and Tamil Nadu, there were cases where the rules for selection were changed after the process was underway.

Similarly, there appeared to be much confusion on the pay scale and calculation of seniority under the service rules for teachers in the different states. Adding to this confusion was that there were often different rules for different types of teachers as well as different types of schools (for example, for primary and secondary schools). Consequently, in several cases, teachers approached the courts to extend government orders on service benefits that related to one category or group of teachers to the group to which the petitioners belonged as well. In 2013, the Madras High Court disposed 133 petitions from government schoolteachers in relation to salary scale, all of which were based on a claim that another group of teachers was getting a higher pay scale.[27] Clearer rules on these issues would go a long way in helping teacher applicants understand the appointment eligibility criteria better and in helping teachers understand the benefits to which they are entitled.

There were several cases with remarkably similar fact patterns that were heard by the High Courts. The Madras High Court heard several petitions from qualified computer science teachers who challenged the appointments of what they termed "underqualified" computer science teachers in the state's government secondary schools. Similarly, the Jharkhand High Court heard many cases of "untrained" teachers who challenged orders of the state denying them increases in their pay scale on the grounds that the state had not provided them with the training they had been promised. In all these cases, a lot of time and costs of teacher-related litigation could have been saved if the state governments had implemented the decisions of the High Courts for all similarly situated teachers rather than waiting for individual teachers to approach the High Courts in turn to get similar benefits.

The analysis of the issues raised in this chapter indicates that there is scope for reducing the volume of grievances raised with the state education department as well as grievances that are litigated. This can be done by improving administrative processes, especially with regard to clarity on rules and regulations, their interpretation and dissemination, and, to some extent, delegation of powers and skills to Education Officers at the sub-state levels. The following two observations clearly show that, oftentimes, litigation cannot determine the outcomes of rules and regulations; their ultimate resolution lies within the education department.

First, in analyzing the outcomes of decisions, a common response of the High Courts in many cases was simply to remand the matters back to the state authorities to consider. This practice of remanding some matters is based on a concept in administrative law that a court cannot substitute its judgment for that of an administrative body. The heavy use of remand is understandable, perhaps, with courts often taking the view that they were not the best placed to make decisions on interpreting the eligibility criteria for appointments or the calculation of pay scales. Yet, the prevalence of decisions being remanded reveals that nearly a third of the judgments that were disposed by the High Courts did not actually result in closure of the disputes for the teachers involved, and may have only set off another cycle of teachers making representations to the state authorities and then challenging their orders in the courts (although the study does not have any information on the extent to which this happens in practice).

Second, given the large number of relatively uncomplicated cases that are filed in the High Courts and often languish in the courts for several years, it is worth asking if the grievance redressal forum established by the state education departments may be used more effectively to shift some of these types of matters out of the High Courts altogether.[28] The grievance redressal sessions, carried out through state education department officials, as well as dispute resolution tribunals offer interesting and useful possibilities. Although the grievance redressal drives may provide teachers with a more accessible and, in the case of straightforward matters, efficient grievance redressal forum, the drives are often limited in their mandate. Officers at the block and district levels cannot resolve issues related to eligibility criteria for appointments or other issues that require an interpretation of the relevant rules. Further, any challenges to existing government orders (for example, an order on promotion or pay scale) must be made in the High Court or a tribunal.

Another constraint is the lack of a clear definition of the procedures for these grievance redressal mechanisms. The lack of documentation of cases means that it cannot be seen whether justice is being done or further disputes could be avoided by following the decisions in a given grievance. Yet, dispute resolution tribunals could resolve a wider array of disputes and, thus, replicate the function of a court more closely. However, unless the tribunals are given sufficient resources and a clear mandate, they could suffer from similar delays and pendency of cases that plague the High Courts.

Further research is needed on these grievance redressal forums. A combination of these systems could be used to provide more accessible and efficient grievance redressal and, at the same time, reduce the burden on the High Courts.

Annex 9A Data Sources and Their Limitations

This chapter is based on information generated through (a) state-level reports that use data from the state education departments (including focus group discussions and interviews with officers, teachers, and their representatives), and (b) an empirical study of teacher grievances that were considered serious enough to be escalated to the courts.

The study of the redressal of teacher grievances through the courts entailed analysis of more than 9,000 judgments involving teachers in primary and secondary government and government aided schools since 2009 from the High Courts across eight states in India.[29] The judgments were largely obtained through searches on online databases. All the relevant judgments that the searches revealed between January 2009 to June 2014 were reviewed. In addition, some of the judgments reviewed were collected from the education departments in the study states.

The cases revealed by the database searches may not cover every single reported judgment in the High Courts of the relevant states, as there are limitations inherent in any keyword search. In addition, some cases were not reported and did not find their way to online databases. For these reasons, the study did not carry out an exhaustive review of all the High Court cases that involved teachers of government and aided schools in the eight states studied.

Further, the judgments only provide a picture of the cases that have been disposed by the High Courts. The judgments do not give any indication of those cases that have been filed and are pending before the courts. However, despite these limitations in the data, the searches yielded a broad cross-section of the types of grievances involving teachers in the eight states between 2009 and July 2014. Therefore, this information is helpful in providing an accurate picture of (a) the grievances that cause teachers to approach the High Courts, and (b) how these grievances are managed and resolved in the High Courts.

The decision to focus on High Court judgments as opposed to judgments of the lower courts (that may be more accessible to teachers and, as a consequence, present a more representative picture of the spectrum of teacher-related disputes) was initially based on the availability of data. Reliable data on disputes decided by the district courts and lower courts are not available and cannot be searched on online databases. However, the High Courts are indeed the right forum to study, because a majority of teacher-related grievances are filed as writ petitions in the respective High Courts, making the High Courts the courts of first instance for many of these disputes. In some states, specialized tribunals may be the first forum to hear teachers' grievances, but even in those cases, teachers have the right to appeal against the decision of the tribunal in the High Courts. Thus, the focus on High Court cases provides a good description of the spectrum of teacher-related disputes that get escalated to the courts.

Notes

1. Gauri (2013).
2. Excluding Mizoram.
3. Source: Rajasthan State Report.
4. At present, none of the 150+ teachers' unions in Rajasthan has been recognized by the state.
5. Source: Odisha State Report.
6. Source: Jharkhand State Report.
7. Source: Uttar Pradesh State Report.
8. Source: Madhya Pradesh State Report.
9. Source: Punjab State Report.
10. Earlier School Management Committees were also involved in the grievance redressal process in Punjab. This has changed with the administrative authority over district/panchayat teachers being moved to the state education department.
11. The abolition of the Tamil Nadu Administrative Services Tribunal was a policy decision by the Tamil Nadu government, which decided that two forums (the High Court and the Supreme Court) for trying service-related disputes was sufficient. At the time of its closure, the tribunal had more than 30,000 cases of service matters pending before it, all of which were transferred to the High Court.
12. Disputes involving regularization typically involved contract teachers and other teachers appointed on an ad hoc basis, looking to regularize their appointments.
13. *Rajesh Kumar Meena and Ors. vs. State of Rajasthan and Ors.* 787 others, 2013(1) CDR558.
14. Section 23(1) of the RTE Act allows the central government to prescribe minimum qualifications for teachers. The central government issued Notification 5.04.2010 authorizing NCTE to prescribe these qualifications.
15. *R. Thirunavukkarasau vs. The State of Tamil Nadu* 2012(5)CTC129.
16. *Sanjeev Kumar and Others vs. State of Haryana and Others* 2013(2)SCT78(P&H).
17. See *Vikas Kumar Agrawal and etc. vs. State of Rajasthan & Ors.* 2012 (3) ILR (Raj) 459.
18. *Naresh Kumar & Ors. vs. State of Haryana & Ors*, dated March 30, 2012.
19. *Gopal Chawala vs. State of Madhya Pradesh* 2014(3)SCT56(SC).
20. *VTS Jeyabal vs. State of Karnataka & Ors, W.P.* 19431/2005 decided on October 13, 2006.
21. *State of Karnataka & Ors, vs. VTS Jeyabal, W.A.* 450/2007 decided on November 3, 2009; *State of Karnataka vs. Nagegowda & Ors*, SLP(c) No. 22176-22186/2010 dismissed on August 21, 2013.
22. See Section 3(1), Karnataka Private Aided Educational Institutions Employees (Regulation of Pay, Pension and Other Benefits) Act, 2014.
23. See Statement of Objects and Reasons, Karnataka Private Aided Educational Institutions Employees (Regulation of Pay, Pension and Other Benefits) Act, 2014.
24. The remaining 10 percent of cases had outcomes that included partial relief or were disposed of without an indication of the particular relief (or lack of relief) being granted.

25. *Rajesh Kumar Meena and Ors. vs. State of Rajasthan and Ors.*, 2013(1)CDR558.
26. Of a total of 9,751 cases reviewed, starting dates were available for 7,081 cases (72.6 percent).
27. *S. Arulappan vs. The Government of Tamil Nadu*, W.P. 4505 of 2012 and others, decided on November 13, 2013.
28. During the preparation of this research, many department officials complained about the amount of time they had to spend attending to litigation cases before the courts.
29. The eight High Courts studied were Jharkhand, Karnataka, Madhya Pradesh, Odisha, Punjab and Haryana, Rajasthan, Tamil Nadu, and Uttar Pradesh. Although Mizoram was also included in the research, it was excluded from these findings because the database search revealed only five cases of teacher-related litigation that reached its High Court, making the sample size too small for comparative purposes.

CHAPTER 10

Unanswered Questions

Overview

Traveling across the nine states and meeting teachers and administrators was an enriching experience. The research team realized that there is no ambiguity on some basic requirements for teachers—they are expected to attend school every working day, teach students for an expected number of hours, and take responsibility for their students' learning. Teacher salaries have increased significantly in the past 20 years, from the Fifth Pay Commission (1994) to the Sixth Pay Commission (2006). All regular teachers who were interviewed during the study informed the research team that they were happy with the pay scale.

The past 20 years have also witnessed significant developments in school infrastructure as well as general infrastructure (roads, communication, electricity, and water). The government has paid attention to teachers' working conditions, such as improving pupil-teacher ratio, provision of teaching and learning materials, and availability of libraries and books. It is not as if nothing has happened when it comes to addressing the needs of teachers. In most states, the team asked the teachers if they had seen improvements in their overall status and working conditions and the answer was affirmative from regular teachers.

All this notwithstanding, there is a sense of disquiet across the country, a sense of despair when talking about the schools, teachers, and children's learning. Those who manage the schools, provide resources, and teach in the schools expressed that they had little faith in the government school system. Not one teacher that the team met sent their children or grandchildren to a government school. Likewise, administrators avoid government schools for their children and grandchildren. Political leaders sent their children and grandchildren to high-end, English-medium, private unaided schools. Even after 20 years of reforms, teacher absence remains an important concern; teaching time is worryingly low; and, most importantly, low learning levels among children means they do not have a strong educational foundation for their future lives. In several states, people talked in hushed tones about proxy teachers.

Another unstated issue that was sensed is the attitude of the administration toward government schoolteachers. Across all levels, teachers are seen as government servants at the bottom of a hierarchical system. By virtue of their administrative role, officials exude a sense of superiority. Teachers were not always seen as professionals who are at the forefront of the work that the education system is supposed to do.[1] The relationship between teachers and administrators is contentious, with both trying to work the system in their favor. It is perhaps not surprising that promotions are eagerly sought after.

At another level, the team heard that leadership of the education department—administrative as well as political—is not a sought-after portfolio. In many states, the heads (political and administrative) have been weak, unstable, and disinterested. Some suggested that this situation is perhaps responsible for the lack of administrative and political will to bring about systemic reform in the education sector. Social movements of disadvantaged groups like the Scheduled Castes (SCs), Scheduled Tribes (STs), and Muslims have not actively engaged with educational issues. This finding is ironic, because it is the poor (among them, an overwhelming proportion of SC and ST) who attend government schools. Although the country's policy says that education should be used as a tool for social equality, the government school system, which caters to the poor and marginalized, is crying for an overhaul.

This study focused on the working conditions of teachers. But the study also raised several issues that remain unanswered. This chapter articulates some of them.

Intent and Outcome

This research study started with a list of research questions. Looking back at the research process and the insights that were gained, several unanswered questions remain. There are significant data gaps and, more importantly, it is not always possible to obtain verifiable information on issues like rent-seeking, patronage networks, and the invisible undercurrents that run through the system. The research team wanted to delve deep into the gap between policies and practices. The team was also keen to understand the informal system as it operates on the ground.

As an example, on December 20, 2014, as the team was winding up the study, the Government of Rajasthan announced that the recruitment process for 12,000 subject teachers (mathematics, science, and English) had been completed and the appointment orders were issued.[2] This was reported in all the newspapers. However, the news item also mentioned that no joining date had been specified (there was, instead, an open-ended appointment letter). Thus, teachers who were assigned to rural/remote schools were ensconced in Jaipur or Bikaner to get their appointments reviewed, as most of them did not want to go to rural areas or difficult districts.

Apparently, teachers posted in rural areas receive a lower house rent allowance, do not get a city compensatory allowance, and, over and above these factors, have to spend from their own pockets up to Rs. 30,000 every year to travel from the nearest town to their school. Instead of incentivizing teachers to go to rural areas, the pay structure does exactly the opposite. How do teachers change the appointment letter to work in their favor? This question invariably elicits a smile and "you know how" comment. Research studies like this can, at best, provide qualitative or anecdotal information on such topics. They cannot provide verifiable documentation of this process, as it operates at a subterranean level, away from the glare of researchers.

This was a hurdle that the research team faced across the country. Although it is possible to get the policies and government orders and interview officials and teachers, it is not possible to record the comments and discussions of teachers and administrators and use them as evidence. Instead, the study had to use conjectures: a few quotes (where teachers or administrators permitted doing so).

Another issue that was staring the team in the face had to do with "working conditions." The data collected on infrastructure and facilities do not tell about the actual conditions. In most rural schools, having a "pucca" building, drinking water source, and toilet may not mean much if the building is in need of repairs, the floor is uneven and broken, the windows are small, the room is dark, and there is no electricity (because of power shortage, the school has not paid its bills, or they do not have funds to purchase bulbs). Children sit on the floor and the teacher may have one chair and no table. Perhaps the school has few teaching-learning materials and the library is locked (because teachers are afraid of the annual stocktaking—when they are asked to pay for the missing books). If they are posted in a rural school that is not easily accessible by public transport, teachers must travel long distances every day. They come late and leave early, and even if they want to stay in the village, they do not find proper housing.

The District Information System for Education (DISE) and Unified District Information System for Education (UDISE) are not geared to collect information on teachers' working conditions. The data reveal (for example) whether there is a blackboard and a toilet. However, the data do not mention whether the teachers have a table and chair, a place to store their teaching-learning materials, a common room or staff room, and, most importantly, access to basic sanitation facilities. Enabling teachers to work with dignity is essential. Some of these facilities are important to provide teachers the confidence that the system cares about them.

Another issue that came up in most of the interviews and discussions was the number of teachers who are available in the school on most days. The discussions focused on teaching and non-teaching duties, formal and informal leave of absence, deputation to an urban locale or administrative post (while formally appointed to a school), and, most importantly, the number of days "officially" spent on non-teaching and noneducational tasks.

Several studies (De, Noronha, and Sampson 2001; Dundar et al. 2014; PROBE 1999, 2011; Ramachandran, Bhattacherjea, and Sheshagiri 2008) have tried to map the work teachers do. In the past few years (since 2007), the DISE data have captured the non-teaching duties of teachers (DISE, various years).

Yet, teachers insist that this is an underestimate and they spend more time on these duties. Administrators insist that this is not the case, and post–Right to Education (RTE), the noneducational duties of teachers have been reduced. As discussed in this report (chapter 7), teachers view educational tasks like continuous comprehensive evaluation (CCE) as administrative work. On the other hand, administrators point out that CCE is an integral part of the teaching responsibilities of teachers. This is one area that raised a lot of questions.

The working conditions of teachers are a complex issue and it is not possible to capture all dimensions using DISE or UDISE data. More in-depth, school-based, qualitative studies are required to unravel the complex interplay of location (rural/urban, state-specific, tribal/non-tribal areas, desert areas, and border areas), connectivity (transportation), infrastructure (roads and housing), and other issues that have a direct bearing on the working conditions of teachers in India. This study has just touched the tip of the iceberg.

What Constitutes Policy?

Another obvious issue has to do with policy. During the in-house presentation of a draft of this report to a peer group, the research team was asked what, according to the team, is a "policy." For over 100 years, most state governments have had an education code. The British introduced this during the colonial times. The code clearly specifies many of the parameters related to teachers—the number of working days, roles and responsibilities, and, most importantly, maximum and minimum ages for recruitment and retirement.

For example, in Uttar Pradesh, the Education Act of 1921 provides an overarching framework. After Independence, the state government issued several orders, many of which make a departure from the 1921 Act. On matters that have not been covered by subsequent government orders, the 1921 Act continues to be the guideline. However, when the research team scanned teacher recruitment and transfer policies, it was found that several states issued annual government orders that were not necessarily aligned to any overarching "education code" or policy document. Therefore, the study surmised that states like Punjab, Jharkhand, Rajasthan, and Uttar Pradesh do not have "policies" that frame teacher recruitment and deployment. In some states, like Punjab, the age norms were altered with each new recruitment process.

In another example, the Government of Rajasthan periodically bans transfers. When transfers open up, thousands of teachers are transferred in one stroke—this is not informed by the Education Code of Rajasthan. The situation in Jharkhand is unclear. The vacancy rate in elementary school is as high as 40 percent, and the government has decided that all new recruitments will be contract teachers.[3] There is no policy that seems to guide these decisions, although technically, Jharkhand continues to retain many of the undivided Bihar policies (Bihar Primary Education [Amendment] Act, 1959).

Therefore, the question that begs attention is "what constitutes policy?" In this study, the researchers looked for a comprehensive government document that spelled out the norms for recruitment, deployment, transfer, retirement, and so on. The research team also tried to match recent government orders for recruitment or transfers with the "policy." Where such a document was missing and where each new notification for appointment or transfer set out a new norm or new eligibility criteria, it was concluded that practice in the state was not guided by policy.

Enabling Circumstances for Clear Policy and Transparent Processes

Looking at teacher management issues in this diverse country, some aspects appear prominent. Some states seem to have clearly laid-out policies, have set in motion transparent processes for recruitment and transfers, and, by and large, the teachers who interacted with the team seemed happy with the system. Yes, they continue to complain about delays in obtaining reimbursement of travel claims or getting retirement benefits. But, on the whole, they are happy that they do not have to lobby or pay for transfers and postings. Karnataka, Tamil Nadu, and Madhya Pradesh fall in this bracket. In some other states, the teachers were restive and unhappy. They talked about lack of transparency in deployment of teachers to schools and the importance of nurturing patronage networks. In some states, they openly divulged the amount they had paid to obtain or prevent a transfer.

What were the political and administrative circumstances that led to the development of a transparent teacher deployment and transfer system? In 2009, a team of researchers tried to understand the system in two diverse states—Rajasthan and Andhra Pradesh (Sharma and Ramachandran 2009). The most important advantage that Andhra Pradesh had over Rajasthan was with respect to its teacher-related policies. Andhra Pradesh had a well-developed system of teacher recruitment against the wavering policies in Rajasthan:

> In Rajasthan, teachers' transfers were regarded as ways of 'obliging' teachers who were close to powerful people, or were doled out as rewards (and punishment) for services rendered such as assistance in political campaigns. Subsequently, such teachers were rewarded with 'good' postings or protected even if they neglected their work. In Andhra Pradesh, a similar situation appears to have existed until 1998, when the Andhra Pradesh government decided to regulate teacher transfers through the process of 'counseling,' which entails a transparent allotment of postings based on predetermined criteria. The then Chief Minister of the state projected a pro-development, modernizing image. Rationalization of teacher transfers was in accordance with this image, and at the same time, it cut at the patronage-distributing power of the local Zillah Parishads and reduced their importance. As the then Chief Minister was a dominant figure in his party, it was possible for him to push this agenda through, despite some resistance from other members of his party. Once counseling had been put in place, pressure by strong teachers' unions in the state made it difficult to reverse. (Sharma and Ramachandran 2009, 119–14)

Discussions in Tamil Nadu and Karnataka for the preparation of the present study also revealed that the reform was led by a combination of a strong Chief Minister, who had the full backing of her/his party and the desire to introduce transparency at different levels to regulate the rent-seeking opportunities of officials and elected representatives, and a group of creative and efficiency-oriented administrators.

Karnataka made its first attempt in the 1990s and evolved a transparent teacher transfer policy. This lasted a few years and was withdrawn. It was reintroduced in 2007 and has remained in place. It was also noted that in all three states, reform was not confined to the education department. Rapid economic development created other opportunities for employment outside and within the government. For example, Andhra Pradesh and Karnataka saw a massive information technology boom in the 1990s. Tamil Nadu also experienced rapid industrialization during the same period. In all three states, government jobs as schoolteachers were no longer the only available opportunity for educated youth. In contrast, in states like Uttar Pradesh, Jharkhand, Rajasthan, and Odisha, teaching positions in government are among the largest job openings for educated youth. As a result, the pulls and pressures are many, and political leaders and administrators see teacher appointments and transfers as an opportunity to strengthen their patronage networks.

Similarly, powerful Chief Ministers in Madhya Pradesh and Odisha also drove administrative reform. Discussions with administrators and teachers revealed that the political leaders in these two states (the Chief Ministers) publicly committed themselves to "good governance." The current regimes in these two states have been voted back into power for three consecutive terms. Consequently, both states have had at least 15 years of stable governments. Beyond these broad trends, the study was not able to provide further insights.

What emerges from a comparative study of the nine states is that in states that do not have a transparent policy and process, the aim appears to be to keep "personnel policy out of the spheres of public and political scrutiny" (Sharma and Ramachandran 2009). When the transfer process is opaque and no one takes responsibility for it, and when transfers are done for "administrative reasons" (not as per the stated policy)—then it could be assumed that it is done for reasons that cannot be clearly stated. Unfortunately, when such transfers are done, they do not come under the scrutiny of the legislative committees of the state or the public. *The important point here is that the problem of transfers needs to be seen not in terms of the politics-administration divide and other policy-related arguments, but in terms of a process that does not follow any publicly stated and owned criteria or policy* (Sharma and Ramachandran 2009).

A far more in-depth study would be required to explain the combination of circumstances that led to a more transparent system in some states and why some states continue to manage with ad hoc systems and annual changes in norms and practices. But this study has demonstrated, beyond a doubt, that it is possible to develop and implement transparent systems and there are readily available models to emulate. What remains is to understand how to generate the political will to do so.

Role of Teachers' Unions in Influencing Policy

The study provides a few glimpses of the role played by teachers' unions. The Madhya Pradesh Report is particularly rich on the dialogue between the teachers' unions and the state, and the pressure exerted by the unions to reverse the state's policy on contract teachers. However, this is not the case with the other eight State Reports. Researchers and teachers' union leaders said that to understand the unions' role, the study would have to create a list of teachers' union–led strikes and struggles and juxtapose it with policy pronouncements (especially on teacher recruitment, deployment, professional growth and development, and grievance redressal) of the state government. A more in-depth qualitative study would be required to trace the role played by teachers' unions in policy formulation.

Roots of Administrative Inefficiencies

When the research team asked teachers about delays in promotions or delays in getting increments, the teachers said that the delays were due to bureaucratic apathy and inefficiency. In several states, the teachers talked about how their annual confidential reviews and service books are not updated in time, and that they may even be lost. In most states the annual confidential reviews are maintained at the block or district level, as the Education Officers do not have adequate space for keeping teachers' records. The office of the District Education Officer or Block Education Officer is cluttered; it was noticed that teachers' service books might even be dumped in a gunny bag in a storeroom. Thus, when teachers need to retrieve their service books, they must search for them or create them afresh. This is an issue that has nothing to do with policy—it is an issue of indifference to the vital service-related records of teachers.[4,5]

Discussions with administrators revealed the other side of bureaucratic inefficiency. They all told the research team that the numbers of schools and enrollments have gone up and the overall size of the education system has grown by leaps and bounds since 1990. However, the sizes of the block, district, and state-level offices have remained almost the same. Equally, when new, centrally-sponsored projects were initiated by the Government of India, separate and parallel structures, like the District Primary Education Programme (DPEP) Society and Sarva Shiksha Abhiyan (SSA) Society, were created. This effectively divided the education system into two—project structures and line departments. What the DPEP and SSA did not do in most states was to strengthen the mainframe education administration. As a result, although the numbers and the types of teachers increased, there was little administrative capacity to manage them efficiently. Existing capacity was further stretched by the additional complexity of service rules and conditions introduced by these central schemes.

Another, related issue that came to light was a change in the attitude of administrators toward teachers, who were perceived as those at the lowest rung in a hierarchical bureaucracy. The respect teachers had in society and the system was eroded throughout the 1990s, especially when governments started hiring unqualified youth as contract teachers or para teachers. The growth of the teaching force was haphazard and ad hoc. The system chased numbers and, gradually, started ignoring the pivot of the system—teachers.

Some states have tried to address this issue by bringing in comprehensive policies for the management of teachers, some others have recently reversed their ad hoc recruitment policies. The fact remains that the past two decades of rapid growth has affected the teaching force in many ways. This is an area that merits further research and this study has just touched the tip of an enormous iceberg.

Performance Appraisal versus Assured Career Progression

As discussed in chapter 8, there is no shared understanding of what is meant by "good teacher performance"—especially in the post-National Curriculum Framework 2005 era, where teachers are expected to be facilitators, and the post-RTE era, where children's right to education also entails the right to be taught in an environment without fear or punishment. Although many states take examination results as a performance benchmark at the secondary level, there is little clarity on how to assess the quality of teachers at the elementary level. Some states, like Mizoram, have an elaborate performance appraisal system on paper. However, the administrators, teachers, and headmasters, who are expected to work on the system, do not follow the process that is detailed in a government order. Therefore, even where there is a system on paper, it is not followed, because of (a) fear of disputes and controversies, and (b) lack of knowledge on how to do it in a transparent manner.

International evidence shows that it is possible to make reliable and consistent judgments about the performance of teachers, even if they are "subjective" (that is, based on observations of classroom practices). This is possible because of intensive and long-term training for those managers and head teachers who make such judgments and of the teachers, who are being evaluated (so that they understand the process and know how to improve their performance). It is also most likely to be possible in a system in which there is professional respect between the various groups, which is not something that is generally possible in such a deeply hierarchical system. Just as teachers need support to evaluate their pupils consistently and fairly, head teachers similarly need support to evaluate the teachers they supervise fairly and consistently. Making reliable and evidence-based judgments about teacher performance is not easy—but it is possible and, moreover, it is essential to help teachers improve their performance and identify those teachers who should be removed from the teaching profession.

Teachers' unions have been arguing for an assured career progression system. Essentially, this would mean that teachers would be on an automatic promotion track. How would such a system be reconciled with a teacher management system that recognizes merit and with the right of children to be taught? This is another area that merits further research.

What Role Do Teachers' Associations and Unions Play?

At the outset, this study tried to interview teachers' union leaders and invited the unions and associations to participate in a workshop in which the first drafts of the State Reports were shared. Teachers' union leaders participated in all the meetings and attended in large numbers. In almost all the interviews and discussions, they said that they did not really engage with recruitment or transfer policies. They petitioned the government on specific issues.

For example, in Odisha, they were concerned about the unclear status of teachers of upper primary classes. Some of the classes are part of the elementary cadre (thus earning less), while others are in the secondary cadre (earning more). In Tamil Nadu, the union leaders were more concerned about non-teaching duties[6] and had a problem identifying the right officer to address it. They also petitioned the government to provide a cleaning staff in all elementary schools to maintain the toilets and the school. In addition, they said they take up specific issues related to language teachers (promotional avenue), no-detention policy, CCE, and abolishing the trimester system and reverting to annual examinations.

In Mizoram, the teachers' unions were actively engaged with the administration on policy issues and, simultaneously, on addressing teachers' grievances. In Rajasthan, Uttar Pradesh, Jharkhand, and Punjab, the teachers' unions expressed concern about the nontransparent system for teacher deployment and transfers, but were not engaged in any discussion on new policies and practices. In Rajasthan, the teachers have been demanding a teacher transfer policy, but teachers' union leaders were not sure if they really wanted a transparent policy. They were not aware of the systems in Tamil Nadu, Karnataka, and Andhra Pradesh.

In most states, the research team asked if the teachers and teachers' union leaders who participated in the meetings sent their children to government schools. In almost all cases, they said no. Interestingly, among the reasons they cited for sending their children to private school was that they did not want their children to mix with "all kinds of children who come for welfare schemes," and that they wanted their children to study in English-medium schools.[7]

Effectively, what emerged in this study is that teachers' unions mostly confine themselves to petitioning the government on teachers' grievances and, sometimes, resort to protests and sit-ins (*dharna*). Except for Madhya Pradesh, the study could not go into the role that teachers' unions have played in bringing about change in policy that affects teachers, or even in the complicated process of lobbying for transfers and cushy postings. This remains an unanswered question and may have to be taken up independently.

Downstream and Upstream Impact of the Teacher Eligibility Tests

One of the important insights gained from this study was that all nine states have adopted the RTE-recommended teacher eligibility tests (TETs). They have also adopted the RTE-mandated and National Council for Teacher Education–stipulated entry qualification of teachers. The study has also shown (chapter 3) that the percentage of successful candidates remains extremely low. In some states, like Madhya Pradesh, the availability of qualified candidates remains a major bottleneck in filling reserved seats (SC and ST).

However, the study has not revealed how effective TETs have been in improving the quality of the teaching cadre. Do TETs help the government hire better teachers? Can TETs identify teachers who have mastery over their subject knowledge and pedagogy and, most importantly, whether they have the right aptitude? Given that most states have had to relax the norms for the examination or percentage marks required to qualify, is TET setting a benchmark for teacher education programs? Does it have a backward impact on the institutions where teachers earn Bachelor of Education or Diploma in Education degrees? Have these institutions started screening candidates based on their mastery of subject knowledge? The research team spoke with various stakeholders (administrators, educationists, and teachers) about this issue. The general impression was that the TET has led to the recruitment of more "knowledgeable" and better qualified teachers. However, this study was not designed to assess the "quality" of the teachers who were recruited.

Moreover, in none of the nine states was there discussion of using the TET results to inform pre-service training practices, including curriculum reform and comparing the pass rates of different pre-service training institutions. Finally, very little is known about the quality of the TET in the states. Some grievance cases, for example in Tamil Nadu, relate to the ambiguity of the test questions or scoring sheet, which delays the whole appointment process. Beyond this, there are more technical questions about whether the TET accurately measures knowledge and skills, whether it does so consistently over time (is a 60 percent pass rate equally difficult to achieve in successive rounds of the TET?), and whether the design of the test enables clear distinctions to be made around the passing score (since it is much more important to be confident that there is a real difference between a candidate who scores 59.9 and one who scores 60.1, than between 89.9 and 90.1 or between 9.9 and 10.1).

A dedicated study is needed on the process of TET, its impact downstream (on secondary and higher secondary schools and teacher education institutions) and upstream (on schools where teachers with TET are appointed). This remains an unanswered question that merits urgent and immediate attention.

Equity, Inclusion, and Gender

The education statistics provide information on the number of women teachers, percentage of teachers from SC and ST communities, and, lately, some information on Muslims. The earlier chapters showed unambiguous and significant progress in all the states in hiring more teachers from these categories. What is not known and the study could not explore is the unstated norms and rules that pervade the system. To take one example, which is cited in the introductory chapter, in Rajasthan, there is an unstated norm to post only male teachers as headmasters of co-educational schools and female teachers as headmistresses of girls-only schools (Jandhyala and ERU Research Team 2014). There could be similar unstated practices in all the states, affecting the career progress opportunities of women or specific social groups. A more in-depth qualitative study would, perhaps, help to unravel the unstated norms that affect equity and inclusion.

Another interesting glimpse has been of the participation of women teachers in training (especially when it is residential), being promoted as resource persons at the block or cluster level, or being sent to the District Institute of Educational Training or to become an educational administrator. It is likely that the barriers to career mobility are different in the different states—with states like Karnataka and Tamil Nadu revealing fewer barriers than, say, Rajasthan and Uttar Pradesh. This is yet another area that merits more detailed research and remains an unanswered question.

Pre-Service Training

The results from the TETs indicate that there are some serious concerns about the quality of in-service training providers. While preparing this study, the research team heard lots of anecdotal evidence about the poor quality of private providers, which constitute the vast bulk of pre-service provision. But it seems that no study has looked at the relative performance of the teacher training institutions on the state TETs. Such a study could have the potential to help state governments regulate the sector more effectively and improve the quality of government institutions. At the very least, such a study would enable important questions to be asked about the link between the curriculum and pedagogy used in training institutions and the performance of candidates on the TET.

Do Teacher Policies Result in More Effective Teachers?

The ultimate test of the effectiveness of teachers is whether the children they teach—*all* the children they teach—are able to reach their educational potential. Whether teachers teach in the most effective ways is determined by a complex set of policies and practices and how they interact with the personal characteristics of teachers and administrators. This study has examined some of the most important of these policies and practices, from the selection of teachers to the accountability for their performance. Moreover, the value of the present study is that the multi-state approach offers comparative insights.

As stated in the introductory chapter, however, the study did not attempt to answer directly the question as to whether India has effective teachers. This section returns to see what light this study can throw on this centrally important question.

First, across many policies, all nine states have very similar approaches. For example, the use of the TET, broadly following National Council for Teacher Education guidelines on teacher qualifications, the use of quotas in selection, the lack of performance evaluation of teachers (and head teachers), the absence of merit considerations in promotions, and the lack of a role for schools in the various processes. On the face of it, the last three practices would not seem to promote a link to effective classroom teaching practices. This chapter has raised questions about the need to explore these other approaches in more depth.

Second, the two areas in which states differ most markedly are the processes for deployment and transfers of teachers. Some states are clearly more policy-driven and have a more transparent system. Are teachers who are managed with respect and care more motivated than teachers who are pushed around by the system? What are the major differences between Tamil Nadu and Karnataka on the one hand, and Uttar Pradesh and Rajasthan on the other? Do the former have more effective teachers in the classroom? Is the deployment and transfer system enough to make a significant difference in the performance of teachers in the classroom? One measure would be teacher absence rates. Here the evidence is, to say the least, mixed: Karnataka is among the worst performers (at 80 percent in primary) alongside Uttar Pradesh (78 percent) (table 10.1).

There is some evidence about the teaching practices in Madhya Pradesh and Uttar Pradesh and teachers' attitudes toward teaching and learning processes, based on the work carried out for World Bank (2014). But it was not possible to compare the practices found in that study with other states in this study. The focus on how individual teachers behave in the classroom is the key dimension and leading indicator of student learning outcomes.[8]

Table 10.1 Pupil and Teacher Attendance Rates, 2013
Percent

State	Average pupil attendance rate		Average teacher attendance rate	
	Primary	Upper primary	Primary	Upper primary
Jharkhand	67	65	91	91
Karnataka	89	89	80	79
Madhya Pradesh	76	73	84	80
Mizoram	93	95	89	81
Odisha	77	78	90	88
Punjab	82	92	85	82
Rajasthan	71	74	85	77
Tamil Nadu	91	92	89	85
Uttar Pradesh	65	63	78	78
India	76	78	84	81

Source: Independent study by Technical Support Group of SSA (housed in Educational Consultants India Limited), 2013, as reported in Ministry of Human Resource Development 2014, "The Right of Children to Free and Compulsory Education Act, 2009."

Conclusion

This study has provided some insights and some unanswered questions—leaving the researchers wondering why there has been so little work in the field of teacher management in India. Although the study describes what does not seem to work, it does not explain why some strategies work in some places and not in others. Although context certainly matters and each state has its own administrative and political specificity, the challenge for researchers is to understand how and why the system works and enables key stakeholders to engage with these issues. That is the first step to search for the ways and means to turn the system around.

Notes

1. Unfortunately, this is not the case with teachers alone—evidence from other sources indicates that medical professionals (doctors and nurses) also experience the same attitude.
2. Dainik Bhaskar, Jaipur, January 21, 2014.
3. As a latest decision of the state government (dated July 10, 2014), 50 percent of vacancies are to be filled through contract teachers with the same qualifications and training parameters outlined for regular teachers.
4. The study team was not in a position to investigate whether the availability of the service records of the educational administrators is significantly better than that of the teachers whom they supervise.
5. Technical solutions are available: for example, Bihar has just completed a Teacher Education Management Information System, which maintains the service records of all teachers through a web-based platform.
6. Record of state workshop held on August 27, 2014, Chennai.
7. Notes and minutes of state-level workshops in the nine states, by Vimala Ramachandran.
8. It is tempting also to look at student learning outcomes as a measure of the success of the teacher management system. Here we would be a little more cautious. We know from studies in India and many other countries that student learning outcomes are the results of a complex combination of factors, of which teachers and the classroom environment are a subset—one that does not explain all the variations in student performance (the family characteristics of students tend to be very important also).

CHAPTER 11

Some Ideas to Take Forward

Overarching Message

This chapter captures some ideas that emerged from the study by way of recommendations. The study has shown that the broad guidelines drawn up at the national level (such as the qualifications for teachers set by the National Council for Teacher Education and the development of the Unified District Information System for Education (UDISE) database) have had and will continue to have an important role in facilitating a dialogue on issues related to teacher management. That said, the vast majority of teachers are state government employees, and it is the states that ultimately determine teacher recruitment and deployment policies, finance salaries, decide promotion criteria, and provide teachers support in the form of professional development and grievance redressal structures. As a result, the primary onus of reforming the teacher management system falls on the state governments, which must incorporate national developments into state policy and practice.

The overarching message emerging from this study is that there is an urgent need for each state to develop a comprehensive teacher management policy—one that includes a clearly laid out recruitment protocol, transfer regime, and clear guidelines for related matters, like teacher deputation to non-education duties (as block- or cluster-level administrative official), education-related duties (such as working with the District Institute of Education and Training (DIET), Cluster Resource Centre (CRC), or Block Resource Centre (BRC), as a key resource person) and promotion (as headmaster or head teacher). But a comprehensive policy is not enough; it needs to be supported by structures that allow practice to follow in a transparent manner, reducing the stress, delays, and confusion associated with non-transparent processes. This chapter identifies five key teacher management issues on which state governments could focus to improve their school education systems. The five issues are related; changes in one are likely to affect the others. Where available, the chapter provides examples from states that have addressed key problems in management, such as opaque and time-consuming transfers.

Streamlined and Transparent Recruitment and Deployment

The study suggests that, barring two exceptions, Karnataka and Tamil Nadu, teacher recruitment, deployment, and transfers are relatively ad hoc processes across the states, often subject to political influence. This ad hocism and uncertainty has given teaching a non-serious image, discouraging applicants from investing systematically in building pre-service teaching skills, and attracting applicants with little long-term interest in teaching in these states.

In contrast, in Karnataka and Tamil Nadu, teacher recruitment, deployment, and transfers share some common features: (a) there are clear policies for each; (b) the processes are transparent and largely conducted online, using sophisticated software and a management information system (MIS); (c) there is a clearly defined timeline for recruitment and transfer processes, which is stable across years; and (d) teachers at the elementary level (where most cases of corruption are reported in other states) are a block-level cadre, with considerable choice in their first assignment. Teacher transfers have been especially politically contentious issues in Karnataka and Tamil Nadu as well—but both states have found solutions and provide the other states an example of how to move forward in this regard.

From a systemic perspective, recruitment policies and practices must address two issues that have complicated teacher management considerably. The first relates to the existence of multiple cadres of teachers in the same state teaching the same level. There are Zillah Parishad or Panchayati Raj Institution teachers and some project-specific teachers (funded from Rashtriya Madhyamik Shiksha Abhiyan or Sarva Shiksha Abhiyan). Rationalization of the teacher cadres and planning for all teachers teaching the same level/grades in one cadre would greatly enhance the position of teachers. More broadly, the multiplicity of cadres makes it more difficult for managers of the system to cope, for example a head teacher of an elementary school with primary and upper primary cadre teachers or a Commissioner of Education trying to establish a clear promotion policy.

The second issue relates to the distribution of pupil-teacher ratios (PTRs) within states, and indeed within districts and blocks. A major finding of this study is that although progress has been made on the overall PTR across states, these averages conceal major inequities in the distribution of teachers across schools. All the states had significant numbers of elementary schools with very low PTRs (below 1:10) and very high PTRs (above 1:100). Therefore, there is an urgent need for the states to investigate the distribution of teachers *at the school level* and rationalize accordingly. At the secondary level, the states need to develop a metric for assessing the need for teachers, as the standard PTR used at the elementary level does not work (such a metric is probably also needed for upper primary teachers).

Easy Access to Support Structures for Teachers

The isolation of teachers in their schools and the absence of a supportive structure for academic as well as other kinds of support (substitute teacher when a teacher has to go on leave or duty) have been discussed in policy documents for a long time. To some extent, the BRC and CRC structures were conceptualized as a peer support system for teachers. However, the feedback from teachers is that there is no support system. In this context, there is a need to think afresh about providing teachers the necessary support to break their isolation, enable them to access academic support, and create a sensitive management system. Three things are important to highlight in this connection.

First, the institutions of headmasters and school principals need to be strengthened, so that they become the first port of call for teachers for administrative as well as academic matters. State governments have an important role in "professionalizing" the position of school principal. Governments can start by recognizing the importance of the role and ensuring that all schools have a principal (the number of unfilled posts is disconcerting) who is competent and motivated (simply appointing the most senior teacher is not a good enough policy). Governments also need to identify training providers who can offer capacity building for all those who are serving as school principals.

Second, there is a need for a systematic induction program for teachers. At present, new teachers are simply expected to learn their roles and responsibilities on the job, with little formal guidance or support. This is unfair on the teachers and unfair on the children they teach. To begin, states should develop a single booklet containing all the information a new teacher needs about their roles, responsibilities, and rights. Next, new teachers should be assigned a mentor—a more senior teacher with responsibility for helping to guide the new teacher and responding to questions. And the states should develop a formal series of workshops to help new teachers understand their job, and to bring together new teachers to share experiences and learn from each other.

Third, and more boldly, the national and state governments should engage in a dialogue about the siting and size of schools. The spread of schools to many rural and remote communities has had a positive impact on access for children. However, it has also had the effect of creating small schools without sufficient teachers (and without adequate support and often without sufficient physical infrastructure) to create *good quality* schools. Not only would teacher management be easier within fewer, larger schools—it is very likely that such schools would offer better quality education for the children.

For teachers to perform effectively, they must know that there are systems in place to protect their professional interests and aspirations. The Government of India could initiate a nationwide dialogue on grievance redressal mechanisms by drawing on good practices in the states, and encourage states to adopt these good practices. The systems in Karnataka, Tamil Nadu, and Odisha are at a nascent stage. They signal a new beginning. However, a lot more needs to be done to strengthen them and institutionalize the process from the cluster and block levels upward. The Government of India could also encourage the state governments to make sure that all schools and education-related institutions like the CRC, BRC, DIET, State Council of Educational Research and Training, and so forth come under the "Sexual Harassment of Women at Workplace (Prevention, Prohibition and Redressal) Act of 2013."

Incentives for Effort and Performance

As discussed in other studies, there are no incentives for teachers to put in more effort. Promotions depend entirely on seniority and the accumulation of qualifications, not on the work teachers do to help students learn better. The exception is Madhya Pradesh, where policy pronouncements suggest that confirmation of contract teachers depends partly on the exam results of their students. However, the study found little evidence to suggest that the policy had translated into practice. Even in states where teachers are given awards based on how well their students have performed on examinations, such as Rajasthan, this is not taken into account in determining a teacher's career path. For teachers to be effective, it is important that career progression structures reward effectiveness versus (poor) proxies for effectiveness, such as experience and qualifications.

Especially important in this connection is that there is no positive incentive for teachers to work in rural and remote areas, with the exception of Karnataka, where years of service in a remote area count in a teacher's transfer opportunities. It may be a good idea to build in incentives in the form of additional allowances, housing in the school compound or in the same village, priority for posting in an urban area after a stipulated number of years, and so forth. State policy should see teaching in rural or remote areas as a positive choice that can be made by good teachers, rather than a to-be-tolerated necessity while waiting for a "good" posting.

A final point on career progression: the multiplicity of cadres also makes it more difficult for teachers to navigate their professional progression, as they usually must leave their present cadre to obtain a promotion and cannot move back. Hence, a teacher cannot build a diverse set of experiences (as primary teacher, upper primary teacher, and member of the BRC team) to be a more effective primary teacher. This situation needs to be addressed.

Accountability and Feedback on Performance

Teacher appraisal is, perhaps, the most underdeveloped but also the largest missing piece in state systems of teacher management. What is expected of a teacher remains ambiguous. In the absence of clear expectations by way of teaching-learning processes, learning outcomes, and nurturing a nondiscriminatory environment for children (among others), teacher appraisal remains an undefined and weak area. The lack of an effective appraisal system means that teachers get no feedback on how they are performing and, thus, no guidance on what their professional development needs are; and system administrators cannot design or contract for necessary training programs.

An appraisal system would also enable promotions to be a reward for good performance rather than simply time served. A further advantage would be to enable the small minority of teachers who continue to perform poorly to be removed from the teaching profession. A lot of work needs to be done in this area. The work that Government of India has started with a handful of states is to be commended; widening the debate and understanding is essential and urgent.

Robust Teacher Information System

Transparent and merit- and experience-driven management of the teaching cadre would be greatly improved by an integrated teacher MIS, where information on the personnel and their deployment history is available, training history is recorded, and other teacher-specific information is available. Although it was not one of the states covered in this study, Bihar has recently developed such a system, and technical solutions are readily available. A combined and comprehensive teacher MIS is essential to make the system work efficiently and effectively. Equally, it would be extremely useful to administrators and researchers if the District Information System for Education and UDISE captured teacher-specific information. A unified MIS could make this possible.

A robust teacher information system would address several issues that teachers and administrators have raised in the course of this study, namely (a) delays in promotions, increments, and transfers due to administrative inefficiencies, like maintenance of service books and teacher records; and (b) deputing teachers for training on the basis of their needs and past training experience. The system would also enable the government to include information that could be used for teacher appraisal, thereby bringing more clarity to whom and what teachers are accountable.

It is well established that teacher accountability, motivation, and development are not only interlinked, but also inextricably linked to the way the system manages the teaching cadre. Many of the issues related to accountability to whom and for what could be addressed if an integrated teacher MIS were able to capture the professional trajectory of teachers. Or to put it the other way around, the development of such an integrated teacher MIS is dependent on having a shared understanding between the teachers and the state government of what teachers are accountable for and, therefore, what types of information should be collected through the MIS.

But having a well-designed MIS system is not enough; it must be used regularly for the purpose for which it has been designed. One such purpose could be for state and district officials to have greater capacity to use and handle data, so that they understand the significance of their policy decisions and how to calculate the number of teachers needed.

Finally, as the report shows, several administrative problems in the various states were caused by poorly developed policies or practices (for example, lack of clarity over service rules leads to delays in payment of teacher benefits and generates court cases). One way to address this issue would be for state governments to consult on new policies and procedures, by publishing the draft documents and inviting comments within a specific period. Beyond enhancing administrative efficiency, this approach would have the added benefit of promoting transparency.

APPENDIX A

Political Economy of Teacher Reforms in Karnataka and Tamil Nadu

Introduction

Chapters 4 and 5 looked at teacher recruitment and transfers in nine Indian states. Except for two states, Karnataka and Tamil Nadu, the states in the study share characteristics that weaken the recruitment system as well as the transfer system. Although across the states the standards for who can become a teacher are relatively low, the other seven states face additional challenges. First, recruitment is unsystematic, with recruitment timelines changing from year to year, terms varying across recruitment cycles, and rampant evidence of patronage. Second, there is generally poor needs analysis of how many teachers are needed in specific subjects. Third, the administration is inefficient, with some states involving too many departments in decision making, delaying the process, and others setting temporary committees without adequate background knowledge of the process. Finally, the recruitment system often comes to a standstill, as teachers file court cases challenging the criteria used for recruitment, such as exam performance and rank.

Transfer practices fare no better. First, and most importantly, they are generally ad hoc. Second, in most states, only regular teachers in government schools can be transferred. Third, teachers report needing powerful connections to get a transfer of their choice (or impede one against their interest) or to get a transfer relatively quickly. In Odisha, for example, political leaders are formally represented on transfer committees. In Rajasthan, transfers were given as rewards to politically helpful teachers. Payment of bribes was also reported in some states. Fourth, if teachers who want a transfer to another school cannot be transferred because no vacancy exists, they can nevertheless get to their location of interest by requesting a deputation to an administrative office. Finally, transfers can be used to discipline errant teachers (although in practice these remain rare, the threat may be real).

As chapters 4 and 5 illustrate, Karnataka and Tamil Nadu buck the trend. This appendix summarizes the key historical and political features in both states that allowed them to undertake relatively more efficient practices in a domain that is heavily influenced by patronage politics across the world.[1] Specifically, this discussion focuses on the following questions. (a) What were the key triggers and facilitating factors underlying the reforms? (b) How was technology used? (c) What is replicable and what is not replicable?

Karnataka

Background

Karnataka has 61,628 schools, with 74 percent managed by the government (Unified District Information System for Education State Report Cards, 2014–15). The total number of teachers in the state is 3,14,595, with 58 percent employed in government schools. Since the state government has 50 percent reservation for women, the state's teacher force is 59.4 percent female. Reservations for social categories have also ensured that teachers from Scheduled Castes (SC), Scheduled Tribes (ST), and Other Backward Classes (OBC) constitute the workforce.[2]

The current practice pertaining to teacher recruitment in Karnataka has been in operation since 2001, when the cadre and recruitment rules were redesigned such that elementary school teachers became a block-level cadre and secondary school teachers became a district-level cadre (see chapters 4 and 5).

Karnataka's recruitment process has two critical features: transparency and inclusiveness. Transparency is ensured because of the clearly laid down criteria and norms for every step, and by publishing the lists in the public domain at key points. An effort is made to ensure quality through the teacher eligibility test (TET) and Common Entrance Test. The differential norms for various social categories promote inclusion. There are differentials in the application fee, which is Rs. 400 for the general category; Rs. 200 for the SC, ST, and OBC categories; and no fee for physically challenged candidates and the minimum marks for being eligible. Candidates from disadvantaged communities get an opportunity to select the placement of their choice first from the available places.

The process is also fair from the perspective of the needs of the children and the school. That everyone has to serve their first five years in a rural area ensures availability as well as stability of teachers in rural areas; this used to be a major concern before this policy. A clause in the rules ensures that in case there are fewer approved positions than vacancies, the positions are distributed for all the districts and for blocks within the districts in a manner that the proportion of unfilled positions remains the same in every block and every district.

The process has been critiqued on two counts. One is the delays in the process. Delays are especially encountered for secondary school positions and direct recruitment of headmasters. Although it is common for the normal teacher recruitment process to take one year, direct recruitment at times takes much longer. The second critique comes from the general category candidates, who have last priority in the counseling process and therefore can select postings only from among those that are not chosen by anyone else (CBPS 2015). There have been cases when the verification process took more than a year or so without any justifiable explanation (CBPS 2015). Although the system can be more efficient to make the process less lengthy, there is no solution to the second critique, as it is the result of a social inclusion policy.

All transfers of teachers in primary and secondary schools, including headmasters, are guided by the Karnataka State Civil Services (Regulation of Transfer of Teachers) Act 2007 (Karnataka Act No. 29 of 2007, Government of Karnataka 2007a). The Act outlines the norms for first posting based on geographical categorizations. The state is divided into Zones A, B, and C, with Zone A being the most urban and Zone C the most rural.[3] Teachers must serve the first five years of their service in Zone C before they can apply for transfers. The entire transfer of teachers takes place on request barring a few exceptions. Once transferred, the next application for transfer can only be made after five years (see chapter 5). Mutual transfers and transfers for disciplinary purposes (rare, but possible) are not conducted through the computerized process.

As is the case for recruitment and placement, the transfer process is largely transparent, inclusive, and fair. The presence of norms allows everyone to know and understand the bases for deciding the priority list. There is general agreement that the priorities as defined by the Act are fine and inclusive except that the cap of 5 percent that existed earlier was believed to affect teacher couples adversely (CBPS 2014). This was then raised to 8 percent (Government of Karnataka 2015). That a teacher becomes eligible for transfer only after completing five years of service in a rural area helps ensure that rural area schools are not without teachers and there is some stability in the position. The sanctioned posts in urban schools where the enrollment of students has declined due to various reasons are frozen and not made available for transfers; this helps ensure the availability of teachers in peri-urban and rural areas. Sometimes this is perceived as "hiding" sanctioned posts by teachers. The provision for punishment posting, although practiced only rarely, is an element of the Act that goes against the general principle of justice from the children's or the school's perspective. If a teacher is found to be wanting for whatever reason in Zone A, why should a school in Zone C be made to accept that teacher?

Historical Context

The first major institutional reform in the school education sector in Karnataka, after the formation of the state, can be traced to the Karnataka Education Act passed in 1983. The Act and its subsequent amendments provided for better organization, development, discipline, and control of educational institutions, in the government and nongovernment sectors, in the state. With all the further amendments, this continues to be the main Act that determines the management of educational institutions in Karnataka.

The reforms in the education sector in Karnataka need to be understood in the context of a broader climate of reform in the state. Two elements of this climate are especially important. The first is the advent of information technology (IT) in the 1980s and the emergence of India as a major player, with Bangalore (Karnataka) changing to become a major IT hub. The presence of many science and technology institutions, including engineering colleges, in and around Bangalore is believed to have facilitated this growth in addition to the state government's policies, which have been very supportive of the IT industry. In the latter half of the 1990s, the state started exploring the use of IT in governance and passed the Karnataka Transparency in Public Procurement Act, 1999, to remove irregularities in processing tenders. Karnataka started the process of digitizing land records in 1989 as part of a centrally sponsored project on a pilot basis, and became the first state to digitize all land records in rural areas in 2007. Other supportive policies range from the allocation of land and development of infrastructure, to exemptions and tax concessions. Starting with the then Congress government in power, all successive governments have been very supportive of the IT industry, which has emerged as a major revenue contributor for the state.

The second element is that Karnataka emerged as one of the reform-oriented states when it passed the Panchayati Raj Act in 1985. This Act is still considered a landmark in the history of the decentralization of power to the third tier of government. This reform was also incorporated into the school education sector.

Teacher Recruitment

Table A.1 summarizes the evolution of teacher recruitment and transfer policies in Karnataka. From 1956 and until the early-1990s, district-level recruitment committees conducted the recruitment of primary school teachers and state-level recruitment committees conducted the recruitment of secondary school teachers. Local members of the Legislative Assembly and other influential political leaders played an important part in teacher recruitment through the district-level committees; hence, patronage was a critical feature of the process.

With the expanding state sector in education, the pressure to recruit a large number of teachers through a transparent process was also gaining momentum in the state. This was especially true for the primary school sector, where the numbers of teachers to be appointed were large. As teaching became a major source of employment, people started questioning the role of patronage in district-based recruitments. The interview-based process was open to maneuvering and hence a subject of criticism and dissatisfaction. To change this, the Government of Karnataka abolished district committees and made teacher recruitment entirely based on "merit" in 1991–92. Merit-based selection meant that teachers were selected based on the use of predetermined, weighted criteria for their marks in academic institutions, including high school and professional degree college. Additional weight was added for candidates coming from rural areas. The power was largely concentrated in the hands of the Commissioner of Public Instruction (CPI) in Bangalore.

Table A.1 Timeline of Major Reforms in Teacher Recruitment and Transfers

Major reform or shift	Ruling party and key political figures	Year or period	Sector and department
Karnataka Education Act 1983	Janata Party Chief Minister: Rama Krishna Hegde Education Minister: Govinde Gowda	1983	Education, Department of Primary and Adult Education
Abolition of district committees; abolition of interviews for teacher selection; recruitment of teachers through "merit"	Congress Chief Minister: S. Bangarappa Education Minister: Veerappa Moily	1991–92	Education, Department of Primary and Adult Education
Introduction of Centralized Entrance Test and computerized admission through counseling in engineering and medical colleges	Congress Chief Minister: S. Bangarappa Education Minister: Veerappa Moily	1991–92	Education, Department of Pre-University Education
CAC created for admission in B.Ed. and TCH and D.Ed. colleges	Janata Dal Chief Minister: Rama Krishna Hegde Education Minister: Govinde Gowda	1996–97	Education, Department of Primary and Secondary Education
Centralized recruitment through use of CET and computerized counseling for teacher recruitment	Janata Dal Chief Minister: J. H. Patel Education Minister: Govinde Gowda	1998	Education, Department of Primary and Secondary Education
Demand-based teacher transfers using transparent criteria and computerized process	Janata Dal Chief Minister: J. H. Patel Education Minister: Govinde Gowda	1999	Education, Department of Primary and Secondary Education
New service rules introduced to back CET and computerized counseling through legislative measure	Congress Chief Minister: S. M. Krishna	2000–01	Education, Department of Primary and Secondary Education
Offline computerized counseling for D.Ed. and B.Ed. admissions and teacher recruitment introduced through CAC	Congress Chief Minister: S. M. Krishna	2003	Education, Department of Primary and Secondary Education
Teacher Transfer Act 2007 passed	Janata Dal Secular Chief Minister: H. D. Kumaraswamy Education Minister: Basavaraj Horetti	2007	Education, Department of Primary and Secondary Education
Transfer of Medical Officers and Other Staff Act introduced	BJP Chief Minister: Sadananda Gowda (also in charge of Health and Family Welfare)	2011	Health, Department of Health and Family Welfare
Transfer Acts introduced for Technical Education	Congress Chief Minister: Siddaramaiah Education Minister: Kimmane Ratnakar	2013	Education, Department of Technical Education

table continues next page

Table A.1 Timeline of Major Reforms in Teacher Recruitment and Transfers (continued)

Major reform or shift	Ruling party and key political figures	Year or period	Sector and department
Transfer Acts introduced for Collegiate Education	Congress Chief Minister: Siddaramaiah Education Minister: Kimmane Ratnakar	2014	Education, Department of Collegiate Education
TET introduced in 2014, based on RTE guidelines; educational qualifications required also changed as per RTE guidelines	Congress Chief Minister: Siddaramaiah Education Minister: Kimmane Ratnakar	2014	Education, Department of Primary and Secondary Education

Note: B.Ed. = Bachelor of Education; BJP = Bharatiya Janata Party; CAC = Centralized Admission Cell; CET = Common Entrance Test; D.Ed. = Diploma in Education; RTE = Right to Education; TCH = Teacher's Certificate Higher; TET = Teacher Eligibility Test.

Many senior bureaucrats who served in the education sector in the state perceived the removal of interviews and making the selection "merit based" as the "most important reform" pertaining to recruitment. According to a former CPI[4] and later Principal Secretary (PS) and Chief Secretary, "What followed later is more about the use of technology to streamline the process, making it more transparent. But this single initiative had made the whole teacher selection process transparent without any aid of technology; this was also politically a more difficult decision as it hurt the interests of the MLAs."

Following the introduction of merit-based selection, another problem surfaced in the form of duplicate applications. Teacher candidates started applying in different districts to enhance their chances of selection. Since the process was manual, it was not easy to weed out duplicate names; therefore, several candidates, especially those with higher ranks, would be selected for more than one district. Once they made their final choices, the department was left with the vacancies that were rejected by these candidates. In 1994–95, with the help of the National Informatics Centre (NIC) cell in the CPI's office, an exercise was undertaken to identify "duplicate candidates," using the name and date of birth combination, and it was realized that nearly one-sixth of the total applications were duplicates. This became the basis for centralizing the process where all applicants applied at the state level and chose their district. Although it helped in weeding out duplicate candidates and controlling the political influence of the local politicians, this solution also made the process highly centralized and time-consuming. "There used to be a kilometer-long queue in front of the CPI's office; and CPI's office was doing only this for several months," shared the then CPI who played a major role in introducing the first phase of the reforms in the recruitment and transfer of teachers in Karnataka. The number of vacancies to be filled was large; therefore, a process that could quicken the pace of recruitment was needed.

In 1998, the state introduced a computerized process for teacher recruitment, leading to the appointment of 90,000 teachers in a period of six months, a feat that is remembered even today. For this centralized process of recruitment, the list of applicants received through the direct recruitment process was merged with the list of eligible candidates shared by the employment exchange. A common merit list for each social category was generated separately. Candidates were finalized based on the reservation roster for social categories as well as the marks secured in their respective degrees (Class XII, Diploma in Education, Teachers' Certificate Higher, Bachelor of the Arts, Bachelor of Science, or Bachelor of Education). Apart from the reservation based on social category, half the seats were reserved for women. The merit list as well as domicile details of the candidates were used to finalize the allotment of schools at the state level. Those securing higher ranks on the merit list were recruited first until the requisite numbers, as per reservation norms and existing vacancies, were achieved. Merit applicants from the SC, ST, and OBC categories were given first preference during allotment. Post-allotment of schools, selected candidates were sent selection letters with the specific school's name. They were not given a choice to select their district, block, or school.

Teacher Transfers

Until the late 1990s, teacher transfers were undertaken for punishment or as reward for those with "connections." The transfers were approved at the discretion of the Chief Minister, based on suggestions by the Education Minister and other officials of the Education Department, including the Deputy Director of Public Instruction, Joint Director (JD), Director, CPI. This often led to contradictory orders. Moreover, the belief was that only teachers with contacts or influence could use the provision of transfer for getting postings in desired areas. However, teachers were prohibited from transferring to their own villages. Such transfer practices led to widespread dissatisfaction among the teachers, especially those serving in rural areas and with no "connections"; they felt that they had no recourse to justice, while those with "connections" could easily get a transfer to an urban area and stay there until retirement. In an effort to reduce the corruption, nepotism, and injustice prevalent in the system, the government ordered that all transfers would be done at the level of the CPI. Although this reduced corruption, it brought in a lot of administrative strain, as it required the CPI to collate information from each school, document the representations received for transfers, consider the recommendations received from ministers, Members of the Legislative Assembly (MLAs), teachers' unions, and other local representatives, and take into account directions received from the government through an elaborate manual process. The system was imperfect, and there were discrepancies due to incorrect information. Further, third and fourth lists continued to be generated, based on representations made by MLAs for cases that had not been considered. Inundated by this voluminous administrative work, the CPI and his establishment ended up spending two to three months each year almost exclusively on this exercise.

Addressing the dissatisfaction among the teachers was the trigger for the reform in the transfer policy. The successful use of similar processes in admission to teacher training colleges as well as recruitment of teachers led to the idea of developing a new transfer policy that used technology for handling multiple criteria and levels at the same time on a dynamic basis.

The state introduced a new transfer policy brought through an executive (administrative) office order in 1999. The main features of this policy have been retained in the 2007 Act with some modifications. The most important elements of the 1999 policy were that (a) all teachers now had an opportunity to apply for transfers, (b) priorities for creating the list were clearly outlined and transparent, and (c) transfers were executed through a process of counseling using a computerized list of teachers ranked as per the priority. The counseling process gave them the choice to select their posting from among the available positions. The list of available positions was dynamic, showing changes after the last person had selected her/his school (Jha, Saxena, and Baxi 2001).

The 2007 Act was different from the earlier policy mainly on three counts. First, the notion of zones was introduced, something that did not exist earlier. This was an important shift, as it tried to ensure that rural areas do not suffer from lack of teachers. Nobody would choose to go to remote areas if they had a choice. Second, the Act introduced the system of equalizing the vacancies; if the number of transfers was not to exceed 500, and the available positions are 1,000, then this 1,000 will be distributed in a manner that all blocks make only half the positions available to be filled on transfer. This was to ensure that remote blocks do not end with a higher proportion of unfilled positions whereas all vacancies in other blocks get filled. Third, the provision for punishment transfer was added. Although the first two counts were to ensure the availability of teachers in remote and rural areas, the third was to protect the right to use transfers in some cases.

The success of the 2007 Teacher Transfer Act led to the passing of similar Acts for other subsectors in the Education Department, as well as later in other departments. The Karnataka State Civil Services (Regulation of Transfer of Staff of Department of Technical Education) Act 2012 used the concept of zones to ensure the availability of teachers and non-teaching staff in government engineering colleges, polytechnics, and government junior technical schools in rural areas. The Karnataka State Civil Services (Regulation of Transfer of Medical Officers and Other Staff) Act 2011 and the Karnataka State Civil Services (Regulation of Transfer of Staff of Department of Collegiate Education) Act 2012 were passed with similar objectives.

Note on Technology

All these Acts could be implemented due to computerized counseling. The use of technology allowed the handling of large numbers and use of multiple criteria on a dynamic basis while ensuring transparency at the same time. With the spread of technology and wide use of the Internet in Karnataka, the application process was made online for admissions to teacher training colleges and applying for a teacher's job in 2008 in the state. Since the Centralized Admission Cell

(CAC) handles both these processes, the change was implemented simultaneously. The e-Governance Cell at the Department of Public Instruction manages the transfers of teachers. In 2011, the Transfer Act was amended to make the application process also online. Karnataka has developed the software and processes without outsourcing any of the services. In the initial phase of transfers, the NIC personnel who developed the software and assisted the process were located in the CPI's office. District NIC offices and District Primary Education Programme (DPEP) offices provided the technical support. In later years, the CPI's office hired its own technical staff, reducing the need for support from NIC. The easy availability of software engineers helped in this process. The details of the transfer process are presented in appendix B.

Political Economy of the Reforms: Who Were the Champions in Karnataka?

Overview

The foundation for later education reforms in Karnataka was laid in the early 1990s when Mr. Veerapa Moily was the Education Minister in the Congress regime led by Mr. Bangarappa as Chief Minister. Mr. Moily disbanded the practice of MLA-headed district-level interview boards for teacher recruitment. It was during his time that computerized counseling–based Common Entrance Test admission was successfully introduced. Mr. Moily later became Chief Minister and continued his support for reforms in the education sector.

Reforms in Karnataka happened in two phases: the first was during the late 1990s when recruitment rules were modified and a new transfer policy was brought through executive orders, and the second in 2007 when the legislative measure was brought in the form of the Teacher Transfer Act, which affected placement and transfer norms and practices. Analyzing both periods from the political economy perspective brings out the following: (a) the government was led by the Janata Party/Janata Dal during both phases, although some critical reforms and extensions took place during the Congress regimes as well, before and after these phases, and the reforms were continued and supported by subsequent regimes; (b) the Education Ministers in both phases were very keen and enthusiastic about the reforms, taking personal interest and using their influence to push the reforms, and the Chief Ministers supported the Education Ministers despite opposition within their respective parties; and (c) senior bureaucrats, especially in two key positions—PS and CPI—were committed to the reforms and open to the use of technology, and themselves conversant with technology.

The combination of the three top positions—Education Minister, PS, and CPI—coupled with the presence of in-house technical expertise helped initiate, push, and sustain the reforms in both phases. Chief Ministers were also important in giving final nods. There were, of course, plenty of negotiations in each of the phases, resulting in modifications. However, the modifications did not dilute the reforms. The paragraphs below describe these processes for both phases, to the extent these could be recreated through conversations with key stakeholders. The key stakeholders in this case included a former minister, secretaries, commissioners, other key officials, software engineers, and teachers' union representatives.

First Phase (1996–99)

One of the well-known champions credited with reforms in education was H. D. Govinde Gowda, a well-known Gandhian leader and known as the "Gandhi of Malanad."[5] He served as the Minister for State for Primary Education and Adult Education between 1983 and 1986, when Rama Krishna Hegde (Janata Party government) was the Chief Minister. Later, H. D. Govinde Gowda was Primary and Secondary Education Minister in Deve Gowda's and J. H. Patel's Cabinets (Janata Dal government) during 1994–99. He quit politics in 1999, as his term as MLA came to an end. It was during his first term as minister when the 1983 Education Act was brought. And later, several of the first phase reforms came during his regime in the late 1990s. The abolition of the district recruitment committees, followed by the removal of the interview as the main process for the final selection of teacher candidates, however, had come in the early 1990s during the Congress regime. Yet, it was during his regime that a common entrance test and computerized counseling were used to recruit a large number of teachers. He is credited with appointing more than 90,000 teachers in a single year, as almost every newspaper mentioned this fact on his death.[6]

Govinde Gowda had the support of senior bureaucrats. The bureaucrats who played an important role during that period were S. V. Ranganath, Sanjay Kaul, Anita Kaul, and Upendra Tripathi, all high-ranking officers in the Indian Administrative Service. All belonged to the Karnataka cadre. An important feature of the state bureaucracy in that period was the continuity of senior officers in the same department, something that is no longer true for Karnataka. Mr. Ranganath, who served as CPI during the early 1990s and worked with Mr. Veerappa Moily (when he was the Education Minister), had started some groundwork for the reform and later became the Principal Secretary (PS) in the mid-1990s. Mr. Sanjay Kaul, credited with bringing in the reform of the first phase, was the CPI during 1995–97, and later became PS during 1998–99. Mr. Ranganath was the PS, when Mr. Kaul was the CPI. And then, when Upendra Tripathi took over as CPI during 1998–99, Sanjay Kaul became the PS. This ensured continuity and it was easy for the new officers joining to continue with the process of reform. Upendra Tripathi was reportedly a technology enthusiast who continued and strengthened the processes started by Sanjay Kaul. Ms. Anita Kaul was the State Project Director of DPEP during the late 1990s phase. DPEP was instrumental in making the teacher issue central, and provided a professional support base in the form of research. DPEP provided the technology support in districts where it was operational, and NIC provided support in other districts.

One of the major stakeholders whose interests were affected was the MLAs who played an important role in recruitment and transfers. The local MLA had been a member of the district-level transfer committee and was influential in decisions pertaining to recruitment and initial placement. Local MLAs were also the most important persons for recommending transfers. Even other MLAs and MLCs "recommended" transfers, especially for more sought-after vacancies in urban areas. The department at times received several recommendations for one position, and it was difficult to keep track of and act on those. During the early 1990s, when Mr. Ranganath was the Commissioner who later became the Secretary and pushed the reforms, the department started maintaining records to be able to explain to the political bosses the difficulties associated with such a process. These records later came in handy to push the reforms, as it was important to assuage any apprehension the MLAs had, to minimize their opposition to the reforms.

Govinde Gowda personally tried to convince the MLAs. His personal image, simplicity, and commitment helped in this process. The minister, along with senior bureaucrats, visited most of the districts to convince the MLAs and Zillah Panchayat office bearers about the new policy and its rationale and advantages. Following the introduction of centralized recruitment, placement, and transfer through counseling, it was ensured that the order for the placement or transfer was delivered by the local MLA or district Panchayat president to the teacher on the same day. This was to recognize their role and create an atmosphere where they did not feel left out. The immediate success and applause for the measure also helped in gaining their support. According to one senior retired official, "the issue of patronage was a big concern for the MLAs; once it was clear that the teachers were happy, MLAs were also happy and did not resist the move; teacher is a major constituency and hence their happiness matters to political leaders."

Teachers' unions were ambiguous in their position in the beginning, but later they also supported the moves. In the case of recruitment, that 90,000 teachers were recruited in less than one year without any significant glitch also earned the team of the minister and senior bureaucrats a good name and silenced their critics. The state had money from Operation Blackboard to appoint new teachers; DPEP had also led to the creation of posts. But in previous years, without a clearly laid out process and in the absence of technology, teacher recruitment took between one and two years.

In the case of transfers, that teachers for the first time had an opportunity to apply for them and there was a fairly transparent process that allowed them to choose for themselves was a great relief for most teachers. The Congress government led by S. M. Krishna that came after the J. H. Patel–led government in Karnataka was all for the use of IT in governance, and therefore supported the continuity of these measures.

This period also witnessed another development that directly helped in the conceptualization and execution of recruitment- and transfer-related reforms. The state tried to streamline teacher grievances in a significant manner and took measures to resolve hundreds of cases in a short period. Teachers' records were streamlined and seniority lists, which in some cases had not been updated for decades, were updated. The Minister, Mr. Govinde Gowda, personally went to every district with the PS and CPI, and resolved 300 to 400 cases in one visit; this expedited the process, which would have otherwise taken months. This also increased teachers' motivation, which in turn helped in acceptance of the reforms. In general, this was a phase of overall reforms in the education sector, largely dependent on executive orders and individual initiatives.

Second Phase (2007–08)

Although the philosophy of "no aggrieved teacher" guided the drafting of the transfer policy in the first phase, and measures were also taken to block or freeze the urban positions where enrollments had decreased, two complaints surfaced in a few years. One was linked to the lack of teachers for schools in remote areas, as no one chose to go there. Teachers had and continue to have a choice of saying no to a transfer if they do not get a school they prefer to their present posting. Another concern was from those teachers who were low priority and if they were serving in remote areas, they never got the opportunity to move anywhere else. By the time their turn came, only remote areas would be available for transfer. As a result, teachers started protesting and there were cases reported from many districts where not all transfers followed the policy using the software-based priority list. That the policy was based only on an executive order was a bottleneck in preventing such violations.

In 2006, Janata Dal (Secular), led by Shri H. D. Kumaraswamy, came into power with the support of the Bharatiya Janata Party (BJP) in Karnataka. Basavaraj Horatti, a member of the Legislative Council through the teachers' constituency, the Upper House of the Assembly,[7] became the Minister for Primary and Secondary Education. This time, he played a very critical role in modification of the executive order to a legislative measure as well as in bringing the changes in the policy that addressed the limitations experienced earlier. This time again, he had the support of two senior civil servants: the PS and the CPI, who were both perceived as committed and competent officers of the Karnataka cadre.

Mr. Horatti, who continues to be a member of the Legislative Council in the state, shared that the immediate trigger for the reform came from a teacher named Pavitra who was posted in a remote block in Hassan and had a mentally challenged son. She wanted to be transferred to Mysore where her husband was posted and where better medical facilities were available for her son's treatment. She approached the minister for help and that made him think about ways to strengthen the transfer process in a manner that takes teachers' grievances into consideration without harming the interests of the students. Along with the senior bureaucrats, PS, and CPI, they examined the 1998 policy and revised it to be able to address some of the concerns that had emerged before converting it into a legislative measure to institutionalize the process.

The most important change was the introduction of the concept of zones and making it mandatory to serve for five years in Zone C before applying for a transfer. Several MLAs had expressed their apprehension about remote areas not getting an adequate number of teachers; therefore, the introduction of zones was the solution. The priority list was also changed to accommodate teachers' feedback. Since couples were not able to get a posting in the same place, the clause of three years was added (to be used once during the entire service) (table A.2).

The Assembly rejected the bill twice and the Council also rejected it twice. Mr. Horatti shared that he personally met the MLAs and Members of the Legislative Council (MLCs) who voted against the bill to understand their opposition and assuage their apprehensions. In the process, some clauses were dropped and some added. The provision of punishment transfer was added later and so was the inclusion of the elected office bearers of teachers' unions in the priority list. In addition, non-cadre positions (positions above senior specialists at the district level are non-cadre positions) were excluded from the ambit of the Act. Interestingly, when the bill was finally passed in the Council, JD, and BJP, the ruling coalition opposed it and Congress, which had a majority in the Upper House, supported it; that is how the Act was finally passed. Mr. Horatti enjoyed the support of the Chief Minister, Mr. Kumaraswami, all along during his efforts to see this bill through.

The combination of minister-bureaucrat mattered in this phase as well. Each of the three crucial decision makers—Education Minister, PS, and CPI—owned the Act and described the processes with similar passion and ownership during the interviews. That made it clear that they were actively involved and keen on bringing this change. These bureaucrats also played a critical role in taking the reforms to other sectors, such as health. An Education Department officer, who later became the PS Health, was instrumental in taking the reform to the Health Department. However, he also shared that the support from the minister was

Table A.2 Changes in the Priority Criteria for Transfer of Teachers

Priority criteria as per the 1998 policy	*Priority criteria as per the 2007 Teacher Transfer Act*
i. Terminal illness cases ii. Physically handicapped cases iii. Other serious medical ailment cases iv. Teachers occupying surplus posts that have been transferred to other schools v. Husband and wife cases where both are in government service vi. Female applicants with fewer than three years of service left vii. Male applicants with fewer than three years of service left viii. Other female applicants who completed three years of service in the same place ix. Other male applicants who completed three years of service in the same place	i. Cases of terminally ill (open-heart surgeries, cancer, and kidney failure) applicants; self and family members included ii. Cases of physically handicapped/disabled teachers with more than 40 percent disability (medical certificate required) iii. Cases of widowed female teachers iv. Cases of married teachers whose spouse is posted outside the seniority unit and has completed three years of service (they can only avail this provision once during the service); highest priority is given if both spouses are government employees v. Other female teachers vi. Elected office bearers of recognized associations of government schools vii. Other male teachers

Sources: Jha, Saxena, and Baxi 2001; Teacher Transfer Act 2007.

essential to take the reform through, especially if it had to be a legislative measure. An earlier attempt to bring such reform in the health sector by some senior bureaucrats (in 1999) had not been successful because of the lack of support from the then Health Minister.

Lessons from Karnataka

Karnataka presents a neat case of progression in introducing key reforms for teacher recruitment and transfers in the school sector. Changes brought first through the executive order route were followed by legislative measures that also addressed the limitations and failures of the experiences. All this was achieved through the intelligent use of technology. Beneath this neat story lies the tale of hard efforts and negotiations, highlighting important lessons, which are described in the following paragraphs.

First, consensus among the stakeholders is the key for success. Although consensus among the top-level decision makers (for example, minister, secretary, and commissioner in Karnataka's case) was important for the reforms to be initiated, building consensus among other stakeholders (MLAs, elected representatives at the district level, teachers, and education administrators) at all levels was critical for sustenance. Commitment, openness, and concerted efforts together with a clear strategic approach by decision makers helped build consensus at various levels. For instance, in both phases of the reforms in Karnataka, the ministers as well as senior officials personally approached and convinced various stakeholders. Although senior bureaucrats as well as the ministers of the concerned departments can be identified as real champions, without the Chief Minister's support none of this would have come to fruition.

Second, the process of negotiation calls for strategic decisions on what and where to give, while knowing well what the non-negotiables are. For instance, certain provisions were added to the 2007 bill to gain the support of MLAs and teachers' unions, without which it would have been impossible to pass the bill and sustain its implementation. However, these provisions did not affect the fundamentals of the Act and therefore did not negatively affect the reforms.

Third, the success of the reforms also depended on the complementary measures that could lay the foundation for the reforms. For instance, that Karnataka also initiated a teacher-friendly process of addressing teacher grievances and managed to address several cases at the district level before the introduction of these reforms played a role in wider acceptance of the reforms.

Fourth, although reform is an iterative and incremental process, it helps to experiment through executive orders and seal it with legislative measures. Although teacher recruitment and transfers did not start as a well-thought-out process, the hiccups and limitations faced during the executive order phase were addressed before the legislative measure was taken. This made the implementation of the legislation smooth.

Fifth, the use of technology must be judicious and facilitative of the process, and must ensure inclusion and efficiency. For that, adequate preparations at the level of design and checks at the level of implementation are a must. It is also important to ensure that enough measures are undertaken for data security and avoidance of any leaks leading to violation of rights or any misuse of data. Karnataka's reliance on in-house expertise and measures for data security helped in building the confidence of teachers and other important stakeholders. Other factors that helped were the use of technology for recruitment, placement, and transfer as part of a larger move of the government toward such usage and not an isolated move. The easy availability of trained human resources also facilitated the process.

Sixth, the economic condition and political economy of a state plays a role in the success or failure of an initiative. Although money power played a role in transfers, interviews suggested it was never a major source of income for the officials or bureaucrats in Karnataka. Almost all those who were interviewed for this study suggested that loss of opportunities for patronage was a bigger issue than loss of "source of income," as was reported in several states in other regions in the nine-state study. Therefore, once teachers supported the move, it became easier to gain the support of others, including the elected leaders at different levels. That all the political parties supported a move that was seen as progressive and successful shows that it is difficult to undo reforms if they have already shown results and been widely appreciated.

Finally, it is also important to build systems for in-house institutional memory of reforms. The concerned individuals remember their own role, initiatives, and experiences, but there is weak knowledge or memory of the earlier or following measures. This is a major barrier in creating the full story and understanding the links. This also colors individuals' perspectives as they view the measures known to them in isolation. It would help to build systems that make it compulsory for civil servants to document the processes and measures taken during postings. It would also help to smooth the transition from one person to the other and contribute in maintaining continuity in the process of reforms and changes, in addition to creating better information sources for understanding the processes of reforms.

Tamil Nadu

Background

The teaching force in Tamil Nadu comprises the biggest group of government servants. Although government schoolteachers are employees of the state government, teachers in aided and unaided private schools are not, as is shown in table A.3.

The state has a high percentage of women teachers. Approximately 80 percent of all teachers in urban areas are women, and approximately 70 percent of all teachers in rural areas are women.

Until 1981, all primary school teachers (known as secondary grade teachers (SGT)), including headmasters, were employees of the Panchayat Union. They became regular government employees on June 1, 1981. High school and higher secondary school teachers were already employees of the concerned directorates.

Table A.3 Number of Teachers in Tamil Nadu

School type	Government	Private aided	Self-financed	Total
Primary schools	64,855	23,446	54,866	143,167
Middle schools	50,508	15,312	12,919	78,739
High schools	27,891	6,855	39,466	74,212
Higher secondary schools	73,616	36,820	102,773	213,209
Total	216,870	82,433	210,024	509,327

Source: School Education Statistics Book, Tamil Nadu Government, 2014.

Therefore, the historical status of primary school teachers was different from that of high school and higher secondary teachers. Gradually, the notion of primary and upper primary schools gave way to elementary. Upper primary and secondary school students are taught by graduate teachers, known as BT, which stands for bachelor degree teachers. There are two categories of graduate teachers. One category is part of elementary school and comes under the Directorate of Elementary Education. The other is BT, who come under the Directorate of School Education. The former is a block-level cadre and the latter is a district-level cadre. The difference in the cadres has implications for the promotional avenues of teachers. For example, the scope of promotion is limited for a block-level cadre teacher unless they seek promotion to a high school with an elementary section.

Teachers in Tamil Nadu are not transferred in an ad hoc manner; most transfers are initiated only on the request of the teachers. Unlike states like Rajasthan where administrative transfers have been the norm for over six decades, all four South Indian states (Tamil Nadu, Kerala, Andhra Pradesh, and Karnataka) adopted more teacher-friendly policies (Ramachandran et al. 2005; Sharma and Ramachandran 2009[8]). Transfers are normally initiated on the request of teachers or for promotion (as a head teacher or when teachers upgrade their educational qualifications and become eligible to move to a high school). Transferring teachers from one district to another is uncommon, and similarly, even within a district, transfer of teachers from one block to another is not easy.[9]

Historical Context

From 1960, teacher recruitments in Tamil Nadu were done through the state and district employment exchange. In the early years, seniority was the only criterion for selection as a government schoolteacher. Seniority pertains to the number of years since applying for the job. However, M. G. Ramachandran (MGR) (who was the Chief Minister from 1977 to 1987) introduced written examinations for the recruitment of BTs and post-graduate teachers (PGTs). Discussions with a few senior retired civil servants who worked in the MGR administration revealed that when the Chief Minister received complaints about the quality of teachers recruited through the employment exchange, he introduced the entrance examination. However, conducting examinations led to inordinate delays in the recruitment process. For example, in 1984–85, it took over two years to recruit PGTs. To mitigate such delays, M. G. Ramachandran asked what could be done to improve the situation. This study's interviews suggested that a committee of senior officials advised him to set up a "Teacher Recruitment Board" along the lines of a state public service commission. M. G. Ramachandran passed away suddenly in 1987, but, in keeping with his directions, the Teacher Recruitment Board was created in 1988 when Tamil Nadu was under President's Rule.

Recalling the Kamaraj and MGR years, retired officials opined that school administration was an important area of focus of the government. Since the late 1960s, education has been perceived as an important input to ensure the social mobility of underprivileged castes and classes. Therefore, senior officials had to pay close attention to educational administration. This likely explains the attention education reform received from time to time, which included popular measures like the noon meal or incentive schemes, as well as unpopular measures that were taken to streamline the recruitment and transfer of teachers.

In Tamil Nadu, the Dravidian parties, which came to power in 1967, were deeply influenced by a common ideology, including the importance of female emancipation, the eradication of caste distinction, reservations for backward groups, and family planning to promote development. Welfarist ideology emerged as a major ingredient of social policy in Tamil Nadu under the Dravida Munnetra Kazhagam (DMK) and All India Anna Dravida Munnetra Kazhagam (AIADMK) in the post-1967 period. Electoral incentives pushed both parties into supporting similar policies and programs. The defeat of the Congress Party in the 1967 state elections in Tamil Nadu, over the issue of food scarcity, convinced the DMK and AIADMK to create a social safety net through the adoption of a universal system of public food distribution and noon midday meal programs for schoolchildren and other groups. The DMK and AIADMK engaged in a process of active one-upmanship to extend the benefits of these programs to a wider set of beneficiaries.[10]

Several examples across different departments of the government were cited. Apart from the fact that the school meal program started in the state in 1956 and became universal in 1982, Tamil Nadu was the first state to introduce 24 Hours Primary Health Centres, in 1994. This was made possible by linking admissions to post-graduate specialization to rural service after the Bachelor of Medicine and Bachelor of Surgery degree. The municipal administration was revamped through computerization of all records, especially accounting, in 2005, and computerization of land records, also in 2005. In the early years, political leaders like Anbazhagan (of DMK) permitted the bureaucracy to try out new ideas, like activity-based learning (ABL), and new ways of doing old business. It would be difficult to say whether other political parties would have followed a similar course, but, looking around, it is quite evident that all four (now five) South Indian states have introduced a range of administrative reforms in the social sectors.

Teacher Recruitment

Recruitment

Before getting into teacher-related policies, it is useful to lay out the terminologies used in the state. There are several categories of teachers in Tamil Nadu, as shown in table A.4.

Teachers at different levels are governed by different state government rules, as shown in table A.5.

As is evident from the timeline in table A.6, teacher recruitment policies were not enacted in one act of the legislature. Instead, the policies evolved over time, incrementally, and step by step. They were introduced as executive orders by the office of the PS, with the approval of the office of the Chief Minister.

There were several specific features of Tamil Nadu's experience with teacher recruitment. First, the establishment of the Teacher Recruitment Board in 1988 set Tamil Nadu apart from other states. This was promoted by MGR to reduce delays in recruitment. Second, there was continuous oscillation between recruitment through examinations and recruitment through the employment exchange based only on seniority, with the former associated with periods of AIADMK and the latter with DMK. Third, there is no "policy" that spells out the teacher deployment and teacher transfer system of the state. Annual government orders (GOs) are issued by the PS's office that notifies recruitment. This is similar to the process followed in Rajasthan and Punjab. The difference is that the norms that are agreed upon are followed annually and there is not much scope for

Table A.4 Categories of Teachers

Staff	Level	Qualification
Secondary Grade Teachers (Grade II)	Primary	Higher secondary plus two years Diploma in Teacher Education
Graduate Teachers (they were earlier known as Secondary Grade Teachers Grade I)[a]	Upper primary	Bachelor degree with B.Ed.
Graduate Teachers	Secondary	Bachelor degree with B.Ed.
Post-Graduate Teachers	Higher secondary	P.G. degree with B.Ed.
School Inspectors, Junior Inspector of Schools	Elementary	Promoted from BT teacher cadre
Pandits, Munshi (Tamil, Arabic)	Elementary	Higher Secondary Certificate plus a two-year diploma Teacher Education Certificate
Vocational Teachers, Grades I and II, including part-time teachers, recruited on contract basis	Elementary	Higher Secondary Certificate and relevant vocational degree
Administrative posts, like DEOs, superintendents, or clerical posts, such as assistant or junior assistant typist	All	Bachelor's degree with B.Ed.; BTs and PGTs could be promoted to some administrative posts; however, SGTs do not have this option, unless they upgrade their educational qualifications

Note: B.Ed. = Bachelor of Education; BT = Graduate Teacher; DEO = District Education Officer; P.G. = Post-Graduate; PGT = Post-Graduate Teacher; SGT = Secondary Grade Teacher.
a. In 2002, a government order notified all SGTs teaching classes VI to VIII as BTs.

Table A.5 Rules Governing Different Categories of Teachers

Category of staff	Governed by the rules
Teaching staff	
Elementary and middle schools	Elementary Education Subordinate Service Rule, enacted in 1955 and subsequently updated; latest updates in 2009 and 2011
High schools	Tamil Nadu School Education Subordinate Service Rule, 2008
Headmasters, District Education Officers, Chief Education Officers, Directors	Tamil Nadu Educational Service Rules
Higher secondary schools, including headmasters	Tamil Nadu Higher Secondary Educational Service Rules
Non-teaching staff	Tamil Nadu Ministerial Service Rules
	Tamil Nadu General Subordinate Service Rules
	Tamil Nadu General Service Rules
	Tamil Nadu Basic Service Rules

Table A.6 Timeline of Teacher Recruitment Policies and Practices

Date, party, Chief Minister	Teacher recruitment policies
1967–69 DMK, C. N. Annadorai	• 1960 to 1991. Recruitment of SGTs, PG Assistants, and BTs done at district or municipal corporation level. The district employment exchange provided a list of potential candidates based on district-level seniority of enrollment in the employment exchange. Interviews were conducted by the concerned Education Officers.
1969–76 DMK, K Karunanidhi	• 1960 to 1991. SGTs recruited by the district but appointed by the Block Education Office. This cadre had a block-level seniority list based on the date of enrollment in the employment exchange and date of appointment as a teacher.
1976–77 President's Rule	• No change.
1977–87 AIADMK[a] M. G. Ramachandran	• 1981. An important change was introduced in June 1981. Teachers who were hitherto employees of the Panchayat Union or Municipal Corporation became government employees. Although BTs and Assistants were employed by the district administration, SGTs became employees of the block administration of the government. • 1985. The recruitment of BTs and PGTs was transferred to the Tamil Nadu Public Service Commission. • 1985. The state government introduced a written examination to enable recruitment of qualified, trained, and knowledgeable teachers. • 1986. The Directorate of Elementary Education was established. This was done on the basis of NPE 1986.
1988 AIADMK Janaki Ramachandran	• No change.
1988–1989 President's Rule	• 1988. TRB was created in 1988 (*GO Ms.No.1622, Edn (HS2) Dept, dt.21.10.1988*). This was initiated by the administration (based on the approval given by late CM, MGR) as a measure to reduce the delays in recruitment. TRB mandated to recruit BTs and PGTs.[b] TRB recruited teachers on the basis of a written examination and interviews. Government documents reveal that more than 20,000 appointments were made and a huge backlog was cleared.
1989–91 DMK K. Karunanidhi	• No change.
1991 President's Rule	• 1991. Responding to complaints about lack of transparency in the interview process, the government decided to discontinue interviews in 1991 through a government order (GO MS No 204 dated 25.2.1991). • 1991. The District CEO was made the nodal point for transfers and postings (including initial deployment) of SGTs and BTs.[c]

table continues next page

Table A.6 Timeline of Teacher Recruitment Policies and Practices *(continued)*

Category of staff	Governed by the rules
1991–96 AIADMK J. Jayalalitha	• 1992. GOM 1251, 1992: CEO was made responsible for appointing teachers based on the district seniority of candidates registered in the employment exchange. The minimum qualifications stipulated were SSLC and TTC specified with 50 percent marks. The CEO was made the appointing authority for SGTs. • 1992. Recruitment of SGTs to the TRB. Tests and interviews were introduced and the selected candidates were appointed to various districts irrespective of place of residence (native place). Preference was given to women candidates for primary schools.[d] The government notified that men could be appointed only if women candidates were not available.
1996–2001 DMK K. Karunanidhi	• 1996. When the government changed in 1996, the new government decided to reverse the decision taken in 1992 to recruit SGTs through TRB (GOM 447, July 16, 1996). The recruitment of SGTs through district-level employment exchange seniority was reintroduced, as were interviews.

2001–06 AIADMK
J. Jayalalitha and
O. Paneerselvam
	• 2002. Interviews were discontinued again and TRB authorized conducting examinations for recruitment of BT and PG teachers.
	  – TRB to conduct the examination and prepare subject-wise rank list
	  – No oral test or interview
	  – Rural area weight would be given to those who studied in rural areas
	  – Final selection on merit and communal roster
	  – TRB to publish answers to objective-type questions in newspapers
	  – In 2002, teachers teaching grades VI to 8VIII were made BTs.
	• 2002. TRB was asked to recruit Block Resource Teachers and Educators and Graduate Assistants (junior SGTs approved under the Government of India grant to the SSA program).
	• 2002. 50 percent of teachers appointed under SSA would be women and they would be absorbed into government schools thereafter.
	• 2002. Posts of Block Resource Teachers and Regular BT Assistants and Language Pundit are interchangeable. They were to be recruited directly through competitive examination (persons who were qualified to be PG Assistants were also eligible to compete).

2006–11 DMK K. Karunanidhi	• 2007. Some policies were reversed again. BTs and PGTs were appointed on the basis of district-level seniority by TRB. Entrance examinations were discontinued and TRB was expected to verify certificates and prepare the district-wise seniority list for appointment. • 2007. The government notified that direct recruitment on a preferential basis would be done for persons who studied in Tamil medium. Of 200 seats, 40 seats were set apart for those who studied in Tamil medium. • 2007. Ratio of 1:1 prescribed for those recruited directly and those by transfer, provided both meet qualification requirements. • 2008. The Supreme Court, by W.A. No. 119 / 2008 and W.A. No. 122 / 2008, quashed the earlier order of the Tamil Nadu government restricting the selection and appointment of SGTs by district-wise seniority in the employment office as ultra vires and unconstitutional. This paved the way for state-level seniority for appointment of SGTs. • 2008–09. TRB was assigned the responsibility of collating the state-level seniority and making appointments. 5,581 SGTs were appointed using state-level employment seniority.
2011 onward AIADMK J. Jayalalitha and O. Paneerselvam	• 2011. The state government notified the RTE Act and the TET was introduced for SGTs and BTs (G.O. Ms. No.173, School Education (C2), 8th November 2011). • 2011. TET notified (G.O. (Ms) No. 181, School Education (C2) Department, Dated 15.11.2011).[e]

table continues next page

Table A.6 Timeline of Teacher Recruitment Policies and Practices *(continued)*

Category of staff	Governed by the rules
	• 2011: computerized counseling introduced for BTs and PGTs, by the Directorate of School Education. There was no policy decision to this effect.
• For a brief period, two examinations continued; however, by the end of 2012, only the TET was retained (G.O. Ms. No. 252, dated 05.10.2012).
• 2012. Competitive examination is conducted by TRB for PGTs.
• 2012. TET weight for SGTs and BTs/Graduate Assistants announced, as follows:

SGTs		BTs/graduate assistants	
Qualification	Marks	Qualification	Marks
HSE	15	HSE	10
D.T.Ed.	25	Degree	15
TET	60	B.Ed.	15
–	–	TET	60
Total	100	Total	100

- 2012. The pass percentage for TET was fixed at 60 percent.[f]
- 2012. Appointment of SGT recruitment handed back to TRB.
- 2012. Recruitment-related counseling was refined to make sure that the posts for which recruitment is done do not figure in the transfer list. This is to ensure that teachers who are deployed remain in that post at least for one full year. This decision was also taken to ensure that deficit schools (those with fewer than required number of teachers) are not disturbed. This process was further refined in 2013 and 2014.
- 2014. All BTs and PGTs were to be appointed through examinations. The pass percentage in the TET was fixed at 60 percent, with a 5 percent relaxation allowed for specific social groups, like SC, ST, and other specifically notified groups.

Note: AIADMK = All India Anna Dravida Munnetra Kazhagam; B.Ed. = Bachelor of Education; BT = Graduate Teacher; CEO = Chief Executive Officer; CM = Chief Minister; DMK = Dravida Munnetra Kazhagam; DTEd = Diploma in Teacher Education; GOM = Government Order of Madras; HSE = Higher Secondary Education; MGR = M. G. Ramachandran; NPE = National Policy on Education; PG = Post-Graduate; PGT = Post-Graduate teacher; RTE = Right to Education; SC = Scheduled Caste; SGT = Secondary Grade Teacher; SSA = Sarva Shiksha Abhiyan; SSLC = Secondary School Leaving Certificate; ST = Scheduled Tribe; TET = teacher eligibility test; TRB = Teacher Recruitment Board; TTC = Teacher Training College.

a. The party was founded in 1972 as Anna Dravida Munnetra Kazhagam (ADMK) by MGR, as a breakaway faction of the DMK led by M. Karunanidhi, the then CM of Tamil Nadu, owing to serious differences. Later, MGR prefixed the All India (AI) tag to the party's name. Today the party is known as AIADMK.

b. As the recruitment process in 1985–86 took almost two years, this delay affected the schools. Reviewing the cause for the delay, the CM took a decision to create a Teacher Recruitment Board along the lines of the Public Service Commission.

c. Although when TRB formally recruits teachers it does not formally send out the appointment letters and initial deployment, the concerned cadre authority does the posting: district CEO for BTs and state-level directorate for PGTs.

d. There was a reservation for women in primary schools of 50 percent, which was increased to 75 percent in 2001.

e. Notification: "In accordance with the provisions of sub-section (1) of section 23 of the RTE Act, the National Council for Teacher Education (NCTE) had vide Notification dated 23rd August, 2010 laid down the minimum qualifications for a person to be eligible for appointment as a teacher in classes I to VIII. It had been inter alia provided that one of the essential qualifications for a person to be eligible for appointment as a teacher in any of the schools referred to in clause (n) of section 2 of the RTE Act is that he/she should pass the Teacher Eligibility Test (TET) which will be conducted by the appropriate Government in accordance with the Guidelines framed by the NCTE…Teachers Recruitment Board is designated as the Nodal Agency for conducting of Teacher Eligibility Test and recruitment of Teachers as per G.O. (Ms) No. 181, School Education (C2) Department, Dated 15.11.2011… The following categories of candidates should write the Teacher Eligibility Test: (a) The Secondary Grade and Graduate Teachers (BT Assistants) appointed with the prescribed qualifications in Government, Government Aided and Un-aided Schools on or after 23rd August, 2010. (b) Teachers working in Unaided Institutions without the prescribed qualifications shall acquire such minimum qualifications within a period of 5 years and should pass the TET. (c) All Candidates with necessary qualifications and seeking for appointment as Teachers for Classes I to VIII." (http://trb.tn.nic.in/TET2012/08032012/Notification.pdf)

f. "In 2011, only 0.39 percent candidates were able to clear TET. Hence, the Chief Minister gave another opportunity to the candidates and asked the TRB to increase the duration of the examination from 2 ½ hours to 3 hours. As a result, 2.9 percent candidates were able to clear the examination and in the 3rd TET, the percentage increased to 4.37 percent. While 60 percent remains the passing marks for all categories, for SC and ST candidates, it is 55 percent." (Inbaraj and Manivel 2015).

tinkering with the basics (reservations, entrance examination, and recruitment through Teacher Recruitment Board (TRB)), as seems to be the practice in Rajasthan and Punjab. When the government changes, there is a good chance that some elements of the annual GO will be revised without diluting the basics.

The oscillation in the recruitment practices for SGTs is worth emphasizing. The recruitment of SGTs was done through district-level employment exchange seniority for a long time. The reasons for the difference between the recruitment of Post-Graduate (PG) and BT teachers and the SGTs is not recorded in any document reviewed. Retired officials said the numbers involved were very high and, given the need for a steady stream of teachers in primary and upper primary schools, the established method was the most efficient. As a result, SGTs were recruited by the employment exchange and this was done at the district Chief Executive Officer's (CEO's) office, using district-level employment exchange seniority. The Block Education Officer issued the appointment letters.

However, there was widespread unrest among teachers who could not get placed in their district exchange. This led the unions to file a court case, and the case went up to the Supreme Court of India. The court decided in favor of the SGT teachers in 2008. Recruitment was now to be done through state exchanges, but examinations were done away with and only seniority was considered. This created problems. Two senior officials explained that when hiring was done on the basis of state seniority in the employment exchange in 2008, the schools had to deal with older (age 45+) teacher recruits who would have done their Diploma in Education over 15 years back. This happened because there were many qualified candidates who had registered in the employment exchange of the more educationally forward districts of Thirunelveli, Kanyakumari, Virudunagar, Thootukudi, and Madurai. Registration on the employment exchange[11] (at the district level) was deemed to be enough for selection. The interview for final selection was considered a mere formality. As older candidates became eligible for teaching jobs, there was introspection in the Directorate, *"because new recruits who were over 45 years of age were not able to grasp the curriculum and their content knowledge was inadequate."*[12] Equally, it is important to remember that the ABL program went to scale in 2007 and many of the older teachers, including older recruits, were resistant to the new approach, which involved sitting with children on the floor and working with them in groups. Teacher educators and teachers' union leaders the study interacted with in 2008–09 were uncomfortable about "providing employment to educationally qualified but unemployable candidates."

Closely related to the dilution in standards for recruitment was the sudden expansion of private teacher training institutions after 2004. The numbers increased exponentially, from 83 in 2003–04, to 665 in 2007–08 (table A.7). Retired officers who were in TRB and the Directorates during that time said, *"there was a lot of pressure on both sides—from the powerful teacher constituency in the forward districts as well as the private teacher training institutions that were churning out teachers across the state (including the educationally not-so-forward districts)."*[13]

Table A.7 Expansion of Private Teacher-Training Institutions in Tamil Nadu

Year	Type of institution				
	DIET	Government TTI	Govt. aided TTI	Unaided TTI	Total
2003/04	29	9	43	2	83
2004/05	30	9	43	126	208
2005/06	30	9	43	415	497
2006/07	30	9	43	477	559
2007/08	30	9	43	583	665

Sources: Ramachandran et al. 2009; data from DTERT, Chennai 2008.
Note: DIET = District Institute of Education and Training; DTERT = Directorate of Teacher Education, Research and Training; TTI = Teacher Training Institute.

Among the schools that suffered the most were those run by the Adi-Dravida Welfare Board. An official who was familiar with the situation said that in 2010 the Adi Dravida and Tribal Welfare Department identified about 1,045 vacancies in Adi Dravida Welfare (ADW) and Government Tribal Residential (GTR) schools across Tamil Nadu. TRB was authorized to appoint SGT teachers. However, the task was not simple, especially after the state government changed the basis of teacher transfers in the ADW board from district seniority to state seniority. Soon after being posted in tribal areas or ADW schools, teachers from other districts go on vacation or seek transfer. Most teachers who remain at GTR schools are from neighboring blocks. "*No teacher from another district usually wants to come, stay here near the forests and work here. It rains for six months every year and unless one is used to living on the hills, it could be difficult*," said Mr. Samuthirapandian, who did his Master of Philosophy on the livelihood issues of the Panniya tribes living in the district (*The Hindu*, October 22, 2011).

When the government changed in 2011 and AIADMK came into power, the recruitment of SGTs was handed over to TRB and the TET was introduced. A senior official argued that with the notification of the Right to Education (RTE) Act and the introduction of the TET, new governments cannot turn the clock back and revert to employment exchange seniority as a method of recruitment.

Counseling for Initial Deployment after Recruitment

In 2001, counseling was introduced for the deployment of newly recruited BT and PGT teachers. This was done manually. The list of vacancies was displayed on the notice board 48 hours before the counseling and posts were allotted sequentially, starting with the first on the merit list. According to the teachers' union leaders, *manual counseling* was introduced on their request. Since PG and BT teachers belong to the district cadre, counseling was done at the district.

The situation for SGTs is opaque. According to a senior official in the EE Department, manual counseling has been done since 2001 at the block office, after the block-specific list of teachers is given to them. Prior to 2001, the Block

Education Officer deployed newly recruited teachers. Often the teachers who did not want to work in the block would immediately apply for transfer. From 2001, the rules for transfer were modified (this is discussed in the next subsection, on teacher transfers), under which newly recruited teachers cannot request a transfer for a year. At the time of the study, no official documents were found that could illustrate the counseling norms for SGTs.

The counseling process is an administrative decision and there is no policy enacted by the legislature. The respective directorates took decisions to introduce counseling to enhance efficiency as well as transparency. For several decades, teachers jostled for transfer soon after deployment, because they were allotted to schools that were far from their home. However, this trend reversed after they were consulted on where they would like to be posted, as most teachers were able to get a post of their first or second choice.

Currently, the following sequence of counseling is being followed in Tamil Nadu. First, counseling for fresh appointments and deployment for rationalization are conducted. Second, counseling is done for appointments through promotion. And third, counseling is undertaken for transfers. However, the counseling process is often skipped in the hilly areas of the district. For example, although counseling is conducted in Hosur of Krishnagiri district, it is not done in Talli (or Tally), a hilly area that comes under Denkanikottai Taluk of Krishnagiri district.[14] Equally, since 2011, vacancies in the southern districts are not displayed during recruitment counseling. This is done to ensure that new recruits are allocated to districts and blocks where teacher shortages are severe.

Teacher Transfers
Transfers

For several decades (since the 1960s), Tamil Nadu has followed an unwritten norm of only transferring teachers on request by the teacher, for promotions, or for specific reasons related to rationalization. Unlike the northern or eastern states, there are no mass transfers driven by political strategies. Formally, teacher transfers remain the prerogative of the state government. Table A.8 outlines the evolution of the policy in Tami Nadu. As per the RTE norms, the pupil-teacher ratio in elementary schools should be 1:30. For example, in a school with 60 students, there should be two teachers and one headmaster. According to two main guidelines (Rc. No. 13275 / C1 / 2012, dated 23.07.2012, and RTE Act 2009 on Elementary Education, as of 01.09.2011), surplus teachers were identified across the state and vacant posts were filled. In recent years, especially after the notification of the RTE, special attention has been paid to deficit schools and surplus schools. Notwithstanding this claim, officials in Tamil Nadu say that shifting teachers from surplus schools to deficit schools is not easy and continues to pose a challenge to the educational administrators. Officials who were interviewed said that teachers in well-located schools resist transfers and most of them are reluctant to relocate to "deficit schools." Therefore, the government has adopted a practice of deploying new recruits to such schools by transferring surplus school positions to deficit schools. Another interesting trend is that

Table A.8 Timeline of Teacher Transfer Policies and Practices

Date, party in power, Chief Minister	Teacher transfer policies and practices
1967–69: DMK (C. N. Annadorai)	• *1960 onward.* Transfers made on the request of teachers. The teachers submit application at the DEO/CEO office. SGTs apply to BEO and others to CEO. Annual GO issued specifying who is eligible for transfer and the timeframe. No general policy for transfers.
1969–76 DMK (K. Karunanidhi)	– Teachers must obtain a no-objection certificate from their respective HOD. – Annual transfer notification issued by the government. – Transfers done without any consultation with applicants.
1976–77 President's Rule	• Same process continues.
1977–87 ADMK M. G. Ramachandran	• 1997. No fundamental change in the transfer system; however, it was made more systematic. Two registers maintained at the CEO/DEO office: – A register has the transfer request by date and seniority. – B register is confidential and gives a consolidated picture of transfer requests and vacancies. • CEO or BEO transfers teachers on the basis of the B register. • Teachers not consulted before transfer order is issued.
1988 ADMK Janaki Ramachandran	• Same process continues.
1988–89 President's Rule	• Same process continues.
1989–91 DMK K. Karunanidhi	• Same process continues.
1991 President's Rule	• 1991. District CEO made nodal person for transfer of primary and upper primary schoolteachers. Transfers of SGTs (elementary) done at the block level (as they belong to a block cadre). • 1991. Teachers drawing a consolidated emolument are not eligible for transfer. • 1991. Vacancies displayed on the notice board of the BEO/CEO office. Teachers can withdraw request for transfer after they see the displayed vacancies.
1991–96 AIADMK J. Jayalalitha	• Same process continues.
1996–2001 DMK K. Karunanidhi	• 1997. The annual GO specified that teachers who seek and are given transfer lose their seniority and become the junior-most in their school.
2001–06 AIADMK J. Jayalalitha and O. Paneerselvam	• 2001. Counseling for teacher transfers introduced. The CEO office at the district calls the BT and PG teachers who request transfer to their office. All vacancies displayed 48 hours before manual counseling, which is done by teams constituted by the CEO. • 2001. Similarly, for SGTs the counseling was done at the office of the CEO, with the BEO of specific blocks present in the committee. • 2001. Transfer on promotion to headmaster is done at the block level. When there is no vacancy for specific subjects, then transfer requests pertaining to that subject could be done by the CEO. • 2001. For district-to-district transfers, and for AEOs, BTs, and SGTs, a state-level seniority list is prepared using date of appointment and date in the last school. • 2001. The sequence of counseling is specified. Transfer counseling is done after new appointments are made. First transfers within the block or district are conducted. Inter-block or inter-district transfers come next.
2006–11 DMK K. Karunanidhi	• Same process continues.

table continues next page

Table A.8 Timeline of Teacher Transfer Policies and Practices *(continued)*

Date, party in power, Chief Minister	Teacher transfer policies and practices
2011–onward AIADMK J. Jayalalitha and O. Paneerselvam	• 2011. Computerized counseling introduced by the Directorate of School Education in 2011 for PGT, BT, Special Education, Physical Education, and others in the same category. • 2011. Noncomputerized manual counseling continued for all SGTs who seek transfer within the block or district. Only inter-district transfer of SGTs is done through computerized counseling at the state level.

Note: ADMK = Anna Dravida Munnetra Kazhagam; AEO = Assistant Education Officer; AIADMK = All India Anna Dravida Munnetra Kazhagam; BEO = Block Education Officer; BT = Graduate Teacher; CEO = Chief Executive Officer; DEO = District Education Officer; DMK = Dravida Munnetra Kazhagam; GO = government order; HOD = Head of Department; PG = Post-Graduate; PGT = Post-Graduate teachers; SGT = secondary grade teacher.

additional posts are created so that teachers are not uprooted from their districts. Only in cases where no vacancies are available and where no additional posts can be created, surplus teachers are transferred to other districts through online counseling (Inbaraj and Manivel 2015).

Approximately 100 to 200 teachers ask for transfer in every district. The numbers may vary from year to year. Senior officials said that the average number of transfer requests rarely exceeds 200 per district. There is also a practice of not encouraging more than one teacher to seek a transfer from each school. Transfer applications are entertained only when they are countersigned and forwarded by the head teacher or headmaster. This is to ensure some degree of continuity in the school. In the past decade or so, since the introduction of Sarva Shiksha Abhiyan (SSA), teachers from "deficit schools" (where approved posts are yet to be filled or where there are few teachers) are discouraged from applying for transfer unless they can identify a fellow teacher who would be willing to come on mutual transfer.

Teachers' union leaders said that obtaining a no-objection certificate is not easy. There have been many instances when the Head of Department (HOD) (or the head teacher) does not give the certificate. Agreeing with this observation, a retired officer said that given the high level of centralization in the hands of the Directorate, there have been times when "camps" have had to be held to clear the backlog of requests for the no-objection certificates necessary to apply for transfer. He added that this kind of "harassment of teachers will come down if application for transfer is made online and approval/no-objection of the HOD is also done online."

The Director of SSA explained that the teacher transfer system has improved over the years and that there have been significant changes in the past two years (2014 and 2015) (table A.9). According to her, "*Earlier there was no objective process of deployment or transfer. These used to get mixed up—going back and forth. Now we decided to do deployment first and there is no choice in deployment when it is done to rationalise posts. We can even transfer a post during rationalisation and this is based on student strength. When we review PTR [pupil-teacher ratios] we can shift a post from one school to another. This happens in 2 ways: (i) compulsory*

Table A.9 Excerpt from 2014 Government Order

Excerpt from GO (1D) No. 137, School Education / SE5 (1) Department, dated 09.06.2014

Teachers who have completed one year in the present post are eligible for transfer. However, the following categories of teachers are exempted:

a. Those who were redeployed in 2013–14
b. Teachers who are visually impaired
c. Teachers with disability (more than 40 percent disability) who are certified by the District Rehabilitation Centre
d. Wife of a military soldier for ensuring her safety
e. Teachers who have undergone a heart transplant or kidney transplant surgery before June 1, 2011, but are still affected by it
f. Widows and unmarried women over age 40 years
g. Teachers who have been to other schools on promotion
h. Parents who have children who are physically or intellectually challenged
i. Teachers working in the same school for more than three years (appointed prior to June 11, 2011); those who have already availed transfer under this policy can apply but their current station seniority will be considered while examining their transfer
j. Spouse employed 30 kilometers or more from the place of posting
k. As a special case if a spouse of a teacher is dead, transfer can be given after submitting a detailed report to the Director.

Special conditions for transfer:

a. Those who seek unit-to-unit transfer, that is, transfer from government to corporation or municipality schools, would be treated as a junior-most teacher in the new place of posting.
b. Only those who have successfully completed their probation can apply for unit-to-unit transfer.
c. Importantly, if there are three teachers in a school, all three will not be transferred in the same year because it would affect the learning of students adversely.

Timing of transfer:

May to June every year, all transfers to be completed by end of June.

Source: Inbaraj and Manivel (2014).

transfer from excess to deficit; and (ii) a post itself can be transferred. We identify schools with excess posts and then transfer the post. This process takes place before the transfer counselling. The deployed posts do not enter into the transfer counselling process. Once deployment is complete, we start transfer counselling. Teachers in TN [Tamil Nadu] can withdraw their transfer request after they see the available posts that are displayed 48 hours before transfer counselling. The process is refined every year." The Director added that there is considerable political as well as administrative commitment to enhance efficiency. Equally, transferring posts from surplus to deficit schools is an effective mechanism for rationalization.

Counseling for Teacher Transfers

In Tamil Nadu, manual counseling was introduced in 2001 to introduce some degree of transparency. Manual counseling is a system where the lists of vacancies (some subject-wise in the case of upper primary schools and high schools) are displayed in the concerned nodal office (block, district, or state) and teachers are called according to their rank on the transfer list. This rank is prepared taking into consideration the priority list notified by the government from time to time. Although manual counseling has given way to computerized counseling for BTs and PGTs, the manual system continues for SGTs. There is a lot of resistance to introducing computerized counseling for SGTs, for several reasons: (a) given that data for computerized counseling have to be entered afresh for each round of transfers, and given the number of entries, this was seen as cumbersome; and (b) as SGTs are a block-level cadre, consolidating lists from all the blocks was also cited as a reason for the reluctance. A few retired officials said that there is little political or administrative will to introduce computerized counseling for SGTs.

Although the manual transfer system in Tamil Nadu is fairly straightforward, there are some important questions: (a) Is the system transparent? (b) Are all vacant post displayed?[15] (c) Has computerized counseling reduced avenues for corruption? (d) Does patronage still play a role in teacher transfers? According to the officials who were interviewed, the scope for rent-seeking and corruption is minimal, as all the transfer requests and posts are displayed in the computer system or on the notice board. However, some retired officers believe that although corruption has been reduced significantly, there are a few "sought after" posts that are not displayed. Hence, while over 85 to 90 percent of transfers are done in a transparent manner, the remaining transfers are done at the discretion of the administration.

By contrast, teachers' union leaders maintain that only 70 percent of transfers are done in a transparent manner. They cited a recent High Court order: "The Madras High Court has observed that despite its earlier order, transfer and posting of teachers are being done by the authorities in a secret manner. *The purpose of counselling is to ensure that transfer or promotion should be done in a transparent manner and the teacher should not have a grievance that the juniors are transferred or promoted unduly. But the situation has not changed much*," observed Justice D. Hariparanthaman in June 2014 (*The Hindu*, June 28, 2014[16]).

As the data on transfer requests and vacant posts are entered in the CEO's office, posts that are in high demand may not be displayed. According to one teachers' union leader, "*Our union supported the counselling system. Before the computerisation, the CEO hid some posts and this practice continues with respect to Secondary Grade Teachers. Online counselling is more transparent and local/district level people cannot hide or manipulate the posts. Teachers Unions have always demanded the vacancy lists should be publicised. The GO says that the vacant posts should be publicised at least 48 hours before counselling and we (the unions) collect information and compare with the publicised list. If we come across 'hidden vacancies' we make a big noise... we have to be vigilant.*" Another teachers' union leader added: "*When it comes to graduate teachers (BT), there are more teachers than available posts. Admissions are going down in government schools. Therefore, teachers (or teacher posts) have to be shifted to deficit schools and the government has to redeploy teachers. This is good, but we need greater transparency when it comes to re-deployment. This is an urgent issue because enrolment in government schools is coming down...*" The phenomenon of declining enrollment in government schools is a serious issue in many other states in India. A senior official explained that many children shift from aided to unaided schools; however, the proportion of children in government schools has remained steady since 2011.[17] In Tamil Nadu, a combination of declining child population due to demographic transition and declining enrollment in government and government aided schools could (in the future) exert great pressure on recruitment and transfers. It would be worth watching if this would lead to greater transparency or not.

Commenting on the timeline (which was shared with retired and senior officials for validation), one retired officer said that full transparency could only be assured if the entire process of teacher deployment and transfer is system driven. According to him, "TN has adopted a half-hearted approach. Every time a counselling is planned, the data is entered afresh, in an external server of K Labs. We do not know how secure this is. TN needs a comprehensive MIS [management information system] that is housed in a government server, one that is secure and one that is used for counselling." Agreeing with this analysis, a serving officer said, *"The present system does not insulate us from hiding posts or tinkering with information. The software we use is not a guarantee against hiding information—because the data is fed afresh every time a counselling session is scheduled. The government has already procured a server and Anna University was supposed to have developed the software a year ago… we are still waiting for the software."*

Note on Technology

In Tamil Nadu, the use of technology for teacher management was first introduced for teacher recruitment counseling in 2006. The process for introducing technology was like a pilot project. At that time, the software was developed internally. However, there is no institutional memory about this software, as it is not being used currently and seems to have been lost. In 2012, then Chief Minister of Tamil Nadu, Ms. J. Jayalalitha, wanted quick appointment of teachers. She announced the dates for the same while the team had to work in a hurried manner to conduct recruitment counseling for around 21,000 teachers.[18] The major issue that they needed to solve was conducting these processes on a large scale. Since mass recruitment had to be conducted in a short period, utilizing earlier offline processes would have been highly inefficient. Prior to the introduction of the technology, they were preparing appointment letters using typewriters. Another hurdle was to ensure that candidates from various districts traveled to a central location for the counseling. Hence, online counseling was sought as an easy solution. The candidates, across districts, needed to travel to their district centers for counseling. Since they had a time crunch, they decided to outsource the online counseling process to KLabs, Chennai. This is how computerized counseling for teacher recruitment started.

Political Economy of Reform: Who Were the Champions in Tamil Nadu?

The two main Dravidian parties of Tamil Nadu championed greater autonomy for state governments and were in the forefront of campaigning for greater decentralization since 1967. Ironically, both parties have resisted devolution of authority to elected bodies at the district and sub-district levels.

As Kumar argues, "The stronger the regional parties, the weaker would be the local self-governments" (Kumar 2009[19]). Important administrative reforms related to recruitment and transfer policies were not only aimed at reducing localized corruption, but also striking at the root local patronage networks of local leaders (Sharma and Ramachandran 2009). Political commentators agree that Tamil Nadu's Chief Ministers were able to cut the patronage network of MLAs as well as Zillah Parishad leaders. The Dravidian parties (DMK, Anna Dravida Munnetra Kazhagam, and AIADMK) put a lot of emphasis on governance at the state level, and the Chief Ministers depended a great deal on the bureaucracy to reach out and get the job done.

A senior official explained that this is possible because these reforms are not necessarily identified with a single civil servant. Comparing the Tamil Nadu scenario with that of Rajasthan, one senior official said that in the latter case educational initiatives that were identified with one civil servant were invariably dismantled by her/his successor, leading to a culture of *"undo what my predecessor did."* Discussing a range of reforms in Tamil Nadu, a senior officer said: *"Any system improvement done in one sector then it is taken to other sectors. What we have done in education is not reform, but it is system improvement to enhance efficiency. It is not a grand one-time policy initiative, but a step-by-step effort to improve the system."* The Director of SSA confirmed this analysis and added, *"meritocracy has been an important driver in appointments in Tamil Nadu and this has become more pronounced since the 1990s. Maybe it has to do with the administrative culture and the larger social culture and practices in the state."*

The response of 15 officials interviewed for this study was quite similar. All of them said that reforms were driven by the bureaucracy and had the political support of the Chief Minister and the Education Minister. However, teachers' union leaders said that mobilization by the unions and their ability to place their demands during election time convinced the political leaders, who in turn asked the bureaucracy to initiate the reforms. The Directorates of Elementary Education and School Education have been the champions of teacher recruitment and teacher transfer policies. Interestingly, the reforms are not identified with any one civil servant—these reforms have had widespread support across the bureaucracy. It is also noteworthy that teachers' unions have sustained pressure on the government to expand the reforms to cover SGTs and deepen the reforms through a comprehensive teacher management information system (MIS) that is housed on a government server, but this is yet to happen.

The officials who were interviewed for this study, serving and retired, said that Chief Ministers rely on civil servants they trust for advice, especially the PS in the Education Department and the directors of elementary education and school education. The former are invariably Indian Administrative Service officers; the latter are Education Department officials who have had long tenures in education administration. The teachers' union leaders who were interviewed agreed with the officials on this point and added that union leaders maintain close links with both Dravidian parties. On specific issues, such as transparency in the counseling process, the government elicited the views of teachers' unions.

Another significant factor is the bipartisan consensus across party lines on a wide range of policies, from midday meals to not disturbing teachers through regular transfers (World Bank 2006). Although there has been some back and forth with respect to SGT appointments, by and large the two state parties have continued with many of the policies of their predecessors. A case in point is the introduction of ABL in 2003.[20] It was taken to scale in 2007 and has survived changes in governments, although the teachers' unions have not been happy with it (NCERT 2011). Equally, when computerized counseling was introduced during the tenure of one official, it continued even after he demitted office. This was possible because of the support of successive Chief Ministers.

Discussions with various stakeholders did not reveal any active support of civil society groups or teacher aspirants in reforming recruitment processes. Although entrance examinations and publication of answers in newspapers have made the system more transparent, teachers' unions are unhappy with recruitment-linked examinations.[21] Three teachers' union leaders who were interviewed said that they would prefer a recruitment process based on performance on the qualifying examinations. However, they agree that with the notification of the RTE, there is no scope to roll back TETs. Therefore, they *"just have to live with it."*

Lessons from Tamil Nadu

The overarching lesson from Tamil Nadu is that institutional reform can be done in an incremental manner. The bureaucracy across different levels needs to support it and promote it. Reforms that do not have a wide support base may not be able to succeed. In any government, there are multiple cadres of officials—the Indian Administrative Service, state civil service, education service, and so on. A buy-in to reform is essential across all the cadres, from the state capital to the school.

Another significant lesson from Tamil Nadu is that the absence of legislature-approved policy does not come in the way of institutional reform. In many states, like Rajasthan and Punjab, there is a feeling that a transfer policy approved by the legislature is essential to bring about institutional reform. The Tamil Nadu case clearly illustrates that more than a formal policy, broad-based agreement across parties can create the conditions to sustain reforms. In some ways, step-by-step initiatives can quietly change the system in a way that a grand one-time policy may not. More than formal policies, it is the nitty-gritty of administrative processes that can sustain and deepen reform. Bipartisan support for key reforms has historically been an important feature of the state. There are many differences between the major political parties, but from 1967 onward there has also been a continuity of commitment to specific reforms. The management of midday meals, teacher recruitment through examinations, and drug procurement process are examples of agendas that cut across party lines.

Finally, the bureaucracy in the state has considerable autonomy to tweak the system to make it more efficient. Most of the officials who were interviewed did not use the word reform, but preferred to use "system improvement." This speaks a lot about how they view their role. It is not surprising that the bureaucracy in the state is seen as the steel frame that holds up the system. Whether "system improvement" also makes the system more transparent remains a big question. The teacher recruitment process is definitely transparent. The same cannot be said for teacher transfers. Notwithstanding the introduction of computerized counseling, between 10 and 30 percent of transfers remain opaque.

Is this a good practice that could be emulated by other states? The nine-state study included a more detailed historical study of the evolution of teacher recruitment and teacher transfer policies in Karnataka and Tamil Nadu. The initial impression was that Tamil Nadu (like Karnataka) had adopted transparent and technology-driven systems. However, on detailed scrutiny, it emerged that some elements of the Tamil Nadu system, especially teacher recruitment and computerized counseling for BTs and PGTs, are fairly transparent, but others, such as transfers, are not. As it stands today, the policies and practices adopted for teacher transfers need more work. A consolidated teacher MIS system (which is in the making) and a technology-driven teacher transfer system hosted on a government server could enable the system to become transparent.

Discussion: What Can States Learn from the Karnataka and Tamil Nadu Experiences?

At the outset, it is important to clarify that there are significant differences between Karnataka and Tamil Nadu. In the former, policies evolved over time and were institutionalized by the government through legislative means. Equally, the system in place has a high degree of acceptance across the political spectrum. In the latter, elements of a transparent system for recruitment and transfers exist, but are yet to be institutionalized. There are major differences across the main political actors in Tamil Nadu and time alone will tell if the institutionalization of teacher recruitment and transfer policies will be sustained. That said, the two states offer important lessons:

1. In both states, consensus was built across the political spectrum, levels of administration, and the community of teachers on the need for reducing individual discretion and promoting transparency in teacher recruitment and transfers.
2. For reforms to work, familiarity and comfort with technology and readiness to engage with it is fundamental.
3. Finally, the willingness to work through the system in an incremental manner over time and stabilize processes is a feature in both states, versus trying to achieve results overnight. While Karnataka introduced a teacher policy through an act of the legislature, Tamil Nadu opted for executive and administrative orders. In both cases, bipartisan consensus on key reform measures has been important.

Karnataka started its reform process in recruitment and transfers of teachers through executive orders, but moved to legislating those by incorporating all the lessons from the experiences of the implementation. The transfer and recruitment policies are complementary to each other and have been drafted in a manner that addresses systemic challenges while being sensitive to teachers' needs at the same time. For instance, recruitment and transfer policies address the issues of shortage of teachers in remote areas and the need for redeployment from excess-teacher schools to others jointly. The estimation of vacancies takes into account the transfers that have taken place and the provision of first posting only in rural areas together with the rule of no-transfer for the first five years to ensure that schools in far flung areas do not face shortages of teachers in Karnataka. The introduction of the concept of zones has also helped in addressing the issue of teacher shortages in remote areas in Karnataka. The practice of equalizing the proportion of unfilled posts in all blocks and districts has ensured that, at any given time, the percentage of unfilled positions remains largely the same in all blocks and districts in the state.

Another issue that merits serious attention is the need for ongoing dialogue between the government and the teachers' unions. Karnataka has built-in measures to address the needs of the teachers' unions (members of such associations also have priority in the criteria for transfers) and the bureaucracy (inclusion of penalty transfers from one zone to the other). It could be questioned whether these are fully justified; however, the fact remains that that they have been incorporated in a transparent manner as part of a legislative measure and represent a process of negotiation among various stakeholders. There is no such transparent process of consultation with teachers' unions in Tamil Nadu. What exists in practice is informal.

Since the reforms are highly dependent on technology, it is important to envision the role of technology while drafting policy documents. If policy documents already exist, it is important to ensure that the software developed incorporates all the features of the policy. Learning from the experiences of these two states, it can be concluded that drafting a clear roadmap for the use of technology for recruitment and transfers would help in this process. A formal Product Requirements Document should be created. The technology needs to be owned and managed by the government to minimize the risk of misuse and ensure the safety of the data.

Notes

1. This appendix draws heavily from Vimala Ramachandran, Jyotsna Jha, Saurabh Minni, and Puja Minni, 2016, "Teacher Recruitment and Transfer Policy and Practice in Karnataka and Tamil Nadu," background note prepared for the World Bank, New Delhi.
2. Karnataka had a system of seven years of primary (first four years known as lower primary and the next three years known as higher primary) and three years of secondary education at the school level. This has been changed to eight years of primary (first five years known as lower primary and the next three years known as higher primary) and two years of secondary school. The official documents use "primary" for the first

eight years, unlike other states in India where primary generally refers only to the first five years of schooling. This report uses primary and elementary interchangeably. Primary refers to elementary unless otherwise specified. The subdistrict unit, the block, is referred to as taluka. This report uses these two interchangeably.

3. Zone A includes Zillah HQ, Taluk HQ, Highways, and Bangalore City area; Zone B covers the area within a radius of 5 to 15 kilometers from Zillah HQ, Taluk HQ, Highways, and Mysore-Hubli-Dharwad Municipal Corporations; and Zone C covers all areas that are more than 15 kilometers from Zillah HQ, Taluk HQ, and Highways, and areas with population less than 5 lakhs (Government of Karnataka 2007b).
4. The directorate of education continues to be known as the Department of Public Instruction in Karnataka, as was the practice during the colonial period.
5. Malanad is a region surrounding Western Ghats in Karnataka; H.D. Govinde Gowda belonged to this region.
6. Mr. Gowda recently passed away at the age of 90. For a newspaper report published on his death in a national daily, see http://www.thehindu.com/news/cities/bangalore/govinde%ADgowda%ADdead/article8072989.ece.
7. The Legislature of Karnataka consists of two Houses, the Legislative Assembly and the Legislative Council, known as the Upper House. At present, among the 75 members of the Legislative Council, 25 are elected by the Karnataka Legislative Assembly members, 25 are elected by local authorities, seven are elected by the graduates, seven are elected by the teachers, and 11 members are nominated by the Governor of Karnataka.
8. Sharma and Ramachandran (2009); Ramachandran et al. (2005).
9. The Director of Sarva Shiksha Abhiyan pointed out this important historical dimension of teacher transfers on August 22, 2016.
10. The World Bank 2006, http://www1.worldbank.org/publicsector/anticorrupt/feb06course/EsReformingPublicServicesIndia.pdf.
11. While seniority of registration on the employment exchange matters, there is also a reservation quota which is: General (31 percent); Scheduled Castes—SC (18 percent); Scheduled Tribes—ST (1 percent); Most Backward Castes—MBC (20 percent) and Backward Castes—BC (30 percent, of which 3.5 percent each is for Muslim and Christian candidates). The number of years that an applicant has to wait before being appointed also depends on the category of application.
12. Interview by K. M. Sheshagiri with the Director of Elementary Education in 2008, cited in Ramachandran, Bhattacharjea, and Sheshagiri (2009).
13. Interviews conducted in November 2015 and February 2016, Chennai.
14. The Director, SSA, explained this phenomenon during a review of the draft of this report on August 22, 2016.
15. In a discussion to review the correctness of the processes described in this case study (August 22, 2016), a senior official explained that vacancies in educationally forward districts and surplus schools are not displayed. This is to ensure that teachers are deployed in deficit schools on a priority basis.
16. "The petitioner was posted as a B.T. Assistant (Science) at Madukoor Boys Government Higher Secondary School, Thanjavur district. After a counselling in 2011, he was transferred to Kadalkudi in Tuticorin district… From 2012, he was eligible for consideration for promotion as P.G. Assistant (Biology.) When counselling was held for the post of P.G. Assistant (Biology), he opted for a posting in

T.M. Kottai, Ramanathapuram district… His grievance was that if three vacancies that existed in Tirunelveli district had been notified, he could have been posted there. At the stage of appeal, the court directed the authorities to conduct transfer counselling in a transparent manner and also consider the petitioner's case as per rules." "The authorities seem to act arbitrarily and in a whimsical manner to accommodate the persons of their choice," observed Mr. Justice Hariparanthaman. Mr. Vaiyanan has approached the court to quash the order of August last year transferring him to a school in Ramanujam Pudur in Tuticorin district and for a direction to the authorities to conduct a fresh counseling for the post of P.G. Assistant (Biology) there. As another person had already joined the post, the petitioner said that at the next transfer counseling he should be allowed to participate. The judge directed the school education authorities to conduct the next counseling in a transparent manner. (*The Hindu* June 28, 2014)

17. Discussion with State Programme Director, SSA, August 22, 2016.
18. State Programme Director, SSA, explained that when this recruitment was done, vacant posts in the four southern districts were not displayed and the government focused on districts where shortages of teachers were severe.
19. Source: http://www.isec.ac.in/WP%20-%20208.pdf.
20. ABL was implemented in classes I and II in 2002–03 in 13 schools run by Chennai Corporation (phase I). It was further extended to classes III and IV and implemented in all schools run by Chennai Corporation in 2003–04 (phase II). It expanded to 37,500 schools in 2007–08. (NCERT 2011)
21. Text of the discussion with officials in TRB on November 19, 2016: *We have ensured transparency. Candidates can take away the carbon copy of the answer key. We publish the key online on the TRB website. Candidates can check their answers. Most legal cases on recruitment are about validity of certain answers. From 2012 the system has become fool proof and ever since there has been incremental improvement every year. Even the Union Public Service Commission of the Government of India does not publish the answers and TRB does it even though we have only 20 people on our staff. Now there can be no turning back—there will be public uproar if anyone tries to tinker with the system."*

APPENDIX B

Teacher Transfer Technology in Karnataka

Introduction

In Karnataka, teacher transfers are conducted as per the Teacher Transfer Act 2007. This Act defines the criteria for when a teacher can apply for transfers (first posting in a rural area and minimum five years of service) as well as the priorities that guide the listing/ranking for the sequence of transfers. For primary school teachers, the seniority unit is the block (for those recruited before 2001, the seniority unit is the district). For secondary school teachers, the seniority unit is the district (for those recruited before 2003, the seniority unit is the division). This Act also specifies that an upper limit of 8 percent of teachers in each cadre/seniority unit can be transferred within their seniority unit. Transfers outside the seniority unit have an upper limit of 1 percent of seniority unit strength. Two kinds of transfers on request are conducted through computerized counseling: transfers within the seniority unit and transfers outside the seniority unit. The e-Governance Cell at the Department of Public Instruction manages the transfers of teachers.

This appendix describes (a) the flow of the software; (b) vendor selection; (c) technology, data, and network requirements; (d) data entry and verification processes; and (e) a demonstration of the software. The appendix concludes with suggestions on improvements to the current technology.

Flow of the Software

Online application for transfers within the same unit of seniority and the computerized counseling process are conducted for transfers of elementary and secondary school teachers. For elementary school teachers, computerized counseling is held at the district level; for secondary school teachers, it is conducted at the division level. However, the software program used and the processes followed are the same for both. The following flowcharts describe the processes and steps conducted for teacher transfers at the backend (source: e-Governance Cell, Department of Public Instructions).

Figure B.1 shows that after applications are received, the software checks for cadre, primary/secondary, and sends it to the Block Education Officer or Deputy Director of Public Instruction for verification. If the application is not rejected, then it proceeds to the next phase.

In the next phase, accepted applications are listed as per priority defined in the Teacher Transfer Act 2007. This is used to generate the Provisional Selection List, which is displayed for objections, if any. After all objections are addressed, the Final List is prepared (figure B.2).

During counseling, candidates are called as per their ranking in the priority list. The transfers are also dependent on their cadre and year of recruitment (pre/post 2001 for primary school teachers and pre/post 2003 for secondary school teachers[1]) (figure B.3).

Figure B.1 Transfer Application Processing within Seniority

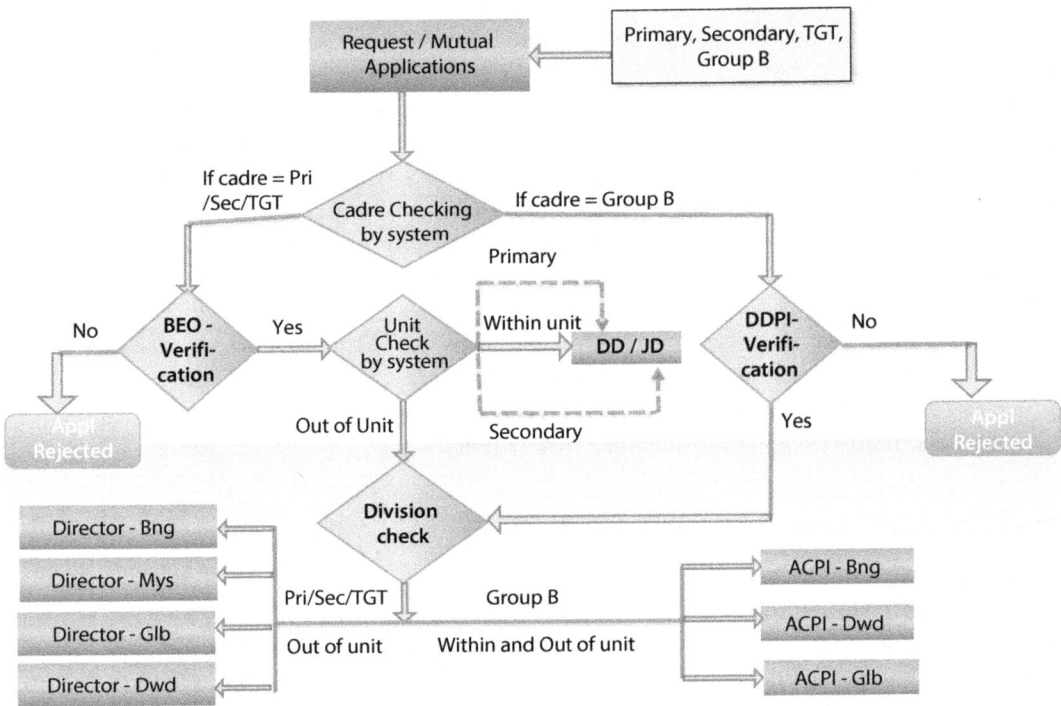

Source: Management Information System Section, Sarva Shiksha Abhiyan Karnataka.
Note: BEO = Block Education Officer; BNG = Bangalore; DD = Deputy Director; DDPI = Deputy Director of Public Instruction; Dwd = Dharwad; Glb = Gulbarga; JD = Joint Director; Mys = Mysore; TGT = Trained Graduate Teacher.

Figure B.2 Provisional and Final List Preparation

PROVISIONAL AND FINAL LIST PREPARATION

Criteria used for list preparation

1. Terminally ill cases
2. Physically challenged
3. Widow
4. Defence cases
5. Couple case - **Husband and Wife both in Govt.**
6. Couple case - **Husband or Wife in Govt.**
7. Other teachers – women
8. Representatives of Recognized teachers association
9. Other teachers – Men

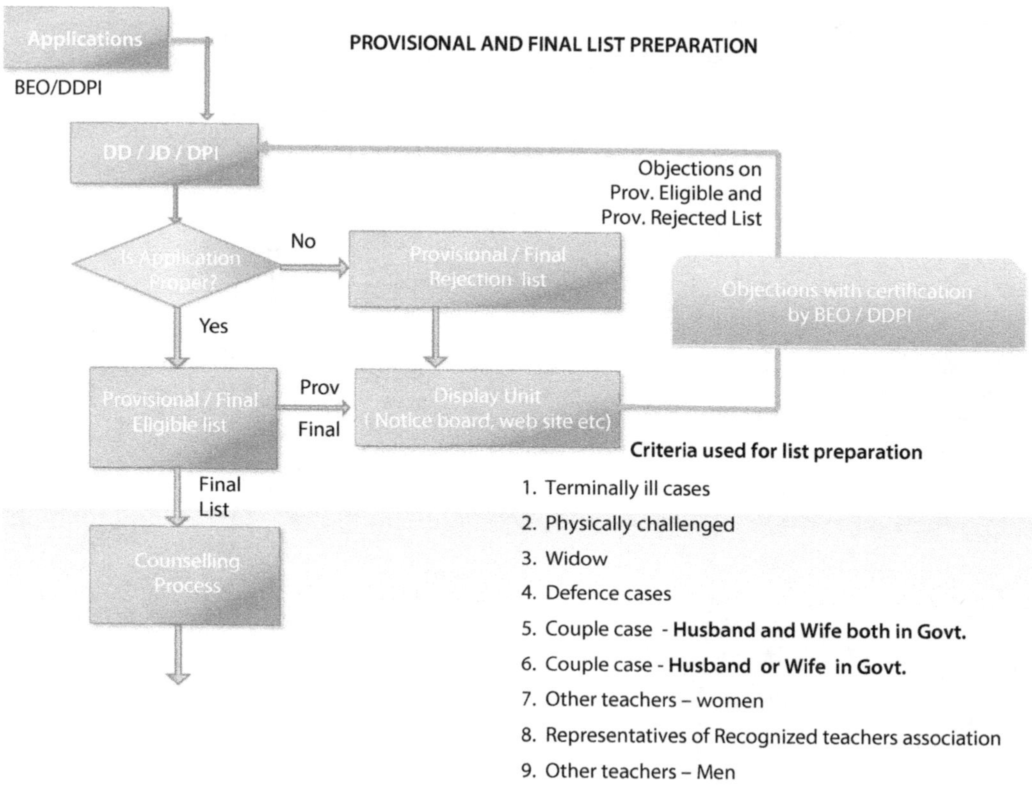

Source: Management Information System Section, Sarva Shiksha Abhiyan Karnataka.
Note: BEO = Block Education Officer; DD = Deputy Director; DDPI = Deputy Director of Public Instruction; DPI = Director of Public Instruction; JD = Joint Director.

For redeployment of excess teachers, similar counseling is conducted (figure B.4). However, the selection and listing of teachers is based on criteria defined by the government order issued for redeployment. Based on the school type and criteria (usually, the pupil-teacher ratio), excess teachers in each school are calculated and listed post-verification of school by block-level officials. This is categorized as per the Priority List and used for counseling.

For transfers outside the unit of seniority, a simultaneous counseling process is conducted at all division headquarters.[2] Ranking of all the applications (from all divisions) is done using the priorities defined in the Act (figure B.5). This is used for counseling.

Use of the Technology

Vendor

The software was developed in-house with assistance from the National Information Centre (NIC). The e-Governance Cell at the Department of Public Instruction maintains the current software and extends support to the districts

Figure B.3 Counseling Process

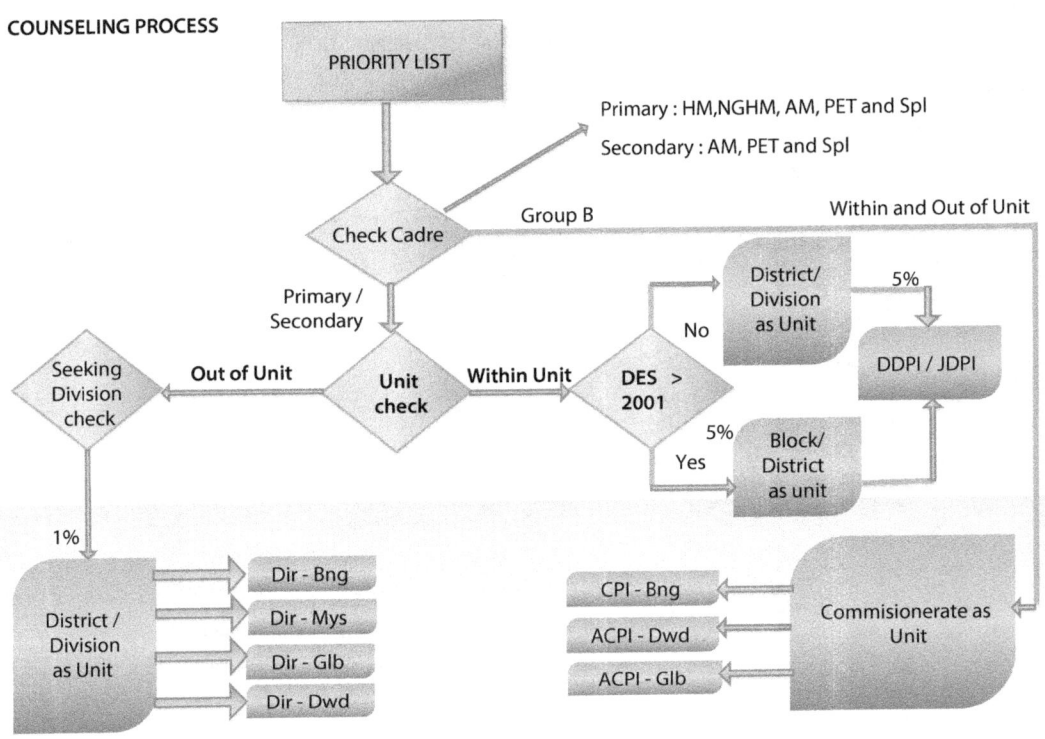

Source: Management Information System Section, Sarva Shiksha Abhiyan Karnataka.
Note: ACPI = Assistant Commissioner of Public Instruction; AM = Area Manager; Bng = Bangalore; CPI = Commissioner of Public Instruction; DDPI = Deputy Director of Public Instruction; DES = District Education Service; Dwd = Dharwad; Glb = Gulbarga; HM = headmaster; JDPI = Joint Director of Public Instruction; NGHM = Non Gazetted Head Master; PET = Professional Entrance Test; Spl = Special.

and divisions for conducting transfers within seniority units. The e-Governance Cell manages the transfers outside the seniority unit, as it is an online software with simultaneous counseling across locations.

Technology

The team did not have a formally documented Software Development Life Cycle but followed the Teacher Transfer Act 2007 as the basis for developing the software. The teacher transfer software is currently built using Microsoft SQL and ASP.net. Since the software was needed for transfers between districts, it had to be converted online. The team was more conversant with these technologies and hence chose to implement them using these tools. Software testing was done internally, wherein only basic testing was conducted. No formal secure coding or similar training was specifically provided to the developers. But basic sanity checks for SQL injection attacks and so forth were ensured during development. No formal process was adopted for tracking and fixing issues. Development and fixes are done in an ad hoc manner.

Figure B.4 Redeployment Process

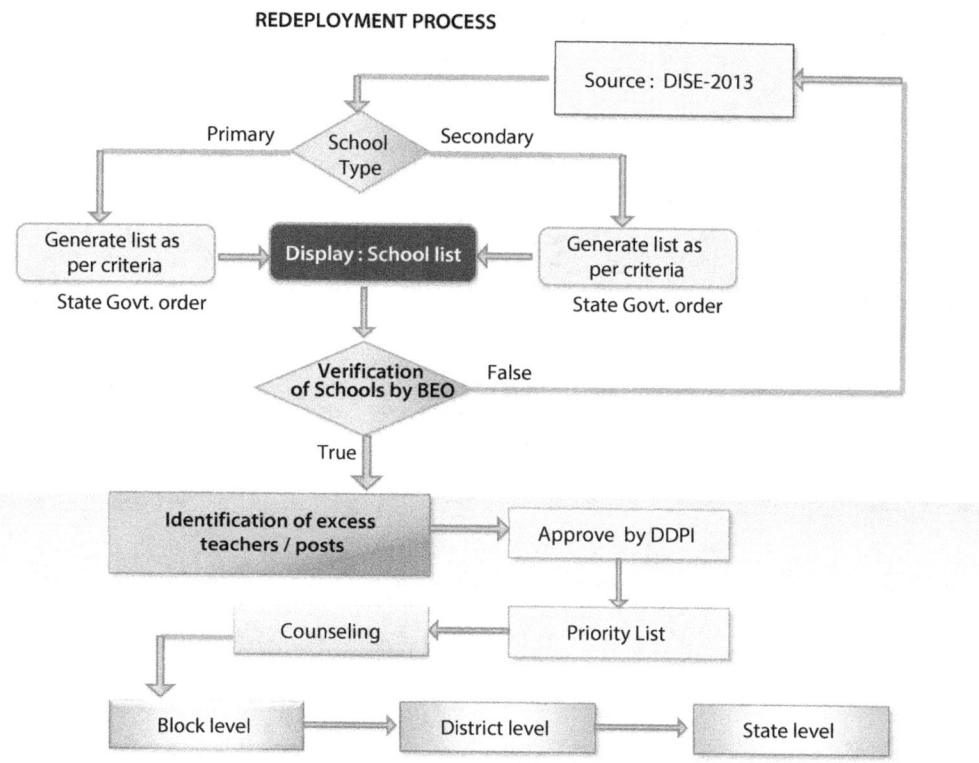

Source: Management Information System Section, Sarva Shiksha Abhiyan Karnataka.
Note: BEO = Block Education Officer; DDPI = Deputy Director of Public Instruction; DISE = District Information System for Education.

Data Requirements

Data are stored on a server provided by the Centre for e-Governance, Government of Karnataka. The Data Centre is located within Vikash Soudha (State Assembly Annexure). The e-Governance Cell follows strict protocols laid down by the Centre for e-Governance with respect to security of server and data. However, insecure HTTP service, instead of the more secure HTTPS, is being used. Hence, the data traverse through the public Internet in an unencrypted format. As per policy, regular tape as well as server backups are taken. No remote access is provided to the servers and the software can only be accessed on the premises. Access to USB and other devices is also restricted in the Data Centre to prevent loss of data.

Network Requirements

The Data Centre of the Centre for e-Governance, Government of Karnataka, provides state of the art Internet and physical security. A firewall and intrusion detection systems are in place to thwart any attempt to compromise the data on the servers. A port scan revealed no port other than the webserver being open.

Figure B.5 Redeployment Process outside the Unit of Seniority

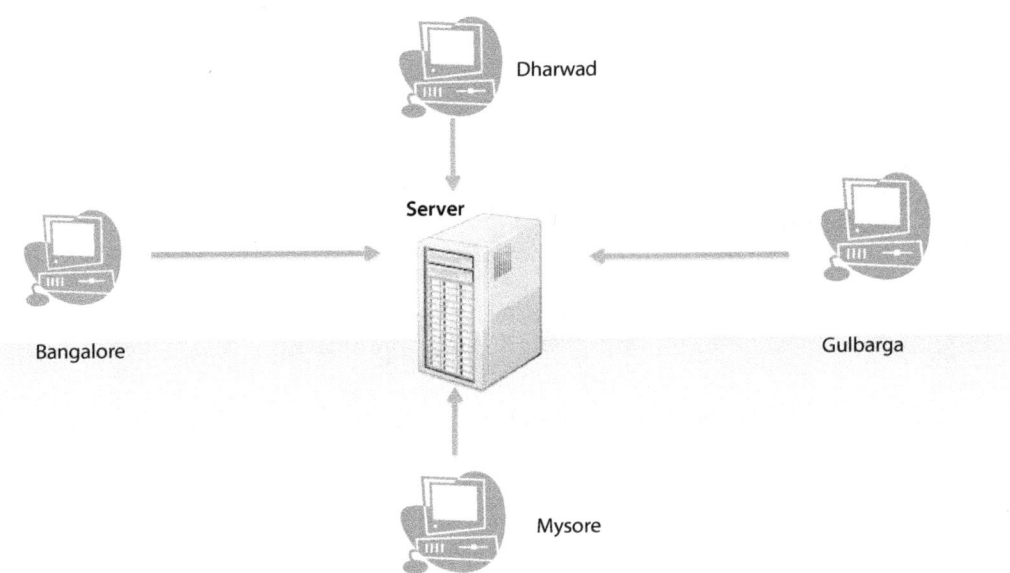

Data Entry and Verification

The data are directly entered into the system through the online applications. They generate the provisional selection list. The candidates have seven days to file objections for the list. While entering the data, basic checks are ensured so that the candidate does not fill in some details incorrectly. Some fields are auto-filled based on information already available. For example, school name, address, and so forth are filled automatically after the school code is entered. Various dropdown menus prevent erroneous entry of data.

Demonstration of the Software

A demo of the software explains the user interface. This has been captured through the screenshots described in the following.

1. Teachers use their unique Karnataka government ID number to fill in the application for a transfer. They can view their application status (that is, whether it has cleared the basic eligibility criteria of a minimum of five years of rural service, has reached the competent authority, has been cleared for transfer as per service records, and so forth).

Teacher Transfer Technology in Karnataka

2. After receiving the application, the system processes it according to the cadre and seniority unit. The system forwards the application to the respective competent authority's login/dashboard where it can be viewed for review. The dashboard requires a login, which is given to each competent authority.

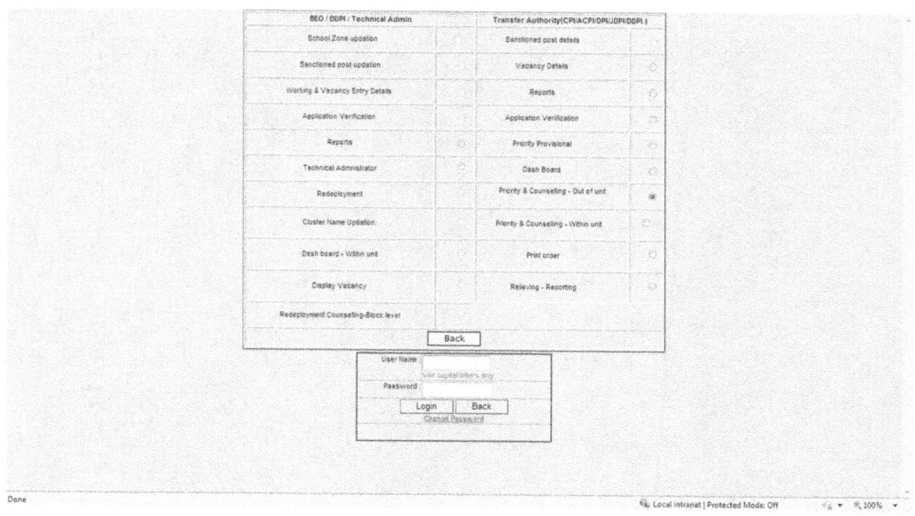

3. Post login, the competent authorities can view and approve the applications based on the service records of the teachers. If rejected, the program deletes the application and the teacher's application status is updated as "Application Rejected." If approved, this is added to the final list, which is generated based on the priorities defined.

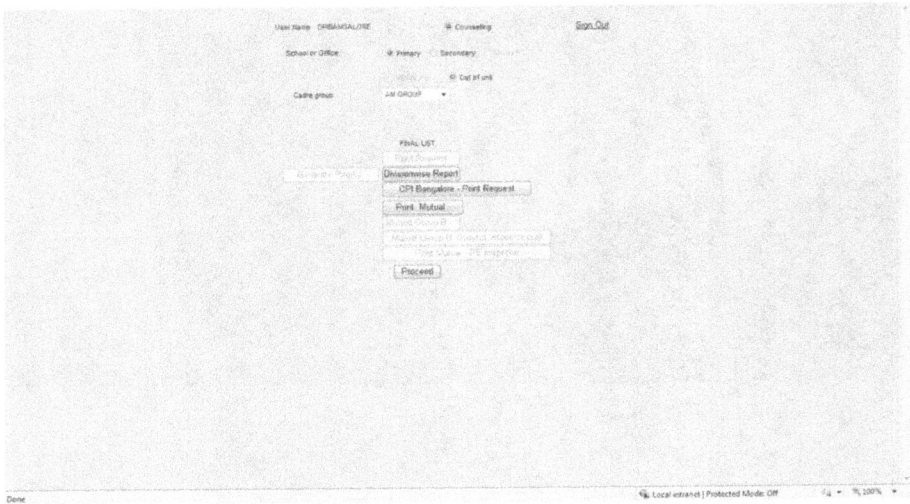

4. During counseling, the competent authorities can view the service records of the approved applicants, which are used for granting transfers. In the top left section, the details of the applicant are visible. This also gives the priority ranking of the applicant and the reason for seeking transfer/priority ranking.

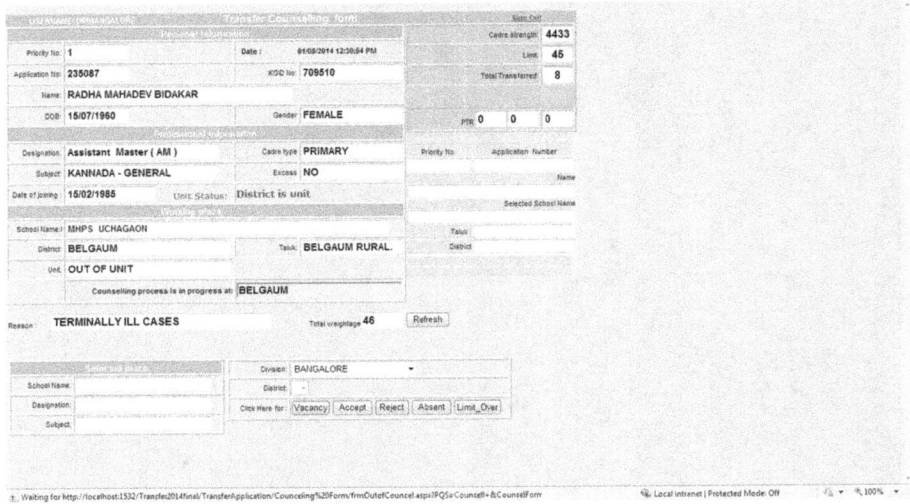

5. When a seniority unit (block or district) is selected, a list of vacancies in the block or district is in the same window.

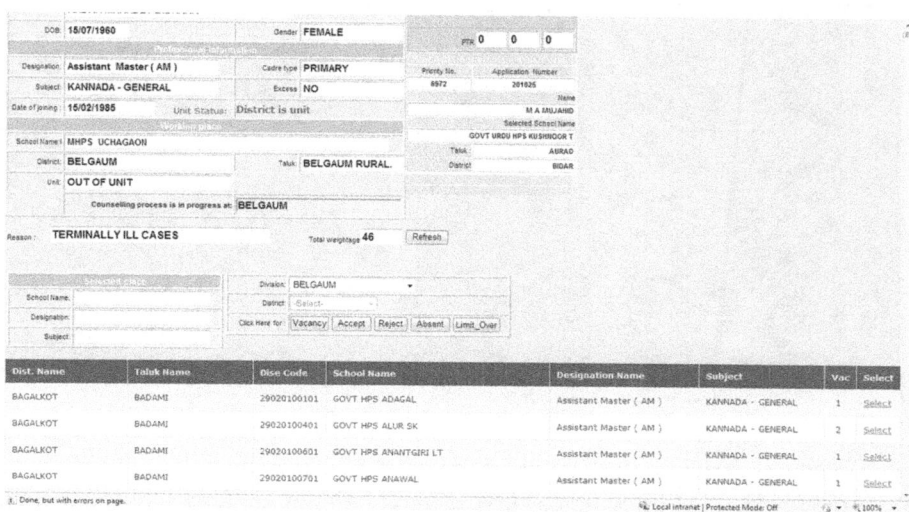

6. The applicant can select any of the available options from the list and verify the details. After selection of a school, the details of the same can be verified and accepted or rejected by the applicant. After accepting a school, the program is updated automatically, changing the number of transfers undertaken, creating a new vacant post in the list, and adding the transfer completed for a single applicant in the final list.

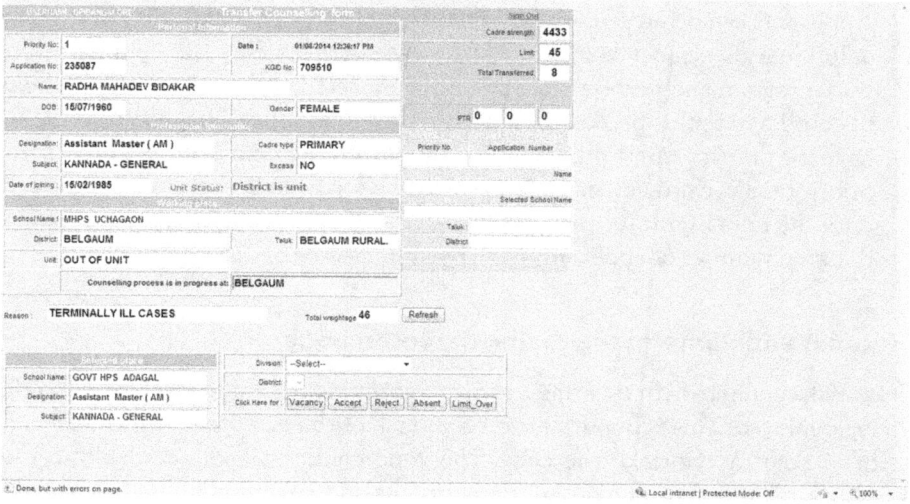

7. A final list of transfers with each applicant's name, present and transferred school details, date and time of transfer approval, cadre type, and transfer authority is generated using the software program.

8. The same software is utilized for transfers requested outside the unit of seniority. After the procedure is completed (that is, the 8 percent limit has been reached or the total number of applicants have been transferred), requests for transfers outside the unit of seniority are conducted, based on available vacancies. A state-level priority list is developed for transfers outside the unit of seniority. Online counseling is held simultaneously in all four divisions. Applicants can be present in any of the venues and a priority list is followed to determine the sequence in which they choose their school. A common software program and four separate systems connected with the same server help in coordinating this process. Due to simultaneous counseling, it is possible to have the priority rank 1 present in Bangalore, priority rank 2 present in Mysore, priority rank 3 present in Gulbarga, and so forth. This process is continued until the upper limit for transfers (1 percent of unit of seniority) is reached or the total number of applicants have been transferred.

Recommendations for Improving the Technology

Karnataka could benefit by using a proper versioning system to monitor the code being deployed. This is important to keep track of the evolution of the code and help in security audits of the code. The code could be made available in the public domain and used by other departments and governments. It would help to prepare the roadmap for technology upgrading, so that outdated tools can be replaced by the latest version. The state would also benefit by securing web access using https rather than unsecure http protocol.

The technology should be accompanied by proper security protocol. Codes and processes need to be audited for security by a third party to ensure that there are no loopholes. Upgrading the software needs to be inbuilt and done regularly. All web access points must be secured with SSL and all web traffic should use secure https protocol instead of unsecure http. Proper logs must be maintained on the server for audit of any changes made to the data. It would help to have a proper versioning system, such as Git, to maintain the history of product development. All code should ideally have backup on a central server with proper backup policy, and codes and process should be audited by a third party for the security of the system. All systems where data reside should be secured with proper access policy. There should also be a policy to upgrade the versions of the tools that are used, based on end-of-life support.

Notes

1. For primary school teachers recruited before 2001, the seniority unit is the district. For those recruited after 2001, the seniority unit is the block. For secondary school teachers recruited before 2003, the seniority unit is the division; for those recruited after 2003, the seniority unit is the district. Hence, the transfers are dependent on teachers' year of recruitment, which defines their seniority unit.
2. There are four divisions in Karnataka: Bangalore, Mysore, Gulbarga, and Dharwad.

Bibliography

Altinok, Nadir, and Geeta Gandhi Kingdon. 2012. "New Evidence on Class Size Effects: A Pupil Fixed Effects Approach." *Oxford Bulletin of Economics and Statistics* 74 (2): 203–34.

ASER (Annual Status of Education Report) Survey. 2005–2014. *Annual Status of Education Report*. http://www.asercentre.org/.

Atherton, P., and G. Gandhi Kingdon. 2010. "The Relative Effectiveness and Costs of Contract and Regular Teachers in India." *Centre for the Study of African Economies Series* (Ref: CSAE WPS/2010-15). Centre for the Study of African Economies, Oxford, United Kingdom.

Azam, M., and G. G. Kingdon. 2015. "Assessing Teacher Quality in India." *Journal of Development Economics* 117 (C): 74–83.

Béteille, T. 2009. "Absenteeism, Transfers and Patronage: The Political Economy of Teacher Labour Markets in India." PhD thesis, Stanford University.

Blum, Nicole, and Rashmi Diwan. 2007. "Small Multigrade Schools and Increasing Access to Primary Education in India—National Context and NGO Initiatives." CREATE Monograph No 17. Institute of Education, London, and National University of Educational Planning and Administration, India.

CAC (Centralised Admission Cell). 2014. CAC, Government of Karnataka. http://www.schooleducation.kar.nic.in/cac/cell.html. Accessed June 21, 2016.

CBPS (Centre for Budget and Policy Studies). 2014. "Evaluation of the Educational Leadership Development Programme (ELDP)." Bangalore, India.

———. 2015. "National Study on Working Conditions of Teachers: Karnataka." National University for Education Planning and Administration, New Delhi, India.

Chaudhuri, S. H., and N. Mathur. 2015. *Working Conditions of Teachers in Mizoram*. Institute of Advanced Study in Education, Aizawl, and National University of Educational Planning and Administration, New Delhi, India.

Cheney, G. R., B. B. Ruzzi, and K. Muralidharan. 2005. *India Education Profile*. National Centre for Education and the Economy, Washington, DC.

Cheney, Gretchen Rhines, Betsy Brown Ruzzi, and Karthik Muralidharan. 2005. "A Profile of the Indian Education System." Paper Prepared for the New Commission on the Skills of the American Workforce. National Center on Education and the Economy, Washington, DC. http://www.teindia.nic.in/files/articles/indian_education_sysytem_by_karthik_murlidharan.pdf.

De, Anuradha, and Tanuka Endow. 2008. "Public Expenditure on Education in India: Recent Trends and Outcomes." Working Paper No. 18. RECOUP, London.

De, Anuradha, Claire Noronha, and Meera Sampson. 2001. *India: Primary Schools and Universal Elementary Education*. India Education Team Report No. 3. New Delhi: World Bank.

DISE (District Information System for Education). 2014–15. "State Report Cards 2014–15."

Dongre, A. A., A. Kapur, and V. Tewary. 2014. "How Much Does India Spend Per Student on Elementary Education?" Working Paper Series 1, Accountability Initiative India, New Delhi.

DPEP (District Primary Education Programme). india.gov.in Archive. Accessed June 22, 2014.

Dreze, J., and H. Gazdar. 1996. "Uttar Pradesh: The Burden of Inertia." In *Indian Development: Selected Regional Perspectives*, ed. J. Dreze and A. Sen. Oxford University Press, New Delhi.

Dundar, H., T. Béteille, M. Riboud, and A. Deolalikar. 2014. *Student Learning in South Asia: Challenges, Opportunities and Policy Priorities*. Washington, DC: World Bank.

Ganimian, A. J., and E. Vegas. 2011. "What Are the Different Profiles of Successful Teacher Policy Systems?" SABER Teacher Background Paper No. 5. Education Sector, Human Development Network, World Bank, Washington, DC.

Gauri, Varun. 2013. "Redressing Grievances and Complaints Regarding Basic Service Delivery." *World Development* 41: 109–19.

Gottelmann-Duret, Gabriele, and Amina Yekhlef. 2005. "Teacher Management: A Bibliography." International Institute for Population Sciences, Paris.

Government of India. 1976. *The Constitution* (42nd Amendment) Act, 1976.

———. 1986. *National Policy on Education, 1986*.

———. 2009. "Right of Children to Free and Compulsory Education Act." Ministry of Human Resource Development, New Delhi, India. http://ssa.nic.in/rte-docs/free%20and%20compulsory.pdf.

Government of India, MHRD (Ministry of Human Resource Development), and SSA (Sarva Shiksha Abhiyan). 2009. "Attendance of Students and Teachers in Primary and Upper Primary Schools: Synthesis Report of the Study Conducted in 20 States." TSG, EdCIL, New Delhi, India.

———. 2012. *Report of the High-Powered Commission on Teacher Education Constituted by the Hon'ble Supreme Court of India*, volumes 1 to 3. Ministry of Human Resource Development and National Council of Teacher Education, New Delhi, India. http://mhrd.gov.in/sites/upload_files/mhrd/files/document-reports/JVC%20Vol%201.pdf.

Government of Karnataka. 1957. "Karnataka Civil Services (Classification, Control and Appeal) Rules, 1957." Bangalore, India.

———. 1996. Karnataka Civil Services (Appointment on Compassionate Grounds) Rules. Bangalore, Karnataka, India.

———. 1999. Karnataka Educational Institutions (Recruitment and Terms of Conditions of Service of Employees in Private Aided Primary and Secondary Educational Institutions) Rules 1999. Bangalore, Karnataka, India.

———. 2001a. *Cadre and Recruitment Rules (No. DPAR.41.SRE.2001, Bangalore, September 8, 2001*. Bangalore, India.

———. 2001b. *DPAR 41 SRE 2001, August 9, 2001 (Karnataka Education Department Services (Dept. of Public Instruction) (Recruitment) (Amendment) Rules 2001)*. Bangalore, India.

———. 2001c. Transfer Guidelines (DPAR 4 STR 2001 Bangalore, dated 22-11-2001). Bangalore, Karnataka, India.

———. 2005. Transfers on Request outside the Seniority Unit (ED 298 DPI 2005, dated 04.05.2005). Bangalore, Karnataka, India.

———. 2007a. "The Karnataka State Civil Services (Regulation of Transfer of Teachers) Act 2007 (Karnataka Act No. 29 of 2007)." Bangalore, India.

———. 2007b. Karnataka State Civil Services (Regulation of transfer of Teachers) Rules (ED173 ETR 2007 Bangalore, dated October 15, 2007). Bangalore, Karnataka, India.

———. 2007c. *Exemption of Physically Challenged Candidates from Fee Paying for Teachers' Post Application (DPAR:142:SRR:2006, May 5, 2007)*. Bangalore, India.

———. 2011a. *The Karnataka Scheduled Castes, Scheduled Tribes and Other Backward Classes (Reservation of Appointment etc) (Amendment) Act 2011 (Karnataka Act No. 7 of 2012)*. Karnataka, India.

———. 2011b. The Karnataka State Civil Services (regulation of Transfer of Medical Officers and other staff) Act 2011. Bangalore, Karnataka, India.

———. 2012a. *Recruitment Notification (Secondary School Teachers) (No. A(1)/PRA SHA SHI NE/01/2012-13 Bangalore, February 4, 2012)*. Bangalore, India.

———. 2012b. The Karnataka State Civil Services (Regulation of Transfer of Staff of Department of Technical Education) Act 2012. Bangalore, Karnataka, India.

———. 2013a. C3(1) PraShi A: Admission: 15 2011-12, February 2, 2013 (Recruitment Notification Elementary School Teachers). Bangalore, India.

———. 2013b. *Conducting Teacher Eligibility Test (TET) for Elementary and Secondary Schools (ED 238 PTI 2012, January 21, 2013, Bangalore)*. Bangalore, India.

———. 2013c. *Karnataka Educational Institutions (Regulations of Admission in the Hyderabad-Karnataka Region) Order 2013*. Bangalore, India.

———. 2013d. *Recruitment Notification (GO No. C3(1) PraShi A: Admission:15: 2011–12, February 2, 2013)*. Bangalore, India.

———. 2013e. Circular for Appointing Honorarium Teachers (C3(1) PRASHINE 15/2011-12, dated 27/08/2013). Bangalore, Karnataka, India.

———. 2013f. "GO No. FD 14 SRP 2013 dated September 2, 2013 (Reclassification of Places and Revision of the Rate of the House Rent Allowances for State Government Employees)." Bangalore, India.

———. 2013g. Appointment of Guest Lecturers (S.N. C4(1) PROSHASHI: ATINE 01: 2013–14). Bangalore, Karnataka, India.

———. 2013h. Karnataka Educational Institutions (Regulations of Admission in the Hyderabad-Karnataka Region) Order 2013. Bangalore, Karnataka, India.

———. 2013i. Recruitment Notification (GO No. C3(1) PraShi A: Admission:15: 2011–12, dated 02/02/2013). Bangalore, Karnataka, India.

———. 2015. Karnataka State Civil Services (Regulation of Transfer of Teachers) Amendment Rules 2015, dated May 13, 2015. Bangalore, Karnataka, India.

Government of Punjab, Department of School Education. 2002. Punjab Education Policy (PEP 2002).

Government of Rajasthan Krishna Bhatnagar Committee on 6th Pay Commission. http://finance.rajasthan.gov.in/doc/bhatnagarcommittee/chapter-I.pdf.

Government of Tamil Nadu. 2012. Tamil Nadu Teacher Eligibility Test (TNTET) Notification / Advertisement No 04/2012, dated March 7, 2012. Chennai, Tamil Nadu, India. http://trb.tn.nic.in/TET2012/08032012/Notification.pdf.

Goyal, Sangeeta, and Priyanka Pandey. 2010. *How Do Government and Private Schools Differ? Findings from Two Large Indian States.* Report No. 30. SAHDS. New Delhi, India: World Bank.

Goyal, Sangeeta, and Sangeeta Dey. 2014. "Teacher In-Service Training in Rashtriya Madhyamik Shiksha Abhiyan." World Bank, New Delhi.

Hanushek, Eric. 2003. "The Failure of Input-based Schooling Policies." *The Economic Journal* 113: 64–98.

Hom Chaudhuri, S., and Nikhil Mathur. 2015. "Working Conditions of Teachers in Mizoram." Institute of Advanced Study in Education, Aizawl, and National University of Educational Planning and Administration, New Delhi, India.

Inbaraj, J., and S. Manivel. 2014. "Tamil Nadu State Report on Working Conditions of Teachers." University for Education Planning and Administration, New Delhi, India.

Inbaraj, J., and S. Manivel. 2015. "National Study on Working Conditions of Teachers: Tamil Nadu." State Council for Education Research and Training, Chennai, and National University for Education Planning and Administration, New Delhi, India.

Inbaraj, J., and S. Manivel. 2015. *Working Conditions of Teachers in Tamil Nadu.* State Council of Educational Research and Training, Chennai, and National University of Educational Planning and Administration, New Delhi, India.

Institute of Development Studies and Knowledge and Skills for Development. Undated. Research report contributed to a multi-country study on "Teacher Motivation: A Case Study of Rajasthan." Sussex, UK.

Jain, P. S., and R. H. Dholakia. 2009. "Feasibility of Implementation of Right to Education Act." *Economic & Political Weekly* 44 (25): 38–43.

Jain, Pankaj. 2009. "Education Budget Allocation and National Education Goals: Implications for Teacher Salary Level." Paper presented at the International Conference of Indian Academy of Social Sciences, held at Homi Bhabha Centre of Science Education, Mumbai, India.

Jandhyala, Kameshwari, and ERU Research Team. 2014. "Women Teachers and the Achievement of Gender and Equity Goals in Secondary Education: An Exploratory Study in Rajasthan." Mimeograph, MacArthur Foundation, New Delhi, India.

Jandhyala, Kameshwari, Nishi Mehrotra, Niti Saxena, Rajni Patni, R. S. Sharma, Spana Goel, Shobhita Rajagopal, and Ul Ojha. 2014. "Women Teachers and the Achievement of Gender and Equity Goals in Secondary Education: An Exploratory Study in Rajasthan." ERU Consultants Pvt. Ltd., New Delhi, India.

Jha, Jyotsna, K. B. C. Saxena, and C. V. Baxi. 2001. "Management Processes in Elementary Education: A Study of Existing Practices in Selected States in India."

Jha, Jyotsna, Neha Ghatak, Sandhya Chandrashekaran, Shreekanth Mahendiran, Puja Minni, Shubhashansha Bakshi, and R. Thyagrajan. 2013. "Challenges in Implementing the Right to Education: The Karnataka Case." Centre for Budget and Policy Studies. Bangalore, Karnataka, India.

Jha, Jyotsna, Puja Minni, GVSR Prasad, and Neha Ghatak. 2015. *Working Conditions of Teachers in Karnataka and Jharkhand.* Center for Budget and Policy Studies,

Bangalore, and National University of Educational Planning and Administration, New Delhi, India.

Joshi, Lohitakshaya, Abani Mohan Panigrahi, and Prasant Kumar Panda. 2015. *Working Conditions of Teachers in Odisha*. Lokdrusti Naupada, Odisha, and National University of Educational Planning and Administration, New Delhi, India.

Justice Verma Committee Report. 2012. "Report of the High Powered Commission on Teacher Education Constituted by the Hon'ble Supreme Court of India." Ministry of Human Resource Development, Government of India, New Delhi.

Kingdon, G. G. 2010. *The Impact of the Sixth Pay Commission on Teacher Salaries: Assessing Equity and Efficiency Effects*. RECOUP Working Paper 29, Department for International Development, London.

Kingdon, G. G., and M. Muzzammil. 2008. *A Political Economy of Education in India: The Case of Uttar Pradesh*. Oxford Policy Institute.

Kingdon, Gandhi. G. 2010. *The Impact of the Sixth Pay Commission on Teacher Salaries: Assessing Equity and Efficiency Effects*. RECOUP Working Paper 29. Department for International Development, London.

Kumar, V. Anil. 2009. "Federalism and Decentralisation in India: Andhra Pradesh and Tamil Nadu." Working Paper 208. Institute for Social and Economic Change, Bangalore, Karnataka, India.

Mathur, Nikhil, Ajay Singh, and Sanjay Agarwal. 2015. *Working Conditions of Teachers in Uttar Pradesh*. State Council of Educational Research and Training, Lucknow, and National University of Educational Planning and Administration, New Delhi, India.

MHRD (Ministry of Human Resource Development). 2016. *Draft New Education Policy*. National Council of Educational Research and Training, New Delhi, India.

Mpokosa, Chikondi, and Susy Ndaruhutse. 2008. "Managing Teachers: The Centrality of Teacher Management to Quality Education: Lessons from Developing Countries." Centre for British Teachers and Volunteers Overcoming Poverty, Reading, UK.

Mukherjee, A. N., and S. Sikdar. 2012. "Public Expenditure on Education in India by the Union Government and Roadmap for the Future." In *India Infrastructure Report 2012 Private Sector in Education* (Infrastructure Development Finance Company), 17–29. Routledge: New Delhi.

Muralidharan, K., J. Das, A. Holla, and A. Mohpal. 2014. *The Fiscal Cost of Weak Governance: Evidence from Teacher Absence in India*. Working Paper 20299, NBER Working Paper Series, Cambridge, MA: Massachusetts Avenue.

Muralidharan, Karthik, and Venkatesh Sundararaman. 2010. "Contract Teachers: Experimental Evidence from India." Working Paper, World Bank, Washington, DC.

Nagpal, Nagendra. 2015. *Working Conditions of Teachers in Rajasthan*. Centre for Education Research & Practice, Jaipur, and National University of Educational Planning and Administration, New Delhi, India.

NCERT (National Council of Educational Research and Training). 2011. "Programme Evaluation Report: Activity Based Learning, Tamil Nadu." New Delhi, India.

NCTE (National Council of Teacher Education) Act. 1993. Notified by Ministry of Law, Justice and Public Affairs, Government of India. http://www.ncte-india.org/NCTEACT/chp1.htm.

———. 2011. Notification of August 2, 2011. Government of India. http://www.ncte-india.org/Norms/RTE-4.pdf.

New Indian Express. 2010. "Education Tribunal Gets New Teeth." *The New Indian Express,* August 10. http://www.newindianexpress.com/states/odisha/article202277.ece?service=print.

Noronha, Anjali, Arvind Jain, and Pradeep Chaubey. 2015. *Working Conditions of Teachers in Madhya Pradesh.* Eklavya Bhopal and National University of Educational Planning and Administration, New Delhi, India.

Pachauri, Anupam, and M. S, Sarkaria. 2015. *Working Conditions of Teachers in Punjab.* State Council of Educational Research and Training, Chandigarh, and National University of Educational Planning and Administration, New Delhi, India.

PAISA (Planning, Allocations and Expenditures, Institutions Studies in Accountability). 2012. *Do Schools Get Their Money?* Accountability Initiative. PAISA, New Delhi.

PROBE. 1999. *Public Report on Basic Education in India.* New Delhi: Oxford University Press.

———. 2011. *A Report on Elementary Education in India.* Oxford University Press.

Rajendran, S. 2013. "Reservation in Education, Jobs in Hyderabad-Karnataka Notified." *The Hindu.* November 6.

Ramachandran, V., K. Jandhyala, N. Mehrotra, L. Krishnamurthy, V. Periodi, and A. Saihjee. 2004. *Snakes and Ladders: Factors Influencing Successful Primary School Completion for Children in Poverty Contexts.* South Asian Human Development Sector Report No. 6. New Delhi: World Bank.

Ramachandran, V., M. Pal, D. Jain, S. Shekar, and J. Sharma. 2005. "Teacher Motivation in India and a Case Study of Rajasthan." Research report contributed to a multi-country study on Teacher Motivation coordinated by IDS Sussex (UK) and Knowledge and Skills for development (UK). http://www.teindia.nic.in/efa/Vimla_doc/TeacherMotivation_in India_2008.pdf.

Ramachandran, V., S. Bhattacharjea, and K. M. Sheshagiri. 2009. "Primary School Teachers in India: The Twists and Turns of Everyday Practice." Azim Premji Foundation, Bangalore, Karnataka, India. http://www.azimpremjifoundation.org/sites/default/files/userfiles/files/Teacher%20booklet.pdf.

Ramachandran, Vimala, M. Pal, S. Jain, S. Shekhar, and J. Sharma. 2005. *Teacher Motivation in India.* New Delhi: UK Department for International Development.

Ramachandran, Vimala, Suman Bhattacherjea, and K. M. Sheshagiri. 2008. *Primary School Teachers in India—The Twists and Turns of Everyday Practice.* ERU and Azim Premji Foundation, Bangalore, India.

Ramachandran, Vimala, Tara Beteille, Tobias Linden, Sangeeta Dey, Sangeeta Goyal, and Prerna Goyal Chatterjee. 2015. "Teachers in the Indian Education System: Synthesis of a Nine-State Study." National University for Education Planning and Administration, New Delhi, India.

Ramachandran, Vimala, Taramoni Naorem, and State Research Teams. 2012. *Inclusion and Exclusion of Students in the School and in the Classroom in Primary and Upper Primary Schools in 6 States of India.* New Delhi: Teacher Support Group, Ed CIL, and Government of India.

Right to Education Act 2009. *Right to Free and Compulsory Education Act 2009.* Ministry of Human Resource Development, Government of India. New Delhi.

Sandamerswaran, K. T. 2014. "HC Orders Transparent Conduct of Teacher Transfer Counselling." *The Hindu.* June 28. http://www.thehindu.com/todays-paper/tp-national

/tp-tamilnadu/hc-orders-transparent-conduct-of-teacher-transfer-counselling/article6157163.ece.

Sankar, D., and T. Linden. 2014. *How Much and What Kind of Teaching Is There in Elementary Education—Evidence from Three States*. Report No. 67. New Delhi: World Bank.

Sankar, Deepa, and Toby Linden. 2014. *How Much and What Kind of Teaching Is There in Elementary Education in India? Evidence from Three States*. Report 67, World Bank, New Delhi, India.

SEMIS (Secondary Education Management Information System). 2011–12. SEMIS Online Report Card. New Delhi, India. http://www.semisonline.net/.

Sharma, Rashmi, and Vimala Ramachandran. 2009. *The Elementary Education System in India: Exploring Institutional Structures, Processes and Dynamics*. New Delhi: Routledge India.

Singh, A. K. 2011. *Study of the Role of VEC/PTA/SDMC/Urban Local Bodies in School Management and Supervision in the Context of SSA—A Report*. New Delhi: National University of Educational Planning and Administration, India.

Singh, Prabal Vikram, Anand Tatambhotla, and Rohini Rao Kalvakuntle. 2012. "Replicating Tamil Nadu's Drug Procurement Model." *Economic and Political Weekly*, September 29, xlviI (39): 26–29.

SSA (Sarva Shiksha Abhiyan), Government of India. 2009. *Attendance of Students and Teachers in Primary and Upper Primary Schools—Synthesis of the Study Conducted in 20 States*. Ed CIL, New Delhi, India.

State Reports. http://www.nuepa.org/New/completed%20reaserches.aspx.

The Hindu. 2013. "Government Concedes Aided School Teachers' Demand." *The Hindu*, December 18. http://www.thehindu.com/todays-paper/tp-national/tp-karnataka/government-concedes-aided-school-teachers-demand/article5472431.ece.

———. 2016. "Govinde Gowda Dead." January 6.

Vegas, Emiliana, Alejandro Ganimian, and Analia Jaimovich. 2012. *Learning from the Best: Improving Learning through Effective Teacher Policies*. Education Notes. Washington, DC: World Bank.

Visaria, Leela. Undated. "Innovations in Tamil Nadu." http://www.india-seminar.com/2000/489/489%20visaria.htm. Accessed June 21, 2016.

World Bank. 2006. "Reforming Public Services in India: Drawing Lessons from Success." Report No. 35041-IN. World Bank, Washington, DC.

———. 2009. "Teacher Motivation, Incentives and Working Conditions." Policy Brief 8. World Bank, Washington, DC.

———. 2014. "How Much and What Kind of Teaching Is There in Elementary Education in India? Evidence from Three States." Report No 67. South Asia Human Development Sector, World Bank, New Delhi, India.

Environmental Benefits Statement

The World Bank Group is committed to reducing its environmental footprint. In support of this commitment, we leverage electronic publishing options and print-on-demand technology, which is located in regional hubs worldwide. Together, these initiatives enable print runs to be lowered and shipping distances decreased, resulting in reduced paper consumption, chemical use, greenhouse gas emissions, and waste.

We follow the recommended standards for paper use set by the Green Press Initiative. The majority of our books are printed on Forest Stewardship Council (FSC)–certified paper, with nearly all containing 50–100 percent recycled content. The recycled fiber in our book paper is either unbleached or bleached using totally chlorine-free (TCF), processed chlorine-free (PCF), or enhanced elemental chlorine-free (EECF) processes.

More information about the Bank's environmental philosophy can be found at http://www.worldbank.org/corporateresponsibility.

www.ingramcontent.com/pod-product-compliance
Lightning Source LLC
Chambersburg PA
CBHW081802300426
44116CB00014B/2207